Appalling Bodies

Appalling Bodies

Queer Figures Before and After Paul's Letters

JOSEPH A. MARCHAL

OXFORD
UNIVERSITY PRESS

OXFORD
UNIVERSITY PRESS

Oxford University Press is a department of the University of Oxford. It furthers
the University's objective of excellence in research, scholarship, and education
by publishing worldwide. Oxford is a registered trade mark of Oxford University
Press in the UK and certain other countries.

Published in the United States of America by Oxford University Press
198 Madison Avenue, New York, NY 10016, United States of America.

© Oxford University Press 2020

First issued as an Oxford University Press paperback 2022

CIP data is on file at the Library of Congress
ISBN 978-0-19-006031-2 (Hardback)
ISBN 978-0-19-766896-2 (Paperback)

1 3 5 7 9 8 6 4 2

Paperback printed by Marquis, Canada

Contents

Acknowledgments

It seems only fitting for a project thinking queerly about our relations to and with the past that I cannot summon one seamless narrative or singular starting point for this book, so long in the making.

It is at least partially tied to an overly ambitious dissertation proposal drafted at the end of my comprehensive examinations, and the moment Mary Tolbert, as sage and as snarky as ever, announced that it sounded like a proposal for not one, but three different books! This book arrives after that dissertation and a few other projects that got in the way, but it grew out of many of those initial ideas, and many of the things I learned in Tolbert's Feminism, Queer Theory, and the Bible seminar. Glimmers of this also shimmered behind a truly horrible undergraduate honors thesis, patiently supervised by Mary Rose D'Angelo, and even my amateurish work in Mark Jordan's seminar on Christianity and sexuality (in which I swore I would never ever read Augustine or Aquinas again—only to find myself recurrently poring over Paul's letters, and a dozen years later, subjecting students to all three of these problematically prominent figures). Yet, I may have been on those campuses, in those rooms, looking to those brilliant people because of the way (other) people have long responded to me and several contours of my embodied existence and attempted negotiation within the world. So, this book might have an even clearer origin in those moments when I first began to notice how people responded to me, my body, my mannerisms, habits, refusals, obliviousness, or (un)chosen comportments in appalling ways.

Because this has been long simmering, too many friends and colleagues to name or even count have contributed to its final shape. Those who have suggested sources or strategies, prodded with questions, read drafts, portions, or proposals, or otherwise improved this through their engagement include Efraín Agosto, Randall Bailey, Jennifer Bird, Ward Blanton, Sheila Briggs, Denise Kimber Buell, Sean Burke, Allen Callahan, Susannah Cornwall, Ben Dunning, Neil Elliott, Lynne Gerber, Jennifer Glancy, Megan Goodwin, Rhiannon Graybill, Sally Gross, Holly Hearon, David Hester (Amador), Jacqueline Hidalgo, James Hoke, Dick Horsley, Ted Jennings, Johnathan Jodamus, Gwynn Kessler, Uriah Kim, Cynthia Briggs

Kittredge, Jennifer Knust, Laurel Koepf-Taylor, Jennifer Koosed, Maia Kotrosits, Kwok Pui-lan, Tat-siong Benny Liew, Davina Lopez, Karmen MacKendrick, Anna Miller, Kelsi Morrison-Atkins, Monique Moultrie, Jorunn Økland, Angela Parker, Todd Penner, Christina Petterson, Jeremy Punt, Robert Seesengood, Katherine Shaner, Mitzi Smith, Shanell Smith, William Smith, Will Stockton, Max Strassfeld, Eric Thomas, Gillian Townsley, Jay Twomey, Caroline Vander Stichele, Gerald West, Heather White, and Demetrius Williams.

Some of their feedback contributed to or responded to earlier versions of the ideas presented here, portions of which appeared as "Bodies Bound for Circumcision and Baptism: An Intersex Critique and the Interpretation of Galatians," *Theology and Sexuality* 16:2 (2010): 143–161; "The Usefulness of an Onesimus: The Sexual Use of Slaves and Paul's Letter to Philemon," *Journal of Biblical Literature* 130:4 (2011): 749–770; " 'Making History' Queerly: Touches Across Time Through a Biblical Behind," *Biblical Interpretation* 19 (2011): 373–395; "Female Masculinity in Corinth? Bodily Citations and the Drag of History," *Neotestamentica: Journal of the New Testament Society of Southern Africa* 48:1 (2014): 93–113; "The Exceptional Proves Who Rules: Imperial Sexual Exceptionalism in and Around Paul's Letters," *Journal of Early Christian History* 5:1 (2015): 87–115. Before an unexpected right turn from above thwarted us, Doug Mitchell's robust support buoyed the initial development of this manuscript. Gratefully, Steve Wiggins immediately recognized the value of this work, and seamlessly brought us over to Oxford University Press. Since then, Steve and the whole team at OUP, including Hannah Campeanu and Asish Krishna (at Newgen) have been an immense help in making this manuscript an object in the world. This arrival would not have been possible without the impeccably astute suggestions of Katie Van Heest in a key, penultimate phase of editing.

The completion of this project was supported by research and writing funding from several sources, starting with my home department at Ball State University, but most especially the Religion and Sexuality Initiative run by Mark Jordan at Emory University (with support from the Ford Foundation), the Wabash Center for Teaching and Learning in Theology and Religion, and the Institute for Research in the Humanities at the University of Wisconsin-Madison, under the magisterial leadership of Susan Friedman. The year in Madison was crucial for this project, and it bears traces of the insights, questions, and good humor of several colleagues made in that year together, including Justine Andrews, Ayelet Ben-Yishai, Leslie Bow,

Nan Enstad, Ramzi Fawaz, and Molly Zahn. The unflappable staff at several libraries, at UW Madison, Ball State, the Graduate Theological Union, and particularly Lorna Shoemaker at the Christian Theological Seminary (here in Indianapolis), made this idiosyncratic project possible. Beyond the eternally useful annual meetings of the Society of Biblical Literature and the American Academy of Religion, a range of speaking engagements at conferences, workshops, and seminars at Bates College, Christian Theological Seminary, Council for World Mission (in Mexico City), Drew University, Eden Theological Seminary, Emory University, Marian University, Pomona College, University of California-Riverside, University of Kent, University of Kwa-Zulu Natal, University of Manchester, University of Oslo, University of Sheffield, and the University of South Africa (Pretoria) provided invaluable insight, inspiration, and motivation.

All of these could be seen as still further queer starting points for the contents to follow. While I do not know how much they will approve of this appalling book, this project and my life, indeed my overall disposition as a scholar and a person, are irrevocably shaped by the passionate commitments of two of my mentors: Antoinette Clark Wire's roving, but indefatigable curiosity, and Elisabeth Schüssler Fiorenza's persistent efforts to counter kyriarchy in its varying forms. My intellectual debts to Bernadette Brooten should be apparent to any who read this, as her work is all over this manuscript. Methodologically, I could not have imagined any of these queer approaches to these materials without the extraordinary paths cleared by Erin Runions, Ken Stone, and Stephen Moore. To this point, I do not think anyone has been asked to read this manuscript more frequently than Stephen. The final version of this is much improved by this reading and the attention of other, still anonymous readers at OUP (and elsewhere). My sanity in these years has been saved multiple times by the continued mentorship-turned-friendships of Melanie Johnson-DeBaufre and Shelly Matthews. It was further buoyed in key moments by the generosity of Elizabeth Freeman, Judith Butler, and Jasbir Puar. This generosity has been matched and multiplied by the gracious permission Peter Lyssiotis gave for us to re-use a photomontage out of *From the The Secret Life of Statues . . .* on this cover—a visceral hint of the haunting juxtapositions I have tried to summon and negotiate.

As once marked by a series of epigraphs, a passion for queer punk, queer theory, and queer hermeneutics shared with Lynn Huber and Teresa Hornsby animates this book. In the background of chapter 2, I can still hear the Scissor Sisters throw off lines like: "She's my man, and we've got all the balls we need" ("She's My Man"). Some of the outrage seeping through chapter 3 echoes those expressed by Sleater-Kinney: "I'm no monster. I'm just like you. All my life is before me. Call the doctor. Call the doctor. Call the doctor" ("Call the Doctor"). As I struggle with the haunting histories of bodily contact in chapter 4, Magnetic Fields rings through: "If you think you can leave the past behind, you must be out of your mind. If you think you can simply press rewind. You must be out of your mind, son. You must be out of your mind" ("You Must Be Out of Your Mind"). The urgent words of The Gossip, "There's an equation—you plus me equals death—to the science of those who dare to forget" ("Eighth Wonder"), cut through the phobic, even terrorizing readings I aim to counter in chapter 5. In these and in many other ways, music has kept me alive now for years, in ways that the biblical never has or ever likely will, as my partner knows all too well. As my queer historical narration here indicates, this project predates our relationship and hopefully will persist somehow well past our time here; but in the meantime I cannot imagine anyone with whom I would rather share this strange mess of a life. I am sorry for the appalling attention I have been giving to a book when we have been trying to read each other for so long now. The duration of this project stretches back so far that Kent Brintnall is the one friend and colleague who has walked with, commiserated over, and cheered on its development longer than anyone. It is almost here; I am sorry it took so long, but I am forever grateful for your companionship through all of these appalling turns.

My work as a teacher and a scholar has in turn been shaped by so many students, colleagues, friends, and companions—particularly those who have shared how their own gender, sexuality, and embodiment have been figured as appalling, often (but not always) in relation to biblical texts and traditions. I would not be so foolish to claim that this book does, or even could, represent the response of all who have been touched across time by such texts and traditions, so I hesitate to say that this book is for them. Yet, this project is motivated by their (and sometimes our) disclosures and resistances, wounds and outrages, debilities and desires, troubles and tricks, particularly when we have been targeted with or simply *as* figures of vilification or stigmatization. I try to find alternative angles on these figures as one kind of intervention (or one set of provocations) to these scenes that shape so many of our lives. This book, then, is dedicated to who and what haunts it—what has already happened, what has been done, those who have and have not survived, echoed in my not so elastic heart, in my ears when I am overcome by the wails of Sleater-Kinney or The Gossip, in my mind's eye when I remember Carol and too many to name and adequately honor, but who still touch me. This may not be worth the trouble, but it is well past time I tried.

Prelude

Before and After

Paul is probably the least interesting thing about Paul's letters.

Perhaps confusion is now setting in—*isn't this a book about Paul?* The shortest answer is: not really. It is, in part, about Paul's letters, though. But those epistles are not particularly interesting to me for their own sakes. *Oh, but certainly it's about the sex, then, right? All I know about Paul, sorry, Paul's letters, is that they condemn homosexuals. Those are the parts I want to know more about. This should get juicy.* Yes, indeed, I will be discussing sexual matters along the way, at times in great, even excessive detail, which is sure to please some and trouble others. This difference is one of the first lessons of queer studies, a close companion to the project of this book: "Most people find it difficult to grasp that whatever they like to do sexually will be thoroughly repulsive to someone else, and that whatever repels them sexually will be the most treasured delight of someone, somewhere."[1] Here, in a signal essay that also ends up serving as a prelude (to queer studies), Gayle Rubin highlights people's inordinate preoccupations with sex—their own and others'—and traces a "fallacy of misplaced scale" about this variation in erotic tastes. Not only do these tastes and their embodied practices vary but also they are ordered in hierarchical valuations, with only some counting as natural and normal, healthy and holy.[2] In the wake of Rubin's work, then, the naturalization and normalization of some practices of gender, sexuality, and embodiment, typically in order to discipline, stigmatize, or exclude other practices, become persistent, even defining features for queer critique.

In a striking, if brief connection to biblical studies—the other, possibly strange book-fellow with queer studies in this present project—Rubin lays the responsibility for our overwhelming sex negativity that generates these fallacies and hierarchies at the feet of Paul and those who follow him.[3] I actually think this would be a relatively difficult case to make, as the letters themselves reflect more ambivalences and tensions than most users of these texts are willing to admit. This is, in part, why this book is not primarily dedicated

Appalling Bodies. Joseph A. Marchal, Oxford University Press (2020). © Oxford University Press.
DOI: 10.1093/oso/9780190060312.001.0001

to figuring out Paul's stance(s) on sexualized topics. There are already some excellent studies about this.[4]

Instead of figuring that out, then, I will be reaching past Paul toward other, far more fascinating figures, before and after these letters: androgynes, eunuchs, slaves, and barbarians—each depicted as perversely gendered and strangely embodied figures in their own distinctive, though interrelated ways, before and after the letters. Once called up, these people can be used to call out others in the audiences, figures targeted by the letters and often ignored in traditions about these texts. The rhetorical figures called up by the letters were circulating in the Roman imperial context *before* the letters were dictated and directed to their respective assembly audiences around the northern and eastern Mediterranean. The potential historical figures addressed by these letters gathered together in these assemblies (rather than "churches") *before* anyone sent such epistles, and likely persisted *after* their arrival, even as it now looks like the letters were sent to target them, to call out and pursue these people—to come *after* them.

In seeking out these other figures, we encounter variations and valuations not entirely distant from the kinds Rubin highlights for more recent contexts. Yet, the distance in space and time between the "there and then" of these first-century epistles and audiences and the "here and now" of those twenty-first-century people who receive, interpret, and use them has also proved troubling. Our expectations around these texts and indeed studies of them (like this one) are conditioned by present-day assumptions, as people are still most likely to hear biblical, and specifically Pauline, arguments when groups are disputing matters of gender, sexuality, and embodiment. The most common positions taken in such conflicts involve primarily condemnatory or defensive responses and invoke a biblical past as either obviously applicable or distantly outdated. Neither is exactly correct, especially because the continued citation and use of Paul's letters demonstrates an ongoing impact and influence that is outsized in comparison to the historical contexts of these ancient epistles. We need another approach, savvier to the before and after of this present-day context.

To start, this approach requires treating the letters as rhetorically sophisticated objects, situated within longer exchanges between Paul and a range of communities in cities and regions within the Roman empire—Corinth, Galatia, Colossae, and even Rome itself. Yet, one of the goals of this book is to find new ways to reach out and know more about the historical figures targeted by the letters to these assembly communities. This entails situating each of the ancient figures deployed in these letters in their specifically Roman imperial settings, an ambience that cast each of these rhetorical figures as complicated, debased, and dangerous. Such contextualizations can begin to trace how the letters and their audiences would have known and heard references to androgynes, eunuchs, slaves, and barbaric foreigners, at least on one level.

However, these figures are deployed to address specific historical figures in these audiences, to convince them and those around them of a course of action outlined in the letter. This ancient context is more helpful in presenting the perspective of the epistle, but not necessarily those targeted by these argumentative and figurative practices. In short, any attempt to reach out and know more about the people within such ancient collectives will meet some rather clear limits if it does not make efforts to reposition the kinds of figures deployed and then targeted by the letter. Paul's letters recurrently repeat and reinscribe ancient (often Roman imperial) ideas about a constellation of perversely gendered and strangely embodied figures. Certainly, greater familiarity with these figures and forms of argumentation provides key contexts for approaching and reimagining those "others" still so marginalized within both these epistles and their interpretations. In an effort to find alternative angles on the arguments and especially the audiences for these letters, angles aside from the perspective presented by or as Paul's, I suggest juxtaposing these ancient figures against or alongside other, more recent figures of vilification or stigmatization—like drag kings or trans butches, or people with intersex conditions, or those engaged in BDSM practices, or those targeted as terrorists.

By implementing key insights about these people and practices from queer studies, my project defamiliarizes and reorients what can be known about both these other historical figures active in these ancient assemblies and those rhetorical figures that continue to be activated in contemporary settings. In tracing the (potential) traffic between these ancient and more recent figures, the aim is not to claim that they are somehow identical to each other. Rather, it is through these subversively anachronistic juxtapositions that this book highlights the particular, but still only partial connections between them: a set of shared features shaped by their practices of gender, sexuality, and embodiment that depart from prevailing perspectives (in both the times we call "then" and "now").[5] Such a strategy takes the biblical interpretation of such topics beyond the most common practices of condemnation or apology, in between assumptions of historical alterity or identity, toward a critical "elsewhere" that reflects more consistently and capaciously on those before-and-after figures who have been targeted by biblically based claims across the centuries.

Such an approach involves disorienting or reacquainting different readers with one or more of the elements this project arranges within and beyond an admittedly audacious ancient, queer, and Pauline threesome.

Romosexuality

Our sources on the larger Greco-Roman context for these epistles and assemblies, for instance, definitely display different attitudes and ideas about human bodies and behavior. Starting with the work of Amy Richlin, scholars of the Roman republic and empire have described their sexual terms and practices as following a Priapic protocol, named after a hypermasculine, superphallic deity Priapus.[6] Males at the top of the sociopolitical, Romosexual hierarchy are imagined as akin to this violent, vigorous, and threatening deity, and thus were expected to be "active" in all things, including sexual acts, where they should only take insertive roles.[7] Elite Romans traditionally tended to think hierarchically about bodies, assuming and then reinforcing claims of elite, free, Roman imperial, male superiority.[8] This prevailing view shapes the belief that sex is not a mutual activity; it is not done with someone else, but to someone else: a superior can, even should make use of an inferior in sexual practices.[9]

In delineating the boundaries between superior and inferior, the Romans tended to hold different ideas about the physical characteristics and sociopolitical significance of bodies, not just around gender but also around ethnoracial, free, and economic status as well as imperial and geographic location. Thus, insertive and receptive roles did not map exclusively on males and females, but on superior and inferior along multiple, intersecting trajectories. Unlike more recent expectations, then, just surviving to become an adult male does not make one a "man" in the Roman imperial context. For the free, elite, adult, Roman imperial male, masculinity is incredibly hard (no pun intended) to achieve and maintain. A good Roman man (a free, elite, adult, male, citizen) would need to constantly demonstrate that he was unlike his social inferiors because he was an exception, part of a relatively small group of people who can be, in the words of Jonathan Walters, "the impenetrable penetrators."[10] (This exceptionalism will be an important topic in the fifth and final chapter.)

All the rest are women and what scholars of Roman antiquity have dubbed "unmen." These are the people who apparently cannot control or preserve the boundaries of their bodies. The unmen might appear to be masculine in one way or the other to twenty-first-century people, but the traditions reflected in Roman imperial sources presume that young, peasant, enslaved, castrated, conquered, foreign, and/or receptive males were not masculine.[11] They were something else and more than a little like women, feminized in this system. Their inferiority is reflected in ideas about their gendered, embodied, and sexualized status, making all of these less problematic receptacles for the "real" man's use than his peers among elite, freeborn, Roman imperial figures.

Such "receptacles" are precisely the kinds of figures I consider in much greater depth in successive chapters. From this politically prevailing perspective, gender-variant females, castrated males, sexually available enslaved people, and barbarically gendered foreigners were ostensibly inferior and degraded figures. Yet the same traditions that cast them in such roles also reflect anxieties about masculinity and a related set of complicated ambivalences around these other figures. The prevailing perspective itself leaves hints that it is not the whole picture.

Queer Reconfigurations

Such alternative angles can be developed with some key concepts and reconfigurations from queer studies. But which part of queer studies suffices for such a task? To attempt a brief overview of the places queer studies can be used for projects in religious or even just biblical studies would be daunting, possibly foolish (as I among others can attest).[12] Even the term "queer" twists people into knots, some embracing, many others loathing it and its connotations as perverse or abnormal. To be sure, such connotations are the point for those who use it, a deliberate strategy to reclaim it from pejorative or derogatory uses.

In early twenty-first-century English the term is used as both a form of identification and a mode of critique or analysis. One can identify as "queer," marking oneself as a sexual or gender minority. In practice, this use of queer often functions as a shorthand for a series of abbreviations from LG, to LGB, LGBT, and LGBTIQA, for lesbian, gay, bisexual, trans, intersex, queer or questioning, and ally (though asexual also appears in some contexts). These growing practices of affiliation, tethering different potential identities to each other, reflects a certain politic that seeks to cross specific practices of gender, sexuality, and embodiment. Those groups and scholars who have reclaimed this word do not dispute that it connotes abnormality or nonconformity; rather, they dispute that such a contrary relation to "the natural" and "the normal" is negative. Queer, then, can also indicate a challenge to regimes of the normal, a desire to resist and contest such a worldview. In this second sense, queer is less an identity and more a disposition, a mode of examining the processes that cast certain people and practices into categories of normal/ natural and abnormal/unnatural and then of interrogating the effects of such processes. Figures, then, can be queer because they self-identify under such an umbrella sign or because they twist, turn, challenge, and reconfigure processes of naturalization and normalization. In what follows, I mostly tend toward the latter sense (a kind of critique), but leave open possibilities for the former (a form of identification).

Various scholarly and activist trajectories fed into the emergence of the subdiscipline of queer studies in the 1990s, as the work of a kinky trinity of Judith Butler, Michel Foucault, and Eve Kosofsky Sedgwick found wider audiences by bringing critical attention to ideas and practices that seemed normal or natural.[13] I grapple with each of these in the following, first full chapter, in order to establish the contours of a queer approach that can reach past Paul, toward other, before-and-after figures, and negotiate between the presumed poles of either continuity or discontinuity between the first and twenty-first centuries. As my preceding discussion of the ancient, Roman imperial context indicates, questions about the historical differences of gender and sexuality remain prominent, which accounts for why Foucault has been more regularly engaged in biblical and classical studies than any other figure in queer theory.[14] Yet, Butler more persistently informs my project, as reflected by the continued discussion into the second chapter and the important, if more implicit role her work plays in framing each of the chapters that follow. Her influential explication of performativity and citationality merits wider consideration within biblical interpretation, particularly wherever alternative historical and political horizons are sought.

All three of these scholars helped to define queer studies' interests in troubling identity and history, bodies and power, representations and effects. One can see their influence in many directions, including later in my second chapter, where Jack Halberstam troubles the attachment of masculinity to men (in ways ancient elite males appeared not to imagine) and underscores the difficulties and ambiguities of bodily practices. Yet, because I remain interested in figures before and after "canonical" lodestars, including those who have emerged as central to queer studies, my engagement with queer interlocutors is also more eclectic, even idiosyncratic, reflecting that there are actually multiple, alternative, even competing genealogies for queer studies. My selection of partners and influences is mostly strategic and intentional, even as it is frankly often just affective and intuitive—these interlocutors are a sampling of available resources (often crossing queer genealogies), those who help me to make sense of the worlds I cycle between, including those in the first and twenty-first centuries.

Indeed, for a project that crosses time like this one, I cannot help but build on the foundation of the historians and social scientists who established the social construction of sexuality (like Mary McIntosh and Jeffrey Weeks).[15] As the first chapter demonstrates at length, the shape of my own approach is as informed by the historical efforts of Bernadette Brooten and David Halperin as the aforementioned "canonical" thinkers in queer studies. In the chapters that follow, still other historians, sociologists, and anthropologists of gender, sexuality, and embodiment provide crucial insight and context for trans and butch practices (Susan Stryker and Rubin), the treatment and response of people with intersex conditions (Alice Domurat Dreger and Katrina Karkazis), and BDSM practices and the continuing legacies of slavery (Rubin, Margot Weiss, and Saidiya Hartman).

Of course, queer studies is inspired and informed by the audacity and irreverence associated with and deployed by the radical, initially gay and lesbian, political actions of groups like ACT UP (AIDS Coalition to Unleash Power) and Queer Nation. Such actions led the way in intentionally reclaiming stigmatizing terms like "queer" for an explicitly confrontational, subversive, and resistant form of advocacy. This accounts for the activist tendencies in queer studies, even as activists "outside" the academy were informed by and generated their own kinds of theoretical practices. One can see this influence in the chapters to follow, given the queer strategies of those working on trans (Leslie Feinberg and Kate Bornstein), intersex (Cheryl Chase), sex-positive (Pat Califia), and race-critical (Isaac Julien) forms of advocacy.

In many instances the lines between academy and activism are not as clear as this basic survey of my project's interlocutors initially indicates, particularly when one considers queer studies' emergence alongside, out of, and from within other projects that blur or cross such lines, as feminist, anti-racist, and postcolonial studies tend to do. These interconnections suggest still other starting points for queer studies, particularly given the necessity for thinking of gender and sexuality as inherently shaped and mutually informed by race, ethnicity, economy, and empire. As several scholars have highlighted,[16] the work of women of color feminists, like Gloria Anzaldúa, Audre Lorde, Barbara Smith, and Hortense Spillers, precede and exceed the focus of the more commonly canonized queer work.[17] Their bodies of work mark a longer critical engagement with the operations of gender and sexuality as they are profoundly delineated by and necessarily intertwined with the dynamics of race, ethnicity, and economy (among others). In what follows, this mode of critique comes especially into the foreground in the discussion of enslaved people and barbarians (in chapters 4 and 5) aided by the work of Spillers, Jasbir Puar, and Jacqui Alexander. Yet, it not only reconfigures our approach to captive, enslaved, conquered, and incarcerated bodies, branded as slaves or religious/racial minorities, but also underscores that other figures of gender and sexual variation (including the androgynes and eunuchs considered in chapters two and three) were always already marked by ethnoracial difference, monstrously gendered and perversely racialized.

Many might expect more psychoanalytically influenced kinds of approaches when a project addresses ideas like perversion or deviance, as this one occasionally does. To be sure, Butler, Foucault, and Sedgwick each respond to and work with elements from Sigmund Freud, Melanie Klein, or Jacques Lacan. Freud is lingering in the background of the third chapter's discussion of castration—with a focus on male genitalia and Jewish-Gentile difference, how could he not be? For the present project, however, I find some of the more recent, psychoanalytically informed queer work on desires and death drives less compelling than those projects that focus on queering our relations to time and history.[18] Thus, I use the first chapter to jump off from Butler, Sedgwick, and Foucault and split the difference between presumptions of historical alterity or identity. Here, the insights of Carla Freccero, Elizabeth Freeman, and most especially Carolyn Dinshaw expand the relational possibilities for reaching back and reckoning with the haunting force of the past on our present. Dinshaw's beautifully juxtapositional ruminations enact a desire to "make relations with" elements of the past, seeking a "touch across time."[19] I find that my own efforts to know queer figures before and after Paul's letters link up with Dinshaw's efforts to make "connections across time between, on the one hand, lives, texts, and other cultural phenomena left out of sexual categories back then and, on the other, those left out of current sexual categories now."[20]

Such touches and connections offer more than crude conflations of people and practices across the centuries. Indeed, the image of a touch across time entails rather contingent connections that split the difference between the continuities and ruptures that have disciplined historical discussions of gender, sexuality, and embodiment. After further discussion of this approach in the first chapter, then, each chapter stages its own touch across time through anachronistic juxtapositions of figures before and after Paul's letters: androgynes with trans and butch, eunuchs with intersex, enslaved people with the bottom in eroticized bondage practices, and barbarian foreigners with the monstrous terrorist.

Past Paul

Such juxtapositions can trouble oversimplified notions about the present's relation to the past and reconfigure the political, cultural, and religious significance of these biblical epistles. These letters have already proven to be quite influential, as even a brief survey of their use in historical and often ongoing disputes—about the roles and status of women, enslaved people, Jews, foreigners, racial minorities, religious dissenters and minorities, the poor, children, the government, and, yes, also LGBTIQ people—shows. Of course, these letters are also among the scriptures of the Christian New Testament. More materials are traditionally attributed to Paul than to any other author or community (fourteen of the twenty-seven books) within the New Testament. For Christians the letters are also valued as the work of a sanctified figure— *Saint* Paul—and, thus, important sources on communal organization, ritual practice, and theological belief.

Historically inclined interpreters highlight the letters' place as the earliest surviving materials within and about the early Jesus movements. Some of the more enthusiastic interpreters have dubbed Paul the "founder of Christianity," given his epistolary and (presumed) evangelizing labors among the communities that would eventually become, or at least be treated as the predecessors of, early Christianity. Many stress the ways Paul worked among non-Jewish peoples (or Gentiles) as particularly important for the growth, even survival of this movement, a claim with an uncomfortable, but clear resonance with Christian claims of supersessionism (their replacement of Judaism as God's true people). Historical or theological claims about the epistles or their author, then, are never purely academic or simply spiritual, as they often have significant social and political consequences.

Thus, these letters do not map smoothly onto more expected configurations. They are neither field manuals, theological treatises, nor autobiographical accounts, even when they make claims about their recipients, refer to theological ideas, or shape Paul's claims about himself. They are rhetorically sophisticated objects, situated within longer exchanges between Paul and a range of communities. In short, when we read the epistles now, we are reading other people's mail! More specifically, though, they are attempts to persuade, likely meant to be read out loud, to be performed. Among the more circumspect, then, these letters are valuable because they provide one, albeit specific angle on the author and these audiences, one perspective on the assembly communities in action.

Still, their importance never simply resides on the historical horizon, as resources for reconstructing debates and deliberations in the middle decades of the first century CE. It remains important to grapple with Paul's letters because they continue to be used; they are not just artifacts from the past, creating arguments with and for others long ago. This also suggests why these epistles are not just for Christians or even for people living in Christian-majority cultures. Because biblical ideas have become central to the planet's most populous religion, and because people from Christian-majority cultures have gone virtually everywhere else on the planet, often claiming a biblical basis for doing so, it would be inadvisable to ignore the impacts of biblical, and especially Pauline, argumentation and figuration. As I will discuss in greater length in the chapters to follow, the biblical already crosses time and space. Why not, then, try a different, if intentionally anachronistic strategy of juxtaposition, in an attempt to reach out and know more about the historical figures targeted by the letters and those rhetorical figures circulating before and after the letters?[21]

For those unacquainted with Pauline epistles or interpretations, though, some further winnowing of the materials and approaches is necessary. While fourteen texts are attributed to Paul, the scholarly consensus treats only seven as among the "authentic" or "undisputed" letters: Romans, 1 and 2 Corinthians, Galatians, Philippians, 1 Thessalonians, and Philemon. The first four of these (in canonical, not historical order) are traditionally described as *Hauptbriefe*, the essential or more important letters, not because they are among the longest, but because Protestant scholars hold that they stress important concepts, like justification by faith, more than the others.

The second chapter reconsiders aspects of 1 Corinthians, a relatively long letter that ranges over a number of topics. Traditional approaches focus on the letter's calls for unity, discussions of the cross, the Lord's supper, and resurrection, and instructions about sex, food, and living among "outsiders." It is often cited because it also contains two passages that aim to circumscribe the speaking roles of women in the community (in 1 Cor 11 and 14). While 1 Corinthians signals conflicts, Galatians (the subject of my third chapter) strikes an even more polemical tone. Though it narrates a select number of events in Paul's life, it does so only to address his concerns about circumcision among the Gentile members of the audience, potentially indicating multiple, even competing teachers and leaders. It contains a famous formula, likely recited at baptisms: "no longer Jew or Gentile, slave or free, not male and female, for you are all one" (Gal 3:28).

The fourth chapter may examine the shortest of these letters, Philemon, but its allusions to the enslaved figure Onesimus (Phlm 10) has led to an inordinate amount of interpretation on slavery and freedom. However, the letter is not only brief, but its exact purpose is also difficult to determine, given the more evasive, even diplomatic approach it takes toward Philemon, the potential addressee and owner of the enslaved person in question. The fifth and final chapter returns to 1 Corinthians, while also reconsidering Romans. Romans is traditionally treated as an elaborate theological statement either because it was meant to be Paul's last testament of his beliefs or his introduction to a community he has not already visited. Both approaches tend to focus on the letter's arguments about salvation and justification, again treating concerns about Jewish and Gentile difference in the community.

Yet the aim of this book is to reach past Paul and toward those figures before and after these letters. Any such attempt will be thwarted in advance if it only seeks to follow the perspective presented by the letter, if it does not work to find alternative angles on these figures. This interest in people beside Paul is inspired by and indebted to a significant body of feminist historical and rhetorical work. Starting especially with Elisabeth Schüssler Fiorenza and Antoinette Clark Wire, feminists reading for the perspectives of women, among others, demonstrated how Paul's letters are not descriptive of a first-century reality, but are attempts to be prescriptive of a reality they are seeking to construct.[22] This opens the way to decentering Paul, and treating him and the letters attributed to him as representing only one among many voices acting and negotiating within the contexts of the assemblies and the wider world.[23] This approach also requires swerving away from the predominant politics of identification with Paul and against nearly any other figure mentioned in the letters.[24] With a different set of commitments, one can factor for the persuasive function of a letter, recognizing the points of considerable strain, conflict, or tension, to move beyond Paul's perspective and see another side to those addressed.[25]

Thus, my queer approach is also a specific kind of feminist project.[26] As I have already suggested, each of the ancient figures deployed in Paul's letters—the androgynes, eunuchs, slaves, and foreigners—would fit with Roman imperial characterizations of unmen. From the perspective of the Priapic protocol, they are defined negatively, they are not like the "real" (read: elite, free, Roman imperial, citizen) men, they lack the ability to control or preserve the boundaries of their bodies, thus they are lower in the prevailing sociopolitical hierarchy. Since males like these are marked as inferior by their association with womanliness or femininity, this could also suggest the potential for rethinking their positionality from below. Schüssler Fiorenza suggests the term "wo/men," to indicate not only the differences within and among females, but also the potential connections between most females and subaltern, or nonelite males.[27] Wo/men highlights that not all females experience intersecting dynamics of power in the same way (consider nonelite, enslaved, and/or foreign females) and may often hold more in common with males toward the bottom than females toward the top. Adopting this understanding, rather than a prevailing perspective disciplined by identifications with Priapus, helps to instead identify these figures before and after the letters as wo/men.

This also signals that the complexity of the sociopolitical dynamics within both ancient and more recent settings is not easily summed up by terms like "empire," "sexual penetration," or even "patriarchy." The Roman imperial era is shaped by all of these dynamics, and more. This is why Schüssler Fiorenza coined the term "kyriarchy" to describe and analyze the multiple, intersecting, and mutually influencing pyramidal structures of power and oppression.[28] Kyriarchy is a system where only certain kinds of males are "men"—elite, educated, freeborn, propertied, imperial, and typically from particular racial/ethnic groups—who rule all who might be wo/men—females but also nonelite, uneducated, enslaved, subaltern, and/or often racially or ethnically oppressed groups of males. Imagining these dynamics as pyramidal visualizes steep angles, where very few reach an apex, while more and more people subsist under multiple forms of subordination and marginalization in the spaces below.

These are the spaces where one would find gender-variant females, castrated males, enslaved people treated as sexually available, and barbarically gendered foreigners, even as scholars typically remain stuck on the prevailing perspective of texts written by and for those toward the apex as descriptive. Thinking and looking with a concept of kyriarchy presents another tool for approaching these figures from a different angle, from below.[29] This book, then, is also a counter-kyriarchal project.

After This Before

The following chapters pursue alternative angles on appalling bodies. The first chapter, "Touching Figures: Reaching Past Paul," further situates queer approaches to history and temporality as a way forward and out of persistent debates about whether and how the past is different from the present. Dinshaw's queer touches across time provide an inspiration that directs the four, more extended chapters, each structured by a specific anachronistic juxtaposition to reach out for those figures cast as appalling bodies, before and after Paul's letters.

Chapter 2, "A Close Corinthian Shave: Trans/Androgyne," grapples with 1 Corinthians 11:1–16, one of the letter's attempts to limit women's prophetic speech in the community. Allusions to androgyny appear in a couple of places in this text, but most especially in strange references to head hair (11:5–6). This is just one vexed marker of gender variety and multiplicity, which can be reimagined with more recent figures of female masculinity like drag kings, butch lesbians, transgender dykes, or gender queers (especially as examined in transgender studies). Chapter 3, "Uncut Galatians: Intersex/Eunuch," reconsiders the multiple ways Galatians argues with and about bodies and two practices of genital cutting—circumcision and castration. Though it quotes a baptismal tradition (3:28) prized for its scrambling of several embodied factors (Jew/Gentile, slave/free, male/female), it also violently wishes for those seeking circumcision to be castrated (5:12), bringing the eunuch as a lingering point of contrast into the foreground of the letter's argument. Critical reflections on the meaning of modifying bodies with intersex conditions contrast with such uses of eunuch figures, subverting the persistent scholarly focus on Paul focusing on the circumcised penis, a focus that reinstalls a normative view of "member"-ship in the community.

Chapter 4, "Use: Bottom/Slave," seeks another way to approach Onesimus, the enslaved figure and object of negotiation in Philemon. Onesimus is also the butt of another casual "joke," this time about the bodily vulnerability of slaves, including for the sexual use by the owner (Phlm 11). To work more creatively with this slim epistle, the coordinates of such arguments are rearranged by a juxtaposition with an alternative ethic that reconfigures constraint in relation to consent. The role of the bottom in BDSM practices (bondage, discipline, dominance, submission, sadomasochism) can help to challenge the ancient ethos around slaves, without swerving away from its horrors and lingering heritages, most especially when it attends to the role of race and historical reference in such practices. Chapter 5, "Assembled Gentiles: Terrorist/Barbarian," resituates figurations from both Romans and 1 Corinthians, particularly within the two "clobber" passages more recent users claim condemn homosexuality (in Rom 1:18–32 and 1 Cor 6:9–10). The role of Gentiles in Pauline epistles and interpretations is troubled by the figurations of the barbarian and foreign Other that appear in both of these "bashing" passages, highlighting a larger role for sexual exceptionalism than sexual orientation. The unexpected resonances between those people addressed in these passages and named in the conclusion of Romans (16:1–16) and those targeted as especially barbaric or terrorizing today provide an alternative angle on assembly and the intersecting dynamics that bring contingents together.

The discussion of these texts was not delayed until the fifth chapter simply because sometimes deferring the desired heightens the pleasure of an encounter (though that might be a happy fringe benefit of this deferral). Rather, I hope it underscores this book's efforts to not focus on prevailing perspectives or figure out "what Paul tells us" about gender, sexuality, embodiment, or, in this case, homosexuality. Just as importantly, however, the analysis of the figures before and after these two passages requires the work on the ancient figures considered throughout the preceding chapters. Gender-variant females, castrated males, and sexually available enslaved people fold into and fill out the figurations of the barbarian and foreign Other and demonstrate retroactively the racializing and colonizing dynamics at work in all of the figurative practices discussed in this project. It's not just about the sex, though there's plenty of it here, even as these intersections highlight the ambivalences of our reaches, remembrances, and touches.

This also accounts, in part, for the concluding epilogue, "Biblical Drag," about how our encounters with the biblical can be such a drag. In reaching past Paul's letters, seeking a touch across time with and through these before-and-after figures, we encounter appalling bodies. The reason for such troubles will undoubtedly vary among those who encounter the figures and arguments with these chapters, but let's all try, even for a little time, to get into trouble together.

1

Touching Figures

Reaching Past Paul

There are many ways to "make history."[1] In setting a precedent, advancing a cause, or achieving something once thought unimaginable, one is said to have made history. In a contrary vein, demonstrating the outdated or out-moded status of an idea or practice, or relegating a person or thing to the past (and likely the past alone) are also ways for something to "become history." ("That way of looking at things? It's history." Or: "My relationship with him? Oh, he's history [or we're history].") Historiography, another, more familiar form of "making history" for scholars, can often be caught between these first two senses: the advances of precedent and the relics of the past.[2] History making, then, can involve the call of the present to discuss the past, often for the future, or it attempts a look back in order move onward and away from this past. Indeed, grappling with how historiography might do such things can also make yet another kind of history; or, rather, it can remake this history: the history of interpretation when it comes to norms, applications, and practices of gender, sexuality, and embodiment.

The challenges of queer theory and the persistently troubling historical practices of biblical citation indicate that it is time once again to make history: to reformulate the history of interpretation, refocus historiographic endeavors, bring some practices to an end, and still others a new beginning. This book moves within and between two different trends in thinking and writing the history of sexuality: the altericist position that views and stresses past formations as different and as "over" in a new present that disrupts any identification with the past, and a more continuist position that recognizes and highlights how the present is after, yet out of a history, a response to the past through which subjects identify (and disidentify).[3] Most positions and practices within this tensive and ostensible "divide," expressed, refracted, and likely contorted by the many senses of "making history" (presented and uninvoked earlier), consider the past, present, and future in virtually simultaneous or at least overlapping fashion. Within

Appalling Bodies. Joseph A. Marchal, Oxford University Press (2020). © Oxford University Press.
DOI: 10.1093/oso/9780190060312.001.0001

them temporally divided states make contact with and graze against each other, if only so that some might disavow or embrace some small sliver of this contingency.

A third way of grappling with ancient arguments about gender, sexuality, and embodiment begins with examining the work of two scholarly precedent-setters, Bernadette Brooten and David Halperin. While both scholars present options for historiographic efforts, both also set a series of limits on these options where one might still tap into a more resistant or disruptive strain in queer theory. Some of these limits at least partially map onto, match up with, or accompany the aforementioned narratives of alterity and identity, reflecting the limits then of some wider trends in history-making.

This study, then, aims to chart another approach, indebted to but departing from these two options, invested in, but not bound to historiography in generating a body of queer *and* feminist interpretive strategies.[4] The trajectory of this approach is further complicated by its focus on biblical argumentation, since historical questions and answers typically and traditionally enjoy pride of place in biblical scholarship, while queer studies have made glancing, compelling, yet oft-ignored forays into the biblical. Thus, one finds queer interrogations of and approaches to biblical materials posed, received, and identified as against this biblical-historical norm, underscoring additional potential tensions as the relationship between the biblical, the historical, and the queer are not at all straightforward.[5]

A particular disciplinary phenomenon—what might be called the "biblical behind"—is the continual lag of biblical studies' engagement with critical theoretical interventions in domains like feminist, race-critical, postcolonial, and/or queer studies.[6] This project aims to mix different scholarly temporalities: certainly biblical studies with queer studies, but also the work of some of the "early" or "first" queer scholars with "recent" queer reflections on temporality and historicity. Biblical image and argument have potently (if often problematically and oppressively) crossed time and exceeded periodization, thus exemplifying what some queer scholars would call multiple, even simultaneous temporalities. Functionally the biblical draws on and partakes of its historical home in our antiquity, slides comfortably in modern periods pre and post, and persists in a range of contemporary effects and affects, where the biblical frequently works to compare, prioritize, reinforce, prescribe, or, in short, normalize specific concepts and practices of gender, sexuality, and embodiment.[7]

Between Brooten and a Halperin Place

If ever there was a work that made history, in many of the senses delineated thus far, while grappling with how the biblical crosses history and
its periodizations, it would be Bernadette Brooten's groundbreaking *Love
Between Women*. In this volume, Brooten assembles an impressively expansive range of ancient sources in order to reframe our contemporary understanding of both ancient female homoeroticism and one particularly
influential passage from ancient scriptures: Romans 1:18–32. As most informed readers and reviewers of this text have attested, the book is sure to
remain a starting point for any future efforts to discuss the topics contained
in its voluminous pages; thus, dutifully and appropriately I also begin here.
Brooten's aim is to contribute to multiple contexts, including especially
women's history and the history of sexuality.[8] Given these contexts and
the ample sources collected in her project, Brooten describes two tasks for
her work and, I suggest, for our continued consideration: "(1) to understand ancient conceptualizations of female homoeroticism in the context
of cultural constructions of the female; and (2) to reconstruct the history of
the women against whom these authors were reacting."[9] In Brooten's analysis, understanding the rhetorical constructions of female figures, whether
engaged in sexual practices or not, can be one resource for the historical
reconstruction of the "Other" of such conceptualizations (including especially the *tribas*).[10]

Brooten's study of the primary sources, mostly generated by elite males,
demonstrates what appears to be a marked rise in awareness about female
homoeroticism in the Roman period. When it comes to the "proper" roles
of women relative to subordination and transgression, she posits that there
might be more continuities between the views of the ancient world and those
of our own than once believed. Furthermore, Brooten shows how Paul's
arguments can be better understood against this background, as Paul's condemnation in Romans 1 reflects a set of assumptions, shared with the wider
Greco-Roman world, about gendered subordination and asymmetrical
sexual practice. In Brooten's capable hands, these continuities disturb trusty
truisms about Christian difference and challenge historical visions, opening
a vista on the possibilities of female homoeroticism in the ancient world and
in the communities to which Paul wrote.

Brooten opens this work by contrasting her results with the claims made
by classical scholar David Halperin in *One Hundred Years of Homosexuality*.

More recently, Halperin has returned to these topics in *How to Do the History of Homosexuality* as a way to develop a slightly altered set of methodological reflections, addressing along the way his own concerns with Brooten's approach. This work attempts a perhaps inconsistent rapprochement with Brooten's assertion of historical continuities, while seeking a more thoroughly historicist engagement of queer resources, including especially the work of Michel Foucault. In the face of his previous, persistent insistence on the discontinuities between ancient and more recent forms of sexuality, Halperin seeks to admit the utility of accommodating both the ruptures and continuities in a queer kind of historiography.[11] Nevertheless, the evident effort and focus on his part in this more recent work suggests that Halperin still has far greater facility in charting the differences and discontinuities.[12] For Halperin, the tasks for our consideration are threefold:

> The real question confronting the historian of sexuality is how to recover the terms in which the erotic experiences of individuals belonging to past societies were actually constituted, how to measure and assess the differences between those terms and the ones we currently employ, and how to deal with the conceptual, methodological, political, and emotional consequences of the conclusions we draw from the evidence—the consequences for ourselves, for others, and for the history of sexuality that we hope to create (and, by creating, to be changed by).[13]

Though Halperin commendably, if but momentarily notes the importance of reflecting on the contemporary consequences of history-making (in his third task), the elements of distance and difference are stressed in the first two tasks, reflecting the predominant tendency of his work, here and elsewhere.[14] In seeking new queer strategies, one might be initially encouraged by this third task of Halperin's, yet in what follows he fails to discuss how one might evaluate these consequences or generate a consequential strategy for a provocative and lively queer present.

In focusing on these first two issues, Halperin limits the potential tasks of the historian of ancient materials in comparison to the efforts of Brooten and others influenced by various models of women's history, social history, or history from below.[15] In explicitly contrasting his approach with Brooten's, for example, Halperin highlights how his aim is just to reconstruct the ancient discourse in all of its cultural specificity and faithfully reproduce its point of view.[16] Halperin adopts this strategy believing that simply presenting the distinctiveness and difference of ancient modes and models for sexual ethics and practice will generate the necessary dissonance within and from those more recent heteronormative claims of timelessness, traditionality, and naturalness. In attempting to adapt Foucault's genealogical analytic for his own history of homosexuality, though, Halperin is forced to admit the clear limitations to his procedure[17]:

> I will make no attempt here to recover the variety of discursive silences, the subjugated knowledges, the non-represented voices that must figure significantly, or at least be taken into account, in any substantive history of male homosexuality. The preliminary genealogy offered here will inevitably overrepresent dominant or elite discourses.[18]

Both Brooten and Halperin note the predominant influence of elite males on most of our sources for the ancient world, but Halperin does little to mitigate this influence by expanding the base of his investigations (to include biblical or "religious" materials, for example) or altering his methodologies to either address or seek subjugated knowledges.[19]

This more recent work finds Halperin trying to engage and implement elements from queer theory for historiography, addressing critiques made by Eve Sedgwick among others, but his refusal or perhaps reluctance to address insurgent knowledges leaves considerable gaps, for both the making of ancient histories of sexuality and the expansion of queer strategies for remaking the present. Too often in Halperin's reflections, it seems, the argumentative appeal of altericist historiography for "making history" is taken for granted and assumed to be self-evidently efficacious. Perhaps the most instructive suggestion to be found is one Halperin makes only in passing (in his introduction):

> Even more promising, however, is the tactic of asserting a continuity with whatever features of ancient, exotic, or culturally distant societies may be at odds with contemporary institutions, practices, and ideologies of homophobia. It is possible, after all, to recruit the queerness of past historical periods not in order to justify one or another partisan model of gay life in the present but rather to acknowledge, promote, and support a heterogeneity of queer identities, past *and* present. There is more than one strategy for entering into a queerer future.[20]

We might still expand on these strategies by rethinking issues of continuity, not through a focus on homosexuality, but on queerness, the nonheteronormativities that crop up across a range of times and spaces.[21] Thinking through the biblical, ancient, or historical indicates that one might productively discuss norms "before" heteronormativity, or the function of normalizing arguments "before" the modern troubles with normal.

How to Get Stuck in "the Middle" with Sedgwick and Butler

The tensions and methodological differences between Halperin and Brooten at least partially correspond to the drift of many approaches to the history of sexuality: one either stresses historicist difference or a transhistoricist similarity. Halperin, for one, has been influential in his insistence on the alterity of the antique past, often implicitly (if inconsistently) for the sake of a present.[22] Yet, scholars attending to textual and contemporary constructions of temporality like Louise Fradenburg and Carla Freccero have questioned this supposition: "Is it not indeed possible that alteritism at times functions precisely to stabilize the identity of 'the modern'?"[23] Staking their claim on the same turf as Halperin (namely Foucault), Fradenburg and Freccero argue: "precisely if we are to honor Foucault's insistence on the unpredictability of political strategies, we should not discount the oppositional potential even of grand narratives and continuist histories."[24]

To the extent that Brooten's work deploys such gestures, these moves might be as Foucauldian as Halperin's repetition of the narrative of rupture (selectively stressed and possibly misread from Foucault's *History of Sexuality: An Introduction*).[25] Carolyn Dinshaw suggests that "our choices as queer historians are not limited simply to mimetic identification with the past or blanket alteritism, the two mutually exclusive positions that have come to be associated with Boswell and Foucault."[26] For the purposes of queerly biblical approaches to history-making, such positions could be further extended in a chain of associations where historical similarity attaches to Boswell and Brooten and differentiation to Foucault and Halperin.[27] Yet, I have already aimed to trouble such a mapping of distinction and association, just as Dinshaw qualified and clarified an "opposition" between Boswell and Foucault.[28]

Though Dinshaw is working on and within a space-time that is "distanced" from and yet also "close" to my present project and to the biblical, her efforts to think through a queer historical impulse prove to be both instructive and provocative.[29] Dinshaw's beautifully juxtapositional ruminations enact a desire to "make relations with" elements of the past, seeking a "touch across time." Asking after and about history need not be an either-or affair of "are they like us or not?" Dinshaw's answer to such a query is paradoxically both and neither, since "history is both incommensurate with and mimetic of our era."[30] Further, as respondents like Ann Pellegrini see it, Dinshaw would rather ask and answer queries like "What other kinds of relations to the past are possible? Must we choose between the comforts—the pleasures—of identification and the cold, hard facts of difference, if that is what they are?"[31] Such a line of questioning both splits and exceeds the difference between alterity and identity in a way that one might call queer. Dinshaw posits that "queers can make new relations, new identifications, new communities with past figures who elude resemblance to us but with whom we can be connected partially by virtue of shared marginality, queer positionality."[32]

If one notes more than a partial connection between this point about queer positionality and Halperin's suggestion to "recruit the queerness of past historical periods," this is because Halperin's compelling (if isolated) foray is sparked by Dinshaw's "careful, responsible, and socially sensitive example."[33] One might be especially inclined to think that Halperin, in his engagement with queer studies, would be uniquely situated to advance further alternatives for interpreting and negotiating historical resources like these.[34] Indeed, like Brooten before him, he is aware of queer theorist Eve Sedgwick's critiques of historical analyses (like his own, including his use of Foucault's) that generally take "homosexuality as we conceive of it today" as self-evident and clear.[35] Yet neither Brooten nor Halperin adequately addresses what Sedgwick has highlighted as the "unrationalized coexistence of different models" in contemporary definitions of sexual identity and conduct.[36] What Sedgwick's analysis indicates is that dissonance, difference, instability, and even contradiction embedded within most contemporary conceptions of gender, sexuality, and embodiment do not unmake or dismantle their argumentative force. Indeed, strikingly, Sedgwick claims that it is precisely the incoherence of such conceptualizations that has made them effective for a variety of rhetorical situations.[37] Simply highlighting the alterity of the past, then, as a form of noncorrespondence will not be sufficient for disrupting the normative force of a model or for sparking a proliferation of resistant options.[38]

In the context of biblical studies, Sedgwick's critical insight might explain why it is that most historically oriented interpretive projects have yet to make the kinds of public impacts that one might have hoped or even expected.[39] The biblical still persists, even proliferates, as its own kind of argument: the transparent and untroubled use of the biblical as timeless, eternal, primordial, and thus contemporarily relevant is still quite effective in a range of contexts. In order to have such an impact, then, the interpreter could follow Sedgwick's queer impulse and recognize that the more significant factors might involve who has the "material or rhetorical leverage" for shaping and deploying definitional force (no matter its degree of internal coherence or historical continuity).[40] Since various LGBTIQ populations have not typically been the bearers of such argumentative leverage, Sedgwick warns us to be both cautious and critical about our strategies for resistance or recognition.[41] In such a context, for example, any focus on questions of "gay origins," historical, social, cultural, biological, or even biblical, however discontinuous its findings might be with widely accepted norms, can be easily redeployed in the predominant cultural trajectory of eradication, not affirmation.[42]

For Sedgwick, there is no place outside of these conditions that "have unfolded both the most generative and the most murderous plots of our culture."[43] Similarly, but perhaps more hopefully, queer and feminist theorist Judith Butler views our enmeshment with and as subjects of gender, sexuality, and embodiment as practices of improvisation in a scene of constraints.[44] As Butler highlights, both of these scholars seek alternatives for our contemporary context: Sedgwick "to show possibilities for sexuality that are not constrained by gender in order to break the causal reductiveness of arguments that bind them" and Butler "to show possibilities for gender that are not predetermined by forms of hegemonic heterosexuality."[45] What Butler stresses, however, is that the currently hegemonic forms and norms constitute the scene from where the subject emerges (constraint) and can still rework or exceed the norms (improvisation). Following this insight, one might enter a context where normative claims have been set (and at least partially through claims of biblical citation, authority, and adherence), but the response to and use of the terms of this context are not at all fixed. As actors in history, then, contemporary people can make partial connections with texts, cultures, and lives that set, yet exceed those constraints (like those of or from the "biblical") in a past constantly and performatively reiterated in and for claims about and constitutions of "contemporary" presents. Queer subjectivity allows for and is conditioned by these kinds of touches across time, on terms not quite predetermined, but contingently and partially enacted.

For Butler, then, it is the doubled task of one with feminist and queer commitments to simultaneously interrogate and use these terms to different ends,[46] asserting "an entitlement to conditions of life in ways that affirm the constitutive role of sexuality and gender in political life"[47] while continuously and critically examining the terms by which this affirmative argument is articulated. In attending to the rhetorical context also described and addressed by Sedgwick, Butler's theorization of concepts like performativity applies where a practice demonstrates both the workings of a presupposition and its openness to rearticulation.[48] A normative presupposition is open to rearticulation precisely because it always only works through its repeated use, its ongoing citation as that "what" which is to be practiced. In the play of identification, then, one might only partially connect with the prior presupposition (whether it is a life, a text, or another entity that lays a claim upon one), thus identifying with the prior, but not being or becoming identical. Identification, similarity, and continuity, after all, presuppose a difference to and from which one must connect but also approach.[49]

With every repetition, a practice can demonstrate that norms can be malleable, contestable, even transformable, since they are always in the process of being realized, but never fully or completely so.[50] Since these are embodied practices, Butler demonstrates that:

> As a consequence of being in the mode of becoming, and in always living with the constitutive possibility of becoming otherwise, the body is that which can occupy the norm in myriad ways, exceed the norm, rework the norm, and expose the realities to which we thought we were confined as open to transformation.[51]

Butler suggests, then, that the operation of norms need not exclusively function to normalize, but it might also be the site of continuous efforts at collective resignification and transformation.[52] Butler's work indicates how much an "alterity within mimesis" persists so that processes of identity formation as identification are never seamless nor complete, functioning as much as a *dis*identifying process not unlike an appropriation.[53] Indeed, Fradenburg and Freccero have noted how queer theorists like Butler have debated about the deployment and repetition of norms, roles, and practices as potentially transgressive in this fashion and questioned whether it might apply to the making of history. Is it possible that "identifications with the past, with earlier communities and sexualities" might "constitute the historiographical equivalent of subversive reinscription?"[54]

Through various acts of improvisation in scenes of constraints, of partial connections, and of disidentifying identifications, the biblical interpreter engaged with historical questions might find other ways to make a troubling kind of history. As Butler argues for gender, the task in the encounter with and on various scenes conditioned by the biblical is both "historical and performative"; it both precedes and requires the imperfectly repeated practices of identification and connection.[55] Butler's description of one such scene might apply, though oddly, to this biblical-historical quandary:

> The prevailing law threatened one with trouble, even put one in trouble, all to keep one out of trouble. Hence, I concluded that trouble is inevitable and the task, how best to make it, what best way to be in it.[56]

Certainly, one could say that a number of biblical texts—like the letters treated in the following chapters—are troubling precisely because they threaten us with trouble if we do not heed its call to stay out of it.

Yet a queer, gender-troubled response to the trouble of how to make history with this text expands the possible tasks with and beyond those delineated by Brooten and Halperin. Both scholars agree that understanding the terminologies and conceptualizations of the ancient world is one such task, while tracing both the dynamics of continuity and difference.[57] Where they most diverge, however, is over the propriety of seeking, as Brooten does, to reconstruct the historical "Others" of this ancient discursive context, particularly tribadic women.[58] This second, reconstructive task might still have compelling interconnections with the third way initially proposed in this study and occasionally suggested by Halperin's own rather sporadic engagement with queer theorists besides Foucault. The effort to reconstruct subjugated parties and formations might, in fact, link up with Dinshaw's efforts to make "connections across time between, on the one hand, lives, texts, and other cultural phenomena left out of sexual categories back then and, on the other, those left out of current sexual categories now."[59] Such reconstructions do not compel unthinking acceptance or repetitions of mimetic exactitude but rather have their appeal in contributing to queerly nonidentical identifications, unanticipatable similarities, and unconventional temporal copresences.[60]

Both Brooten's and Halperin's manifest topical foci and methodological preferences, though, have led to only cursory treatment of the resources of those queer theorists, like Butler and Sedgwick, who also grapple with a range of feminist issues. This set of resources provided by thinkers queer and feminist can help the biblical scholar contest processes of normalization and generate alternatives for the practices of disruption, resistance, and transformation of contemporary culture(s) too often bent against the safety, survival, and social justice of those troubled and targeted by biblically based claims. While the remembrance and reconstruction of the others in the normative and normalizing impulses of biblical claims is clearly important in this process, it operates not for its own sake, but for the goal of transformation. Thus, in this approach a priority is placed on developing transformative practices and assessing how suspicious strategies and critical evaluations of "history" (both the product and the process) can contribute to these practices.[61] In suggesting this third interpretive approach to the hermeneutical options available, this book pursues a route more precisely attuned for meeting and exceeding those conceptions of "making history" delineated in the opening of this chapter.

Does this approach open up the possibilities for that elusive "touch across time" between people positioned queerly in, by, and perhaps partially against the marginalizing arguments? What more can we know about prophetic women or baptized bodies? Can we make contact with people like Onesimus or groups like the assemblies gathered behind and before these letters? This will only be possible if interpreters learn from the feminist biblical scholars who have attended to the rhetorical dynamics of these letters. They have stressed that one cannot begin with a position of simple acceptance or acquiescence (either in historical presuppositions about the past community or ethical-political considerations of the present and the future). Paul's authority is (and was) far from final or ultimate; his arguments reflect that he is one out of many. This might indicate the utility of feminist historical conceptualizations for a range of interrogatory practices, as it pluralizes the visions and authorities of and in structures of the ancient assembly communities.[62] The audience, then and perhaps both now and later, is not confined to the perspective Paul attempts to norm through these letters. This indicates that my aim is not limited to "finding" these lost "them," even as I could be seeking partial connections, contingent touches, and dissonant identifications with various audiences. The aim is as much about generating what "we" who are now an audience (of a sort) to this rhetorical act in history can do, possibly with the connection of a queer kind of coalition: not in corresponding with this correspondence (Paul's letters), but in any noncorrespondences to the letters that nonidentically touch on other noncorrespondences.[63]

In and through these letters, concepts of exclusive authority are decentered, as Paul often acknowledges by appealing to so many different leaders and participants in these assembly communities. These figures and their communal formations precede Paul, so for Paul to participate in and declare his own kinds of precedence, he must perform it through citation. Such citations are more open to reconfiguration than most interpreters are willing to consider.

Toward Some Touching Connections?

Paul's vision is only one out of many, and the other members of the community seem likely to have improvised differently than he given the constraints presented by both the letters and the ancient figures they cite in addressing these other figures, these other members of the assembly community. Assemblages now can also improvise similarly, approximately, but not identically to the epistles or the figures deployed or addressed by them.[64] Butler's formulation of a gendered, sexualized, and embodied subjectivity that is performatively produced stresses this openness to the rearticulation of norms and the possibility of different modes of living. Performativity always leaves room for a differently produced subject, both then and now. Whether in these epistles, their interpretations, or circles wider than (but still possibly affected by) these, the expression of norms leaves possibilities for different citational and (dis)identificatory practices, ones that are not solely confined to a faithful repetition of the norms. An interest in antique historiography or Pauline rhetoricity does not necessitate a loyal and exacting reproduction for contemporary contexts; but this interest can become a site of transformative rearticulation.[65]

Butler's conceptualization cautions, though, that this practice cannot be enacted by the solitary genius or the individuated subject, operating voluntarily, freely, even wildly. You or I come to be and know ourselves as subjects (we live) in the paradoxical conditions of constraint and improvisation. The necessary deterritorialization of norms through their citation will not be the result of heroically isolated and grand gestures of subversion, but requires a persistently critical reflection on our practices at and as "collective sites of continuous political labor."[66] We need less of heroically adventurous and saintly subversive solitaires like Paul and more of oddly assembled and critically reflective collectivities like those assembled in the pages to follow, with and through whom one could find contingent connections in, as, and with history. Only then can we embark on the tasks of continuously assessing our assertively affirmative practices, submitting them to critical scrutiny with regard to their effects and consequences, intended and unintended.

Any reach to touch people within such ancient collectives will meet some rather clear limits if it does not make efforts to reposition the kinds of figures deployed and then targeted by the letter. Paul's letters recurrently repeat and reinscribe ancient (often Roman imperial) ideas about a constellation of perversely gendered and strangely embodied figures, including androgynes, eunuchs, slaves, and barbaric foreigners. Indeed, greater familiarity with these figures and forms of argumentation provides key contexts for approaching and reimagining those "Others" still so marginalized within both these epistles and their interpretations. Juxtaposing these ancient figures against or alongside other, more recent figures of vilification or stigmatization—like drag kings or trans butches, or people with intersex conditions, or those engaged in BDSM practices, or those targeted as terrorists—suggest alternative angles on the arguments and audiences for the letters (aside from the perspective presented as Paul's), particularly when they share particular, if still only partial connections on the basis of their practices of gender, sexuality, and embodiment that depart from oppressive perspectives (then and now).

The history of others from and in the elite male normalizing argument can trouble and exceed the norms, as they help us to imagine other possibilities than once thought possible. But a further queer inquiry presses us to consider what kind of troubling history can be made if we might still rework those norms arrived through historical means, through the citation of either normalizing rhetoric or subjugated histories. Though this citational practice is always malleable and open to resignification, it is also never conclusively finished or fixed, either in its normalizing or its queerly regenerative forms. The norm's citationality entails that a queerly feminist critical process matches a process of and for living: it must persist for us to subsist and it must be cautiously and critically reflexive for us to be reiteratively responsive to the functions of alternative figurations. There will be still other possibilities enacted in and through these traces tracked historically and argumentatively, but each must be evaluated in terms of its contemporary rhetorical leverage. In biblical studies, such a practice could make a new history of interpretation, but more importantly it could be history-making for our own ongoing practices of being, doing, and living.

2

A Close Corinthian Shave

Trans/Androgyne

Because it contains a notoriously difficult passage about women prophesying, Paul's first letter to the Corinthians is typically one of the principal
texts enlisted in debates and deliberations about gender, sexuality, and
embodiment. The section of the letter that argues about women's roles in
the assembly community at Corinth (11:1–16) is convoluted and persistently characterized by interpreters as obscure, contradictory, even impossible.[1] Ostensibly, the women are acting in ways Paul saw as unbecoming,
but on close investigation the potential situation of the audience and the
outcome sought by Paul become rather difficult to discern. The strange
figures and forms cited, constructed, and addressed by the arguments
of the letter do, however, provide an opportunity to reconsider a series of
perversely gendered figures, those circulating in the ancient world
and deployed to particular ends in Paul's letters as well as those in more recent contexts.

Paul's arguments about prophetic females repeat problematic aspects of
Roman imperial traditions. Androgynous figures took a range of forms in
Greco-Roman antiquity, many of which will be considered here. Because
Paul's perspective presents only part of the ancient context of these assembly communities, though, the introduction of more recent figures of
female masculinity (especially as examined in transgender studies) can
provide an alternative angle on the figures deployed and targeted within
this letter. By juxtaposing them against more recent figures of vilification
and opprobrium, other aspects of these marginalized figures targeted by
Paul's arguments can emerge, and the traffic between the figures from
seemingly disparate sites can be traced, as they resonate both before and
after Paul's letters.

Appalling Bodies. Joseph A. Marchal, Oxford University Press (2020). © Oxford University Press.
DOI: 10.1093/oso/9780190060312.001.0001

Corinthian Citations, Pauline Performativity, and Echoes of Androgyny

In chastening women who had the audacity to prophesy and pray—heads uncovered—in their assembly, 1 Corinthians 11:1–16 makes an argument about natural gender roles and proper bodily comportment, contending over authority and imitation. These topics are often tightly woven within Judith Butler's analysis of performativity, a concept that challenges many of the commonly received notions about the sexed body, the seemingly stable basis for arguments about gender, desire, sexual practice, and (what we now call) sexual orientation. It is surprising how rarely the imitative, repetitive, and citational elements of performativity are considered or deployed in queer engagements with biblical argumentation.

Recall Butler's idea that, because it must always be repeated to be recognized as normal and natural, gender is unstable.[2] Yet, if gender is itself unstable, so too are constructions of sexuality like heterosexuality, requiring as they do stable genders and a corresponding desire for an "other" (*hetero-*) gender. What appears as only "natural" or "normal"—one's gender, body, sexuality—is not a straightforwardly innate part of one's identity; rather, this sense of identity is only an effect of the incessant doing that must be done in order for one to be readable in the regulatory frame. Sexual normativities (like heterosexuality) are revealed as inherently unstable, even panicked, needing constant explanation and reiteration to produce themselves (or itself) as the natural. This process requires copies of copies of copies of what it is producing as the "natural." It requires incessant repetition.

Such a recurring operation leads Butler to observe that "*gender is a kind of imitation for which there is no original,* in fact, it is a kind of imitation that produces the very notion of the original as an *effect* and consequence of the imitation itself."[3] Butler is turning on its head the heteronormative claim that homosexuality is a secondary, derivative, or imitative form of sexuality (after the "naturally" occurring heterosexuality). Performativity shows that any gender and any sexuality is an imitation, an attempt to copy the cultural process by which it is regulated.

In Butler's conceptualization, while these cultural processes that produce our ideas of genders, sexualities, and bodies are never complete, one cannot exactly get "outside" such processes of regulation. Because this regulatory frame conditions everyone's subjectivity, one must "cite" the normalized and naturalized practices in one's actions. Yet their instability and repeatability can make them sites to "trouble" norms; their citationality provides opportunities for subversion—to repeat, but "fail to repeat loyally."[4] The issue is not *whether* one repeats gendered scripts or cites erotic norms, but *how* one does so. Normalization and naturalization are open to rearticulation precisely because they always only work if they are constantly being reinstalled as the normal or the natural, as the practice that must be cited and repeated. Since they are always requiring repetition, norms are never fully or completely realized. Arguments that (attempt to) establish the nature or the norm are sites for trouble, and can be cited to transform norms and resignify bodies. There is room within this process for subversive improvisation through repetition, imitation, citation.

The importance of the imitative aspect to Paul's argumentation is brought into clearer relief by beginning slightly earlier than where scholars have typically divided this passage from previous arguments. I maintain that, in a more linear fashion, Paul concludes one argument, but also continues it and, thus, begins this section on women's behavior in the assembly community by explicitly calling for imitation: "Become imitators of me, just as I am (also) of Christ" (11:1).[5] Paul seeks the community's imitation, while claiming that he imitates Christ. If this argument is successful, it establishes Paul's authority in the eyes of the audience, but he is also constructing an image of what it means to be imitating Christ, what it means to belong to *his* version of a Christ-like community. This establishes what will be an ongoing dynamic of conformity and difference, the potential similarity between parties and a hierarchical order that structures their roles differently. Thus, when Paul presents a threefold hierarchy of heads in 11:3, it both repeats this hierarchical sort of argumentation, but it also stresses that there are correspondences between the three pairings (Christ over man, man over [his] woman, God over Christ), that they somehow repeat each other. The authority of a claim that males are over females derives its authority from its functional repetition of other relations, which seem to be more accepted in the community (the supernatural over the human). Not so incidentally, the shorter argument from correspondence and imitation in 11:1—imitate me, just as I imitate Christ— might just be echoed and, thus, slotted within this hierarchized series of correspondences, giving Paul a share of Christ's authority through his imitation and implicitly generating a God—Christ—Paul—man—woman chain.[6]

If Paul is building on an understanding that God and Christ are over humans, generally, and even inserting the man over (his) woman into this understanding, then he does something that many biblical communities try to do: cite a tradition. Indeed, Paul cites all sorts of things to build his argument and vision for the community. He cites himself (11:1, 2) and claims that the Corinthians have done so too, since they "remember me in everything," keeping traditions in just the way he gave them (11:2). He cites a potential tradition about heads (11:3) and cites aspects of the two different creation stories to account for why only men are in the image of God (11:7, referencing Gen 1:27), and women were made from and even for man (11:8, 9, referencing Gen 2:22–23). He cites the angels (a reference that still befuddles biblical interpreters, 11:10) and practices of propriety (11:13). Reaching the end of his rope, he cites what nature should apparently teach (11:14) and what all of the other communities do (11:16; everyone else is doing it, so why don't we?). Paul repeatedly does this, repetitively appealing to all kinds of arguments (arguments that just might be outside of the community but, Paul holds, must reflect the true meaning of their communal identity).

All of these arguments are meant to address one major concern about what women are doing when praying and prophesying within the community (11:5). Unlike the interpretation presented by Gillian Townsley (the only other application of Butler's ideas to this passage I have found),[7] though, I do not think the primary rhetorical concern of this passage is with the Corinthian men.[8] Of course, the Corinthian women are praying and prophesying, just like the Corinthian men are (11:4). The concern for Paul seems to be that these two groups are doing the same things, and doing them in the same way, without covering their heads. The argument represents an effort to try to keep the women from repeating this practice; or, rather, it aims to get them to repetitively pray and prophesy, but from within a regulatory frame that reinforces a gendered difference. The letter is repeating that dynamic of conformity and difference: the women should conform to a differentiated gendered role that hierarchically structures their place in the assembly community. The letter, however, reveals the work it takes to generate and reinforce these gender-differentiated roles. These arguments are already unstable, no matter how much Paul (or others) might insist on a naturalized order or the proper place of supposed social inferiors. Paul's repeated citation of various arguments and his attempt to get the Corinthians to imitate himself and his vision of the community reflect the hurried, harried, even panicked condition of performativity. Paul is only the authority he claims to be, if the Corinthians confirm this role by repeatedly and loyally performing their circumscribed roles that would ostensibly naturalize the regulatory order that Paul tries to generate as constant and proper, original and God-given. Of course, the arguments for these origins reflect that Paul seeks the imitation of this vision without an original: they are not already doing and repeating and citing the way he wants them to. (Else why expend this effort?)

Passages like this one aim to prescribe certain embodied practices as natural. The need to cite, repeat, and even imitate the arguments made in this text indicate their continuing instability, the possibilities for claims about nature to function in ways besides naturalization. Here, Paul is arguing that when the Corinthian women are doing these same things, repeating the practices of prayer and prophecy, but without covering their heads, they are confusing gender roles. Scholars have long puzzled over the potential background of this dispute about gendered comportment between Paul and members of the Corinthian assembly community.[9] Often, they have speculated as to whether and how Paul could be calling up figures and forms of androgyny in this passage. Given the frequent references to the creation stories found in Genesis (in verses 7, 8, 9, and 12), several previously postulated that community members were appealing to a "Gnostic" myth of a primal androgyne to explain their identity as transcending or mitigating gendered differences after baptism.[10]

One advantage for a reconsideration of this passage as performative is that the primordial-androgyne suggestion raises questions about how the recipients of this letter thought and acted, particularly before the letter was even sent. To his credit, Dennis MacDonald seeks just such information by opening his discussion of primordial androgyny by noting: "Perhaps the most fascinating but vexingly elusive issue of all is: Why did the Corinthian women uncover their heads?"[11] For MacDonald (and a few others) the answer lies in an attempt to overcome gender distinctions, as inspired by a myth of primal androgyny that lies behind the baptismal formula of Galatians 3:28 ("no longer Jew or Gentile, slave or free, not male and female") and their ecstatic worship practices. While some biblical scholars, like Wayne Meeks, were more optimistic about the social and political effects of such traditions about gender transcendence or reunification,[12] MacDonald maintains that "the androgyne myth is not antiquity's answer to androcentrism; it is but one manifestation of it."[13] "Gnostic" perspectives on the devaluation of the body and the desire to overcome the feminine mean that an androgynous unity is still a male kind of androgyny, to which the female should try to conform.

Here, however, is where the hypothesis encounters problems. To build a case for an original (and originating) myth, MacDonald, Meeks, and others must refer to a range of texts and traditions from periods later than the mid-first century. In fact, their sources are primarily the later texts of early Judaisms and (eventually) Christianities: rabbinic texts, Irenaeus, Tertullian, Clement, and those texts classed as "Gnostic" (like *Exegesis on the Soul, Gospel of Philip, Gospel of Thomas*). It is especially in the last of these that one finds a stress on the necessity of females becoming male in the process of redemption. This association with "Gnosticism" is likely one of the main reasons this hypothesis about the early existence and influence of a myth of primal androgyny on the first-century Corinthians finds few advocates, given more recent critiques of the term as a problematic conceptualization for dividing and assembling a range of different practices and ideas.[14]

Beyond these conceptual and historical-categorical problems, however, feminist scholars like Elisabeth Schüssler Fiorenza have noted a range of problems with trying to separate out the "social significance" of baptismal traditions or prophetic practices from a communal "religious" or "ecclesiastical" order, including a new or restored order of "spiritual" androgyny.[15] Antoinette Clark Wire specifically objects to MacDonald's effort not only to separate such realms but also to claim the priority of an original, primordial androgyny behind the exchange reflected in 1 Corinthians 11 and even before any social significance to baptism practices (that call up a "not male and female" existence). On the contrary, Wire argues that Paul's rhetorical effort in this passage "presupposes an earlier social function of the claim to be *not* male and female in Christ. His unquestionably social struggle with the women prophets in Corinth is good evidence of this."[16] For now I will admit that I remain agnostic (no pun intended) about what meaning or use of the baptismal tradition, repeated in Galatians 3:28 and reflected in this passage's *different* reuse of the first Genesis creation narrative (in 11:7), could have been original or even just earlier. We cannot know the original function of what was likely an oral tradition in these developing assembly communities. However, it was probably not "Gnostic" (however that term might still be used) during or before the middle of the first century and it appears to have been taken to have some sort of social, political, or otherwise practical significance in at least the Corinthian assembly before Paul writes this letter. (If not, how else can one account for Paul's intense efforts in this particular passage?)

Methodologically, in examining the potential meaning of androgyny (of primordial or of other varieties), it is not surprising to find androcentric attitudes or hierarchical forms when the sources considered are primarily, or even exclusively from elite male perspectives.[17] This is a problem not only with those earlier studies about androgyny (from the 1970s or 1980s), but also within more recent work stressing "unequal androgyny," such as Dale Martin's.[18] In such instances perspective matters—the perspective taken by ancient texts and by contemporary scholars. Like most interpreters and users of Paul's letters, Martin's focus remains resolutely on Paul in statements like: "neither Paul's androgynous statement in Galatians 3:28 nor his admission of women to important positions within his churches demonstrates that he was a gender egalitarian."[19] Here, Martin assumes that only Paul was active in these issues and adopts his perspective (or the perspective Martin constructs for him), aiming only to identify (with) his position, not the women's (nor their reason or motivation for action).[20] This is potentially problematic, or at least ironic, considering that it attributes actions and authority to Paul in two matters where it is not at all clear he did or had them. The baptismal formula is more frequently considered to be pre-Pauline in composition and use, while there is no evidence that the various positions in local assembly communities (not "his" churches) were "Paul's" to give. Like many others, Martin does not ask why or how the Corinthian women led prayer and prophecy activities, the kinds of questions Wire and even MacDonald do ask.[21] Scholars have not only used a likely later set of traditions to limit primal androgyny's (prior) meaning(s), but also accepted the perspectives reflected in kyriarchal ideas and arguments as a primary influence.

The figure of the androgyne actually lurks in the background and, briefly, wells up into the foreground of the argument in this 1 Corinthians passage, but not where scholars have typically focused: on the image of the divine and the reworking of the Genesis creation narratives. It might be more helpful to look earlier in the passage, when Paul first labors against (what he sees as) the potential for confusing varieties of gender in the Corinthian assembly community. When Paul first mentions the Corinthian women doing particular things with their bodies—praying and prophesying uncovered—he claims that such behavior is the same as if the women's heads were shaved (11:5; cf. 6). Scholars often trivialize or pass over this particular rhetorical move, characterizing the argument as ridiculous or absurd, as an exaggeration, perhaps even intentionally so on Paul's part. A range of commentaries declares that Paul is being sarcastic in making this equivalence (or in arguing that a woman should cut her hair short if she will not cover).[22] Wire combines two common scholarly estimations when she describes Paul's equivalence of prophecy uncovered with head shaving as a "shocking aside."[23] When this portion of the text is not treated as some kind of hyperbolic shock treatment,[24] then it is most frequently passed over in due haste to get to other verses and (ostensibly) more pressing matters, like the meaning of *kephalē* (head) or *exousia* (authority).[25] When considered, Paul's argument about shortly cut or shaven hair is seldom deemed relevant for the historical situation in Corinth. Richard Horsley insists that this argument is "hypothetical. It does not presume that some women were cutting off their hair."[26] For Wire, the rhetorical efficacy of Paul offering a "reasonable concession" (head covering during prayer and prophecy) is dependent on shortened head hair being "an unthinkable alternative."[27]

Yet, what if the argument Paul is making is dependent on women's shaved heads being a distinctly recognizable, thus thinkable practice and possibility?[28] I intend to treat this particular rhetorical move as more than just an aside, a peripheral or incidental gesture, completely unmoored from historical dynamics. Lingering over the potential premise "it is shameful (or dishonorable) for a woman (implied: a women's head hair) to be shortly cut or be shaved" (11:6) calls up images of gender variation (and before one gets to the sentences that ostensibly reflect on a myth of primal androgyny). This is the first claim Paul makes after attempting to establish three hierarchically arranged "head" relationships. Given the rarely used terms for hair cutting, shaving, and covering (*keirō, xyraomai,* and *katakalyptomai,* respectively),[29] Paul's argument in these two verses could just be an unacknowledged contributor to the entire passage's oft-noted difficulty.[30] Rather than pursuing the image of an androgynous deity, this more explicit, if still potentially ridiculed, image indicates that the forms of gender variance that have been (inconsistently) classed under the category of "androgyny" can still be insightful for discerning alternative angles on the argument and the audience reflected in 1 Corinthians 11. It is worth starting over again with any reflections on androgyny and 1 Corinthians.

Ancient Androgyny, Reconsidered

In starting over again, one must admit that there is some degree of confusion within and between studies of ancient androgyny, possibly because their terms were deployed in ancient contexts to a number of different ends. The meanings tied to *androgynos, androgynus,* or *androgynē* encompassed a variety of behaviors and ascribed bodily conditions. Androgyny is a confused category from the start, and, to the degree it was tied primarily to gender variation, the Roman imperial elite were uncertain what to do with examples of it. On the one hand, from within a hierarchically ordered sex-gender system, gendered variations would seem to be both common and expected. There are males at the top of this order, but there are plenty of males who are not: foreigners and the enslaved, just to start. Females depart from the excellent or even perfected human, the male, by matters of degree—in at least two meanings of the term, heat and hierarchy—but not entirely by kind.[31] Since the elite, free Roman imperial males, *viri*, could lose a heightened (= masculine) status by demonstrating an inability to control themselves or others, the possibilities of males who fail at manliness, or of their various Others potentially rising in status, remain an ever-present possibility. This model appears almost as a zero-sum system of power, with better and more excellent humans who are more controlled and in-control-of-others' bodies at the top, over a range of such bodies requiring their rule, those that depart from this standard of excellence as lesser embodied entities.

On the other hand, it is also clear that these elites encountered figures of gender variance for which they felt that they must somehow account, in both positive and negative ways. Indeed, these conditions are where androgynous figures appear and reappear in ancient contexts like the Roman imperial. In the Greek cultures the Romans inherit and adapt, for instance, *androgynos* was already an insulting term for males, indicating some kind of "womanly" quality. Aristophanes knows it to be an insult (in Plato, *Symposium*, 189e), likely because it was a term that was applied to an elite male who showed he was cowardly, particular in war.[32] This association of *androgynos* as a signifier of a weakness in masculinity survives into and through the Second Sophistic, where if a man even breathes like a coward, he is likely an *androgynus*.[33]

The parameters of ancient figures or forms of androgyny are not always clear to scholars of more recent centuries. One of the few sustained studies dedicated to androgyny, by Luc Brisson, often seems to merge, even conflate androgyny with hermaphroditism. Unfortunately, Brisson rarely interacts with a great deal of the emerging literature on gender, sexuality, and embodiment in Greco-Roman antiquity, leading to his often idiosyncratic use of terminology including "bisexuality" and "dual sexuality."[34] Brisson prefers the latter (which could be better termed in English as "dual-sexed"?) in delineating his area of focus: "the simultaneous or successive possession of both sexes by a single individual."[35] This definition can account for many of the contexts in which androgynous figures appear. Androgynes are linked to differences in the sexed body, for instance, in the Hippocratic corpus, where *androgynoi* are a third-tier category of male newborns (the lowest), resulting from the mother contributing a male body that masters the father's contribution of a female body.[36] Indeed, in some places *androgynos/us* appears almost as a synonym for *hermaphroditos/us*, as when Diodorus Siculus suggests that an *androgynos* (in 32.12.2) is like a previously mentioned *hermaphroditos* (in 32.10.4). In this vein, Brisson cites Pliny the Elder, who explained, "Persons are also born of both sexes combined—what we call 'Hermaphrodites,' formerly called '*androgynoi*.'"[37]

Particularly if the Romans were looking for portents of trouble, the birth of a gender-variant child was often categorized as a monstrous prodigy.[38] Brisson assembles a table of sixteen such references to dual-sexed newborns between 209 and 92 BCE.[39] The appearances of these children were viewed as bad omens, then, given the frequency of war and conflict in this period. Cicero, for example, argues for the prophetic power of such occasions, like "when that unlucky prodigy, the *androgyni*, was born."[40] Livy as well describes when "at Sinuessa a child was born of uncertain sex, as between male and female—the populace call them *androgynos*, as it uses many similar terms, since the Greek language is more apt at compounding words."[41] Here, not only is the intermediary figure (*inter marem ac feminam*, between male and female) requiring atonement, but also it makes a distinctly Roman imperial claim about the correspondingly strange Greek antecedents.[42]

Yet, the uses for androgyny were not limited to those bodies of (ostensibly) indeterminate or intermediate form. *Androgynos* remains an effective term of reproach for males who are not "man enough" in public settings. According to Suetonius *androgynoi* were males that were lacking in ways that mark them as feminine, they "have something of the shape of a man, but are feminine in all other respects."[43] Even when there is some sort of intermediacy, as with the Hippocratic corpus earlier, it can be marked as a certain kind of male departure from his masculinity: "He who is between man and woman."[44] In fact, given the role of this sort of characterization in the competitive culture reflected in ancient physiognomic training, Maud Gleason regularly prefers to translate *androgynos* in terms of effeminacy, a male's gender deviance, a man's deficit or loss of masculinity, rather than a body's intermediacy or indeterminacy.[45] This is how the *androgynos* can, at times, appear to be indistinguishable from the *cinaedus*, a figure whose gender deviance or transgression was often (but not always) indicated by his playing the receptive role in sexual acts.[46]

Strikingly, androgyny played a similar role in distinguishing certain kinds of females from others, but with occasionally different evaluative results than when attributed to males. When Valerius Maximus praises a group of elite women's oratorical skills, he describes Maesia Sentina as an "Androgyne" because she had a "masculine spirit beneath a feminine appearance."[47] To the eyes of elite males, the practice of masculine skills or virtues by their women was often a source of praise and admiration. What was once the distinguishing practice between "real" (elite, imperial, free, Roman, or Greek) men and unmanly figures (like *androgynoi*) can become the marker of special kinds of women. Like its Greek counterpart *andreia* (manliness, virtue, or courage), the preeminent virtue for Romans was, well, *virtus* (manliness, valor, or virtue), derived from the Latin word for man, *vir*. "*Virtus*," as encapsulated by Craig Williams, "is the ideal of masculine behavior that all men ought to embody, that some women have the good fortune of attaining, and that men derided as effeminate conspicuously fail to achieve."[48] Whereas earlier, in the Hippocratic corpus, the third-tier category of female newborns are equated with the second-tier of male newborns (as *andreiai* and *andreioi*, respectively), by the time of Seneca, elite females who demonstrate *virtus* are on the same level as great men.[49]

As a result, Plutarch was able to describe Cato's daughter Porcia as lacking in neither prudence nor *andreia*.[50] Valerius Maximus offers further perspectives on these exceptionally virtuous (masculine) women, including Porcia. He describes the lengths to which Porcia went to kill herself, swallowing live coals from a fire, as "having imitated the manly death of her father with a woman's spirit."[51] Valerius Maximus goes even further in describing Lucretia's suicide as reflecting the mean error of fate of her possessing a "man's soul," but receiving a "woman's body."[52] As Judith Hallett has rather carefully demonstrated, elite Roman men were often pleased to describe elite Roman daughters as similar to their fathers, or to other male kin.[53] Cicero, for instance, calls his daughter, Tullia, "the image of my speech and mind."[54] By their speech and their studies, daughters were said to bring their deceased fathers back to life.[55] As Hallett highlights, Pliny the Younger also argued that "the recently deceased daughter of his friend Fundanus was her father's exact living image in appearance and ways."[56]

Still, masculinity as *virtus* belongs to (particular) males and naturally so. Such virtuous women, however, are hardly the rule, but an occasional (though frequent) exception, reflecting the virility of their kinship.[57] After all, the positive evaluation of gender variation only goes in one direction: when females are more masculine (or androgynous), not when males are more feminine or androgynous.[58] In a certain way, the relative virility, masculinity, or perhaps androgyny of elite, free, Roman imperial women presents no problems for the sociopolitical order (which kyriarchally weaves together not only gender and status but also race, ethnicity, sexuality, economy, and empire). Indeed, it seemed one way that elite, free, Roman imperial families managed their place in the increasingly imperial and thus more precipitously hierarchical environment, as Rome moved away from being a republic.[59] A number of social and legal changes, involving marriage, dowry, and inheritance practices, meant that many elite, free, Roman imperial women were tightly integrated in the economic networks at the top of the sociopolitical order.[60] They would have been benefactors, patrons, and investors.

As Hallett terms it, a "bipartite" conceptualization of gender, status, and kinship—bouncing between similarity and difference, universalizing and minoritizing tendencies—remained embedded within Roman imperial ideologies.[61] On the one hand, the Roman imperial elite perspective projects the potential that many relatives (even females) could aspire to and embody *virtus* or *andreia*, the similarity between kin demonstrates their entire family's superiority. From a more negative perspective, however, the fact that *virtus* or *andreia* must be achieved and repetitively enacted also means that many (even males) could cease, or simply fail at being a "real" *vir*, could just be an *androgynos* in disguise, a *cinaedus* in private, an unman in waiting. On the other hand, this kyriarchal perspective also insists that masculinity is (almost) entirely the exclusive purview of the "real" (read: elite, free, Roman imperial) man; it belongs naturally to him, even if he has to (paradoxically) work to achieve and maintain it. The flipside of this system requires kyriarchal masculinity to have its Others, its inferiors, including women; this system needs there to be significant differences between those at the apex and the many varieties of people below them. There are the few, the exception, who rule, and the many below, who are ruled.

Not all females who somehow act or simply are androgynous are characterized positively, particularly to the degree that this sort of androgyny is associated with the figure of the *tribas*, a sexually assertive, even aggressive female. *Tribades* are often treated as possible sources for ancient forms of female homoeroticism, as and among other departures from the dominant ethos of penetration.[62] However, their transgressive behavior is particularly treated as a form of gender variation (that is, a deviation), not simply an erotic departure, to which the terms of androgyny can apply. So while Martial ridicules Philaenis as the ultimate *tribas* (*tribas* of the very *tribades*),[63] she is later described by Pseudo-Lucian as a prime example of androgynous loves, or desires (*androgynous erōtas*).[64] Both characterizations of Philaenis ascribe masculine activities and qualities to "her," including Greek athletic activities of wrestling and jumping and (implied Greek) erotic activities of penetrating both young females and males. In females, androgyny is marked by their adoption of some masculine quality or activity.[65]

As in Bernadette Brooten's discussion of these figures, Philaenis is often considered alongside other named *tribadic* or gender transgressive figures. One of Martial's epigrams (1.90.5) is addressed to Bassa, who he once thought was virtuous like Lucretia. This poetic depiction potentially calls up the "good" form of androgyny Lucretia represented: her *vir*-tuous suicide reflecting her bravery and her misfortune to have a "man's soul" in her womanly body.[66] But, in fact, Martial presents Bassa to the poem's audience as a *wrong* kind of masculine disposition—she is a penetrator (*fututor*, or "fucker," 1.90.6), exploiting the opportunity afforded by her all female surroundings. Bassa is a dire prodigy, whose "monstrous lust imitates a man" (1.90.8). While some female forms of imitation of masculinity deserve praise, there are limits to what elite males can accept, and one such limit is the possibility of females playing an "active" or insertive sexual role. As demonstrated by scholars like Brooten, this characterization of females somehow becoming masculine or imitating masculinity, then, is one of the main ways that many ancient sources explain female homoeroticism.[67]

The apparent impossibility of erotic contact without the masculinization of one of the females is driven home by stories like Ovid's account of Iphis and Ianthe (*Metamorphoses*, 9.666–797).[68] Born as a female, but raised as a male (to avoid the threat of a paternal infanticide), Iphis is engaged by her father to her beloved friend Ianthe. Iphis cannot be happy about this potential match, because she knows that her love for Ianthe is "monstrous" (*prodigiosa*, 9.727) and "nature" (9.758) does not allow it.[69] Iphis recognizes that sexual contact with Ianthe is impossible; it requires that one of them be or become male (9.735–44). In this scenario the only positive resolution requires the act of a god (Isis) transforming the body of Iphis (9.782–91).[70] Yet, the seemingly tragic set-up of this tale is mitigated by the virtue demonstrated by Iphis: despite being Cretan and female, her piety, composure, and self-control demonstrate that her qualities have a great deal in common with the ideals of *virtus* prescribed for elite Roman males.[71] In some ways, even before the divine transformation of certain physical characteristics, the tale reflects some of those positive possibilities in particular kinds of gender variation. Iphis was already exceptional before Isis lengthened her stride, gave her greater strength and vigor, sharpened her face, and even shortened her hair, making her male (9.782–91).

Nevertheless, the divine masculinization of Iphis only occurs after she repeatedly affirms the natural and divinely given status quo of gendered hierarchy mapped onto sexual contact. Like the Roman matrons discussed earlier, Iphis can be the virtuous exception because they reflect and perpetuate the order's own claims about its virtue. More frequently, though, the elite imperial perspective presumes the monstrosity of a physical masculinization that they believed must accompany female-female erotic contact. In short, they imagine that one woman's body must have a longer or larger clitoris, a mini-phallus, for penetration. This accounts for the eventual prescription of clitoridectomies for multiple forms of sexual excess.[72]

Unlike Ovid's portrayal of Iphis, Martial's depiction of both Philaenis and Bassa as penetrating prodigies fit the phallic, but tribadic type. Still, the elite imperial mockery of masculinizations can extend to scenarios where the phallic penetration is conspicuous by its absence, as in Lucian's fifth *Dialogue of the Courtesans*. In this dialogue the satirist depicts a wealthy and aggressive woman from Lesbos named Megilla and her persistent efforts at seducing another courtesan, Leaina. In just one short dialogue, Megilla is described over a dozen times with terms of masculinity: *anēr*, *andrikos*, or *andrōdēs*. For her part Leaina knows that this behavior is strange and shameful (5.1), but goes to bed with Megilla and Demonassa (the other host, from Corinth, 5.2). Once they kiss Leaina ("like men"), Megilla removes a wig to reveal a closely shaven head (*apokekarmenē*), "just like the most excessively masculine of athletes," causing Leaina to pause (5.3). At length she tries to determine exactly what kind of gender variation she is encountering in Megilla, until Megilla insists: "I was born a woman like the rest of you, but I have the mind and the desires and everything else of a man" (5.4). As in Martial, Megilla demonstrates an inadequate kind of masculinity—having the desire for this female courtesan, but an inability to control the desire. The tale teases the reader with titillating possibilities, but mocks Megilla as the mode for presenting them.[73]

Though most of these tribadic figures of gender variation are evaluated negatively, the wealth of figures like Megilla or the assumed virtue of those like Bassa indicate their connection and potential proximity to the androgynously virile women who were positively evaluated as vir-tuous. Those positive female figures of androgyny were viewed as assets in elite Roman imperial families and examples of the superiority of their male kin. At the same time, though, the changing social, political, and economic conditions for these women and their families could be posed as a threat, a problem of gender variation that destabilizes rather than reinforcing the hierarchical order. If some women can be like men, can be images of their fathers, imitating their manliness, raising the rulers to come, and managing their own affairs to exercise virile influence at the highest rungs of the empire, what makes the imperial masculinity of elite Roman men superior to these women? As the Roman republic was looking increasingly like an empire, accusations of these women's sexual improprieties, like adultery, become one way to express this anxiety.[74]

The social impropriety of some women's higher status is matched by their sexual impropriety, these improprieties made manifest even in their bodies. Martial's often raunchy poems could have been one attempt to contain the influence of these, elsewhere-positively depicted, androgynous women.[75] Seneca complains that these kinds of women have conquered their nature (or physique, *natura*) and are now rivaling the worst licenses of men: excessive drinking, vomiting, wrestling, and ultimately finding ways to be sexual penetrators (*Ep.* 95.20–21). Seneca twice stresses that such activities result in heretofore unseen hair loss among these women: their baldness showing that they now have all of the worst parts of being a male, including male diseases (or vices, *morbis virilibus*, 95.21).

The figure of the "mannish woman" thus becomes a handy caricature for those elite, free, Roman imperial males anxious about change. This tribadic type is applied especially to those who are elsewhere imagined to be positively virile, especially because of their similarity to elite imperial males.[76] What better way to handle this task of Othering this most akin group than by exploiting their apparent similarity and stress the ways they fail to match the ideal, and thus produce monstrous gender variations? Indeed, it is difficult to imagine this particular rhetorical strategy of casting certain women as "illegitimate men" developing without a preceding recognition of the potential for similarities, similarities demonstrated by such gender variations among elite Roman women.[77]

It is no wonder, then, that ancient androgyny is such a fraught category, sporadically applied to the hermaphroditic body or the phallicized female, an intermediately gendered or dual-sexed figure, the daughter in the image of her elite father or the cowardly male avoiding physical or verbal combat, the bravely virtuous wife and mother or the usurping threat to imperial order, the effeminate, even cinaedic male or the exceptional female, the monstrous prodigy at infancy or threatening portent as a penetrating adult, the female fortunately imitating male virtue (and succeeding) or the female mirthfully imitating male vices (and thus failing), the virtuous female transformed by the gods or the excessive female descending into disease, a male body mastered by the mother's biological contribution or a female body with a manly soul or spirit, the woman who has increased status and influence or the woman who exploits that position. Given this immense range, the *androgynos* and *androgynē* reappear or relate closely to other concepts recognizable in Greek and Roman antiquity: *hermaphroditos*, effeminate, coward, *cinaedus*, virtuous woman, "new women," or *tribas*.

If these figurations were to be rhetorically effective, then an audience would need to accept, first, that such people and practices are possible, and second, that these accusations and characterizations are recognizable to them. Depictions of androgyny would need to connect in some way with types of behavior audiences know. After all, if a claim is entirely implausible, it undermines the person making the claim. The claim may not entirely correspond with already-accepted ideas, but it must resonate with them in some way, it needs to build on that. Specific cases of the elite Roman imperial male ambivalence about elite Roman imperial females signal that the possibilities of androgyny are not precluded but are often assumed to be possible: sometimes praised (if done the right way), and sometimes condemned (if done the wrong way).

Hair-Raising Androgyny and the Corinthian Assembly?

In the notoriously tricky passage in the eleventh chapter of 1 Corinthians, Paul says that a woman praying and prophesying with her head uncovered is the same as a woman having a shaved head (11:5). Altered hair does not call up a primordial androgyny so much as the negative, female forms of androgyny discussed in a range of ancient Greco-Roman texts. Isis, for example, magically shortens Iphis's hair in order to transform her into a male. Seneca worries over the effects of tribadic behavior on women's bodies, including their male-pattern baldness. And in a key moment of Lucian's dialogue, Megilla removes a wig to reveal a closely shaven head (*apokekarmenē*) to Leaina. The description of Megilla's head hair employs the same verbal form (*keirō*) as Paul's premise that "it is shameful for a woman's head hair to be shortly cut (*keirasthai*) or be shaved" (11:6).[78] In encountering a practice that recites (while re-citing) a tradition of becoming not male and female, the prophetic females of Corinth may not have been able to imagine a world beyond or outside gender (or those responding to their practices might not have been able). Their bodily practices were read, then, as variations, even juxtapositions of different gendered ideas and arguments. Paul is deploying a figure that is a masculine female, rather than one that is both male and female.

This, albeit initial connection can be helpful in pursuing alternative angles on the argument and the audience reflected within 1 Corinthians. Like the Roman imperial males positioned above Paul and the assembly community members in Corinth, the first letter to the Corinthians does not pass over these potential figures of gender variance. Rather, Paul also appears to need to account for the prophetic females in the community, both positively and negatively. On the one hand, the type of androgyny to which these verses potentially allude can be seen as a term of reproach or insult, as it was repeatedly used in that fashion for both females and males in the Roman imperial context. Some kind of negative resonance is more than implied by the premise of the argument found in verses 5 and 6, since these modes of bodily comportment are twice marked as shameful. At least some members of the letter's audience would agree that shaved or close-cropped head hair is shameful or dishonorable for females, and Paul attempts to transfer this problematic self-fashioning to another embodied behavior—females praying or prophesying with an uncovered head.[79] Paul begins with a premise that resonates with the perspective of figures like Lucian and Seneca.

On the other hand, Paul's argument also proceeds from the assumption that the Corinthian females are praying and prophesying within this assembly community and the argument does not appear to negatively evaluate females engaging in those speaking activities. In short, this passage is not disputing *whether* females should pray or prophesy, it is prescribing *how* females should be doing these activities. In many communities within the developing movements that some will eventually call early Christianities, women were playing a variety of active, leading, and organizing roles.[80] Paul's own letters refer to a wide variety of both named and unnamed females engaging in such prominent activities within the network of communities he encounters in his travels. Thus, as some elite, free, Roman imperial males commended and some worried about their prominent women, Paul's letters reflect the existence of women prominent within these assembly communities, in a number of roles, including but not limited to those of benefactors and patrons. Letters like 1 Corinthians certainly affirm that there is something different and better about these assembly communities, not entirely unlike the ways the Roman imperial elites imagined their own superiority among other kinds of people. Each group's views of its own exceptionally virtuous women might then be crucial to constructions of the group's relative value.

Though in this passage he does not appear to be especially expressing praise or admiration for the Corinthian females specifically, Paul's argument indicates his acceptance of the prophesying and praying roles for females and he generally commends the assembly community earlier in the passage (v. 2). Intriguingly, Paul's argument here also proceeds on similar terms as some of the (other) ancient texts discussing female forms and figures of androgyny. The transition to this topic stresses the imitation of Paul, just as figures like Valerius Maximus described virtuous women (like Porcia) imitating their male kin. Of course, one of the main ways Paul addresses his audience is through kinship terms, casting himself alternately in the role of brother and father (and occasionally even mother).[81] His arguments explicitly and implicitly prescribe imitating him. Indeed, this passage might just be one occasion where Paul is responding to ways that the assembly community members are imitating, following, repeating, or otherwise citing him (or traditions they hold in common), yet in ways he does not want, nor potentially anticipated![82] What does it mean, after all, to prescribe imitating Paul to females in an assembly community where their prominent roles are already practiced and (at least partially) accepted? Might it affirm such roles, extend them, or constrain them in particular ways? Again, some of the conflicted ways Roman imperial era texts construct figures and forms of androgyny can help.

Paul's arguments likely reflect a dynamic similar to the bipartite view, or unrationalized coexistence, of Sameness and Otherness within this context. The arguments in this passage aim to maintain a twofold differentiation, between Paul and the audience, and between the males and the females in the Corinthian assembly. At times Paul acknowledges, even seeks certain kinds of similarity from both the females and the males in these communities. Yet, he also works to put some distance between parties in this context: Paul makes idiosyncratic use of a Genesis passage about humans being in the image of God (both male and female, in Gen 1:27) by stressing that only males are in this divine image (v. 7). Here, the passage works to put some distance between males and females, and is likely responding to another, very different citation of the same tradition by (at least) the females in Corinth.[83] The letter maintains that males and females were not created simultaneously, nor is their status altered by the likely baptismal citation of this passage (see Gal 3:27–28). Rather, Paul stresses other traditions and posits that woman was created out of (vv. 8, 12) and for the sake of (v. 9) man. The female's status is derivative, though no longer in the image of God, perhaps somewhat in the image of the male (possibly not entirely unlike Tullia in the image of her father Cicero).

With the greater visibility and further integration of prominent and active females into the networks within and between these assembly communities, Paul's contorted argumentation in this passage could just be functioning in analogous ways to (other) conflicted arguments about ancient androgyny. Some elite, free, Roman imperial males came upon ways to manage some of their females' newfound opportunities for independent social, political, and economic action by stressing obligations to their male kin. This passage in 1 Corinthians moves in similar ways to manage the praying and prophesying females, always in relation to their Corinthian male "brothers" in Christ. As within this Roman imperial context, these obligations shape a mode of discipline for these androgynous females: if they seek to be (seen as) virtuous, they will learn to transmit their culture's kyriarchal values to others. Females can speak and lead, teach and run (at least certain) things, but only if they conform to a status quo shaped prior to such activities. The argument in this passage functions in very similar ways: the Corinthian females can pray and prophesy, can play such prominent roles, only so long as they "know their place" relative to the males in the community and Paul's own authority about their bodies. Paul's argument, then, is one attempt to control the behavior of the prophesying and praying females by insisting that certain communally gendered differences be marked on, by, and through their bodies.

Of course, the argument here proceeds from the worry that this form of differentiation is not already accepted and practiced (enough) within the Corinthian assembly community. When set within the significant, rhetorical efforts of this passage, the negative allusion to a female form of androgyny (vv. 5–6) registers an anxiety about certain forms of gender variation, an anxiety that echoes out of the (other) ancient texts about androgyny. Elite, Roman imperial males described *tribades* as monstrous and ultimately failed imitations of males and masculine(-like) behavior. Indeed, monstrosity is a persistent feature of the various rhetorical depictions of ancient androgyny.[84] Paul's premise depends on a similar kind of reaction within his audience at Corinth: horror, disgust, or condemnation of females with shaved or close-cropped hair should be provoked, in order to be transferred to practices that are apparently similar.[85] Perhaps certain kinds of androgynous, or gender-variant activity among females were accepted by Paul. (Indeed, given the way Paul's letters relativize certain forms of kinship and reproduction, they often could be taken to be prescribing rather gender transgressive behavior.)[86] But, in the cases of females who engage in gender variant practices, there is a fine line between being an asset and being a threat to the predominant sociopolitical order. This threat is intimately related to the proximity between some males and some females.

Paul appears to hold simultaneously positive and negative views of certain parts of the prophetic and prayer practices among Corinthian females. He does not object here to females praying and prophesying; the letter seems to presume that these practices can genuinely reflect important ideas about being in Christ, in keeping with traditions that Paul himself claims to hold and transmit. Rather, the issue (from his perspective) is how such praying and prophesying is done. If done the right way, it is worthy of praise. However, if it is done the wrong way, with head uncovered, it is a monstrous threat: it is the same as those female figures of androgyny condemned elsewhere, like the *tribades*. As a result, these bodies would not be prophetic of a changed reality due to Christ, but would become an ominous portent (like other, negative androgynous figures).

It is not hard to imagine that Paul alludes to this figure of reproach—the tribadically transformed body, usurping woman, illegitimate or failed man—as a defensive gesture. Those outside of the assembly community could associate the strange, gender variant practices within this community, even within this letter, with those practices they know from these negative figures in wider argumentation. On the one hand, Paul wants the Corinthian assembly members to depart and differentiate themselves from those around them in certain ways. On the other hand, this argument might just be one attempt to convince them not to stand out too much, or at least not in these particular ways. The argument potentially reflects a view that some are "getting out of hand" and, by alluding to a figure of insult and reproach for the Roman imperial era, aims to get its audience to make the connection between these (similar?) kinds of androgynous practice. Alongside the handy caricature of the "mannish woman" circulating in a few forms, the threat posed by outsiders is another useful tool to get the audience to agree to the modes of control Paul's argument is advocating.

The predominant trajectory of most references to ancient androgyny bends negatively toward condemnation and insult, horror or mockery. Indeed, this is one of the reasons Brooten objected to MacDonald's reconstructions of the meaning of the Corinthian veiling practices through the primordial myth of androgyny: unveiled women praying and prophesying may not have considered themselves any less female, though opponents of their behavior may have.[87] If those practices were in fact readable as a monstrously masculine or ridiculously androgynous behavior, however, why would Corinthian female prophets do this?[88] The numerous ways in which the letter's argumentation reflects and often repeats kyriarchal attitudes to (particularly female) forms of gender variation do situate the content of the letter, but not the potential recipients. The unrationalized coexistence, or bipartite view, embedded within elite, Roman imperial male attitudes about androgyny not only indicate the conflicts and anxieties of this context but also supply the vital hint that practices and people read as androgynous can be conceived as more than just horrific, tragic, nefarious, or pathetic. For claims about such practices to convince, they must resonate in some way. As caricatures or anti-types, figures or stereotypes, the people or practices described as "androgynous" may not exactly correspond to historical practices or people, but Paul likely needed to connect them to at least some historical elements if he wanted his argument to have the desired effect. This constrained connection, then, could provide another vantage point on the historical and rhetorical possibilities of these figures.

Transgender and Other Mobilizations of Masculinity

In many respects, the prophesying Corinthian females correspond with a range of more recent gender-troubling figures, including butch lesbians, female-to-male trans men, transgender butches, and drag kings. Valerius Maximus, Paul's contemporary, claimed that Lucretia had a "man's soul" in a "woman's body" (6.1.1), prefiguring one of the most common narratives about trans embodiment.[89] But out of all of the examples I have already discussed, the dialogue from Lucian proves particularly interesting, not the least because Megilla insists to Leaina: "I was a born a woman like the rest of you, but I have the mind and the desires and everything else of a man"

(5.4). Indeed, passages like these have led classical scholars like Shelly Haley to argue that Lucian's fifth dialogue treats an ancient version of "transgendered lesbianism," inferring that: "Had Megilla been an historical figure, she might well have found herself represented in Leslie Feinberg's *Transgender Warriors* and would have felt at home in the modern transgender community."[90] Though I do not think I can make quite as bold a statement of equivalence as Shelly Haley does here, figures like Megilla and the prophetic females of Corinth could broadly fit within the category of transgender. Perhaps they should be seen as examples not of androgyny but of female masculinity.

"Transgender" as a term crystallized especially in the 1990s in order to describe a set of practices of identification and embodiment that stress some sort of variation, instability, shifting, or change in a person's gender.[91] Like the term "queer," with which it has some overlap, "transgender" functions in at least two ways, as both a category of identity and a mode of political action or analysis. As an identity term, "transgender" seems to have started out as a way to differentiate those who sought shifts in gender identification without as many (or even any) surgical interventions or modifications as those one might categorize as transsexual.[92]

Under the influence of key advocates like Leslie Feinberg and Kate Bornstein, "transgender" also comes to signify a larger alliance or umbrella term that includes postoperative transsexuals among a variety of people and practices, experiences and expressions. Feinberg's now-famous pamphlet on transgender liberation focused on a politicized mode of action by stressing both the potential and the lived alliances between a number of oppressed groups, including "transvestites, transsexuals, drag queens and drag kings, cross-dressers, bull-daggers, stone butches, androgynes, diesel dykes."[93] Feinberg's aim was to counter codes of gender that impose oppressive norms for embodiment, to recognize the intersection of this effort with other struggles for social justice, and to call a wide variety of people to act against such oppression.[94] Working in the same generation as Feinberg, Kate Bornstein discussed the growing changes in transsexual subcultures, where one could meaningfully be neither preoperative nor postoperative, but "nonoperative," or, in other words, "anyone whose performance of gender calls into question the construct of gender itself."[95] Indeed, Bornstein frequently calls for a wider conception of trans as a common ground for all "gender outlaws."[96] Resistant yet fluid, rule-breaking and remaking, if transgender comes to mean "transgressively gendered," then it creates different kinds of alliances and communities.[97]

Like ancient forms and figures of androgyny, transgender is a capacious category that has the potential to describe a range of gender-variant practices and people.[98] Unlike ancient androgyny, though, "transgender" appears to be less riven by fundamental tensions, even as its meanings move between more specific and general, individualized and collective resonances, and even as its uses provoke a range of reactions. If "transgender" can be helpfully applied to ancient figures who might otherwise be labeled "androgynous," the traffic between these constructions of past and present can also be found among those who begin from the more contemporary transgender angle. Because the regulation of homosexuality, hermaphroditism, gender inversion, and other forms of "social monstrosity" has both overlapped and persisted, Susan Stryker asserts that "attending to what we would now call transgender phenomena has been a preoccupation of Western culture since Greek and Roman antiquity."[99] History, then, proves a crucial vector for transgender studies, even if, as Mary Weismantel argues, the pursuit of this history does not aim "to re-populate the ancient past with modern trans men and trans women," but "to replace the narrow, reductive gaze of previous researchers with a more supple, subtler appreciation of cultural variation."[100] In a slightly different vein, Stryker is willing to allow for degrees of anachronism, so long as it helps discern a wider range of gender variations and connect those who are opposed in similar ways to oppressive situations.[101] Tracing, even constructing such connections across and between variations of gender, then, can be just one practice of a queerly transgender history, the touch across time that Carolyn Dinshaw evokes.

Loaded and long-standing dualisms make masculinity a fraught and conflicted category between and within transgender and lesbian communities. The stereotype of the "mannish woman" had purchase not only in ancient contexts but also in a range of more recent contexts, where the lesbian has been and still often is characterized in sexist and heterosexist ways. Yet, Jack (previously Judith) Halberstam insists that masculinity cannot be reduced to forms of male embodiment and their various social, political, and cultural effects in terms of power and privilege.[102] What many presume to be a stable and univocal masculinity is only a hegemonic form of it that subordinates, while depending on, a number of alternative or minoritized masculinities. Masculine women, lesbians, trans men, and (other) gender deviants, for instance, have produced masculinities that do not in advance "belong" to males.[103] In fact, Halberstam posits that an insistence on the equivalency of maleness and masculinity maintains both patriarchal and misogynist formations, reinscribing masculinity as powerful and active against femininity still cast as passive (in accordance with scripts familiar even to scholars of the ancient world).

Gayle Rubin staked out a different position about the utility of masculinity by proposing that butch is "most usefully understood as a category of lesbian gender that is constituted through the deployment and manipulation of masculine gender codes and symbols."[104] Such codes can be used in a variety of ways: to signal a sexual interest in other women or in a more initiatory sexual role with them, to dress or style oneself more comfortably, and/or to indicate a discomfort with one's gender assignment. In this way Rubin recognized the tension, but also the overlaps and traffic, between these different kinds of female masculinity, including lesbian and trans masculinities. Butch was the mode of gender comportment with which Feinberg would have been most familiar among working-class lesbians in Buffalo during the 1950s, and likely accounts for how she could conceive of a multifaceted transgender alliance of "gender outlaws." Indeed, Rubin (among others) argues that butch signifies more things than male forms of masculinity: "there are more ways to be butch, because when women appropriate masculine styles the element of travesty produces new significance and meaning. Butches adopt and transmute the many available codes of masculinity."[105]

Butch is one of the many forms of female masculinity that Halberstam catalogs and considers, arguing that female masculinity intervenes to offer "an alternative mode of masculinity that clearly detaches misogyny from maleness and social power from maleness."[106] Rather than purging any traces of masculinity, female masculinities can present subversive, even transformative possibilities for gender. Indeed, in response to many of the critiques of lesbian and trans forms of masculinity, Halberstam argues that, "far from being an imitation of maleness, female masculinity actually affords us a glimpse of how masculinity is constructed as masculinity."[107] Masculinity is far more mutable and mobile than most assume. This elasticity of gender, though, can be part of its performative effectiveness: the impossibility of anyone ever being adequately and fully male or female keeps these terms dominant. To resist and subvert such gender and sexual systems of signification is not simply a matter of introducing new genders, though it might just be connected to recognizing some of the excessive and strange kinds of gender represented by practices like female masculinity. Female masculinity is not simply a female version of male masculinity, but it does work out (in keeping with the work of Butler) some of the specific ways that masculinity is an imitation without an original.

As a result, female masculinity is not equivalent to androgyny (in either its ancient or more contemporary forms), nor is it ambiguous in its genderings.[108] In some instances, trans men explicitly discuss their discomfort and conflict when their bodies were read in accordance with ambiguities associated with contemporary kinds of androgyny.[109] At the same time, some drag kings make strategic use of the adjective "androgynous" in order to signify how they mix or maneuver within and around codes of masculinity.[110] Even in doing so, the drag kings featured in Halberstam's *Female Masculinity* and *The Drag King Book* enact recognizable aspects attributed to masculinity, impersonating notable male figures or repeating overdetermined tropes of masculinity.[111] Halberstam's study considers other stylized portraits of masculine women who are hardly ambiguous, given how their bodies are clearly presented sporting recognizable facial hair patterns, stereotypically militarized clothing, or shortened or shaved (head) hair.[112] Throughout this work Halberstam presents the complicated forms and figures of masculinity embodied by tribades, stone butches, transgender dykes, and gender queers (who do or do not transition). These widely various forms have the potential to resist the annexation of masculinity for violence and oppression and to change the meaning of gender and sexual identities.[113]

Nevertheless, this work on butch masculinities cannot help but reflect the oft-noted overlaps and anxieties between lesbian and trans codes and communities. Rubin demonstrated how butch works as one such site of both grouping and differentiation. While in many contexts, this is accepted, the transitivity and mutual applicability of such codes of masculinity also engender "frontier fears."[114] The permeability between butch and transsexual generates feelings of both antagonism and kinship. Some of this antagonism was (and still is) encouraged by certain kinds of feminist arguments against transsexuality.[115] In other cases female-to-male (FTM) or (other) transgender people are cast as destabilizing important categories for political action, including those of woman and lesbian. Lesbian butches and FTMs have traded accusations of the others' gender conservatism, normativity, or oppression. In these "border wars" FTMs have been described as traitors to the cause of women, of being butches who believe too much in the anatomically sexed body.[116] In turn, lesbians have been accused of demonizing FTMs, of being butches who are too scared (and implicitly too feminine) to "go all the way" through transition.[117]

Halberstam's concerns about these characterizations are not aimed toward one or the other "side" of these ostensible borders. If butch lesbians seek to pose terms like "woman" or "lesbian" as stable signifiers, they risk ignoring the capability of butch and even lesbian figurations to do important work destabilizing gender and sexual privilege. And FTMs run similar risks if they insist on trans modes of embodiment that stress dissociating one's masculinity from butch or dyke modes of bodily comportment. In the latter case, since the butch has been associated with very short, even punk-styled (head) hair for decades,[118] commonly disseminated tips among trans men for passing as more authentically masculine warn against such haircuts and styles.[119] On this trend in trans comportment, Dean Spade notes:

> this establishes the requirement of being even more "normal" than "normal people" when it comes to gender presentation, and discouraging gender disruptive behavior. The resulting image, with the most "successful" FTMs exiting as khaki-clad frat boy clones, leaves feminist gender-queer trannies with the question, why bother?[120]

Head hair becomes a vexed marker in constructions of female masculinity, strangely echoing the way medicalized institutions, like the *DSM-IV*, focus on girls who prefer wearing "boys' clothing and short hair" as an indicator of gender identity disorder.[121]

While practices like short hair cutting and styling refer to modes of masculinity, these modes are themselves varied, even multiplying, as the traffic between butch and trans indicates. Of course, these practices do register people's investment in categories of gender, sexuality, and embodiment. Rubin, however, casts doubts on whether any such categories, while necessary, are ever anything but limited and leaky: "Categories like 'woman,' 'butch,' 'lesbian,' or 'transsexual' are all imperfect, historical, temporary, and arbitrary."[122] Rather than reinforcing any absolutized or naturalizing differentiations between such categories, Halberstam's reflections on the butch/FTM "border wars" examine the exchanges and continuities between these two different forms of gender variance (among others). Even as people negotiate forms and figures of masculinity differently, Halberstam works to trace and support a kind of "dialogue between FTM and butch subject positions that allows for cohabitation in the territories of queer gender."[123] Some of this can be achieved by pointing out still other modes of masculinity, within and through terms like "transgender," "genderqueer," and "transgender butch." Halberstam introduces the last of these as a category beside and perhaps between butch and FTM, tracing the paths some butch lesbians have taken toward trans treatments and operations, as well as those who do not opt for surgeries but resonate with modes of transitivity and variation.[124]

Where gender variations are detached from gendered hierarchies, as well as from male bodies, female masculinities can present new ways to repeat, embody, and hence rework gender, sexual, and bodily practices and identifications, helping to produce different relationships between gender, desire, power, and embodiment. Given their interests in these specific connections and the broader traffic between butch, transgender, as well as drag king masculinities, scholars and artists like Halberstam and Volcano are in many ways working in the wake of Feinberg's calls for solidarity and action and Bornstein's views of gender variation. Volcano's modes of self-identification themselves vary, "I call myself a 'hermaphrodyke' for now, which I like to think of as my own custom gender blend. . . . I see myself as BOTH male and female; 'either/or' rather than 'neither/nor.' "[125] Volcano repeats this almost biblical reworking of gender in asserting: "I see myself as BOTH (male and female) rather than NEITHER (male nor female). In my case, the two add up to something non-numerical. I am simply gender-variant."[126] Any interest in androgyny is quite muted, quite possibly because its more contemporary connotations of in-betweenness tend to present both masculinity and femininity as falsely stable and monolithic in their operations.[127]

Drag kinging is still another practice of gender variation whose practices and effects are worth tracing, in relation to other forms and figures of female masculinity. Halberstam describes a drag king as "a female (usually) who dresses up in recognizably male costume and performs theatrically in that costume."[128] While Volcano defines a drag king as anyone "who consciously makes a performance out of masculinity," Halberstam's reflections on the practice elaborate and qualify some of Butler's reflections on drag and gender performativity.[129] In contrast to the male impersonator seeking a passing plausibility, "the drag king performs masculinity (often parodically) and makes the exposure of the theatricality of masculinity into the mainstay of her act."[130] In this light, drag practices are not about seamless repetitions or perfect imitations; drag is not successful because the performer "passes" for the gender or sexual identification being enacted. Drag kings can use a performative repertoire or persona to express or simply embody their gender variation, as tied to or dissociated from a sexual identity like lesbian. Alongside other practices of female masculinity, drag king masculinities can be productive places for revealing differences from and dissonances within various forms and norms of gender, sexuality, and embodiment. It moves within and creates its own traffic with other forms and figures of gender variation, like the butch lesbian, the trans guy, or the transgender butch.[131] Drag kinging, then, presents just one of the many ways that female masculinities do differ from male masculinities. Halberstam posits that there are important connections between these alternative practices of masculinity and "diminishing the natural bonds between masculinity and men."[132]

Transgender is particularly helpful for demonstrating how much effort is involved in posing and projecting particular expressions or explanations as "natural." One such intervention proposes the potential affinity between the transsexual body and the monstrous body. In one of the first specifically transgender studies projects to link with queer theories, Susan Stryker describes her own identification with Frankenstein's monster, as something unnatural, but also something more than their surgical "creators" intended them to be.[133] As with the reversal and reclamation of terms like "dyke," "fag," or "queer," Stryker aims to talk back to those, like Janice Raymond and Mary Daly, who are horrified by and condemn transsexuals, by redeploying terms like "unnatural" and "monster."[134] As an "assemblage of incongruous anatomical parts," a transsexual body is no more a seamless imitation than drag is, yet it has the potential to show the "seams and sutures" in all constructions of the apparently natural body.[135]

Picking up where Stryker leaves off, Nikki Sullivan refocuses on the practices of body modification involved with transgender bodies. Sullivan similarly revalues a potentially abject term for embodied practices by elaborating on transmogrification. Here, transmogrification describes "strange or grotesque transformation: transformation that is characterized by distortion, exaggeration, extravagance, and, as the *Shorter Oxford English Dictionary* puts it, 'unnatural combinations.'"[136] Sullivan's conceptual choice could function as a qualification of some of Halberstam's taxonomies of female masculinity, since it is meant to reflect not only the capacities but also the difficulties of inhabiting modified bodies, like (and unlike) a transgender body. It is still very much the case that a great many people respond in disgust, anger, condemnation, horror, and physical violence when they encounter certain forms or figures of gender variation. This makes life difficult for a great many people as well, and not only the drag kings, transgender butches, lesbians, trans men, and genderqueers described (if but briefly) in this chapter.

The risks and the costs of confronting people and reflecting back to them
their estrangement from the forms and the norms (they think) they seamlessly embody are unevenly born by the kinds of gender-variant people
described by Halberstam and Volcano, Feinberg and Bornstein, Spade and
Stryker, most especially trans women of color. Still, this reconfiguration of
the monstrous capacities (and difficulties) of transgender can hark back and
shed new light on the androgynous bodies that troubled the ancient Romans.
Stryker makes such a link explicit, recalling that "monster" relates back to the
Latin for a warning or divine portent (*monstrum*). This potential resonance
would also extend the focus of scholars of ancient androgyny, like Brisson,
since the monster:

> came to refer to living things of anomalous shape or structure, or to fab-
> ulous creatures like the sphinx who were composed of strikingly incon-
> gruous parts, because the ancients considered the appearance of such
> beings to be a sign of some impending supernatural event. Monsters, like
> angels, functioned as messengers and heralds of the extraordinary. They
> served to announce impending revelation.[137]

Stryker's efforts to connect contemporary transgender bodies to ancient,
seemingly incongruous bodies as monstrous can reframe how the females
in 1 Corinthians were and are prophetic—their embodied actions read as
anomalous but also extraordinary and revelatory.

Resembling and Assembling Female (Masculine) Prophets

Grappling with the potential for androgynes, rhetorically and historically, to be more than horrific, tragic, nefarious, or pathetic requires a
depathologizing approach, especially given the ways the Roman imperial
perspective is willing to cast only certain practices of androgyny—those
that affirm, even reinforce the kyriarchal order—as positive.[138] Only then
might it be possible to evaluate the figures and forms that androgyny takes
in the Corinthian community differently than Paul, in conversation with the
Roman imperial perspective, does.

Starting again by seeing these practices as akin to (without being collapsed
into) female masculinities is distinct from the perspective occasionally taken
by more traditional, conservative, evangelical, or even reactionary readings

of this letter as specifically related to homosexuality. Jerome Murphy-O'Connor was one of the first scholars to argue that homosexuality was the problem Paul was trying to address among the Corinthians.[139] Before this, scholars like C. K. Barrett and Robin Scroggs imagined that the situation in the text evoked Paul's horror or fear of homosexuality, without elaborating on this possibility.[140] Like many other takes on this difficult passage, the lack of clarity within 11:1–16 contributes to these suggestions. For instance, when John P. Meier noted that there is no clear reason why cut or shaved head hair should be viewed as shameful (v. 6), he guessed: "There may be a reference here to the practice of lesbians, especially so if Paul's concerns about homosexuality is one of the unspoken reasons for his insisting on visible distinctions between the sexes."[141] The gendered distinctions created by hair length become one of the major foci for the arguments that follow Murphy-O'Connor. At first, he proposed that "long hair was associated with homosexuality."[142] But, because he sought to argue that the problem of the text involves both females and males, Murphy-O'Connor had to do more than (incorrectly) collapse condemnations of male effeminacy with the larger (and modern) category "homosexuality." He then finds parallel problems with these Corinthians, reflected in verse 14 for males and verse 6 for females, since "short hair could mark a woman as a lesbian."[143] Just as effeminacy was the issue with males in this assembly community, so was the unfeminine, mannish behavior of the females: "If a woman is prepared to be 'unfeminine' to the extent of not dressing her hair properly, then she might as well go the whole way and appear 'mannish.'"[144]

Few interpreters have agreed with this reading of the text, beyond the occasional conservative, evangelical, or apologetic circles.[145] Anthony C. Thistelton admits that the allusions to shortly cut hair (in vv. 5–6) could connote "a 'boylike' style, with possible hints of lesbian gender-crossing."[146] Quite possibly the closest and most intensifying repetition of this reading, though, can be found decades after Murphy-O'Connor's original work, in Kirk MacGregor's insistence that "short hair was the sole distinguishing trait that physically marked a woman as a lesbian."[147] MacGregor claims a connection between cross-gender identification and homosexuality throughout his argument, three times explicitly linking the issue in the text to a problem of "female masculinity"![148] In the process he reduces not only the potential meaning of gender variation but also the overall significance of the letter as a whole:

That Paul's remarks concerning head coverings were aimed at the prohibition of male effeminacy, female masculinity, and their implied homosexuality fits like a hand in a glove of the Sitz im Leben disclosed by the remainder of the Corinthian correspondence.[149]

Here, a particularly constrained and heterosexist set of mistaken readings of two words (in just one verse—1 Cor 6:9—out of all of the two long letters to the Corinthians), arsenokoitēs and malakos, is taken as comprehensive and authoritative and, in turn, justified by combining them with another set of confused conclusions about 11:1–16.[150] In spite of a range of errors and exaggerations, such intensely heterosexist apologetics make explicit what is often just a general inclination among interpreters of these letters: there is rarely any question about questioning the picture presented by (or through) the text.[151]

Still, these readings unwittingly support the strong links between Paul's arguments about bodies and behavior and other ancient ideas and arguments about gender variation. In these contexts head hair is a recurrent marker of gender variation, which is occasionally (though clearly not always) associated with contested sexual practices. It may not be that the prophesying females in Corinth are equivalent to modern-day transgender butches, but their juxtaposition can help us zero in on this (sub)cultural variation of gender in a different, even subtler way than simply assenting to the worldview of the letter or using it as a cudgel to condemn lesbian, gay, trans, or other gender-variant people.[152] By both prophesying and uncovering their heads, the Corinthian female prophets were (in the words of Rubin) adapting and transmuting the ancient codes of gender variation to different ends.[153] Along the lines suggested by Halberstam, then, their practices indicate that social power can detach from maleness.[154] Paul notices this (as do we) and needs to address it, because these practices of power are departing the male body in many places in these communities, including when women are taking leading, speaking roles in the assembly (as they are doing in Corinth).

There is something beyond the bipartite view of women reflected in the conflicted ancient perspectives about female practices, cast as androgynous. Instead of comparing how females and males practice masculinity (or androgyny), one can learn more about masculinity by considering a range of female practices of gender variation (cast as either masculinity or androgyny) alongside each other.[155] Indeed, on further consideration of ancient figurations, one encounters a dizzying array that the elite Roman imperial traditions were trying, in part, to avoid.[156] Grouping these wild variabilities in terms of multiplicity alters the perspective on ancient androgyny, which itself takes multiple forms. Texts like Lucian's *Dialogue of the Courtesans* reflect the proximity, the blurriness between multiple forms of ancient androgyny, or even multiple forms of ancient female masculinity. Recall the moment when Megilla reveals a closely shaven head, echoing the shortly cut hair stressed twice in Paul's argument in verse 6 (the same verbal form—*keirō*), and declares, "my name is Megillos" (5.3). Leaina, in turn, tries to understand this bodily practice by alternately asking if Megillos is a cross-dressing man, a hermaphrodite, or a woman transformed into a man, each of these being types known from other stories. Only then does Megillos (not Megilla, as I wrote before) tell Leaina that: "I was born a woman like the rest of you, but I have the mind and the desires and everything else of a man" (5.4).

A range of gender-variant figures were adapted as handy caricatures in ancient Roman imperial settings. The appearance of multiple bodily possibilities within this exchange between Megillos and Leaina resonates with those types recognizable to ancient audiences, but their rhetorical utility does not preclude that people were doing various things read as masculine (or androgynous). Rather, the power of such depictions depends on the possibility, even plausibility, that audiences know of such figures and forms in people's bodies and behaviors. These ancient people or patterns of embodied practices may not have corresponded exactly to these types, but they could have used such typing to proximate, though different ends than presented by mostly elite, Roman, imperial, male perspectives. In a similar vein, I would caution against straightforwardly identifying Megillos as a "transgender lesbian" (as Shelly Haley did)[157] or the prophetic females at Corinth as sporting "mannish," "boylike," or "lesbian gender-crossing" hairstyles (as a few Pauline interpreters have). The stories about contemporary forms of female masculinity and ancient forms of androgyny have the potential to reflect not a continuum, but a constellation arrayed in relation to each other, but not in terms of progression or a hierarchy of value. While Halberstam argues for a space of cohabitation of queer gender for trans and lesbian masculinities,[158] the currents, the touches, even the traffic between ancient androgyny and female masculinity suggest a more capacious space, a cross-temporal cohabitation.

In the spaces created and negotiated by figures and forms of androgyny and female masculinity, head hair is a vexed marker of this variety and multiplicity. The effort to cast the female Corinthians' prophetic practices as akin to shaved or close-cropped hair (11:5–6) is an ambivalent indicator. It might just signal the prophetic females' attempts to resist dominant narratives about gender and embodiment in their contexts, to do and be something else. Yet, if one follows the claims made by Paul, these practices could also be read to solidify the Roman imperial perspective on the exceptionalism of female virtue. Here, it is important to recognize that versions of gender variation are going to be read against and through each other. (The bipartite view persists, even as there is much more at work in these contexts.) Still, shortened hair is not ambiguous: it is a recognizable marker (then and now) of some sort of gender variation.[159] This, then, appears to qualify Wire's claim that Paul was presenting an "unthinkable alternative" to the Corinthian females in this passage. Wire argues that "his expectation that his challenge will be shocking shows that the women he wants to persuade are not social outcasts with no pretensions of honor but consider themselves worthy of respect in the community."[160] Much of this chapter indicates how this practice was thinkable in some specific ways, suggesting that the prophetic females in the Corinthian assembly might just have been interested in being social outcasts (to those outside the community), while retaining a different kind of respect among themselves. Indeed, it is hard to imagine how they would not be at least at risk of social disapproval if their practices and ideas fit the picture Wire develops throughout most of her study.[161]

This highlights the citational quality of female prophetic practices, referencing and reworking assumptions about the nature of gender and of bodies. Such practices also show the artificiality of such arguments about nature, given the effort it takes to prescribe it and propose certain imitations, of those like Paul, as authoritative. One has a clearer view, then, of how Paul constructs masculinized authority, but also of how the practices of the Corinthians were, in Butler's terms, an imitation without an original. Tracing the performative aspects of such arguments and juxtaposing them against contemporary figures of female masculinity help to denaturalize claims about gender difference, bodily comportment, and communal authority. As both Butler's conceptualization and Paul's efforts in this passage indicate, it takes a great deal of effort to pose and then maintain something as "natural." Indeed, what passes for the "natural" can be enacted, embodied, and repeated in rather different ways, as practices like drag kinging (alongside other practices of female masculinity) often highlight.

Of course, drag practices are rarely simply about "passing" as whatever figure or form at work in the practice (the natural, the normal, or otherwise). Similarly, the encounter with regimes of the natural need not produce different claims on or within it. When faced with problematic arguments about nature, perspectives that conflict with another sense of embodiment and community, why wouldn't figures like the Corinthian prophetic females seek to be *un*-natural to such perspectives? The fact that the prevailing political forces would have seen their actions and identifications as troubling, even monstrous, might be part of the point of these actions and identifications—their new life in the assembly community at Corinth was not meant to be business as usual. Stryker and Sullivan pose the monstrous as a figure for contemporary trans identification, given the way the monster assembles unnatural combinations.[162] The prayers and prophecies of the Corinthian females and their androgynous (or female-masculine) comportment appear to be an unnatural combination in Paul's arguments (cf. 11:14–15). That the prophetic females did not object to such combinations in their bodily practices reflects, further, that prophecy is an unnaturally natural phenomenon. It is atypical speech, often within the frame of a liminal experience; it is different from other parts of life. Their actions in the assembly are meant to be revelatory that there is something different about them, about the assembly community. As Stryker highlighted, "Monsters, like angels, functioned as messengers and heralds of the extraordinary. They served to announce impending revelation."[163] If the Corinthian females are unnatural, even monstrous in their prophecies, then they may even be competing with those other messengers, whose appearance in this text (11:10) often mystifies interpreters.

The monstrous possibilities of the particular gender-variant practices of the prophesying females could be read another way within the community itself. Paul's argument presumes that at least some members of the assembly would have found shortly cut or shaved hair shameful or dishonorable for females (the premise in v. 6), since the argument attempts to transfer this problematic self-fashioning to another embodied behavior—females praying or prophesying with their heads uncovered. Of course, the effort to convince some, more, or even all in the audience of this connection also presumes that some, more, or even all of them had not already heard or agreed with this connection (or possibly even the premise on which this connection depends). Instead, it remains a lively possibility that the prophesying Corinthian female members experienced a "transmogrification" as part of their life in the assembly community. Their prayer and prophetic activities marked their lives as different, from what came before and from those around them in Corinth but outside the assembly.

To this day, transgender folks are targeted at much higher rates of harassment and violence than other populations (including lesbian, gay, and bisexual groups), so much so that one scholar has advanced the notion that "genderbashing" takes precedence over (and may more likely be at the root of) "gay bashing."[164] In the ancient Roman imperial setting, most forms of gender variation (cast as androgyny) were received with horror, mockery, or condemnation. Yet the picture constructed by Paul's arguments in this letter is not as seamless or univocally reproachful as the tradition of interpretation has often implied. Admittedly, these are difficult texts—not only to understand but even to hear uttered today. Paul's letters are certainly some of the most cited pieces of Christian scripture, but they are also some of the most reviled pieces of argumentation. As failures, embarrassments, or simply disappointments, the encounters with Paul's arguments or the obscured connections with the prophetic figures in the Corinthian assembly are examples of what Heather Love has described as a "history gone bad."[165]

This is the value of keeping in mind the dynamic of performativity at work in this exchange. If the practices of the Corinthian female prophets were readable as masculine in some ways, if prophesying with uncovered head corresponded to having shaved head hair, the argument attempting to connect these two demonstrates that the limits and meanings of masculine practices are not delineated in advance. Thus, their practices of prophesying and praying were not necessarily derivative, did not in advance belong only to males. Indeed, the letter's argument presumes that it cannot entirely detach women from these practices. The Corinthian women's masculinity was not some female version of Paul's argument for imitating him. Indeed, his argument for imitation seems to depend on their alternative practices of (what appears to him and possibly others as) masculinity preceding the call to imitate. Efforts to proclaim a particularly gendered order as natural are exposed as artificially constructed in this moment. Pauline masculinity is an imitation without an original, or perhaps, an imitation with an unexpected, minoritized, Corinthian female masculine predecessor. Regardless, what one finds by juxtaposing the Corinthian female prophets with forms of ancient androgyny and more recent female masculinity is that there are multiple forms of masculinity, a complicating variety of genders denaturalized from arguments that claim an obvious, God-given, even timeless authority.

To take alternative angles on the figures deployed and targeted by the arguments in letters like 1 Corinthians, one needs to consider carefully queer approaches to history, including what Carolyn Dinshaw describes as the desire to "make relations with" elements of the past, seeking that "touch across time."[166] Those voices from the past who barely leave a trace, if any, might only resemble some contemporary groups because they were marginalized by the prevailing forces of their own times and places. The juxtaposition of the female prophets in the Corinthian assembly alongside transgender, butch lesbian, and drag king figures presents one such effort of this project. These improvised queer communities or coalitions are made by partial connections across time, echoing the never-perfect aspects of identification, the never-foreclosed dynamics of imitation, the alterity embedded within the performativity discussed in both this and the previous chapter.

Strangely, the letter reflects anxieties about such matters of imitation and identification. Paul took notice of these in a way that he did not approve of certain speaking bodies—not of the speaking itself, but how the bodies "spoke" by their appearance. This is likely because the kinds of gendered practices enacted by the prophesying Corinthian females had been left out of Roman imperial ideas about androgyny as a variation in gender. Paul appears to have wished this bodily practice had been left out, but his response to the situation shows not only the marginalization, but also the existence of this practice. Try as he might, Paul cannot erase, let alone control, how the Corinthians organized themselves or responded to arguments like his (before or after the letter).[167] One has more than a hint of these practices if one reads Paul's arguments carefully as responses to the Corinthian female prophets, a response that tried to convince people to see their gender variant activities as the wrong kind of gender variation (like the negative kinds of androgyny). At least some Corinthians did not see things this way, an alternative that is easier to see in the light of the anachronistic juxtapositions I have attempted to stage.

Such juxtapositions reflect partial connections and gendered contingencies, the kinds of connections and contingencies I have hoped to highlight by raising female masculinity as a more provocative and productive practice for understanding these arguments about imitation, repetition, and citation aimed toward the Corinthian women. By juxtaposing drag kings and more contemporary figures up alongside the ancient figures deployed and targeted by Paul's arguments, my aim was not to claim, anachronistically, that these figures are somehow identical to each other. Rather, I hope that through anachronistic juxtaposition I have highlighted the partial, but particular connections between them, their shared features shaped by their practices of gender, sexuality, and embodiment that depart from oppressive perspectives (then or now).[168] Further, these figures are not identical, but do partially connect, citing and repeating each other, shaped by each other, but in ways not entirely determined in advance. Instead of imagining only that we can borrow contemporary drag kings, butch lesbians, transgender dykes, or genderqueers in order to rethink the Corinthian women, it may be that Corinthian female masculinity can help us rethink masculinities without men, or at least nonhegemonic repetitions and citations of masculinity, in the present and the future. One need not resort to androgyny to understand the first century: there are first-century images different from the elite male in control, at the head or in the image of God—there are images of people who are no longer male and female, but not entirely eliminating male and female, working on and within these concepts of gender, males and females who can do masculinity (and likely also femininity) differently.

The ways Paul's authority has been reinscribed, leading to the obscuring of the roles of many, many others (behind and beside the Corinthian female prophets) represent a potential loss that must be negotiated for queer and feminist users of these pasts and presents. But those losses also represent the generative threat of masculine women in the ancient (and contemporary) context(s), exposing as they do the dissonances and (un)natural linkages between genders and embodied practices, and the possibilities for different citations, combinations, and connections. Those marginalized by this text, and ultimately by traditions of reading that ignore them, do make demands on us, reaching and briefly linking us back to the biblical behind. They present or perhaps just represent the possibilities of a differently gendered existence, one derived from previous ingredients, in ways not unlike those conceptualized by performativity and female masculinity. These figurative practices can be repeated, in a number of ways, in rather different ways, reflecting backward to the Corinthian females behind the letter and resonating with the transgender butches, drag kings, and the dyke boys of more recent scenes; figures connected, if only partially, by virtue of shared marginalities, their departures from naturalizing categories of gender,

sexuality, and embodiment, then and now. The touches, even the traffic between the figures and forms of ancient androgyny and female masculinity
suggest a more capacious space, cross-temporal habitation in which one
might find nonidentical correspondences, complicating varieties of gender,
prophetic people, then and now.

3

Uncut Galatians

Intersex/Eunuch

The celebratory declaration of the sex of an infant upon delivery is one of the clearest examples of a performative utterance in contemporary Western culture (which is to say one of the most powerful and historically specific moments). The announcement of "It's a girl!" or "It's a boy!" is most frequently made first by an attending doctor (though increasingly by ultrasound as well) and exuberantly repeated by and to family and friends, thus interpellating the child and the caregiver(s) into particular roles, embedded within cultural expectations and sociopolitical conditions that must be performatively reenacted.[1] This medical declaration concerns more than just neonatal anatomy in that it draws its force from the norms it cites and then spurs to further recitation. The scientific authority granted to the speaker depends on the reinforcement of these norms, while the authority with which medicine is currently imbued legitimizes and maintains those norms. For those eventually drawn around a child, whole patterns of preparation and rearing ostensibly depend on the relation between this authority and these norms. Various, often rather precise futures—relational and even sexual—are imagined after and through this (routinized) pronouncement. And this apparently all depends on a physician's ability to interpret the genital appearance of an infant.

Since medical professionals' cultural authority is constructed on declarations inferred from a rather constrained set of ocular data, the appearance of (ostensibly) ambiguous bodies—or, rather, bodies that do not immediately conform to their specifically gendered expectations for external signs of sexed differentiation—is a cause of medical anxiety. Declarations are deferred or amended. Into the threshold opened by this delay enters other cultural authorities, religious sources that previously held (even) greater sway before scientific, psychological, and medical discourses came to predominate. Families turn to chaplains, ministers, and rabbis, close family, and friends.[2] Given the powerful and historically specific conditions that have

Appalling Bodies. Joseph A. Marchal, Oxford University Press (2020). © Oxford University Press.
DOI: 10.1093/oso/9780190060312.001.0001

shaped religion in contemporary culture, many in the West eventually turn to biblical images, ideas, and arguments for consolation and guidance about what to do with, to, or for people with such bodies: the intersex, for lack of a better word.[3]

In such instances, the uses for the biblical are not just ambivalent but also ambiguous. If humans were created male and female, by God no less, then what kind of human is an intersex person?[4] Some hold that people with intersex conditions are unfortunate signs of the current human condition, corrupted by original sin or the Fall (as variously interpreted from the Genesis creation accounts).[5] This perspective persists even among Christian groups that attempt to provide support services to intersex people, like Intersex Support Group International (ISGI). A US-based Christian group created by and for people diagnosed with intersex conditions, ISGI stresses both that intersex people are God's "unique creation," and that they reflect the "damaged results" of humanity's "fallen nature."[6] Other passages condemning or isolating those with bodily blemishes or other gender-blending features (like Lev 21:16–23; Deut 22:5; 23:1) have been cited to label intersex people as defective or otherwise problematic for religious communities.[7]

Before discovering the details of her own intersex condition, Sally Gross was a Catholic priest. Ordination made her privy to detailed theological deliberations about the relative status of intersex Christians. Her interlocutors connected the "natural" order, as aligned with those creation stories from Genesis, to the necessity of dimorphically sexed (human) bodies with the capacity for baptism. On the basis of Genesis 1:27, these interlocutors fulminated that "determinate maleness or determinate femaleness is the mark, above all else, of what it is to be created human" and therefore that Gross was "not the kind of thing which could have been baptized validly."[8] This religiously, and even biblically, based dehumanization culminated in exclusionary treatment for Gross: when she reported what she discovered from counseling and hormonal testing, she was granted a year's leave of absence until a Papal Rescript annulled her religious vows, stripped her of clerical status, and created significant obstacles for any participation in church organizations or activities even now as a layperson.[9]

Traditions about creation and baptism can be put to rather different uses when considering intersex conditions and people with them. Gross, for instance, highlights the connections between the myth of a primal androgyne and rabbinic Jewish and early Christian traditions about the first human(s).[10] Rather than dividing humans into exclusively dichotomous terms, such traditions highlight that the "original" human was male and female and, thus, hermaphroditic, most pertinently (for some Christians) before the Fall.[11] Others have pointed out that the second of the two Genesis creation stories divides the female from the first human, who therefore could be identified as intersex.[12] Even a prophetic text about the blessings a covenant-observing eunuch receives (Isa 56:4–5) has brought comfort to the parents of a recently born intersex child.[13] A threefold saying about eunuchs attributed to Jesus has allowed some Christian advocates, including ISGI, to argue, " 'Some are eunuchs (genetic intersex) because they were born that way . . . Matthew 19:12.' We know that God made no mistake when He made us."[14]

Of course, some people with intersex conditions and religious motivations seem less taken with eunuch figures,[15] but many advocates specifically link intersex to transgender via the ancient eunuch,[16] for which the baptismal formula found in Galatians 3:27–28 is useful, in that it resituates the creation of humans as male and female (Gen 1:27). This baptismal formula could be an altogether alternative performative utterance, a rather different pronouncement from the gendered interpellation of human infants, particularly since it cites the supposedly determinate "male and female" of creation and relativizes their significance by reciting the words "no longer Jew or Gentile, slave or free, not male and female" (3:28). Meditations on the Galatians formula bookend Virginia Ramey Mollenkott's religious vision for an "omnigendered" paradigm—a nonhierarchical gender pluralism.[17]

The biblical operates in lively ways, reflecting again its temporal persistence. Even in settings where one might expect modern(ist) authority to undercut their force, biblical figures recur in a range of ways, and yet . . . a belief or even just a sense that appeals to the biblical can provide answers or ammunition, increased comfort or certitude, remains. Tracing this persistence promises to be fruitful, but the idea herein is not to reinstall or otherwise reinforce the biblical as authoritative. Not only does the biblical not require my help in its persistence but also I am not yet entirely convinced that the biblical should or even could help with addressing the conditions that generate the stigmatizing and dehumanizing treatment of people with intersex conditions. Yet, the biblical does persist, its images, ideas, and arguments deployed to normalize and naturalize and therefore also stigmatize and dehumanize. But whether this complex of materials speaks to, or even about intersex people is contested and therefore worth addressing directly. Rather than letting the biblical determine what to think, say, or even do with or as intersex people, intersex advocacy—which is informed by feminist and queer principles and practices—interrogates the practical and potential uses of the biblical.[18]

Paul's letter to the Galatians proves to be an especially relevant test case for this effort not only because it contains the baptismal formula that attracts so much attention, but also because it seems primarily concerned with practices of genital cutting, albeit particular ones. Galatians addresses practices of genital cutting in some distinctive, but also troubling, ways: it refers rather explicitly to castration, summoning the variety and ambiguity of ancient eunuch figures in the ancient Roman imperial context, an ambiguity that is also reflected in Paul's deployment of eunuch figures in his letter. The figure of the eunuch comes to the foreground just once, but it appears to be the point of contrast lurking throughout the letter's lengthier reflections on circumcision. In turn, the meanings and limits of baptisms, bodies, and belonging for the first-century contexts of the Galatian assembly communities shift through critical reflection on modifying bodies with intersex conditions in the twenty-first century.

"They tried to write their Gospel on my body": Defining, Treating, Resisting

The term "intersex" simply does not refer to any one kind of person or medical condition; its meanings and connotations vary and its use remains controversial in some corners both clinical and activist.[19] "Intersex" tends to refer to a range of bodily states that have typically been treated as medical conditions. From the perspective of medical practitioners, at least forty and often up to sixty or seventy different diagnoses could classify as intersex.[20] The most common way such diagnoses are made is based on the apparently atypical external appearance of genitalia,[21] but intersex conditions are broadly defined by what are viewed as discordances between the various components of sexed anatomy, components commonly imagined to be strictly and exclusively aligned with each other, including genital, gonadal, genetic, chromosomal, and hormonal aspects.[22]

Although the predominant protocol for treatment is organized around the social significance of the genitalia,[23] doctors have since the 1950s followed an "optimal gender of rearing" model that stresses the importance of a child's socialization as determinative for his or her gender and sexual identity.[24] Though this model grants that gender roles are plastic until the age of eighteen months, it also assumes that a person must have one stable and nonprovisional gender identity, either male or female, in order to be "healthy." The health of the intersex child thus necessitates gender assignment as early as possible, from which point the assignment should be treated with certitude. An aim of treatment is to ensure that when a parent, friend, peer, or even the patient *looks at* the external anatomy, they see (what at least appears to be) "normal" genitalia.[25] Surgery is "required" whenever a medical professional encounters genitalia that do not unambiguously belong to one or the other of the dichotomous genders. In this protocol a failure to act, rather invasively, is to risk causing psychosocial damage; any occurrence of ostensibly ambiguous bodies becomes a medical emergency, primarily because it is a (psycho)social emergency.[26] By the end of the twentieth century, this particular model, along with its affiliated assumptions and theories, so routinely set the terms for treatment that it has been described as "gospel."[27]

Generally, for a child with a 46, XY karyotype, the medical team will evaluate whether the phallic structure is of sufficient length for the child to look and function "like a male." Phallic size has traditionally trumped preserving fertility functions in these cases, so that if the structure is less than 2.5 centimeters (or 1 inch), the child is assigned to the female gender. What might be called a "micropenis" is then surgically altered through procedures like clitoral reduction and vaginoplasty.[28] By way of contrast, a child with a 46, XX karyotype is typically given a female gender assignment, no matter the size and appearance of the genitalia. The medical team will attempt to measure the phallic structure and in cases where it exceeds 1 centimeter (or .39 inches) perform clitoral reduction or recession surgery.[29] The aim is to make the body with an "enlarged" clitoris (clitoromegaly) look and function more "like a female," while preferably preserving fertility. With that aim in mind, the surgeons may also seek to create or lengthen a vaginal opening and begin hormonal treatment at puberty.[30]

These surgical and hormonal efforts to construct a natural and stable social identity are justified as reducing, even preventing the stigma and trauma anticipated for children with intersex conditions (and their caregivers). Yet, as innumerable studies and first-person interviews and essays report, these treatment practices in fact cause (or at least exacerbate) the shame, trauma, and stigma they are ostensibly meant to prevent![31]

Because of the "trauma caused by being repeatedly 'put on display,'"[32] many people with intersex conditions describe medical professionals' behaviors and their own lack of control as patients (often from a young age forward), as forms of physical, emotional, and sexual vulnerability, violence, and abuse.[33] These medicalized practices of (apparent) care also involve indirect, incomplete, misleading, or outright deceptive communication with patients and caretakers alike.[34] Although meant to prevent shame and stigmatization, the surgeries and inspections, deceptions and silence, generate and perpetuate what they claim to prevent—a pattern described in the first newsletter of the Intersex Society of North America (ISNA): "the vicious cycle in which shame [about variant genitals] produces silence, silence condones surgery, and surgery produces more shame (which produces more silence)."[35] Given the effects of the predominant treatment protocol, intersex activists like Cheryl Chase have countered that intersex is "primarily a problem of stigma and trauma, not gender."[36] For most people with intersex conditions, the shame, stigma, and suffering do not originally stem from either an "incorrect" gender assignment or an insufficient surgical technique on the part of the doctors.[37] The medical presumption of the traumatic and stigmatic character of intersex is what stigmatizes.

Given the constancy with which suffering, shame, and stigma are recorded, it has been axiomatic in intersex activism to argue for a delay in any genital surgery until the person with an intersex condition can at least participate in the decision. The physical outcomes of surgeries on genitalia are inevitably damaging and thus harmful to genital sensation, although for decades it was taken as writ that no one had reported loss of feeling after clitoral modification, or even removal.[38] More and more, experts are recognizing that sensation and especially pleasurable genital contact are impaired by the scarring that results from often multiple procedures, making friction painful and preventing lubrication.[39] Indeed, most of the autobiographical intersex accounts reflect the various negative effects of surgery on sexual enjoyment, frequency, and identity.[40] The scarring experience and appearance of surgery has led some intersex advocates to refer to this kind of medical treatment as genital mutilation.[41]

Yet medicalized treatment practices remain persistently fixated on the phallus and remarkably incurious about the clitoris, with corresponding effects.[42] As legal scholar Julie A. Greenburg has succinctly described the difference between the treatment of XX and XY children: "males are being defined by their ability to penetrate and females are being defined by their ability to procreate."[43] Pleasure and reproduction recede into the background, however, where possession and passivity fix these bodies into place. As Morgan Holmes notes: "the goal of surgery on intersexed infants is to produce adults who will function as either female receptacles *for* the penis, or male possessors *of* the penis."[44] A vaginal opening is adequate in its created form only if it is of sufficient depth and/or dimension to receive a (phallic structure judged large enough to be a) penis, reflecting interrelated sexist and heterosexist presumptions.[45] Even as they are the way to assign a female gender, vaginas are still for men![46] Strangely, even as medicalized management is focused on a penetrating penis, the vast majority of treatment practices involve a female gender assignment and the shaping or creating of a vagina. Certain procedures may be relatively more difficult to perform, but the oft-cited surgical common sense of "You can make a hole but you can't build a pole"[47] reflects and reinforces the greater social status and expectation placed on the male member. Being "harder" to construct surgically, the phallus connotes activity and plenitude, while females become associated with passivity and deficiency—their gender is merely a default setting, a fallback, or a lack (a hole).[48] Operating here is a dichotomous view that sorts gendered roles into active and passive, penetrator and penetrated. Once an intersex person, like Kiira Triea, was assigned to the female gender, "The objective was to make the hermaphrodite fuckable."[49] These priorities sound shocking when put as Chase does: "Doctors consider the prospect of growing up as a boy with a small penis to be a worse alternative than growing up a girl sans clitoris and ovaries."[50] Reproductive capacities may not be maintained, but the prerogative and status of the penis—and the bodies that possess them—are.[51] Strikingly, doctors reveal themselves to be "size queens," insisting that a structure must "measure up" in order for it to be preserved and pronounced a penis.[52]

While doctors are laboring to produce a properly penetrating kind of masculinity, they have also been trying to prevent other kinds of masculinity, particularly "virilization" (enlarged clitorises) of females (with congenital adrenal hyperplasia [CAH]). With the development of screening programs to test in utero, some doctors have suggested hormone therapy, even in cases that lack a clear medical need, and despite counterindications in terms of effect and the demonstrated dangers of prenatal dexamethasone use.[53] The possibility of women who are "too active" or who lack interest in male sexual partners may provide enough of a rationale[54] to those who presume a series of links between masculinity, activity, intersex conditions, and lesbianism.[55]

Medicalized efforts to stabilize gender and preserve masculinity for only some members arguably follow from the very treatment of intersex and homosexuality as "conditions."[56] After all, as Anne Fausto-Sterling notes,

"If intersexuality blurred the distinction between male and female, then it followed that it blurred the line dividing hetero- from homosexual."[57] The worldview that presumes that only two possible genders and one possible orientation (heterosexual) are normal is particular but also rather pervasive. As a result, Dreger and Herndon confirm, "the treatment of intersex has historically been motivated by homophobia and transphobia—that is, fear of apparent same-sex relations and fear of people changing or blurring gender categories."[58] These histories persist even into the twenty-first century, a time in which people also persist in turning back to the biblical.

Biblical images, ideas, and arguments have been deployed in both stigmatizing and dehumanizing ways about intersex bodies and belonging. A more careful and sustained engagement with intersex critiques, though, can challenge historical interpretations and contemporary uses of biblical images, ideas, or arguments. To use forms of intersex advocacy, themselves informed by feminist and queer principles and practices, explicitly to interrogate the practical and potential uses of the biblical, we must start with one very particular and important letter from Paul.

An Ancient Pal, Against Genital Cutting?

In the long Christian histories and theologies of interpretation, the letter to the Galatians has been known as a kind of "Magna Carta of Christian freedom."[59] Especially where the letter focuses on circumcision and baptism, Paul is actively engaging an audience in multiple assembly communities about what to do with bodies, including one's own, and how to belong in a community with those other bodies that are so like and unlike one's own. Embodied practices, particularly around circumcision, are the major concerns of Galatians.[60] According to the typical (and traditional) line of interpretation, someone besides Paul is trying to convince the members of these Galatian assembly communities to be circumcised. Ostensibly, Paul writes the letter in response to these events, indicating his deep disapproval of such a practice among the Galatian communities. In short, he appears to be arguing, even insisting (most likely to Gentiles): do not get circumcised. Circumcision as a practice is referenced in several parts of the letter (2:3, 7, 8, 9, 12; 5:2, 3, 6, 11; 6:12, 15), but Paul most directly addresses the matter in the latter chapters (5:2–12; 6:12–16). He uses the language of compulsion to characterize the community members who are apparently seeking circumcision: "those who wish to make a good (or easy) appearance in the flesh, these force you to be circumcised" (6:12).[61] So not only does Paul establish a tone conveying "do not be circumcised"; he is also saying, "do not *let yourselves* be circumcised," as if those who seek to perform such surgeries were compelling or forcing others to accept their view (2:3; 6:12).[62] This reading of Paul could be read today as oppositional to genital surgeries and those, including the medical establishment, who pressure intersex people or their guardians, and who even go forward with interventions without informed consent.

Mere sentences after his admonitions regarding obligatory circumcision, Paul declares, "For neither circumcision nor uncircumcision counts for anything, but the new creation is everything!" (NRSV).[63] Verses like this (6:15; cf. 5:6) have certainly bolstered the view of Paul as crossing, even violating, boundaries in his arguments and actions: some feminist interpretations consider Galatians depolarizing and transformative. His arguments about circumcision had effects on gendered dynamics, alongside and within ethnoreligious dynamics, for the Galatian assembly communities.[64] Brigitte Kahl openly wonders about the "male" members of the assemblies: "Being a Jew and being uncircumcised—wasn't that a description exclusively for Jewish women? Were they not real Jews and not real men either? Maybe a 'third sex' in between?"[65] Non-male in-betweenness could be, and indeed has been, identified with contemporary intersex and transgender people,[66] which is why the baptismal formula of Galatians 3:28 could be so hermeneutically powerful for them.

Indeed, the light from this formula shines brightly for a wide variety of Pauline interpreters, possibly because it was used in a number of assembly communities besides the Galatians' (including the Corinthian community, as described in chapter 2). For many feminist interpreters, the words of this pre-Pauline formula—"there is neither Jew nor Greek, neither slave nor free, not male and female; for you are all one in Christ Jesus"—are "the clearest statement of women's equality to be found in the Christian scriptures."[67] Despite the determination that the baptismal formula predates Paul, the traditional theological view casts the letter as a whole as liberatory in substance and tone.[68] Kahl's work strongly maintains that "Paul's most fundamental statement on border-transgressing unity of race, nation, class and sex" is not some alien exception, but is integral to the whole of Paul's argumentation and attitude in the letter.[69]

If it does infuse all of the letter to the Galatians, then that liberatory transgressiveness should also apply to the letter's argumentation about circumcision. Frequently, Pauline interpreters relate circumcision to baptism by means of comparison: if "the law" and practices like circumcision have been downplayed or delegitimized, then baptism is now the more significant practice, embodying the "freedom" so often highlighted by Paul's readers. Typically, this new practice is viewed as more inclusive, as Schüssler Fiorenza (once) argued, "If it was no longer circumcision but baptism which was the primary rite of initiation, then women became full members of the people of God with the same rights and duties."[70] The phrasing and order of the formula is paralleled in later statements where "neither . . . nor" pairs ("neither Jew nor Greek," in 3:28, "neither circumcision nor uncircumcision," in 5:6 and 6:15) are juxtaposed with positive statements of what matters: oneness in Christ (3:28) and "faith" and the new creation (5:6 and 6:15).[71] Not all feminist interpreters make a direct link to Paul's "new creation" saying (6:15), most *do* see a new relation to the created order reflected in the baptismal formula, particularly in the phrase "not male and female." This third pair stands out in the formula, breaking the rhythm of "neither Jew nor Greek, neither slave nor free": one might have expected to hear "neither man nor woman" next, rather than "not male and female." This departure in phrasing and rhythm in the paired "not male and female" of the baptismal formula echoes the first creation account in Genesis (1:27).[72] This "border-transgressing unity"[73] qualifies previous versions of creation, and the oneness of the baptismal community invalidates divisions and status differences, including those that prescribe particular sexual-social roles for males and females (as indicated by the verse's qualification of Gen 1:27's "male and female").[74]

Kahl argues further, though, that this vision of a new creation is the core and climax of Paul's argument in the letter to the Galatians.[75] In Galatians, this vision of a new creation entails a neutralization of mundane status structures that enables Paul to deploy his own weakened and marked body as an anchor for argumentation. Immediately after insisting that neither circumcision nor uncircumcision is anything (6:15; cf. 5:6), Paul points to his own "marks" or scars, *stigmata* (6:17), as reasons why no one should cause any (more) trouble or suffering for him.[76] Earlier in the letter, Paul describes how he had some kind of "weakness in the flesh" (often translated as a "bodily ailment" or "physical infirmity") when he was first among the Galatians (4:13–14). His visual differences mark him as defeated and distinctly unmasculine in the eyes of the Romans, but in solidarity with others pierced and penetrated by imperial authority.[77]

As Beverly Gaventa has pointed out, Paul shortly delineates his view of the proper communal order by addressing the audience as his children with whom he is in labor pains (ōdinein, in 4:19).[78] While that imagery does re-insert a power differential between the stigmatized Paul and his figurative progeny, it should be noted that visual depictions of the defeated nations, the peoples conquered by Rome, were often personified as women or aberrantly gendered males.[79] So Paul's wordplay, and potential gender play, could reflect a kind of solidarity in suffering with a Paul that depicts his own body as stig-matized and strangely gendered. Paul, after all, briefly appears as a transgen-dered mother![80]

By setting such biblical images and arguments into a context focused on baptism and circumcision, scholarship on Galatians could prove itself useful to an intersex critique, particularly given how biblical arguments have already been deployed in stigmatizing and dehumanizing ways. It becomes more difficult to build an exclusionary argument on the first crea-tion account's "male and female," for example, when it is somehow negated or relativized by a later part of (Christian) biblical argumentation, as in the baptismal formula: not (or no) male and female.[81] Building on some of this feminist work on the letter, interpreters and advocates for intersex and trans-gender people like Mollenkott are confident that this text is egalitarian and inclusive: "It is this category-transcending, passionate, and compassionate vision of the human face divine that will stimulate and sustain our attempts to achieve omnigender justice."[82] Justin Tanis also finds transformative hope in Galatians 3:28's "world beyond gender, in which there is room for infinite variation and infinite grace."[83] Yet, Paul's rhetorical leveraging of circumci-sion in this letter complicates the more enthusiastic approaches to this for-mula and the letter as a whole.

A Cutting Joke

Resonances between an intersex critique and the text of Galatians could offer a kind of inclusion to people with intersex conditions, an inclusion that has thus far been only sporadically offered to some lesbian, gay, bisexual, and (perhaps even fewer) trans community members in (overlapping) so-ciopolitical and religious settings. In this letter, there are arguments made explicitly against genital cutting and against compelling people to conform to this practice. Paul depicts his own body as marked by stigmatization, potentially presenting himself as identifying with the defeated and marginalized. The letter's baptismal formula may even advocate a multiply transgressive vision of a different social order that permeates the whole letter. It is indeed promising that the letter does reflect on the topics of embodied suffering and stigmatization alongside, or within, an effort to limit at least some surgical practices for particular kinds of bodies.

And yet . . . a particularly disturbing turn occurs in the midst of the letter's appeals to (a certain kind of) freedom, when Paul writes (or recites): "I wish those who are unsettling you (pl.) would cut off themselves (*apokopsontai*)" (5:12), that is, castrate or mutilate themselves. To be blunt, Paul flippantly and violently wants those seeking circumcision to have their penises cut off! Among most Pauline interpreters this wish is often seen as trivial, another one of those incidental, sarcastic, but nonrepresentative outbursts (like the apparently joking exaggeration in 1 Cor 11:5–6, described in chapter 2, or the thoughtless punning in Phlm 11, considered in chapter 4). While it is hard to duck how bloody an image this is, some interpreters do characterize it only as a rude and obscene exclamation[84] or a joking "after-thought."[85] Regardless, this joke or obscenity is widely recognized as alluding to the ancient figure of the eunuch.[86]

Unlike some previous claims about other biblical depictions of eunuchs, this reference to the eunuch figure could hardly be said to be positive.[87] The person Paul wishes would be castrated is not blessed (as in Isa 56:4–5) or especially gifted with spiritual identifications or practices (as in Acts 8:26–40 or Matt 19:12).[88] Rather, the people targeted by this violent wish would likely share more in common with those barred from the assembly of the Israelites in Deuteronomy 23:1 ("No one whose testicles are crushed or whose penis is cut off"). The Septuagint even uses a form of the same verb (*apokekommenos*) as found in Galatians 5:12 to describe the latter party barred from the community. Indeed, Paul is expending the bulk of his rhetorical energy in the letter attempting to counter the position they are apparently advocating and to exclude them from (at least his conception of) the assembly communities in Galatia. But why call on the figure of the eunuch to do this?

Though not as broad and convoluted a category as ancient androgyny, under whose sign the eunuch sometimes also dwells (see chapter 2), the eunuch of the ancient Roman imperial context is marked by variety and ambiguity.[89] In the ancient settings that condition and constitute the first century context of Paul's letters, eunuchs are defined in a variety of ways, are created or recognized in a variety of ways, and are imagined to have a range of meanings and effects, for themselves and for others. Even the vocabulary associated with eunuchs varies in both Greek and Latin. While one can find at least twenty different verbs for castration in Latin, Greek has at least seven terms related to these figures besides *eunouchos*, including: *spadōn* (tear, tear off, or remove), *tomias* (cut, castrate, or geld, that is, often of a nonhuman animal), *ektomias* (cut out, cut away, or sever), *thlibias* (squeeze, crush, press, or bruise), *thladias* (or *thlasias*, crush or bruise), *ithris* (eunuch), and *apokopos* (cut off).[90] The last of these is the term used in Galatians 5:12. In most cases, this range of terms reflects the range of techniques one could use to alter male genitalia and, thus, make a person a eunuch.

Yet these labels should not be imagined as precise, referring to discrete types of eunuchs: their meanings overlap, and the Hellenistic and Roman valences can be confusing and contradictory.[91] A seemingly straightforward legal attempt at categorization raises two kinds of ambiguity for the ancient category of eunuch. Justinian notes eunuchs who are *spadones* "by birth" (Justinian, *Digest* 50.16.128), likely referring to those with male genitalia (and/or whom ancient elites might still recognize as male) who are somehow infertile.[92] One well-known eunuch from the Roman imperial period, Favorinus of Arles, was a sexual favorite of the emperor Hadrian, a eunuch by birth, and described as hermaphroditic.[93] This kind of eunuch might even account for the first kind of eunuch described in Matthew 19:12 ("there are eunuchs who have been so from birth"). Mathew Kuefler proposes as much, linking the passage with categorizations in both the Mishnah and the earlier Roman jurist Ulpian, identifying these eunuchs as "men with congenitally undeveloped sex organs."[94] This likely accounts for the wide net Walter Stevenson casts in surveying Greco-Roman settings, preferring to "use the term 'eunuch' in its broadest sense, referring to all the sexually altered or asexual men of the period under discussion."[95] Yet, even as many scholarly discussions recognize this congenital or biological cause for some eunuchs, most treatments of the topic focus on those people whose bodies were altered, surgically or otherwise.[96]

The second kind of ambiguity concerns which part, or parts, of the genital anatomy were altered. When ancient laws, speeches, poems, or plays discuss some part being bruised, crushed, or cut, are they referring to the testicles, or the penis, or even both? In many cases, the focus is on the testicles, as when Soranus discusses the effects of bruising or crushing (*thlibiae* in *Gynecology*

2.40.5). Without having to cut off or into the genitalia, one can press or crush the testes to the point of incapacitation. Rather than removing the testicles, one could, for instance, tie or bind the scrotum so tightly as to cut off the vas deferens. Assuming human castration practices developed from comparable practices with (nonhuman) animals in agrarian settings, compression or removal of the testicles seems to be the safer and more sensible option.[97]

Still, Stevenson reminds us that "*castrati* in Latin refers to those whose gonads (and possibly penis also) were surgically detached from the body."[98] References from the Roman imperial settings are ambiguous, especially in consideration alongside examples from the ancient Near East. After all, the relevant text from the Torah bans a person whose testicles were crushed *or* whose penis was cut off (Deut 23:1). Most of the myths associated with ritual practices of castration focus on the loss of the penis. In Egyptian stories Osiris and Seth are castrated, and replicas of their penises are used in cultic practices of commemoration.[99] There are comparable Greek myths and rituals, focused around the castration of Kronos or the ecstatic tearing off of Dionysus's penis.[100] Over time and into the Roman imperial period, Dionysus will be treated as equivalent to Attis, the castrated counterpart to Cybele. At least some practitioners within this cultic group, the *galli*, were known for castrating themselves. When Martial mocks a *gallus* named Baeticus, he asks, "Why was your dick cut off by a sherd of Samos / if cunt was so appealing to you, Baeticus?" (3.81.3–4).[101] The obscene Roman slang for penis, *mentula*, appears in this and other jokes at the expense of *galli*, one making particularly clear reference to the goddess and her followers: "Geld, if you will, Cybele, hapless queens [*cinaedi*]: this was the cock [*mentula*], yes this, that merited your knife" (9.2.13–14).[102] The association of *galli* with *cinaedi* in this passage is important to notice, as is Martial's crass but persistent joking about penises (not testes).[103]

Recent confusion about what castration could constitute is likely exacerbated by the powerful cultural force of Sigmund Freud's ideas about castration (however precisely or imprecisely known and understood they might be).[104] Freud imagines castration as an operation that removes the whole genital apparatus, then uses that to conceptualize the difference between male and female anatomy and a respective set of psychological negotiations. As with the medicalized protocol for treating intersex conditions, Freud's work suffers from a certain reduction of sexuality, gender, and even identity to the presence and meaning of the penis, even as he multiplies the objects that could symbolize the penis.[105]

Still, the varying techniques for castration had different effects and a corresponding variety of uses for eunuchs in ancient settings like the Roman empire. Such differences could stem, for instance, from the timing of the genital alteration. Castrating a young male before puberty would prevent the development of several features of gendered importance for elite Romans, including increased physical strength, facial (and body) hair, and a deepening voice. Removal or incapacitation of the testicles before puberty typically ensured that the eunuch would maintain a youthful and "effeminate" appearance, making (or simply keeping) him an object of desire. The use of this kind of eunuch was common among the Roman imperial elite, including emperors like Nero, Titus, and Domitian. While one hears a great deal about Domitian's beloved eunuch Earinos in the flattering poems of Martial and Statius,[106] one of the best-known uses of these kinds of eunuchs involves the young freedman Sporus. Because he looked so much like Nero's deceased second wife, Nero had Sporus castrated and took him as a receptive sexual companion, treating him "like a wife" (Dio 62.28.2–3; and Suetonius, *Nero*, 28.1). Even after Nero's suicide, Sporus was used in similar ways by both an imperial rival (Nymphidius Sabinus) and a later emperor (Otho) (see Dio 64.8.3; and Plutarch, *Galba* 9:3).[107]

This same procedure, or at least this same timing of a range of procedures, could also make eunuchs useful for other purposes. The very prepubescent castration practices that made eunuchs sexually desirable to elite males left them physically incapable of erection or insemination. This incapacitation is among the reasons why eunuchs were labeled *semiviri*, or "half-men."[108] Since they were capable of neither penetration nor insemination, enslaved eunuchs were trusted to watch over an extended household of the master's women and children. After all, if one major source of anxiety involves guaranteeing the paternity of children, who better to guard the wife (or wives) than one who physiologically cannot throw the matter into question? The eunuch's placement within the stratified, but tightly woven kyriarchal household is made possible by a bodily state repeatedly marked by a prior moment, a bodily intervention that defers physical adolescence and even forestalls other futures.

The timing of castration practices may not entirely change the eunuch's relation to these temporal dimensions, but the age when the procedure was performed does affect bodily appearance and genital function. While fertility is still foreclosed when the testicles are incapacitated or removed after puberty, the postpubescent eunuch is capable of physical arousal (as indicated by erections) and genital pleasure.[109] Furthermore, those bodily features more recently viewed as secondary sex characteristics, including facial hair and deeper voice, will persist to such a degree in bodies modified after puberty that people complained that one cannot even tell the difference between a eunuch and a man.[110] Capitalizing on such ambiguities is also a recurrent plot point in stories of this period, where nonaltered males disguise themselves as eunuchs in order to get access to women they are pursuing.

The ambiguities do not stop there, however, as the same eunuchs trusted to aid in controlling elite women's sexuality are often depicted as expedient sexual actors for such women. In typically bawdy, yet revealing fashion, Martial asks: "Do you ask why your Caelia has only eunuchs, Panychus? Caelia wants to be fucked, but not to have children" (6.67).[111] The use of these eunuchs may not disrupt claims of elite paternity, but they do undermine the (occasional) notion of elite wives' greater moderation (see chapter 2) or more prominent claims about elite male control over the household. Further, in returning to Martial, this sexual ambiguity circles back around to the ambiguity about which parts of the genital anatomy are altered in ancient castration practices. After all, Martial has been treated as one source for the amputation of the member (for at least one kind) of eunuchs, but here (and elsewhere) it is this genital organ about which elite males jest, worry, and complain as being used to penetrate elite females. There is tension or contradiction in the work of even this one author, as eunuchs were alternately figured as effeminately receptive and incapacitated or capably and voraciously insertive.

The disposability of eunuchs intertwined with their status in society, since enslaved people in Greco-Roman antiquity were considered persistently and ubiquitously sexually available. Many, perhaps even most, castrated people were enslaved; their bodily alterations were involuntary, and performed primarily to support the purpose(s) of their owner-users.[112] The various practices of genital alteration reinforced both the absolute authority of the owner and the natal alienation of the enslaved. The ability to have a body castrated, or acquire a castrated body and participate in the economy that produced its condition, was considered essential to the category of ancient imperial manhood, or *virtus*. Owner-users believed that eunuchs would be even more loyal to or dependent on them than other slaves, since their castration heightened their status as socially dead and natally alienated.[113] While nearly all enslaved people were cut off from any ties to a familial and regional past by their acquisition and displacement into the owner-users' household, enslaved eunuchs were also cut off from any future social or familial ties beyond those associated directly with their owner-user(s). As slaves par excellence, eunuchs were physically marked by particular interventions in time, whether before or after puberty, that forestalled any other futures for them.[114]

Ancient castration practices could make the person already being used as a human tool even more useful, aiding in an elite male's control of the women and children in his household. In the later Roman Empire, court eunuchs would themselves be unable to establish their own families to rival that of the rulers. Eunuchs could act as sexual implements for both their male and female owner-users. A range of ancient texts attests that enslaved eunuchs were "luxury items," more valuable and thus more expensive than most other slaves. Particularly beautiful specimens were especial symbols of the status of those who owned and then displayed them.[115] The only possible fertility or paternity that matters—that even exists—in such a household is that of the Roman imperial, elite, slave-owning man at the top of its structure.

Eunuchs remained a somewhat troubled category, because a genitally altered or asexual male was never perfectly synonymous with the enslaved male. Indeed, the very fact that Justinian's compendium lists different kinds of eunuchs has to do with their paternity.[116] Since inheritance is the main mechanism for perpetuating Roman imperial patrilinearity, there is ambiguity in legal traditions about eunuchs. While the nonprocreative elite male could (at least theoretically) marry and adopt a son to receive the inheritance, generally this would require overcoming a legal tradition marked by suspicion of a castrated father.[117] Eunuchs were commonly enslaved, and therefore by definition illegitimate and ineligible for inheritance, so it seems that other kinds of eunuchs were socially and legally assimilated to such categories. For the most part, a eunuch would be a son and heir of nothing in particular, likely because he was often imagined to be criminally vulgar.

The line that differentiated between slave and free was hardly as stable or clear as the naturalized claims frequently made by elite owner-users, since a freeborn male could become an enslaved person by being conquered or captured in battle, kidnapped, or exposed when young. In these contexts where people are owned and exchanged, the idea of natural-born rulers (and natural-born slaves) is challenged. Slave dealers could and would castrate young enslaved males in order to preserve their desirability and increase their worth (to the dealer and the prospective owner-user). While it was at least theoretically possible to redeem a "mistakenly" enslaved person, the act of castration permanently marked a body beyond such recuperation.[118] One procedure, at one moment in one's life, could forever alter one's status. Given the manifest anxiety that elite Roman men showed about continuously demonstrating their imperial masculinity, the eunuch physically and then socially, politically, and culturally indicated how porous the boundary was that elite males were desperately trying not to cross. As testaments to the separability of man and masculinity, eunuchs represented divergent, but all-too-possible pasts and futures for these elite men and their heirs.

Eunuchs castrated before puberty could, even at one glance, signal what could happen to any male—a loss of status because of a loss in fertility and thus potency. Yet the other set of eunuchs, particularly those castrated after puberty, refused to demonstrate their difference through either appearance or sexual performance. Eunuchs could be anywhere, undermining elite males' sexual control over their women, but without the telltale evidence of their impropriety: pregnancy. In a range of ancient texts, "the eunuch was a human dildo, threatening precisely because he could offer women just as much sexual pleasure as any uncastrated male."[119] Eunuchs evoked anxiety precisely because of how imprecise a threat they represented. Were they a problem because they presented the importance of any instant in which one can be transformed into a slave and a feminized receptacle for penetrative use, or because in many moments they were capable of violating one's wife (one elite possession "having" another possession, like he was as masculine as the husband)? As enslaved people, were eunuchs especially trustworthy or more prone to deception? Were they considerably different from or much too close to their owner-users? Were eunuchs asexual or hypersexual?

As dangerous to social hierarchy as eunuchs could appear, castration was a widespread and well-known practice in the Roman imperial period. The castration of young males apparently outraged ruling males; nevertheless, the demand for such slaves only grew and their numbers were spread throughout the empire.[120] A few emperors (including ones, like Domitian, who kept their own favorite eunuchs) attempted to prohibit first the castration of any citizen and then the castration of young enslaved males.[121] However, the main effects of such laws appears to have been the way they simply reinforced claims that castration happened outside the Roman empire; any eunuchs were ostensibly "foreign" exports of the larger slave trade.[122] This association of eunuchs with foreignness, and especially "the east" is further cemented by the westward movement of religious practices and stories centered around Dionysus, Cybele, and Attis.[123]

This association of religiously motivated body modification with foreignness might also have been strengthened by Roman perceptions of a less popular but relatively well-known practice of genital cutting: Jewish circumcision. While circumcision practices existed more widely in the region, over time Roman elites viewed it as a distinctly Jewish practice and worthy of sexual mockery.[124] Horace, Petronius, and Persius use this affinity in order to make circumcised people a butt of their jokes.[125] Persius even links the circumcised with the *galli* of Cybele as reflecting different superstitions from the east (*Satires*, 5.176–88, especially 184–86). For both Greek and Roman elites, circumcision belonged with the more familiar castration in a larger category of genital mutilation. The understanding of circumcision was shaped by this analogy, even assimilation, including among Hellenized Jews like Philo and Paul.[126] Later Roman law would treat the circumcision of a non-Jew as identical to castration.[127] The potential similarity of circumcision and castration has led to theories about the role of each in creating the other practice. Gary Taylor, for instance, argues that circumcision predates castration because the more preliminary genital marking (of just the foreskin) requires only the development of tools, whereas genital incapacitation (particularly of the testes) requires further knowledge of physiology.[128] Piotr Scholz, however, sees circumcision as a "humanizing" development out of and away from castration.[129] In this light, the prohibition of Deuteronomy 23:1 indicates a familiarity with castration practices among ancient Israelites (or at least among their neighbors).

Though (self-)castration is associated with earlier Egyptian and (other) Near Eastern cultic contexts, the depiction of such practices rises in Greek and then Roman accounts from the Hellenistic period forward.[130] The priestly followers of the Anatolian mother deity Cybele, the *galli*, were familiar, even notorious, across the Roman empire for their ritualized displays of self-laceration and castration—and especially in Galatia, located in the highlands of the peninsula.[131] While the stories told and reasons offered for the castration practices of the *galli* varied, the association of Attis and Cybele/Agdistis with the *galli* as castrated priests was cemented before the first century CE.[132] Romans celebrated an annual festival every April to commemorate the arrival of Cybele, but they attempted to separate Attis festivals to March, likely because *Dies Sanguinis*, the "Day of Blood" (March 24), was a common occasion for *galli* to castrate themselves.[133] Elsewhere, the *galli*

are depicted as itinerant and mendicant priests, whose rituals involving ecstatic dancing and bodily cutting attracted attention.[134] Though Martial and
others associated them specifically with the removal of the penis (discussed
earlier), these priests would also whip their backs and cut (the skin of) their
arms, the latter being performances they could repeat. By thus presenting
themselves as slaves of Cybele beyond temple complexes in either Rome or
Anatolia, the *galli* would take up collections to support their cultic activities.[135] After their initiation into these practices, their scars would make
them recognizable figures, as would their long, bright robes and their long,
often loose head hair.[136] Though persistently cast as foreign and strange,
these eunuch priests would be both recognizable and even esteemed (in certain ways) for their outrageous practices.

Still, elite Roman imperial males often, even uniformly, insisted that these
eunuchs were justifiably targeted as objects of explicitly eroticized ridicules
and specifically gendered jokes. From their perspective the term *gallus*
functions as a mocking diminutive (Martial 11.72), associated with feminized and cinaedic males (Apuleius, *Metamorphoses* 8.25.4; 8.26.1; Juvenal
2.115–16; and Martial 9.2.13–14, quoted earlier).[137] The repetition of this
sort of figuration has led Craig Williams to suggest that "the ultimate scare-
figure of Roman masculinity was the *gallus* or castrated priest of Cybele."[138]
The potency of this scare-figure is intimately related to the interlocking
differences of body, status, gender, sexuality, space, region, race, and religion
the castrated devotee under the sway of an eastern goddess can represent.
In this way the *galli* fit within the larger category of eunuchs, viewed as "the
most extreme type of unmanly men"[139] and "the nightmare embodiment of
men's worst fears."[140]

This construction of eunuchs as sexual scare-figures and nonmasculine
nightmares was persistent, but it was perhaps never quite as uniform as some
elite males presented it. Indeed, the ambiguity of eunuchs also provoked ambivalent responses. After all, the effort to create enslaved eunuchs, for both
practical familial and aesthetically erotic purposes, reflect the ways in which
elites valued eunuchs. These wider sorts of ambivalence around eunuchs,
in turn, affected the reception of religious figures and practitioners in both
Greece and Rome. When Attis emerged as a divine figure associated with
the self-castration of Cybele devotees in the Hellenistic period, the Greeks
viewed him as effeminate and barbaric like other "Oriental" figures from their
east, arrayed in antithesis to their own cultural identities.[141] Such negative
figurations were powerful and persistent, and yet as Susan Elliott highlights,

these figurations do not account for why so many were attracted to this cultic figure and the practices associated with him.[142] Indeed, it would seem that the ritual act of self-castration by followers of Attis and Cybele would be a rather potent display of dedication and attachment to these gods. In thinking about responses to Attis, then, one must become accustomed to looking from (at least) two different directions, from both the west and the east, at once.

The same dynamic of syncretism that facilitated the movement of Cybele, Attis, and the *galli* westward and throughout the Roman empire conditions the response once these figures and practices are known among the imperial elites. The Romanization of Cybele (linking her to their Aeneas epic and thus other female deities from their east) was often accompanied by efforts to dissociate her from her troublesome castrating priests, hence, their persistent depiction as foreign, feminized, and sexually strange.[143] Various Roman rulers also tried, unsuccessfully, to ban castrations within the empire. The stereotyped image of the eunuch and specifically the eunuch priest appears to have greater life than such legal efforts, spreading throughout the empire and projecting a competing set of scare-figures even back into Anatolia. The animated ritual activities of the *galli*, their shouting and scourging, self-lacerations and castrations, could then be received with a similarly doubled vision in the cities and villages of this empire. Just as Attis was simultaneously deified and viciously stereotyped, the actions of the *galli* could have been viewed suspiciously or more receptively. Their scarred bodies and striking behavior could either be vivid confirmations of the widely circulating stereotypes, presented in the surviving Greco-Roman literature, or live demonstrations of the continuing power of the Mother of the Gods.[144]

In Anatolian contexts like those of the Galatian assemblies, her eunuch priests could be seen as elevated, if their association with a once-localized but long-known deity persists, or debased, if the Hellenized and Roman imperial tendencies to ridicule and fear their actions were adopted.[145] The mere survival of this cult and its practitioners indicate that there must have been something appealing about them, even alongside a perception of them as revolting.[146] While most eunuchs were enslaved people and thus involuntarily castrated, the sheer drama of the *galli* was their voluntary and vivid display of self-castration, as dedication to a deity. This is likely why they provoked such a strong response among kyriarchal males, why they were the ultimate scare-figures within constructions of imperial masculinity (and the various others subordinated to it). Though ridiculed and despised for dishonoring themselves and their bodies, in a position akin to (other) enslaved people, the eunuch priests also made a claim to an honor derived from the power of the god and the honor and respect due to her.

When someone in the Roman imperial setting introduces the figure of a eunuch in an argument, the intended rhetorical effect is most likely to present the figure as ridiculous or threatening.[147] Whether they were voracious but sterile penetrators or effeminately receptive, they were sexually transgressive. As slaves or as priests, they were gender-troubled "half-men," even unmen. Eunuchs are a joke or a problem: because they are problematic, they are worthy of ridicule, but because they have the potential to make a mockery of (a range of) ancient protocols of differentiation, they are also a problem that must be contained or explained. This widespread derogation can also, then, be a reflection of anxieties and tensions within the empire, even among elite Romans. On the one hand, the most conceptually troublesome of the eunuchs, the *galli*, can be easily assimilated into Roman imperial constructions of themselves and their Others, since they are a vivid point of contrast, a reminder of what they are not. On the other hand, they are incredibly proximate to these elites, either as the eastern outsiders among them or as striking representations of how parts of their imperial margins have been brought into the very heart of their empire.[148] The *galli* can both shore up and undermine kyriarchal identity.

With all the variety and ambiguity of ancient eunuchs, it is possible that ambivalent visions are circulating around and about them. The figure of the eunuch is meant to call up disgust and mockery, and yet their familiarity across the empire and the variety in their uses signal that they could be more than just such scare-figures. Otherwise, how else can one explain the way this cult survived, even thrived into the first century and beyond? Why would someone voluntarily join this group, let alone castrate oneself? All of which leads back to Paul's letter to the Galatians, where he brings up the practice of castration in relation to his own distinct argument about communal belonging.

Facing the Phallus, Cutting to the Fore(skin)

At times it seems that Paul's letter to the Galatians is arguing rather explicitly against genital cutting, and perhaps especially against anyone who would compel people to undergo such operations. Perhaps that could be liberatory for intersex people. Yet recall Paul's flippantly violent wish for those (apparently) seeking circumcision to have their penises cut off (5:12)! A surgical action could put those whom Paul sees as opponents in their place. He is relating one form of genital cutting—circumcision, the persistent focus of the letter—to another, one that is a source of fascination, exploitation, and anxiety in the Roman imperial period: castration. The verb Paul uses to strike out at these other figures, *apokoptō*, meaning to cut off, appears in other ancient treatments of eunuchs, including within the Septuagint (Deut 23:1), the version of the Jewish scriptures Paul was likely to know in the first century CE. Like many other ancient depictions of castration, Galatians 5:12 is unclear about which part or parts of the genital anatomy were to be amputated.

Setting this verse in the larger context of the whole letter, however, underscores the immense attention to the penis, and specifically the foreskin as removed in circumcision. This attention signals that the cutting Paul seeks most likely refers to at least the penis and possibly the entirety of the external genitalia. For their part, scholars analyzing the letter both admit and avoid this possibility, reflecting their own varieties of anxiety. On the one hand, a magisterial commentary like Hans Dieter Betz's can admit that the verb deployed in this verse "is used here in a specific sense ('castrate') as a caricature of the Jewish ritual of circumcision."[149] On the other, Betz also insists, on the very same page no less, that Paul's harsh "joke"

> does not imply that the Galatians were in fact under the influence of the *galloi* (castrated priests) of the cult of Cybele-Attis, but Paul uses the public disgust with regard to these rituals in order to discredit his opponents and their ritual of circumcision, which, it must be said, had nothing to do with castration.

Castration can be understood as a specific caricature of circumcision, can be based on wide recognition of (at least) one kind of eunuch, yet circumcision has nothing to do with castration (or the disgust around eunuchs)!?! Clearing his throat and crossing his legs, Betz crosses his own arguments here and in his circumlocutionary translation of the verb as "make eunuchs of themselves."[150] Even as later translations and commentaries are more willing to see castration in Paul's argument, it is rarely dwelled on for more than a moment. Castration is given only the slightest treatment by J. Louis Martyn: just a few sentences out of an imaginative and mostly comprehensive commentary of over 600 pages.[151]

The reason this particular passage evokes the kinds of anxieties that produce contradictions and omissions is that the argument one encounters here is more than just sarcastic or even crude: it is cruel. The Paul produced by this obscene, if still ironic "stab" at those he opposes is curt and surprisingly cavalier about genital cutting, incapacitation, and even dismemberment. By way of contemporary treatment protocols for intersex conditions, he wishes to see their genital flesh reduced, excised, and scarred like those bodies judged to have either a micropenis or an enlarged clitoris. In both ancient and contemporary contexts, such people are effeminized. In the letter there is no sympathy for this kind of pain or for the potentially effeminizing (and therefore negatively evaluated) effects of violent cutting. Indeed, Paul offers no challenge to the view that receiving acts of violence is effeminizing, the kyriarchal view that defeat and cut-ability is feminine. Rather, it appears he is deploying it to evoke a particular response to other figures in the assembly communities of Galatia. In doing so Paul makes an associative move similar to those found within Roman imperial traditions, where circumcision and castration are linked as forms of genital mutilation. From within this worldview these practices are particularly characteristic of superstitious and strangely religious people from the Romans' east, including both the circumcised Jew and the castrated *gallus* (see Persius, *Satires*, 5.184–86). Castrated and then circumcised males are the repeated objects of ridicule.

Whether Paul of Tarsus knew Persius of Volterra or this association found in wider Roman imperial settings, his argument links circumcision to castration in similar ways in Galatians. Despite the dual admission and distancing performed by interpreters like Betz, Paul's call to have some figures castrate themselves evokes the notoriously and vividly demonstrative self-castrations of the *galli*. His depiction is consistent with concerns prevailing in Roman imperial settings, where these effeminate eunuch priests from the east appear as the ultimate scare-figures of elite imperial masculinity. Circulating throughout the empire, these scare-figures would have made it back to the region most associated with such self-castrations: Anatolia. Ritual self-castrations would have been recognizable, from at least two directions, to the assembly communities in Galatia, located as they were among those settled within this larger region of Asia Minor and colonized and ruled by Rome.[152]

Mathew Kuefler has suggested that Paul is specifically exploiting the figure of the eunuch priest as a common symbol of gender ambiguity and religious perversion in this passage, linking circumcision and the unmanliness of castration.[153] Rare among biblical scholars, Susan Elliott insists

that, if interpreters consider the details, practices, and motivations surrounding both circumcision and castration more carefully, particularly in
the local setting of the Galatian assembly communities, it becomes clear
that circumcision would have been too similar to the ritual castrations of
the *galli*.[154] As a result:

> circumcision threatens the Galatians with regression, not a regression into
> some vague and generalized form of paganism, but into a specific form of
> popular religion prevalent in their Anatolian context, worship of the ubiq-
> uitous Mountain Mother of the Gods.[155]

Yet, for all the depth and breadth of attention paid to Cybele, Attis, and the
galli in Elliott's contextualizations, her own treatment of the letter's violent
wish for castration is ironically rather slight, beyond asserting that Paul's
mockery in 5:12 is an "important piece of evidence" for ancient associations
between castration and circumcision.[156]

Elliott is correct about this passage's importance but misses out on its significance for the rhetorics of the letter as a whole. Eunuchs are the stigmatized
point of contrast lurking throughout the argumentation about circumcision
and communal identity. That much is clear from Paul's cutting joke, or violent wish, that circumcisers should be castrated. A specifically phallic focus
comes starkly into the foreground with this ostensibly sarcastic outburst, one
strikingly consonant with Roman imperial jokes about sexually uncontrolled
but sterile eunuchs, as well as the more recent surgical shorthand of "You
can make a hole but you can't build a pole." In first- and twenty-first-century
contexts, "male" or phallic genital tissue is overly invested with importance,
and Paul does not contest the worldview that these interventions reduce
subjects to female (or feminized) roles to receptivity. Brigitte Kahl wonders
whether Galatians should be labeled "the most 'phallocentric' document of
the New Testament. Nowhere else in Paul's corpus have we so much naked
maleness exposed as the centre of a deeply theological and highly emotional debate: foreskin, circumcision, sperm, castration."[157] This decidedly
male focus affects the entire letter and potentially even the reception of its
directives.[158]

Paul's efforts in the letter represent a winnowing down of emphasis: only
some surgical procedures, only particular kinds of bodies, and only particular
parts of Torah/law are in view in his epistle's arguments. Unlike intersex activist
Cheryl Chase, for example, Paul is not arguing about the elimination of *female*

genital cutting. Rather, more like the medicalized protocol Chase and others oppose, Paul seems to be particularly focused on the treatment and meaning of the penis and male members (or "members"). It is precisely this focus on the (un)circumcised penis that most Pauline scholars evade or downplay, even if and as they have (ironically) kept their own focus trained on circumcision as a topic and point of contention in the letter. Paul's potentially strange phrase "gospel of the foreskin" (2:7) is sanitized and generalized into "gospel to (or for) the uncircumcised," or even "for the Gentiles," in standard translations and commentaries.[159] Interpreters flinch in the face of the visceral physicality of this, and several other terms used in the letter. Indeed, the Greek word that appears three times in Galatians, *akrobustia* (in 2:7; 5:6; and 6:15), is typically used to describe the part removed in circumcision, the foreskin, not as a term standing for those who have *not* had this surgical procedure, that is, non-Jews.[160] Paul's use of the term to describe the non-Jewish nations (or Gentiles) as the uncircumcised or "the foreskin," then, is distinct from other appearances of the term (including even the majority of Paul's own uses of it).[161]

This atypicality extends to Paul's unique contrast between the "gospel of the foreskin" and the "gospel of circumcision" (2:7), two phrases that appear nowhere else in the Pauline corpus.[162] Even the oppositional pairing of foreskin (*akrobustia*) and circumcision (*peritomē*) is unattested anywhere in ancient sources (Jewish or non-Jewish) before Paul's letters to the Galatians and the Romans. His use of the other side of this opposition—circumcision—as a metonym for Jews also stands out, as Caroline Johnson Hodge notes: "Although it is common to associate Jews with circumcision, and they were known among non-Jews for this practice, no one calls them 'the circumcision' as Paul does. This terminology is striking in that it singles out an ethnic-religious ritual of fertility as a defining characteristic of the Jewish people (even as it only marks male Jewish bodies)."[163] Both Paul's reduction of the groups to one identifying signifier (presence or absence of foreskin) and his totalizing categorization of them into an oppositional pair in Galatians (and his letter to the Romans) stand out historically and rhetorically.[164] A studied reluctance to discuss the penis (and at least this surgical procedure) means that most Pauline interpreters are avoiding or evading precisely what makes Paul's argumentative perspective unique for his ancient context.[165] By accepting and only arguing themselves from this perspective, Pauline interpreters reinforce Paul's reduction of Jews and the other nations to what the males do (or do not) have done to their genitalia. The history of interpretation paradoxically perpetuates yet deflects this Pauline focus on the penis.

From within this tortured reinstallation of Paul's view of embodied practice as normative, scholars often also avoid what makes Paul's argumentative focus not particularly unique, for either the first or the twenty-first
century: its androcentrism.[166] Even as Paul's androcentrism could hardly
be said to stand out in his ancient contexts, the particularity of its expression, fixated on the penis with or without foreskin, does. The letter's phallic
fixation cannot be chalked up to Paul's Jewishness either, particularly since
circumcision was just one practice in a range of factors to be negotiated in
matters of Jewish identity and practice. It simply was not the most important feature of Jewish identity.[167] Yet Pauline scholars frequently presume
the absolute centrality of circumcision to ancient Judaism(s) because they
follow the lead of (at least parts of) Paul's argumentation.[168] However, Paul's
own argumentation and presentation of himself, in Galatians and elsewhere,
seem to reflect a much more complicated understanding of Jewishness. He
demonstrates his status not only by his advancement in "the traditions of
my fathers" (Gal 3:14), but also by his birth as Jewish, not "from the sinning
nations" (Gal 2:15).[169] Even when Paul mentions his own circumcision, in
another letter, he lists it among other factors—including birth, descent, and
his Pharisaic practices—that signal his Jewishness (Phil 3:5–6). This historical and rhetorical landscape, then, makes Paul's repeated isolation of circumcision and foreskin as the communal markers of belonging in Galatians
all the more remarkable. Regardless of what one can or cannot surmise
about his "opponents," one can see that Paul's argumentation persistently
circles around the penis.[170] Male genital appearance is directly connected
to belonging in Paul's specific norms and forms of community. In Paul's
constrained anatomy of belonging, membership is about male members (in
at least two senses of the word).

Of course, one can see why a letter that potentially reduces Judaism(s) to
one practice of genital cutting—circumcision—almost certainly associates
this practice with another, more widely debased practice—castration—and
then dissociates both of these practices from a communal life defined, in part,
by baptism would play a turbulent role in the history of interpretation. Even
rather recently, a number of supposedly "New Perspective" scholars have
argued, as James Dunn does, that: " 'Circumcision' could stand metonymi-
cally for a whole people precisely because it characterised a people's whole
existence, a complete way of life. As Christians today speak of a 'baptismal
life,' so we could speak here of a 'circumcision life.' "[171] Yet, for centuries this
totalization and equivalence are false: Jews did not view circumcision as the

sole basis of salvation and requirement for belonging, as Christians came to see baptism.[172] The stress on circumcision as the definitive marker of Jewish identity in antiquity is much more the result of distinctly Christian interpretations than the lively and long-lasting discussions about the meanings and practices of Judaism(s) among Jews. Historically, this stress is more characteristic of manifestly anti-Jewish polemics, starting with Justin Martyr and influencing figures like Augustine and Martin Luther, each building their claims on Pauline argumentation.[173] In Luther's particularly influential commentary on Galatians (his favorite epistle), circumcision is associated with what he viewed as the negative conditions of his time, where individuals tortured by fleshly desires battle sin. Circumcision presents the epitome of these conditions, and is repeatedly characterized as the "altogether carnal" exemplar of the "horrible terrors of the law."[174]

The association of male genital cutting with sexual immoderation or transgression is much more strongly in evidence in Roman imperial depictions of castration than ancient Jewish ideas about circumcision. In identifying (some) Jews as "the circumcision," Paul's argument in Galatians is distinctive from both of these settings. When the letter links circumcision with castration, it is more consonant with Roman imperial perspectives than (other) ancient Jewish perspectives. Even when his arguments are strangely phrased, Paul's concentration on the details of male genital anatomy is almost entirely at home in an ambient androcentrism that was reflected among Gentiles and Jews, ruling Romans and their various subject peoples. This androcentrism could (at least in part) account for the persistent interest in the capabilities and meanings of male genitalia across a range of ancient settings, including this letter.

Since Luther, however, Galatians is repeatedly cast as about the "faith" of the baptized as opposed to "the works of the law" (particularly circumcision). Yet, for all of their interest in faith versus law or baptism versus circumcision, even modern scholarly readers have remained incurious and imprecise about the recipients of this message, the Galatians, either Paul's "opponents" there or the community members in general. "Pale and abstract figures, they remained faceless and disembodied—except for the one striking male physical feature at the heart of the whole debate: their foreskins."[175] Interpreters focus on the foreskin (its absence or presence), following Paul's own peculiarly predominant focus on the foreskin. Strangely, they then presume that it must be Paul's (and their own) adversaries and "Others" who are excessively focused on fleshly matters. Despite the persistent return to circumcision as the problematic practice at the center of Paul's argumentation in Galatians, scholars seem to become incongruously queasy if they focus on the details, surgical or otherwise, of these particular penises, with their fleshy foreskins (for too long).[176] Instead of flesh as the foreskin that knives can cut, "flesh" must be transformed into a symbol to convey a weightier rhetorical or theological point about topics like works-righteousness or "the law."[177]

The claim that *other people* are focusing too much on the flesh, especially the foreskin of the penis, simultaneously and paradoxically reveals and refuses a particularly Pauline fixation, in both the epistle and its interpretation.[178] The interpretive tradition is one filled by males (and their malestream followers) fixing on one aspect of embodied existence: the presence or absence of foreskin on a penis. It is a lineage of (mostly) males looking at previous, (mostly) male interpreters, both sets of which are looking at a past, saintly someone (the mostly male Paul) looking for the foreskins of the male members in the Galatian assembly communities. However, this collective channel of foreskin fixation—from Paul through Justin, Augustine, Luther, and many, many more—both admits of their focus and disavows their own role in their scopic selection. At each layer of this phallo-focused line, Paul and then the Pauline interpreters insist that they are interested in this small batch of penile flesh because it is some other group who are themselves overly fixated on the forms of the flesh.

Yet it is Paul's letter that repeatedly isolates circumcision and foreskin as the communal markers of belonging. In this constrained anatomy of community, Paul's focus remains mostly on male genital appearance and the male members in the Galatian assembly communities. Indeed, this fixation on the function and meaning of a relatively small amount of flesh as the ultimate determinative factor is shared not only among Pauline epistles and their interpreters but also among ancient Roman imperial elites anxious about castration and more recent medical elites worried about intersex bodies. Paul, most Pauline scholars, and still other malestream interpreters of the body, in the first and twenty-first centuries, have all proven themselves to be "size queens," seeking for a member to be long (enough) to belong. The Roman imperial concern with masculine penetration and potency, in the face of other bodies imagined to be effeminized, displays a surprising degree of staying power.

Most of Paul's argumentative effort is expended in constructing and maintaining one acceptable way to belong in his version of the assembly communities. Yet, one especially large hole in the argument of the letter concerns the absence of those bodies derogatively characterized as "holes" by both ancient and modern medical authorities. If the pictures of the Galatians in this letter are "faceless" except for their foreskins, then how much more are the women in the communities obscured by Paul's rhetorical focus?[179] This Pauline epistle and its interpretation remain remarkably incurious about women in the communal body, again, much like those following the recent treatment of intersex bodies or the ancient concerns about castrated bodies.

Anachronistically juxtaposing ancient eunuchs and contemporary people with intersex conditions makes it easier to trace how female forms of embodiment only come into view as figures of receptivity in all three settings. As Kahl, Gaventa, and Lopez are right to stress, the argumentation of the fourth chapter offers a number of maternal figures. The longest stretch of the text to focus on such females is the allegory of two different mothers, in 4:22–5:1.[180] Yet, this also functions as an extension of the Abrahamic arguments Paul has already presented in the previous chapter: it elaborates on what kinds of male offspring Abraham will "have" (4:22) through these female receivers of his seed. As receivers of seed and bearers of children, these female figures are unlike some of the women elite Roman imperial males criticized for their taste in sterile sex (with eunuchs). The primary role of the free mother ("Jerusalem above," 4:26, implicitly Sarah) and the enslaved Hagar are to produce male offspring of the penetrating Abraham, offspring that will be further submitted to penetrating Pauline arguments of comparison and contrast. So these female bodies are presented instrumentally, as receptacles for the delivery of potential sons and then as figures receptive to representation as wider concepts (freedom/slavery, Jerusalem now/Jerusalem above, spirit/flesh). As Sheila Briggs highlights, the utility of women's bodies is only underscored by Paul's choice of "metaphors taken from the institution of slavery and the sexual use of women in slavery."[181] Neither mother is a model herself, but both are put to bodily and rhetorical use, particularly in defining what kind of community (marked as elite male as inheriting sons) Paul wants the Galatians to be.

The conclusion of this allegorical deployment of two sexually receptive female figures directly states that Paul's fraternal "we" are Isaac (4:28), Abraham's son and heir by the free woman, not the enslaved boy. The deployment of such figures only displays Abraham's patrifamilial prerogative, fertile potency, and virile control of others, those topics of anxiety that Roman imperial elites evinced in their reflections on castration. The meaning of this allegorical argument is connected to the status of this Galatian "we" through another, thrice-repeated contrast with enslaved people (4:30, 31; and 5:1; cf. 3:29–47). Paul even cites a previous scriptural tradition (Gen 21:10) to explain why those who are (imagined to be) slaves must be cast out and cut off, in a position exemplified by the enslaved eunuch.

The practice of castration most explicitly appears as Paul's arguments against circumcision reach a rhetorically striking crescendo with his wish that the advocates for such practices would castrate themselves (5:12). The presence of a eunuch figure in the foreground indicates that eunuchs might just have been lingering all along in the background of the many arguments about slaves and sons (and possibly even earlier). If Paul expects that he can effectively call on an association between two types of genital cutting, castration and circumcision, in this moment, then it appears that he could expect others in his audience to have figures of castration in mind in prior or future discussions about genital modification. Certainly, eunuchs were prominent in elite Roman imperial deliberations about masculinity and embodiment, status and sexuality, most especially if *galli* were the ultimate scare-figures.

Yet, like the figure of the ancient eunuch, this potential identification within the arguments of Galatians presents some of its own ambiguities. After all, the zing of Paul's cutting joke depends on (those he sees as) his opponents castrating themselves. On initial blush, this sounds more like priestly eunuchs than enslaved eunuchs, since the *galli* chose to castrate themselves (they were not castrated by others). This makes sense if Paul is aiming to introduce a stigmatized point of contrast that also resonates with the situation at hand, because he is trying to convince members of his audience(s) not to circumcise their own genital members, like the *galli* who castrate their own genitalia. Paul aims to counteract their voluntary genital modification. However, the edge of this wish for castration, its cutting resonance, also indicates that these other(ed) figures would not have intended their own castrations. Cruelly, but ironically, those seeking others' circumcision would themselves end up castrated! Perhaps, this would connote the way *galli* were portrayed as carried away by their rituals, particularly since some Roman imperial depictions emphasized their regret. Certainly, the point of this violent wish is that the outcome should be negative for those Paul opposes; however, this was not the way most eunuch priests perceived their ritual practices.

If these castrations were meant to be seen as unintended by the castrated, then this would have resonated with their depiction as compelling others to be circumcised (6:12; cf. 2:3): their unwanted castrations as just desserts for forcing other people's circumcision. An involuntary, even unwanted castration, then, sounds much more like the practices applied to enslaved people than the practices performed by *galli*. Perhaps that is the point to which the letter has been leading in repeatedly highlighting enslaved people: this involuntary castration exemplifies the debased status of an enslaved eunuch that an assembly member would have if his member were circumcised.

Paul's wish for these other figures to castrate themselves presents them in a pointed, yet ambiguous manner. Would they be viewed in roles more like the priestly eunuch priests or enslaved eunuch? One probable reading could involve both! The appearance of the eunuch figure in Galatians plays on the ambiguity endemic to the variety of eunuchs in the Roman empire, even or perhaps especially because people in the Galatian assemblies would have known or heard about both kinds of eunuchs. Paul first deploys enslaved versions of this figure to stress an involuntary kind of castration, which aids him with a negative depiction of those who are trying to convince others to voluntarily circumcise themselves, portraying them as actually compelling an involuntary action. It is clear from the arguments leading up to Paul's cutting "joke" that the audience should not want to be like the son of Hagar, should not seek to be placed in the position of a slave (the place Paul constructs for those who fail to conform to his more constrained anatomy of assembly belonging). Paul's vicious wish drives this dissociation home through a callous accentuation: why would you want to be enslaved, particularly if it means that you (too) will be castrated?!? Paul's perspective collapses the position of the self-castrated *galli* into that of the (involuntarily) castrated slave in a manner more like the mocking elite Roman imperial depictions of *galli* as depraved slaves under the sway of an eastern goddess. Just as this depiction of eunuch priests built on the larger category of enslaved people who might also be eunuchs, so Paul's argument in Galatians proceeds from enslaved to explicitly castrated points of contrast.

Nevertheless, just before the allegory of two different mothers (4:22–5:1), Paul depicts himself—albeit briefly—in labor pains (4:19). This kind of gender-crossing, maternal Paul has caused both confusion and excitement among Pauline interpreters, suggesting that it is important to reconsider Paul's self-presentation in the letter. Some interpreters have even suggested that Paul's depiction of his own "weakness in the flesh" in the preceding lines (4:13) reflects a different negotiation of gender, a less masculine, more feminine Paul.[182] Pauline arguments and interpretive claims like these actually reinforce, rather than subvert or scramble, the ancient and modern associations of female or effeminized embodiment with passivity, pliancy, porousness, and receptivity.[183] Eunuchs castrated before puberty were identified by their (relative) physical weakness and were associated with those other features marked as especially feminine in the elite Roman imperial worldview. When Paul is searching for a way to describe a (briefly) weakened condition (from the past), he stresses those things debased in his worldview: flesh that reveals a diminished status (4:13) and the receptive female role in delivering offspring (4:19). These certain kinds of bodies are combined with femaleness, or effeminacy, in the immediately following allegory, where one kind of Abrahamic offspring is born from degrading flesh (4:23, 29). This fleshly kind, associated with enslaved people, must be excised from the communal body, cast out like other expendable enfleshed entities (here, the enslaved female and the potentially effeminized enslaved son, 4:30). Just as modern doctors draw on certain constrained views of a "natural" kind of body to determine what to cut, Paul cuts his kind of community through embodied arguments that reflect ancient views of "natural" differences like fleshly receptive females and hereditarily inferior enslaved bodies.[184] In both domains authorities are strikingly cavalier about cutting in order to affix a (supposedly) stable, gendered communal identity.

This disposition is consistent with the argumentation in most of the letter, where Paul demonstrates his customary kyriarchal character. Even an optimistic interpreter like Kahl must admit it: "Galatians is the most polarizing and angry letter that Paul wrote."[185] In this letter Paul curses and name-calls, insults and isolates, cuts out and cuts off. Rhetorically speaking, Paul is militantly masculine in Galatians.[186] The arguments are volatile and laden with judgment from the abrupt and thankless beginning of the letter forward. Twice Paul delivers a curse, *anathema* (1:8, 9), against those he cast as twisting or perverting the message that he brought. Paul can only make this characterization, though, by insisting that there is only one kind of message, his; there is no other way of looking (1:6–7). From the strength of his response, Paul attempts to defend the Galatian body he sees as his "turf." The claim of another way is a challenge to the authority Paul claims for himself; the letter, then, is his chance to resolve what he sees as a problem and to maintain his status as an authority. The letter represents an insistence that he is the proper interpreter of this communal body.

While Paul describes those who are (apparently) seeking circumcision as compelling or forcing the Galatians (6:12; cf. 2:3, 14), the letter itself reflects a different kind of compulsion in terms of Paul's exclusive claims. The community must resist and refuse this different gospel (which is no gospel) unless they too want to be perverse and accursed (1:8–9), unthinkably foolish (anoētoi) and maliciously bewitched (3:1), and, thus, driven out, ostracized from the community (4:30). In Paul's eyes the audience must resist any visions about the meaning and uses of their bodies different from the one he presents. There is no legitimate difference or acceptable variety; those who argue from different embodied positions are only "pseudo-brothers" (2:4). The possibility of "false" brothers also potentially echoes Roman imperial anxieties about the "fake" masculinity of eunuchs who can initially pass as men (due to their postpubertal castrations). Paul's phallic fixation on only certain forms of flesh, then, represents its own set of constraints. Though arguing against at least some kind of surgical action, Paul's arguments echo the predominant attitudes about the contemporary treatment of intersex conditions. Medicalized management insists there is no different way to treat these conditions, when another way can actually involve no interventionist treatment. Refusing the treatment is unthinkable (anoētoi), particularly in the social conditions reflected and maintained by this protocol that see such differences as perverse and isolating.

The curt, cavalier, even cruel attitudes about the condition of various bodies encountered in these Galatian assembly communities reflect the letter's arguments about genital cutting and about flesh in general. Paul even connects the two, insisting that those advocates of circumcision he opposes are motivated by hypocritical, fleshly motives (6:12–13). Building a contrast between spirit and flesh (3:3; 4:29; 5:16–25; and 6:8), he wants the community members to cut out the fleshly parts of the Galatian body—those he opposes and whoever else does not conform (enough) to his anatomy of communal belonging (4:23, 29–30). Aside from his prior (and brief) weakness (4:13), Paul dissociates himself from flesh (1:16) and seeks to eliminate the influence of flesh in the community. Associated not only with weakness and those Paul opposes but also with enslaved bodies (4:23, 29), improper desires (5:16–17, 24), and the vices that exclude one from inheriting the kingdom (5:19–21), flesh is tainted by its association with desire, weakness, enslavement, inferiority, or, in short, the feminine, all qualities that the eunuch figure potently signifies for elite Roman imperial males.[187] The vilification is ironic, considering Paul's particular focus on the phallic flesh of the foreskinned males in the community. It might be difficult to reconcile, within the "body" of his letter, Paul's blithe treatment of genital cutting or his debasement of enfleshed activities with his notable insistence that foreskins not be removed. This difficulty is heightened if one is unable to recognize Paul is not "anti-circumcision" because he is concerned with bodily integrity, sensation, or safety. From his arguments in Galatians, Paul seems thoroughly uninterested in such matters and much more concerned with keeping certain embodied experiences, sensations, and subjects out of (his version of) the assembly communities. Preserving the possibilities of pleasurable sensation and minimizing pain are not primary ethical impulses in the letter to the Galatians.[188] The only reason even to avoid (unnecessary) pain might be to avoid its weakening and thereby effeminizing impact.

Paul presents no consistent argument about genital cutting per se in Galatians. He can relish the thought of those he opposes being viciously cut, even as he seeks to cut out of the community some who do cut their own foreskins. This issue of a fleshly practice can drive his entire argument, yet he can aim to vilify anyone who focuses on fleshly matters. At times Paul's arguments are as anxious as the Roman imperial setting that conditions them. The letter's claims can be as tensive and contradictory as those made within the predominant protocol for treating intersex conditions: those who cannot leave moderately varied flesh alone, but cut and construct genital flesh ostensibly to reveal the "true" or "natural" meaning inside the body.

"Don't Quote Ovid to Me"
(and Don't Bother with Paul Either?)

The arguments about genital cutting in Paul's letter to the Galatians are ambiguous at best, violent and cruel at worst, quite possibly because they play on the ambiguities inherent to the variety of eunuchs in the Roman empire, a violent and cruel kyriarchal system.[189] In the present-day context of medicalized management, there are a variety of bodily states labeled as intersex because of an apparent ambiguity in the genitalia or between the genitals and other aspects of embodiment. While I am not arguing that the situations of the circumcising members of the Galatian assembly communities (or of the eunuch

figures deployed in Paul's arguments to address these members) are equivalent to those of contemporary people with intersex conditions, I do think
that anachronistically juxtaposing these differently stigmatized bodies can
help one zero in on a set of potential, if still partial, correspondences between
them and their contexts. Such correspondences can help a queer analysis,
in solidarity with intersex efforts to counter stigmatization, recognize and
reconfigure the debasing, even dehumanizing perspectives deployed against
people with these varieties of bodily conditions.

Such reconfigurations can even challenge the notion that the bodies
targeted and stigmatized for their apparently significant differences are
marked by ambiguity. The genitalia of many intersex people clearly fit the
features ascribed to one of the two already recognized genders. Even when
these genitalia do not correspond (enough) to these categories, they are not
then unclear, the "fact that such bodies are neither male nor female makes
them clearly intersexed rather than confused or incomprehensible," writes
Morgan Holmes.[190] Such a body "has an excess of sexual difference—perhaps
a vagina and penis," Iain Morland notes, "rather than a lack of differentiation."[191] Medical protocol must generate an undifferentiated "ambiguity" as
problematic, abnormal, and unnatural in order to justify an intervention that
apparently resolves problems and restores a normal and natural state. Yet by
damaging genital anatomy, sensation, response, and function, "the surgery
creates a sexual abnormality."[192] In making cuts, in leaving traces, the most
common treatments appear to make people *more* intersex—more ambiguous, not less.[193]

Given the constancy with which suffering, shame, and stigma are recorded by people treated for intersex conditions, activists have especially
stressed the importance of a delay in any genital surgeries, at least until the
intersex person can participate in the decision. Ancient Romans recognized
the different effects associated with the timing of castration procedures,
as they seemed especially anxious about those who were castrated later in
their lives. However, these elite Roman imperial traditions are almost entirely unconcerned about the suffering or stigma of the castrated. Indeed, for
those seeking historical resources to advocate against genital surgeries, it is
ironic that the Romans attempted to ban castration practices, since such laws
simply reinforced claims that castration happened outside the Roman empire, any eunuchs ostensibly foreign exports of the larger slave trade. Thus,
anticastration laws did not mean that the Romans were concerned about
those whose bodies were surgically altered, and certainly did not stop them

from acquiring such enslaved people or continuing to associate them with stigmatized qualities and practices. On the contrary, it appears these laws increased stigma around eunuchs!

Both ancient eunuchs and the people we today recognize as intersex can be identified by their scarred bodies. Here, the surgical scarring of intersex people has potentially less in common with the *galli*, known for their displays of self-laceration and castration, than those enslaved people that have been marked by tattooing, scarification, or castration practices enacted by someone else (their owner-users).[194] Beyond the series of physical problems for intersex people, the scarring effects of surgical practices are, as Morland argues, one of several things that marks him (and others) as *more* recognizably intersex.[195] Intervention is never seamless, always leaving traces, including the creation of what Katrina Roen calls "newly queered beings."[196] Still, because the impacts and the impressions of the standard treatment linger, intersex is and "does" more than normalize or naturalize, people with intersex conditions are more than just scarred and stigmatized bodies, are "more complex than what we look like."[197] The treatment "fails" to impress one constrained version of belonging, yet generates the basis for a very different kind of community, one of solidarity and support for surviving the scarring and stigmatizing effects of surgeries.[198]

Perhaps certain kinds of bodily transgressions make solidarities possible. An intersex biblical critique (which one *might* also call queer) has the advantage of recognizing the details of a range of embodied conditions, acknowledging and countering the stigmatizing that predominantly shapes the settings for those inhabiting such bodies. One of the perceived threats of intersex is its blurring of gendered distinctions and destabilizing seamlessly heteronormative identifications—and one of the perceived threats posed by ancient eunuchs was that their subordinately gendered position could both shore up and transgress the presumptively natural and exclusive link between sexual penetration and elite imperial virility, potency, and fertility. Indeed, the history of eunuchs and other "unmen" in antiquity demonstrates that there have been many more categories for gender and embodiment than just men and women, even if the way these are sorted kyriarchally are evidently problematic for more recent settings. This sort of approach to intersex interrogates any attempts at straightforward identification with other altered bodies, from antiquity or otherwise, but it also generates alternative angles on both the argument and the audience of letters like Galatians.

It would be a mistake to presume that Paul's perspective—often in accord with Roman imperial perspectives on figures imagined to be perversely gendered because they are strangely embodied—represents the assembly communities of Galatia. His letter is just one part in a rhetorical exchange. Paul's efforts to depict those assembly members who are (apparently) seeking to circumcise others as akin to enslaved and castrated bodies, as eunuch figures, are reflections of an unstable and incomplete process, neither a complete nor wholly satisfactory vision of bodily variations for either the first or the twenty-first century. Only some parts of (only some of) the members come into the foreground of the letter, where both the epistle and the bulk of its interpretation have reduced their meaning to (a particular portion of) phallic flesh. Most (malestream) writing on this text reproduces this reduction and an accompanying figuration of those Paul opposes, often simply trusting the partial, if politically privileged perspective the letter (comes to) represent.

The countervision produced by intersex advocates and scholars goes a long way toward correcting the faint, faceless, mostly abstracted treatment of these other figures in scholarship on this letter. Though the letter appears to be repeating and reinscribing Roman imperial perspectives on surgically altered bodies, recall that there are other ways of seeing and thinking about figures like the *galli*—vivid, even memorable figures who look reviled, debased, and dishonored to some, yet emulated, dedicated, and elevated by others. Paul's letter likely plays with the ambiguities presented by the variety of eunuch figures, assimilating aspects of enslaved eunuchs into the self-castrating eunuch priests, and then associating this threatening but ridiculed figure with those who were (apparently) seeking circumcision. But this does not mean that all in his audience would have made such connections. Rather, the fact that Paul is anxious to make such connections suggest that he thinks at least some, most, or even all would *not* have made these connections, or would not have evaluated their significance in the way that he has. Many of Paul's arguments, though they build on Roman imperial perspectives, appear to be rather distinctive from both these and other Jewish perspectives of this time and space. It is a strong likelihood that there were countervisions among those assembly members addressed by these adaptations of Roman imperial scare-figures.

The manifest efforts to dissociate the circumcising members from the larger baptismal body of the Galatian assemblies indicate that there is something problematic or even threatening about any members choosing circumcision at this point in their lives, but the threat might not extend much beyond the concerns presented by Paul. To medical elites in the present day, the threat presented by people with intersex conditions lies in their potential to blur gendered distinctions and destabilize seamlessly heteronormative identifications. Analogously but not identically, one of the perceived threats posed by ancient eunuchs was their potential to transgress the boundaries of masculinity and challenge the prevailing ethos of penetration that (they thought) was meant to correspond exclusively to elite imperial free males. For those living further from the apex of the kyriarchal pyramid, this difference could be part of the appeal of assembling together, or could simply be the case that the boundaries that provoke anxieties among elites (especially in imperial centers) do not easily map onto nonelites in Galatia (an eastern province).

Because Paul insists that Gentile male assembly members should not be circumcising themselves upon joining the assemblies, any effort to encourage this activity transgresses or blurs the zones of loyalty he imagines for his own vision of the community. Such a permanent, visceral, and of course painful act would vividly demonstrate how much these and other bodies would not have conformed to Paul's wishes or accepted his authority on this and potentially other matters. Of course, in such depictions Paul may just be the one who protests too much, considering that he first encountered these Galatians because of his own "weakness in the flesh" (4:13). This is striking, considering Paul's own itinerant activities, promoting a strange religious movement from the east. The collection of funds for other, far-flung participants in this movement is a recurrent and at times important topic in other letters and in their presentations of Paul's position in the wider social networks of these assembly communities. But Galatians bears only the slightest of references to this collection, a throwaway allusion about something Paul was eager to do anyway (in 2:10), perhaps because Paul's self-presentation in this letter as both fleshly weakened (4:13) and stigmatically scarred (6:17), as a bodily altered, traveling, and begging figure claiming some charismatic authority, resonates a bit too strongly with figurations of eunuch priests, against which he wants to contrast himself and those who would follow him.

Paul's own stigma (6:17) is remarkable, but not because he is now a model figure to be recuperated, someone who grapples uncomfortably with gendered embodiment, walking a fine line that can admit, and still flee away from fleshly associations. Rather, it is the way Paul describes the occasion for his *interaction with* the Galatians (4:12–15) in such a condition that deserves further reflection. Paul maintains that it was because of his "weakness in the flesh" that he first came to them. Yet, instead of ridiculing, vilifying, or distancing themselves from this weak, even eunuch-esque outsider (as Paul argues one should do in several other parts of the letter), they received him rather favorably (4:14). Though Paul was a "trial to you in my flesh" (his flesh again), the Galatians even received him as a divine messenger, like Christ Jesus (4:14). The argument implies that the Galatians supplied support to this stranger, a diasporic Jew, with his own surgically modified body, physically recovering in a weakened condition (not unlike the support a freshly castrated person would need).[199] The Galatians themselves are modeling an attitude to embodied difference that is distinct from Paul's. These members are not only comfortable with the possible complication that Paul presents to their communal life; they are hospitable to this foreign other, even as he is apparently weak in the flesh. As members of those nations (*ta ethnē*, typically the "Gentiles") that both elite Romans and ancient Jews would see as their "others," the Galatians do not behave like the hostile characters that ancient literature, whether Greco-Roman or Hellenized Jewish, portrays them to be.[200]

If the Galatian assembly members did not view castrated or circumcised bodies as particularly ridiculous, and potentially even deserving of admiration and respect, then this could in part account for why the weakened Paul was read as reflecting not ambiguity but simply variety, a difference that did not particularly perturb the Galatians or signal their superiority (as the Roman rulers would have imagined it). Perhaps this is why Paul cites the baptismal formula familiar to them "no longer Jew or Gentile, slave or free, not male and female" (3:28): because he knows they would recognize it and likely use it differently than he tries to use it in the letter. Indeed, this formula could be deployed to imagine gender, status, ethnicity, and embodiment in more capacious ways than the vision shaped by elites anxious about such dynamics. Paul, however, argues for more stringent communal boundaries, particularly as it relates to what they should do with (at least some of) their bodies and how (perhaps paradoxically) they should avoid everything associated with the flesh. Though Paul might feel the need to account for this (in his view, momentary) weakness, the Galatians apparently received him in the past as if the temporal and spatial co-presence within their community of people in a range of bodily states was not particularly problematic. If Paul's arguments linking enslaved and castrated figures to circumcising members was meant to communicate, "Don't do it! You'll be a eunuch!" then perhaps the response that would fit these Galatians would be a sad recognition of a common Roman imperial stereotype, or even a mystified shrug: "maybe . . . but so what?"

In the ancient Anatolian context under Roman imperial authority, the Galatians could have known castrated people, seen them, or even been them. However familiar that kind of difference would have seemed, Paul's letter works persistently against any notion of harmless (or simply neutral) variation. By framing himself as an exclusive conduit of the gospel, Paul claims a constrained anatomy of belonging. His opening argument insists that there are no other "gospels" (1:7–9), and yet the letter's selected narration of his past reflects that such a matter is quite contested, even by Paul![201] In his depiction of the "Jerusalem council," two different kinds of gospel are accepted (2:1–10). Paul claims he was entrusted with the distinctly and strangely embodied "gospel of the foreskin," while Peter "the gospel of the circumcision" (2:7). Even Paul's own accounts of his interactions with others in these early movements reflect that there is more than one kind of negotiation of this particular, even narrowly gendered aspect of embodiment in the assembly communities. Still, in the same letter Paul objects to a different gospel (as if there were no other) and argues vigorously that only one kind of body is the marker of belonging (as if there was no other kind of body in this communal body).

But what if, despite all of these protestations (by this Protestant hero), these were already communities marked by the co-presence of different bodies, circumcised and uncircumcised, castrated and noncastrated, and not just male bodies, intact or "effeminized?" Of course, recall in the oppressive frame provided by Roman imperial traditions, women's bodies are also imagined in terms of an embodied lack; circumcised and castrated bodies are read alongside women's bodies on such terms. There are clear echoes of these ideas in more recent protocols for treating people with intersex conditions as well. But what if we situated such traditions by specifying them as not only Roman, not only imperial, not only free, but also as specifically male, in interrelation to all of these other components? Castration and circumcision are jokes and threats most especially (and perhaps even only) to such elite free males. Would communities with prominent females, like these assembly communities, care less about genital variety, or just be relatively less interested in male genitalia in general? Despite later Freudian claims otherwise, you cannot have an anxiety over castration if you do not have the genitalia to be cut or incapacitated. If you will pardon the pun, women would not seem particularly attached to this particular member. These alternative starting points would certainly shape the reception of good news about crucified bodies, baptized bodies, and yes, probably also surgically altered bodies, in ways different from Paul's arguments in Galatians.

Paul's rhetorical efforts seem to be less defenses of *the* gospel or *the* community, endangered from the outside than a response, angry and volatile, to a (perceived) encroachment on *his* gospel and *his* (perceived) community, from another potential option about the embodiment of communal life, likely even from within these assembly communities. As even Paul is forced to admit, there *is*, after all, at least one other gospel (a gospel of circumcision), even from among those with whom Paul associates; it is just not *Paul's* version of gospel or community. Paul's response to multiple relations to embodiment in these assembly communities might have been rather different, however, if he had drawn a different lesson from his first interaction with the Galatians.[202]

The fact that the community seemed to have received and practiced this message prior to Paul adds another perhaps paradoxical layer to Paul's insistence of only one gospel (1:6–9). Paul's own argument on this matter trips or hiccups from the start. By beginning with a description of their apparent "turning to a different gospel" (1:6), before quickly correcting, "not that there is another" (1:7), the argument (perhaps unintentionally) reveals that there are different kinds of messages in these communities. Yet, Paul persists with two anathemas, or curses, the latter delivering a curse on anyone who delivers a message "contrary to the one you have received" (1:9). Ironically (and most likely unintentionally), by insisting that the Galatians should now have a different view toward embodiment and the treatment of difference in their assembly communities, Paul offers a message contrary to the one the Galatians lived in their hospitable reception of the weakened outsider, even eunuch-esque Paul. In the letter Paul argues that some people (and practices) must be cut out of the community and even wishes for a particularly painful genital cutting for those he opposes. This certainly seems to be a different perspective from the one the Galatians embodied on Paul's arrival, or even the agreement reached with Peter and others in Jerusalem. Read in this light, then, Paul's curse would curse himself! But, of course, Paul's argument is not the last word; he need not be cursed if one takes seriously that there was more than one negotiation of gendered embodiment circulating among these ancient assembly communities.

Galatian Bodies Beyond Phallic Fixations

Instead of imagining the Galatian audience as an isolated group following exclusively the lines of Paul's argumentation, one can begin again with the assembly members as variously embodied communities, aware of various kinds of surgically altered bodies, deployed figuratively toward different ends. For Paul's argument to make any sense at all, one must presume that assembly community members and particularly those Paul claims to oppose are at least considering these practices and principles differently than how Paul argues. If Paul is attempting to naturalize and even normalize a particular adaptation of Roman imperial figurations, then his argument can also point to other figures, lead to unanticipated collectivities, in various pasts and presents as well as between these spaces and times.

Despite its extensive efforts to naturalize certain perceptions of the body (of the members and of the assemblies), often in ways consonant with a Roman imperial regulatory frame, the letter's performative quality both demands and worries over Paul's citational authority and a repeated reception among these bodies. As with the exchange between the Corinthian assembly members and Paul, there is some value in keeping in mind the dynamic of performativity in the exchange between the Galatians and Paul. If the activities of the circumcising members could be associated with eunuchs and castration, and if accepting such practices and people would be one way to be enslaved (not unlike enslaved eunuchs), then the argument attempting to forge, exploit, and even expand on these associations demonstrates that the merits and meanings of various bodily conditions are not at all determined in advance.

To be accountable to the critique posed by intersex people, one must recognize the ways biblical argumentation (like the sort found in Galatians) reinforces the kinds of naturalizing and normalizing dynamics about such bodily differences found in recent modes of medicalized management: an exclusive insistence on one model of embodiment, a fixation on and overestimation of the centrality of the penis, the debasement of fleshly and femininely receptive bodies, and a disturbing lack of concern about pain or pleasure. Flesh could matter in other ways, and arguments about bodies, and especially genitals, can have stigmatizing and enabling effects.[203] Any argument about if we cut, who we cut, and how we cut our and others' bodies deserves more careful engagement. Just as an intersex critique requires seeing intersex people as participants and not fetish objects, so rhetorical and historical considerations of the Galatians should press beyond the phallic fixation of Pauline epistle and interpretation or celebratory visions of them as exemplary totems of "Christian" universalism. Traces of their communal struggles with the import of baptismal actions lie in the letter Paul writes to them. Since the communities were more likely shaped by the co-presence of foreskin and circumcision—as well as people with neither!—they also involved the coincidence of baptism and circumcision, contrary to later supersessionist and anti-Jewish readings that would have us think the two states were incompatible in early "Christian" groups.

These baptized bodies might have differed from circumcised bodies, or overlapped with them, and perhaps even appeared like eunuch bodies to some, but among the Galatian assembly members it appears not to have mattered—or matters materialized differently than Paul's own efforts toward one meaning of the body and the community. Even when we consider contemporary figures like intersex people alongside these ancient figures deployed and targeted by Paul's arguments, I do not anachronistically claim that these figures are somehow identical to each other. Their juxtaposition does, however, highlight the partial, but particular connections between them, their shared features shaped by their practices of gender, sexuality, and embodiment that depart from oppressive perspectives (then or now). Some disturbing correspondences in the physical treatment and cultural perception link these estranged, even marginalized people to each other. This should sound a word of caution that those queer touches across time can cut and crush as much as (or even more than) connect and enable.

Among religious interpreters sympathetic to or embodied as intersex people, the eunuchs depicted in the biblical corpus have already been used to justify or explain various positions about intersex bodies and their degrees of belonging. Consequently, the question for me is not whether the biblical can be used in arguments about bodies, but how could the biblical still be engaged and used to counter the stigmatizing and dehumanizing treatment of intersex people beyond rather fraught processes of identification. Avoiding or simply papering over the problematic aspects of Pauline epistles and interpretations risks their reintroduction and perpetuation when claims of equivalence to contemporary identities are made. Still, there must be other uses one can make of the nonidentical figurations of these other modified bodies, beyond their ancient treatment as jokes or threats, the ultimate scare-figures. The problem is not that human bodies come in many different forms (surgically altered or otherwise). Problems arise when people are pressed to conform to singular visions that stigmatize any departure or difference—when people try to enforce narrow views of what bodies should be, as Paul and many others over the centuries have tried. It seems likely that members embodied the combination Paul stresses, of baptism and foreskin, as well as those he obscured and marginalized—those bodies baptized but neither circumcised nor foreskinned, like women![204] Baptism and other marks of being and belonging demonstrate that matters do not begin and end with genitals, selected and celebrated, or surgically altered, scarred, and stigmatized, despite the sometimes obsessive focus on them in Pauline epistles and interpretations.

4

Use

Bottom/Slave

The letter to Philemon is by far the shortest letter in the Pauline corpus but, having learned key lessons about the limits of being "size queens" in the previous chapter, I hope that the users of this book will not measure the impact of the letter to Philemon by its (relative) length. This would be a mistake not only given the letter's ambiguity but also given the outsized roles it has played over the centuries, most especially in struggles over the abolition and the maintenance of slavery.[1] Most scholars can agree that Paul is addressing the situation of the enslaved Onesimus in the letter, but matters become considerably murkier from there.[2] The relationships between Paul and the other figures in the letter, the likely enslaved Onesimus and his probable owner Philemon, are unclear, because Paul's arguments here are so fraught. Much as Paul appears to make sarcastic stabs about castration in Galatians, here Paul discusses—even puns on—the sexual utility of slaves, describing Onesimus as "once *achrēston* (useless) to you, but now *euchrēston* (useful, good-for-use) (both) to you and to me" (Phlm 11). The overall background of Paul's brief arguments in the letter to Philemon has long proven elusive, but the grounds for sexual use (*chrēsis*) have been pushed completely to the back (or to the bottom).[3]

A range of texts and traditions shows that the sexual use of enslaved people was both ubiquitous and unexceptional for the centuries preceding and following the creation and circulation of Paul's letters. Particularly in the Roman imperial era, readers can find sentiments attributed to male and female slaveowners, roles demanded of enslaved females and males, and duties expected from the enslaved and freedperson, each reflecting the expectation that enslaved people will be physically accessible and available for sexual use. Some communicate this expectation by presenting idealized depictions of enslaved people willingly offering to comply with the masters' desires, as when the freed slave character Trimalchio notes, "For fourteen years I pleasured him; it is no disgrace to do what a master commands. I also gave my

Appalling Bodies. Joseph A. Marchal, Oxford University Press (2020). © Oxford University Press.
DOI: 10.1093/oso/9780190060312.001.0001

mistress satisfaction" (Petronius, *Satyricon* 75.11).[4] Another slave character, Gastron, also exemplifies the enslaved's default positioning as erotically available by admitting to his female owner-user: "Bitinna, I am a slave: use me as you wish" (Herodas, *Mimes*, 5.6). An enslaved person's acquiescence to this status and mode of use might make owning and using easier, but the will or desire of the enslaved figure is otherwise almost entirely inconsequential. The novelized situation of a nobly born, wrongly enslaved Callirhoe, who must continuously attempt to resist a series of lovestruck masters, prompts one character to remind her owner Dionysius: "You are her master, with full power over her, so she must do your will whether she likes it or not" (Chariton, *Chareas and Callirhoe*, 2.6.2).

Horace's casual, even flip remarks reflect a total lack of interest in the enslaved person's will: "I like sex that is easy and obtainable" (Horace, *Satires*, 1.2.119).[5] The attitude to the sexual use of these people was indifferent and often sardonic; their use in these slave societies utterly conventional and uncontroversial. An excerpt from Haterius's defense of a freedperson even has the feel of an aphorism: "Unchastity is a crime in the freeborn, a necessity for a slave, a duty for the freedman" (Seneca, *Controversies* 4, Praef. 10).[6] Generic and applicable in an almost common-sense way, differences in enslaved status are reflected through a graduated set of sexual expectations. The everyday normalcy of such views explains how Petronius's satirical portrait of Trimalchio can voice the same casual indifference through the formerly enslaved. The indifference in these and other resources extends not only to the gender of which owner uses the enslaved person (as in Petronius) but especially also to the gender of the enslaved person used (in Horace).[7] When Greeks, Romans, and Jews do place limits on or offer moralizing condemnations of some sexual uses, their focus does not fall on what some in the twenty-first century would call homosexual (or "same-sex") erotic contact but on containing elite women's practice in order to preserve matronly chastity and patrifamilial honor.[8] Most texts and traditions about slavery are primarily ordered and oriented around those of the freeborn and slave-owning ranks.

Since the study of slavery is too often seen as divorced or isolated from the study of sexuality (and vice versa), though, the relevance of the sexual use of enslaved people has often been obscured, and not only in Pauline studies. Philemon is a letter that discusses the utility of Onesimus and selects arguments in an effort to gain the consent of an owner. These kinds of rhetorical choices signal the letter's place within, rather than distance from, the imperially gendered slave system reflected in these opening selections and the following discussion. Paul's punning characterization of Onesimus and seemingly deferential appeal to the autonomous authority of an owner-user take on different hues and shades in light of the sharp shadows of the sexual use of enslaved people, especially when we consider alternative bodily approaches to bondage, dominance, and submission.

The Use of Slaves

Paul characterizes the (likely) enslaved Onesimus as "once *achrēston* to you, but now *euchrēston* (both) to you and to me" (Phlm 11). Scholarship on the letter has justifiably focused on this verse's wordplay with Onesimus's name in explicating the likely enslaved status of Onesimus; Carolyn Osiek even notes that Paul is here using a "condescending pun."[9] *Onēsis* is similar to (if not exactly synonymous with) *chrēsis* in describing something useful, beneficial, profitable, or enjoyable. Descriptions of Onesimus as previously "useless" or "not-useful," but currently "good-for-use," "well-used," or even "easy-to-use" strikingly evoke the embodied figurations of the erotically available (or sexually vulnerable) enslaved person in the wider Roman imperial context.[10] Onesimus's name reflects his own placement within an imperially gendered slave system, since it contains a constellation of connotations sought by owner-users in their slaves. The slave exists not for his or her own benefit, profit, or pleasure, but for the enjoyable use of the owner, and Paul's description of Onesimus in terms of his utility (*achrēston/euchrēston*) reinforces the status quo of this erotically kyriarchal system.

Yet most scholarly treatments of Philemon have not even noted that terms of *chrēsis* could connect Onesimus's enslaved (or potentially manumitted) status to the sexual use (*chrēsis aphrodisiōn*) of enslaved people. This gap even includes those scholars (like Osiek, Jennifer Glancy, and Richard Horsley) who note the ubiquity of this kind of use in antiquity.[11] The formation of the elite ancient Greek male self was wholly a matter of how to avoid excess and passivity in the use of food, drink, and sex.[12] This question of right use is about the proper *Use of Pleasure*, the title for the second volume of Michel Foucault's *The History of Sexuality*, for which he borrowed the Greek expression *chrēsis aphrodisiōn*. The correct forms of *chrēsis* relate to and communicate one's status both generally—in a context where there is an "isomorphism between sexual relations and social relations"—and thus, specifically—where women, the enslaved, and other males of lower status and age were the proper objects for use.[13]

Such attitudes and arguments about erotic practice in general and the sexual use of enslaved people in particular persist as similar dynamics in the Roman imperial era. In one of the first studies of sexual language in the Latin and Greek literature of the late republic and early empire, Amy Richlin highlighted the Priapic model of gendered and sexualized practice.[14] Craig A. Williams's work also builds on this Priapic model in detailing a sexual protocol for the maintenance of Roman masculinity that centers around the insertive role as "the prime directive of masculine sexual behavior."[15] This model does not differentiate between the gender or status of the receptive party in a sex act, except to exclude the use of freeborn Roman males or freeborn Roman females who are not one's wife.[16] A relatively early elaboration of this expansive directive and its exemptions can be found in a Plautine comedy:

> In that case nobody stops or forbids you to buy what's in the open market, if you've got the cash. Nobody stops anyone from walking along the public highway. Provided you don't make inroads on fenced-in preserves, provided you keep away from married women, widows, virgins, young innocents, and children of respectable families, love anyone you want (*Curculio*, 33–38).

The analogy with property and other objects available to purchase gives voice to an elite perspective and prerogative about appropriate sexual partners.[17] When the prime directive of penetration meets the exceptions to this prerogative, it also generates a corollary, implicit in Plautus, but made clear by scholars, that

> slaves' bodies were entirely at the masters' disposal, and from the earliest of times it seems to have been understood that among the services that Roman men might expect their slaves to perform was the satisfaction of sexual desires . . . both in the earliest contemporary sources and in later references to the distant past, it seems always to have been assumed that the master would make such use of his slaves of both sexes.[18]

These two parts of the Priapic protocol, aggressive pursuit of insertion and disposability of enslaved people's bodies in this pursuit,[19] thus expound on the formulation found in Seneca: the necessity of receptive use for enslaved people and the reprehensive criminality of the same for the freeborn elite (Seneca, *Controversies* 4, Praef. 10). As these texts and a wealth of classical scholarship are increasingly acknowledging, this sexual use was not sporadic. Indeed, it was so ubiquitous that Williams can fittingly argue that a "comprehensive catalogue of Roman texts that refer to men's sexual use of their male and female slaves would be massive," since "it was simply taken for granted that this kind of freedom (or rather, dominion) was one of the many perquisites of being a Roman slave owner."[20] Given how commonly it is reflected in the literature from Homer up to and through the height of the Roman Empire, the sexual use of enslaved people cannot be limited to any one period of Greek or Roman preeminence or isolated as an idiosyncratically fleeting anomaly.[21] What the owner-user held in dominion is what the enslaved person lacked in slavery; owners demonstrated control of self and surroundings (both locally and more imperially) through their unrestricted control over the body of the enslaved, including sexually.[22] Keith Bradley sums up this ancient kyriarchal perspective: "it is taken without question that slaves can and do become objects of sexual gratification for both the men and women who own them. It is one of the prerogatives of ownership and the servile response is scarcely worth considering."[23]

While this overview provides the broader system and protocol for elite slaveowners' use of pleasure, it does not specify how the terminologies of use (*chrēsis*) specifically relate to and reflect on slavery in antiquity. To clarify, one can return to the depiction of an enslaved figure in Herodas's fifth *Mime*. Here, Gastron's response is given in a context where the female master has already used him sexually and she is currently angry that he has had sexual relations with another (likely also an enslaved person, described as Menon's Amphytea in Herodas, *Mime* 5.3). Gastron links his enslaved status with his availability for use: "use me as you wish" (*chrō hoti Boulēi*, 5.6).[24] Beyond the setting for this mime, the erotic resonance of this verb can be confirmed by its recurrence in the following mime. Two slaveowning women discuss acquiring a particularly finely crafted dildo, but Koritto complains about a third friend who has borrowed it before she even had a chance to use it (*chrēsasthai*, 6.29) herself.[25] Both slaves and dildos are objects that function as substitutes for an absent husband or lover and as tools for these women's own erotic control.[26] As a result, scholars of Greco-Roman antiquity like Page DuBois can characterize "slave bodies as ubiquitous and serviceable . . . as sexually desirable and available," since in Herodas enslaved people fall somewhere in a kyriarchal hierarchy of objects, "as a slightly higher form of dildo for the women of the master class."[27] For male owner-users, too, the *chrēsis* of enslaved males continues to appear in later imperial works like Athenaeus's *Deiphnophistae*, where both Sophocles and Euripides were described as "consorting" with the same handsome boy (*chrēsomenos autō* in 604D and *kechrēsthai tō paidi* in 604E).[28]

In discussing the relevance of this asymmetrically gendered sexual protocol for the interpretation of another of Paul's letters (Romans), Bernadette Brooten stresses that "Greek authors from the classical period through late antiquity use both the noun *chrēsis* and the verb *chraomai* ('to use') in a sexual sense. A man 'uses' or 'makes use of' a woman or a boy."[29] Pseudo-Lucian's dialogue, *Erōtes*, uses this same terminology for both male–female and male–male erotic contact in its debate over the relative merits of women and "boys," Brooten goes on to explain.[30] When Charicles argues that the sexual "services rendered by a woman are far superior to those of a boy" (*Erōtes*, 25), this service is *chrēseōs*. Indeed, he furthers this point by highlighting that a woman can also "be used like a boy" (*kai paidikōteron chrōmenon exestin* in *Erōtes*, 27).[31] Not only does *chrēsis* recur in this discussion, but the more commonly Pauline *koinōnia* becomes associated with *chrēsis*, as it appears several times to describe the sharing of sexual pleasures in this passage (*Erōtes*, 27).[32]

This dialogue on erotic relations also highlights the overlap between slavery and sexuality.[33] In recounting the conditions of Callicratidas and Charicles's living arrangements, the text stresses each of their inclinations through the enslaved people attending them. The "love of boys" advocated by Callicratidas involved enslaved males, since he "was well provided with handsome slave-boys and all of his servants were pretty well beardless" (*Erōtes*, 10).[34] Likewise, Charicles's "love of women" is displayed in "a large band of dancing girls and singing girls" that so filled the house with an almost exclusively female presence (*Erōtes*, 10).[35]

Thus, the Greek Lucianic text illustrates a disposition similar to the one Horace communicates in a fuller version of one of the Latin quotes in this chapter's introduction. There Horace recommends a utilitarian attitude to fulfilling one's desires for food, drink, and, of course, sex:

> Now really, when your throat is parched with thirst, you don't ask for golden goblets, do you? When you're hungry, you don't turn your nose up at everything but peacock and turbot, do you? When your crotch is throbbing and there is a slave-girl or home-grown slave-boy ready at hand, whom you

could jump right away, you don't prefer to burst with your hard-on, do you?
I certainly don't. I like sex that is easy and obtainable (*Satires*, 1.2.114–19).[36]

Here, enslaved people function interchangeably with each other (across
gender) and with other "basics" to keep one sated and out of trouble.[37] The
trouble avoided by the elite male owner-user becomes a repetitive source of
trouble, however, for the protagonists of ancient Greek novels. In these, male
and female owners dispose with enslaved heroes (who show themselves to be
truly noble, because they are nobly born) as they please, arranging for sexual
exchanges or seeking their own fulfillment with both enslaved females and
males.[38] Though the heroes in Greek novels escape without being used sexually, their stories repetitively reflect the utter conventionality of the owner-
user's sexual access to enslaved people.[39]

Normative access to enslaved bodies is part of a more general ethos and
practice of *chrēsis* in the ancient world. Even when figures like Epictetus and
Plutarch argue for an elite male prioritizing of moderation, the terminologies of use and the management of food, drink, and slaves in the household
recur.[40] If one properly manages oneself and others, purity and sexual use
need not be incompatible:

> In your sex-life preserve purity, as far as you can, before marriage, and, if
> you indulge, take only those privileges which are lawful. However, do not
> make yourself offensive, or censorious, to those who do indulge, and do
> not make frequent mention of the fact that you do not yourself indulge
> (Epictetus, *Encheiridion*, 33.8).[41]

Even for a philosophical champion of detached moderation seeking to put
limits on the predominant Priapic protocol, it is not contradictory for one to
be virtuously pure and moderate while making use or "indulging" (*chrē*) in
nonexclusive sexual contact.

Of course, those "privileges which are lawful" include the sexual use of
enslaved people. These privileges are useful because they violate neither
the law nor one's reputation: "Or did the Romans of early times account it
not disreputable nor disgraceful to love male slaves in the flower of youth,
as even now their comedies testify, but they strictly refrained from boys of
free birth . . .?" (Plutarch, *Moralia*, 288A). For Plutarch, the sexual use of
enslaved people is even a sign of a good husband, one who shows respect
for his wife by engaging in debauchery with parties held in much lower

esteem (*Moralia*, 140B).[42] The utilitarian disposition to *chrēsis* in general is on display when Aristippus defends his sexual use of Laïs in the absence of love: "He didn't imagine, he said, that wine or fish loved him either, yet he partook of both with pleasure" (*Moralia*, 750D-E).[43] Thus, not only are virtues of purity, moderation, and even chastity left unviolated by sexual contact with enslaved and other nonelite bodies but also this sexual use could be the means of maintaining one's status as virtuous in the kyriarchal management of one's wider household (and often, by extension, the empire). Though it might sound strange, figures like Virgil can practice a passion for enslaved young males and become sexually involved with a woman and still be so associated with virginity and austerity to be called "Parthenias."[44] The sexual use of enslaved people is itself not a moral problem, so long as the elite participant maintains a proper disposition in this, or any other, activity.

While these authors convey attitudes about preferable practices for the typically elite, mostly male owner-user, the evaluation of these acts also communicates a fair amount about the value of enslaved people. In certain ways, such activities do not "count" as ethically or socially significant, showing in turn the lesser significance of enslaved people in general. This view toward sexual use, in particular, is manifest in the casual glibness of Aristippus's explanation, Trimalchio's exaggerated pride in his days as enslaved, or the jokes that follow on Haterius's explanation in Seneca:

> he said, while defending a freedman who was charged with being his patron's lover: "Losing one's virtue is a crime in the freeborn, a necessity in a slave, a duty for the freedman." The idea became a handle for jokes, like "you aren't doing your duty by me" and "he gets in a lot of duty for him." As a result the unchaste and obscene got called "dutiful" for some while afterwards (*Controversies* 4, Praef. 10).

The sequence described by Seneca illustrates the elite, Roman imperial predisposal to joke about others' sexual vulnerability: *officiosi* becoming a demeaning pun for "doing one's duty" sexually.[45] Even when the Romans are lampooning an elite head of a household, their jests and digs reflect common assumptions about the *auctoritas* of the elite, Roman imperial male:

> Quirinalis doesn't think he should have a wife, though he wants to have sons, and has found a way to achieve this: he fucks his slave girls and fills town house and country estate with home-born knights. Quirinalis is a true paterfamilias (Martial, *Epigrams*, 1.84).

Though "the joke" is on this Quirinalis for his foolish strategy for filling his *domus*, the necessary conditions for Martial's ridicule reveal both the unremarkable access to enslaved girls and the very real kyriarchal authority of male heads of households over wives, children, and enslaved people (even if their roles are interrelated but nonidentical).[46] While the epigram is at the expense of an owner-user, the text reflects rather than detracts from the predominant social system that presumes the owner's access to enslaved people as part of the premise.

In these sources the joke is perhaps even more "on" the enslaved *and* the freedperson. Haterius's words in Seneca reflect the ongoing vulnerability of even the freedperson, the figure presumed to be dutiful in continuing to submit to a sexual use by the owner. This expectation of ongoing service demonstrates how the relative frequency of manumission should not be mistaken for the emancipation of enslaved people from within a flawed, but mostly altruistic institution.[47] Manumission is not a softening, but a tightening strategy for keeping the enslaved under control. The promise or prospect of manumission was apparently enough to keep many obedient until their bodies were worth less than a younger replacement.[48]

By inspecting the *paramonē* contract inscriptions for over twelve hundred enslaved people from 153 BCE to 47 CE at Delphi, Keith Hopkins was also able to discern further patterns linking sexual use to manumission practices.[49] Often, enslaved people were only freed when they could leave children behind in their place.[50] Since these freedpeople typically also owed service to male and female owners until the owners' death(s), even the child born to a freedperson in their period of ongoing service could be viewed as belonging to the owner or the heir of the slaveowning family.[51] Even in instances where the owner is not directly involved in using an enslaved or freedperson sexually, the owner benefits from using the enslaved or freedperson as a body that produces more useful bodies. Indeed, one of the main ways that this ancient slave society discussed slaves as implements is by describing them as bodies, *ta sōmata*.[52] This attitude persists even in the case of freedpeople, so that the sexual use and manumission practices combine with a variety of effects. The infamous murder of the prefect Pedanius Secundus by one of his slaves, for instance, was left ambiguously attributed to either a failure to manumit the enslaved or the enslaved's unwillingness to see the owner involved sexually with another male.[53] The ambiguous extent of the freedperson's obligations and its relation to sexual use is also reflected in the accounts of Dio Cassius. For instance, Nero castrated "a boy of the freedmen" (*paida apeleutheron*, *Roman History*, 62.28.2) and took him as a replacement for his wife Sabina, "and he used [*echrēto*] him in every way like a wife" (*Roman History*, 62.28.3).[54] The terminology of *chrēsis* resurfaces in order to reflect how casually the emperor can use the son or the slave (the ambiguous *pais*) of a freedperson for his own purposes.

As this and so many of the vignettes from ancient texts and traditions indicate, there is often little to no interest in the view of the enslaved or freedperson in these bodily uses, even as dutiful compliance certainly makes it easier for an owner-user to manage their dominion. In Chariton's novel *Chareas and Callirhoe*, the owner Dionysius initially feels spurned by the newly enslaved Callirhoe. Yet he is shortly reminded by his steward that this is mostly irrelevant: "You are her master, with full power over her, so she must do your will whether she likes it or not" (*Chareas and Callirhoe*, 2.6.2).[55] While agreeing to or obeying a master's order would be nice (doing something willingly, *hekousa*), it is not necessary. The enslaved person may be unwilling (*akousa*) but the authority of the master is what counts in such situations.

Even as enslaved people had no legal or cultural right to refuse commands,[56] owners frequently chose suasion as much as force in order to more effectively exercise control. The incentive and promise of manumission and the various stories and sayings that justify the social order described thus far would be just two examples of their attempt to rule through persuasion. In the scheme to get the enslaved hero Habrocomes for his pirate master's sexual use in Xenophon's *Ephesian Tale*, Habrocomes is advised to show affection (*agapan*, 1.16.3) to his new master. Yet, as part of the same attempt at suasion, he is told to obey (*hypokouein*, 1.16.5) his master when he is commanded. Later in the novel, when the other half of the star-crossed couple, Anthia, is sold into prostitution, a similar strategy is applied with the pimp "alternately asking her to cheer up and making threats" (5.7.3). Plautus's comedy *Epidicus* depicts an enslaved person fretting over whether a new captive has usurped his place in the owner's love (64–66). Another enslaved person taunts him in reply: "He loves her more than he ever loved you" (66). Here, love is not incompatible with the buying, selling, and casting off of various enslaved bodies. The language of love, affection, and positive feeling toward the enslaved or between owner and enslaved person are not mitigations of the imperially gendered slave system, but expressions of its inner workings.

Cultivating this feeling of connection to the owner is a savvy strategy for running the hierarchical household in antiquity, especially because the enslaved are people who have been removed from various forms of connection. Orlando Patterson's classical formulation of the constituent elements of slavery stresses enslaved people's permanent natal alienation, their symbolic and social removal from the bonds of their ancestral kinship.[57] Enslaved people are dissociated from their ethnicity, kinship, culture, and locale, so that they might be integrated into a different family (the owner's) and incorporated into a particular role in a stratified household structure. Enslaved people simultaneously "had no family" and were deeply embedded in a *familia* and *domus* to be managed by the *paterfamilias*.[58] Of course, their incorporation in the *familia* has particular consequences for the household management of wives and children.[59] Indeed, Richard Saller has noted how the general sexual availability of enslaved males and females "increased the strain in family relationships by presenting an external source of competition for affection and sexual attention within the household."[60] Saller's point stresses the inherently tensive place of the enslaved person "in" the family. They can cause jealousy and anger in an elite marriage as an "external" factor, yet the occurrence of this threat is likely because the enslaved person is, in Horace's words, "easy and obtainable"—one who is "within" these structures and relations.[61]

Typically, prostitutes were enslaved people whose clientele were lower in status, but owners did not need to go to brothels since their own slaves could serve as "private prostitutes" for them and their friends and family.[62] Just as the sexual use of enslaved people introduced some tensions and concerns in "family life" between husband and wife, providing this service to friends and family can be a matter to be carefully negotiated between friends becoming patron and client. On this matter Horace gives a warning: "Let no maid or boy within your worshipful friend's marble threshold inflame your heart, lest the owner of the pretty boy or dear girl make you happy with a present so trifling or torment you if disobliging" (*Epistles*, 1.18.72–75). Horace indicates that one has to be deliberately prudent when developing a friendship with a powerful man. If one owes the new friend (too much), the minimal gain in political advantage could be outweighed by the loss of self-determination or control in new obligations. The advice, of course, assumes that free men are giving enslaved people for these purposes, even as it advises care.[63] It stresses once more that this sexual use is mostly trivial; the significance of the exchange is not in the treatment of the enslaved person, but in the relationship with the owner and the friend.

Given the Roman imperial predisposal to make light of the sexual vulnerability of others, Onesimus's name and Paul's description of him as "good-for-use" in this letter resonate with demeaning descriptions like Seneca's sexually "dutiful" freedman (*Controversies* 4, Praef. 10) or Horace's preference for enslaved people as "sex that is easy and obtainable" (*Satires*, 1.2.119). The rhetoric of Philemon is more consonant with than counter to such conditions and sentiments, callously indifferent to the fate of the figures behind these asymmetrical dynamics and descriptions. Paul's cleverly connecting argument curls in a colonial fashion, then, conveying rather casually the relative social significance of the enslaved person as not "counting," even from within his vision of an apparently alternative assembly.[64]

The Use of Onesimus: *Chrēsis* and Consent, Puns and Patrons

The ubiquity, acceptability, virtue, and even the occasional political peril (for the owner-user, not the owned and used) of the sexual use of enslaved people puts the letter of Philemon in a different light. Against an ancient background benignly neutral to and even encouraging of the sexual use of enslaved bodies, it is not impossible that in Philemon 11 Paul is arguing that Onesimus is "good-for-use," and thus "easy-to-use" sexually, for the letter's addressee, other community members, but also even for Paul himself.[65] Considering the unexceptional way in which access to slave bodies for sexual use was part of this letter's Roman imperial context and part of ancient slavery more broadly, it would actually seem more prudent to assume this possibility as a likelihood, at least until argued convincingly otherwise. In Romans 1:26–27 even, the meaning of *chrēsis* as sexual is patently uncontroversial, even as different understandings of this passage continue to spark ecclesial and public controversy. One of the most common ancient Greek words for sexual relations is *chrēsis*, so common that the NRSV simply translates (if softens) their appearances in Romans 1 as "intercourse." If there were some consistency across the translations of Paul's letters, Paul's characterization of Onesimus in Philemon could have been translated as "good for intercourse" rather than simply "useful."[66]

If one reads Paul's description of Onesimus as *euchrēston*, it further clarifies other argumentative moments in this brief epistle. Paul's claim that he sought to do nothing without the addressee's consent, knowledge, or judgment (*gnōmēs*, 14) coheres seamlessly with a slaveowner's perspective on the use of enslaved people.[67] Here, Paul appeals to the owner to agree with

Paul's exhortation "not according to constraint but according to a voluntary (*hekousion*) act" (v. 14). The direction of the argument demonstrates whose will matters here: Paul does not speak of Onesimus willingly (*hekousa*) acting, but of his owner's "good" in this exchange. The enslaved person's will is inconsequential; the letter attempts merely to steer a discussion between Paul and Onesimus's owner.

Yet if the letter is seemingly "cold" in instances such as these, one challenge could be how one accounts for some of the "warmer" forms of language employed in the letter, especially when Paul is discussing Onesimus. After all, Paul does describe Onesimus as "my *splanchna*" (typically translated as "heart") in verse 12 and applies a number of kinship terms to their relationship (vv. 10, 16). One may recall that affectionate language is not foreign to the imperially and erotically asymmetrical dynamics of ancient slavery: the mostly elite, free, imperial male, owning (or kyriarchal) texts and traditions frequently describe and prescribe the relations between enslaved people and their user-owners as warm. They comfortably speak of intimacy and harmony in the slaveowning household and society, but these affections do not contradict the harsh coercion of slavery, where "generosity" and "love" are accompanied by force, threats, and fear.[68] As Hopkins reminds: "As in other slave societies, the tie between master and slave could be warm; this warmth did not necessarily lessen exploitation; though it may have softened the slave's feelings about it."[69] That kind of rhetorical strategy is not a mitigation but an expression of the imperially gendered slave system, simultaneously masking and bolstering its social and sexual differentiations and discrepancies. As with the condescending and chilling turn of phrase (in v. 11), even the affection reflected by Paul's perspective (in vv. 12 and 16) aligns comfortably with that of the slaveowners.

While the *splanchna* often functions metaphorically as the location of affections (like the modern, Western "heart"), its ancient anatomical location is lower in the abdominal cavity (more like "the guts"), stressing the vital or internal organs including the bowels or even the womb. The *splanchna* could include those locations on the body affected by sexual contact, not unlike the Latin *viscera* in Juvenal's graphic comparison of roles for enslaved people: "Or is it easy and straightforward to drive a penis worthy of the name into your guts (*viscera*) and there meet yesterday's dinner? The slave who ploughs the soil will have an easier life than the one who ploughs his master" (*Satires*, 9.43–46).[70] Evoking the *splanchna* could not only echo that there is affection between a master and an enslaved person but also invoke one reason why the owner might want to encourage such a disposition in the enslaved: to make sexual use of the enslaved body.

If this anatomy of affection is indeed compatible with the Priapic protocol of penetration followed and maintained by user-owners, then it raises further questions about life in the assembly community greeted in the letter's opening. This assembly gathers in an extended household of the Roman imperial era (v. 2)—one likely to have enslaved members, quite possibly including the previously less "useful" Onesimus. From Paul's perspective, the letter's addressee brings joy to Paul when he releases or alleviates the *splanchna* of the holy ones (v. 7); later in the letter Paul even demands this same refreshing release of his *splanchna* from the addressee (v. 20). In light of the commonly unexceptional sexual use of enslaved people, what could this refreshment of the body entail?[71] When Paul calls for the addressee to prepare hospitality (*xenian*, v. 22) for his anticipated return, it would not be that uncommon for such hospitality to include the availability of the hosting owner's enslaved to serve an honored guest in many capacities, including the *full* range of his bodily needs. For the head of a household, a host, and/or a patron, one of the benefits of having slaves at one's disposal is their availability for uses, sexual or otherwise, to one's family and friends (negating the need for them to visit brothels and move outside of one's sphere of influence).[72] In Paul's calling for hospitality, one cannot rule out that he also meant the hospitality entailed in the sexual availability of enslaved bodies "good-for-use."

Indeed, despite the potential warmth of Onesimus's description as Paul's *splanchna* (in v. 12), the place of Onesimus in Paul's vision of the wider community is made clear in the very verse where he is described thusly. After all, Onesimus is the one "whom I am sending up to you" (v. 12); the anticipated interaction is one of exchange between Paul ("I") and the owner-addressee ("you"). Onesimus is a thing to pass along, to send at Paul's will, even as Paul also claims that he wanted to continue holding or possessing (*katechein*, v. 13) this "good-for-use" animate tool. Such expressions recall a context where humans can be given, sold, or simply exchanged between parties for any number of reasons, including sexual ones.[73] Again, Paul specifies in the following verse that this interaction is between the owning addressee and Paul (v. 14), since Paul is not seeking Onesimus's will or consent, but that of his master. In this matter, two people besides Onesimus are negotiating over the now "easy-to-use" figure sent by Paul.

Rhetorically and historically contextualizing Paul's description of Onesimus as his *splanchna* should also resituate Paul's words to follow. Paul does exhort the owning addressee to "receive him [Onesimus] as (you would) me" (v. 17), indicating perhaps that Onesimus is a substitute of sorts for Paul. Yet the immediately preceding clause stresses the partnership (*koinōnon*) between Paul and the addressee, not one between Paul and Onesimus. The sending-up of Onesimus is a matter between these two parties, stressed throughout this brief letter. Indeed, Onesimus is not really a substitute for Paul, as he makes clear by twice stressing (implicitly in v. 19, explicitly in v. 22) that he will be coming soon himself. Given the likelihood that Paul is here addressing a slave owner-user, in an assembly community that meets in an extended household, scholars might need to rethink exactly what dynamics inhere within the communal sharing or partnership extolled here (v. 17) and elsewhere (v. 6), in this letter and the wider Pauline corpus.[74]

Even when Paul enlists warmly affectionate language like "beloved" (*agapēton*, v. 16) to describe Onesimus as a "brother" to both of the parties negotiating over him, it is from within a context of coercion and the customary *chrēsis* of enslaved people. In the imperially gendered slave system, affection and the many uses of enslaved people can and do go together; love and obedience do in fact work together. Since the enslaved Habrocomes can be advised to show *agapē* and remain obedient (*hypakouein*) at the same time, it is not so strange for Paul to describe an enslaved (or freed) person as beloved while still expecting compliance and obedience, both of Onesimus (v. 12) and of the addressee (v. 21).[75] The rhetoric of affection and emotion can be a subtle support for the social and sexual practices of slave use.

Of course the expression "beloved brother" also raises the issue of Paul's use of kinship terminologies in his letters. In the first and only instance in which Paul explicitly names Onesimus in this letter, he introduces him in the clause "I exhort you concerning my child, whom I begat in chains, Onesimus" (v. 10). Now, one could argue that the potential intimacy of this connection is conditioned and qualified by the clause that immediately follows this introduction of Onesimus: the aforementioned relative clause containing the dual *chrēsis* terms (v. 11). Yet this would pass over and presume that terms of kinship connote the same degrees of warmth and closeness as our contemporary terms (at least claim to) do. That, of course, would be a problematic presumption, given the relatively nonaffectionate and hierarchical view of the ancient *paterfamilias*.[76] In the Roman imperial context, the forms of emotion owed to and bestowed by one's social superior do not negate or "relativize" the heightened positionality and power of those sharing in some form of kyriarchal privilege (lord, owner, father, emperor). Specifically, in the context of enslaved people and their owner-users, diminutive terms were applied to enslaved people so as to demean and even dehumanize them.

Often, when slaveowners used the institutions or terms of kinship with their enslaved, it was a means toward the owner-users' ends.[77] Promises of (albeit constrained) forms of kinship, like permitted sexual relations (with other enslaved people, for instance) or remaining with their own "family" (among enslaved people), were ways to manipulate or maintain acquiescence and obedience. The juxtaposition of terms from kinship and slave domains in Paul's letter should not now and likely would not have been then viewed as generously egalitarian, or even as reducing the power and practice of slaveownership. In instances when family language was used to inculcate a positive disposition, it was part of the flexible asymmetry of Roman imperial forms of rule, including slavery. As a "natally alienated" and "deracinated outsider," the enslaved person is uniquely and oddly positioned to be incorporated into his or her role within the household, somehow "in" the *familia* but not of it.[78] It is possible that just such a tensive flexibility can account for how Paul can claim to be both father (v. 10) and brother (v. 16) and still not disrupt the agenda and arc of his argumentation.[79] From within both the ancient context and the Pauline corpus, such argumentation fits a pattern that comfortably mixes affection with asymmetry, harmony within hierarchy. Such dynamics extend even to the argument Paul attempts with the addressee: one whom he calls his brother (vv. 7, 20) yet still expects obedient action and disposition.[80]

The incorporation of a (formerly) enslaved figure like Onesimus into the language and structures of "family" does not preclude the asymmetrical uses of (freed and) enslaved people. Nevertheless, verse 16 has drawn so much critical attention from Philemon interpreters because of its strange formulation of Onesimus as "beloved brother." Onesimus is "no longer a slave, but *hyper* slave, a beloved brother, especially to me, but how much (more) especially to you, both in the flesh and in the lord" (v. 16). This extended clause has often been the cause of scholarly considerations about Onesimus's fate and even his potential family.[81] Onesimus is somehow "more than" (*hyper*) a slave, yet not necessarily in the sense of moving "higher," but in a role of excess or "more-ness" with regard to slavery. It is possible that Paul argues thusly to insist that Onesimus has become a particular kind of enslaved person, whose role now goes beyond to do more, or it is one performed in excess.[82] By being or becoming a "brother," Onesimus is possibly being described, then, in ways similar to those enslaved people who become the "favorites" (sexual or otherwise) of their owner-users. He now has a particular role, one that a slaveowner and his friends would be comfortable in describing on the terms of "love" and a kind of "familial" belonging.[83] If Onesimus is now *euchrēston*, this could indicate how excessively (or hyper-) useful he has become.

The combination of slave and, or within, kinship terms does not nullify the oppressive aspects of slave use discussed thus far. Of course, the mere presence of kinship terms in a Pauline letter would not do this either. Paul often argues about communal belonging in terms of fictive kin,[84] even negotiating and commending particular uses of "kin" for sexual purposes in the community and for *apostoloi* (1 Cor 7:1-16, 25-40; 9:5; 1 Thess 4:1-6).[85] It seems likely, then, that there was at least some sex "in the family" of the ancient assembly communities addressed by Paul's letters. At least according to the argumentation made available to us through Paul's letters, an enslaved (or freed) person being or becoming a "brother" in an assembly community does not, by itself, rule out sexual relations, or in the ancient terms, *chrēsis*, with this "brother."[86] Indeed, it has been increasingly recognized by scholars that Paul nowhere condemns or rules out the sexual use of enslaved people for such "brothers and sisters."[87]

Building on this ancient context and the rhetorical dynamics within the letter, the strange dual prepositional clauses ("both in the flesh and in the lord") to conclude verse 16 can be clarified. Allen Callahan has pointed to this description of the relationship between the addressee and Onesimus to argue that they are "indeed brothers both literally and spiritually. They are siblings at odds with each other."[88] Yet my present argument suggests a reconsideration of, or at least a particular elaboration on, Callahan's bold hypothesis. It is right to see the two clauses as compatible with each other; they are paired and paralleled. The "fleshly" role goes together with the "lordly" role; it is not inconsistent with the role one would play in the community of the *kyrios*.[89] Might it be more probable that the argument being made here is that fleshly uses of an enslaved (or freed) person are not contrary to, but consistent with being "in the lord?"[90] Objections to this reading might presume that the consistency must travel in another direction: the fleshly uses of enslaved people must fit themselves into the "lordly" practices, including perhaps sexual austerity or moderation (as described elsewhere), not that fleshly uses fit within "lordly" practices. Of course, this obscures what has been persistently delineated earlier, that the sexual uses of enslaved people *are* "lordly" uses in the Roman imperial context.[91] The *kyrios*, or one of his family and friends, is the presumed user; this is simply one of the presumed privileges of being in a "lordly" kyriarchal role. This use has not and cannot yet be ruled out from any particular Pauline argument, here in Philemon or elsewhere.[92]

Of course, none of the arguments and contexts presented thus far can rule out Callahan's claim that Onesimus and the addressee are *actual* kin, either. Callahan's argument has found few supporters among interpreters of Philemon, yet it might still prove to be an illuminative historical possibility if it too is considered in light of the sexual use of enslaved people. This would require that one presumption of Callahan's argument be altered: the apparently mutually exclusive possibilities of Onesimus being enslaved and a "brother." In reflecting on both the history of interpretation and the experiences of African Americans, Demetrius K. Williams concludes his own reflections on Philemon by reminding us that, whether in ancient Roman imperial or more recent North American contexts, one could be *both* brother and slave, someone's biological kin and still enslaved.[93] Given the sexual use of enslaved people by user-owners, enslaved people were "children" if not heirs, they were "brothers" if not equals, they were "loved" if still obedient and useful. Depending on Onesimus's origins (as a "homegrown" product or one otherwise acquired), he could even be an incarnate sign of this use: a product of the use of an enslaved female by an owner-user. This distinct, but seldom considered historical possibility is all the more stark in this epistolary instance, given Paul's own use of a verb of embodied generation earlier in the letter ("begetting," v. 10). From an owner-user's perspective, such a verbal expression might serve adequately to describe the products of his (or even her) use of enslaved bodies.[94] An image often read as affectionate paternity also proves to be quite coherent within an order where *chrēsis* is mostly unexceptional.[95]

If Paul is in fact angling his argument to achieve the manumission of Onesimus (in vv. 16 and 21, for instance), it does not necessarily function as a counter to the coercion and *chrēsis* delineated here.[96] As scholars of ancient slavery have highlighted, manumission is not a lessening of the exploitation of this system, but a continuation of it through the management and replacement of less useful bodies. Paul's exceeding (*hyper*) expectation of obedience (v. 21) and the exceeding (*hyper*) role of Onesimus (v. 16) indicate a similar continuation of kyriarchal dynamics. Such argumentation more likely, then, reflects rather than diminishes the ongoing vulnerability of even the freedperson, as these conditions can require sexual duties, before and even after manumission.[97]

These kinds of arguments, whether focused on manumission or some other outcome, tend not to narrow the hierarchical relations Paul expects between the addressee and himself, between the owner-user and Onesimus, or between Paul and Onesimus. Though the letter implements "warm" and familial language for the relations between these figures, Paul still has particular expectations of the addressee, including the hospitality discussed toward the close of this argument (vv. 20–22). Setting aside whatever Paul seeks with regard to Onesimus, this hospitality could be a further specification of the benefit he expects from the addressee (in v. 20). Of course, as often noted in the exegetical literature, the rare optative verb *onaimēn* ("may I have this benefit") is derived from the same root as Onesimus's name. Though the clause evokes Onesimus and may still be seeking particular uses of this likely enslaved person, it is not addressed to Onesimus. The benefit is to come from the letter's addressee, the likely owner-user. When combined with the presence of another punning wordplay, Paul's presumption of only certain participants in this exchange indicate that his arguments do not move past a mindset of disparaging utility and glib diminution reflected earlier in the letter. In such arguments, Paul casually plays with the name of Onesimus and its connotations; the view on display in the letter is wholly compatible with an ancient context where a person can be used as an animate tool.

While these arguments reflect and maintain a hierarchical difference between Paul and Onesimus, they also seek to negotiate the situation with the letter's addressee to generate a similar, if nonidentical difference. Paul seeks hospitality from this (likely) owner-user (v. 22), a hospitality that typically would have included the fulfilling of the guest's bodily needs by enslaved people. Yet even while accepting such hospitality and in making use of Onesimus (vv. 10–13), Paul also appears to be arguing carefully for how such conditions do not make him the client of the owner-user addressed in the letter. To manage such a situation, Paul stresses that he could command this potential patron (v. 8) and that the addressee "owes" the considerable debt of his very self (v. 20). By the end of the argument, Paul declares his confidence in the addressee's obedience (v. 21), or, as Osiek sums the sentiment of this verse, "if nothing else, you will be obedient."[98] If Onesimus was the property or even a gift of this owner-user to Paul, such an argumentative arc is a savvy way to deflect a focus on the benefits Paul has *already* received from this potential patron.

As commentators often highlight about this letter's rhetoric, it is simultaneously focused and unfocused on Onesimus. This is likely because Paul is attempting to show indifference to the benefits of such a useful tool. Through such a line of argumentation, he shapes an implicit claim that he did not *need* the service of someone else's enslaved (or freed) person, once more stressing that the letter is less "about" Onesimus than the meaning of these exchanges, rhetorical and material, between Paul and the addressee (with the assembly community as witness to at least this portion of the process). Of course, though Paul might want to argue that he did not need or want the good-to-use Onesimus, he did make use of him (v. 11). Though he might not require hospitality, he will seek, even demand it from the addressee (v. 22). If Paul does not want to become someone's client, his actions and arguments indicate that he is willing to take the benefits typically viewed as patronly in the Roman imperial context.[99]

If Paul is seeking to establish (or maintain) a hierarchical relationship where Paul is owed dutiful obedience by the addressee (and not vice versa), then this letter may be preoccupied by concerns similar to the ones expressed by some of the (other) Roman imperial texts and traditions about slavery. As these attest, using someone else's slave, sexually or otherwise, is a matter to be carefully negotiated by the friends and family of the owner-user. Horace's caution is worth repeating: "Let no maid or boy within your worshipful friend's marble threshold inflame your heart, lest the owner of the pretty boy or dear girl make you happy with a present so trifling or torment you if disobliging" (*Epistles*, 1.18.72–75). In both Paul's and Horace's epistles, the significance is not the trifling gift or the object for use in an exchange, but the conditions of advantage and obligation established or expressed by an exchange. In sending this letter, though, Paul attempts to avoid being under any obligations to a patron, even though it appears he violated the advice offered by Horace: he made use of another's enslaved person. This is likely the reason Paul implements the patron-client language of owing and obedience in this brief letter; he is trying to avoid becoming the client and the inferior to the letter addressee.

Further, Paul is not simply seeking to avoid this dynamic but to reverse the ancient expectations about such an exchange by expecting obedience from the potential patron. This explains the oddly emphatic comparative turn of phrase when Paul insists that Onesimus is also "a beloved brother, especially to me, but how much (more) especially to you" (v. 16). The one whom Paul is sending, described as his "child" and his "brother," is *even more* the "brother" of the addressee. Even if and as some differentiations persisted among "kin" in the assembly communities (why Paul addresses the owner-user, not Onesimus), Paul is indicating that he is even further above and much less alike (or "akin" to) the enslaved (or freed) person than the addressee is. This is why Paul expects obedient action from both.[100] Even as Paul may be trying to rearrange the format of patronage through this letter, there are few indications that the forms and practices of the use of enslaved people (sexual or otherwise) are reordered. Indeed, the conditions of such uses have proven to be illuminating to some of the strange or challenging argumentative dynamics of the letter: from this re-arrangement of patronage, to the mixture of warm and cold language toward the (formerly) enslaved Onesimus, and most especially the usefulness of Onesimus. Grappling with the unexceptional historical conditions of the *chrēsis* of enslaved people highlights the striking ways in which this letter deploys and targets enslaved figures.

The arguments found in Philemon (and other letters) demonstrate more than just a lack of concern about the vulnerability of enslaved people to such uses. Paul's thoughtless punning and doubled description of Onesimus in terms of (sexual) use are disturbing precisely because they reflect (yet again) a cold, even flip attitude toward marginalized and stigmatized others, in this instance, toward enslaved bodies. It becomes harder to see stark moments like these sarcastic, even cruel outbursts as nonrepresentative or merely incidental, especially in the light of the apparent joking exaggeration of 1 Corinthians 11:5–6 or the flippantly violent wish for castration within Galatians 5:12. In each instance, Paul's letters reflect Roman imperial tendencies to demean and deploy perversely gendered and strangely embodied figures (androgynes, eunuchs, and now slaves) to target other members of these ancient assembly communities. It would be a mistake to presume that Paul's perspective represents the whole, rather than just one part in a rhetorical exchange with a particular assembly community, likely gathered in the household of Philemon, Apphia, and/or Archippus (vv. 1–2). With such a kyriarchal *ethos*, can other, ethically and politically accountable uses be found for the kinds of *chrēsis* Paul's letter reflects?

Switching Biblical Bonds

Alternative, even unexpected uses for this letter could be developed, though, through a set of queer strategies. Such approaches to Philemon are rare in the scholarly literature, likely because sexual topics are still seen as inappropriate for scholarly projects in biblical studies, perhaps especially so amid treatments of another ethically fraught and politically troublesome topic like slavery. (One hot-button issue at a time!) Yet it is imperative that one confronts the appalling ways Pauline arguments glibly repeat and even joke about the sexual use of enslaved people. Beyond identifying such arguments, I juxtapose them with an alternative erotic ethic that grapples with power and pleasure, connects bonds and bodies, and reconfigures scripts of sensual (even sexual) submission—namely, BDSM communal practices.

Since Philemon so painfully evokes horrifying circumstances around the use of human beings, it might just prove queerly relevant to juxtapose two nonidentical figures of opprobrium and vilification: the ancient slave and the "slave" role played in some BDSM scenes. Reading the *chrēsis* of Onesimus through certain practices within BDSM has the potential to acknowledge, rework, and even transform social imaginaries along the lines of postcolonial and queer strategies of catachresis ("improper use").

The acronym BDSM combines multiple sets of often interrelated practices, including bondage and discipline, dominance and submission, and sado-masochism.[101] BDSM communal practices persistently foreground matters of consent, often while engaging in forms of bodily contact and interaction derived from institutions that downplayed, deflected, or outright denied the utility of consent, institutions like slavery (in both its ancient and more recent forms). The importance of consent for such communities is indicated by its centrality in the two most common acronymic slogans for explaining codes of conduct for "playing" in a "scene" (participating in a BDSM encounter): SSC, or "Safe, Sane, and Consensual," and RACK, "Risk Aware Consensual Kink."[102] The title page of the landmark lesbian S/M collection, *Coming to Power*, puts it plainly, and helpfully: S/M practice is "a form of eroticism based on the consensual exchange of power."[103]

BDSM could be imagined as a set of queer practices, particularly if one underscores the potentially subversive or resistant aspects of BDSM.[104] Patrick Califia, for instance, stresses: "We select the most frightening, disgusting, or unacceptable activities and transmute them into pleasure. We make use of all the forbidden symbols and all the disowned emotions. S/M is a deliberate, premeditated, erotic blasphemy."[105] BDSM's potential seems especially tied to different and disowned *uses*, alternative uses of the body, even alternative uses of history, of the past. For Foucault, what is transformative about S/M practices are their different uses or relations to power:

the S/M game is very interesting because it is a strategic relation, but it is always fluid. Of course, there are roles, but everyone knows very well that those roles can be reversed. Sometimes the scene begins with the master and slave, and at the end, the slave has become the master.[106]

These sorts of reversals, often called "switching" in BDSM communities, are common in explanations of how BDSM practices depart from, rather than replicate social norms and oppressive forms of power. Prior to Foucault, Califia argued that, "During an S/M encounter, roles are acquired and used in very different ways. . . . If you don't like being a top or a bottom, you switch your keys. Try doing that with your biological sex or your race or your socioeconomic status."[107] BDSM encounters confound by resituating seemingly stable sociosexual roles, including stereotyped roles like masculine activity and feminine (or feminizing) passivity or receptivity.[108]

BDSM restages dynamics of power, presenting possibilities for nonoppressive and pleasurable uses of power. These bodily practices of power differentials could even be seen as forms of resistance, reflecting the utopian tendencies of a great deal of organizing and writing about BDSM. A range of BDSM practices display their disruptive potential by departing from heteronormative disciplinary modes—through their disinterest in genitalia, reproduction, and often orgasms as "outcomes," as well as their investments in switching, redistributing, or even scrambling typically gendered positions.[109] When these ideas and practices cross over into theological domains, though, their transgressive or disruptive potential are precisely in their resistance to utility. Building on the ideas of Foucault and Georges Bataille, Karmen MacKendrick stresses how "The break with good subjectivity arises in the *useless* and *excessive* nature of deliberately invoked pain and restraint."[110] In reflecting on those modes of conduct found in BDSM that deliberately move away from gratification or release, MacKendrick repeats and elaborates: "an excessive and useless restraint is already a form of resistance—to power as the disciplinary force of efficiency and productivity."[111] The messy, unmanageable, and excessive dynamics of BDSM, then, signal uses of bodies in relation, in community, separate from the uses demanded by disciplinary economies.

In the face of jokes about sexual vulnerability (again, both in the first and in the twenty-first century), BDSM does not pun, but it does redeploy powerful scenes of bondage and subordination. The version found in Philemon—Paul's arrangements around certain owner-users' consent and the relative utility of Onesimus as an enslaved (or manumitted) person—is not the only possible combination of these features; rather, their strategic use can generate not further sociopolitical subordination, but pleasures across multiple bodily sites. Pleasures in scripts of power and control are not in and of themselves problematic, but (ancient) slavery's coercion and lack of consent are. Onesimus's will is totally absent in the deliberations and declarations of Paul's letter. Consent is more intensely focalized in BDSM practices than most other forms of human behavior, sexual or otherwise.

Certainly, BDSM and this juxtaposition of it alongside Philemon are irreverent, but they are hardly as cold and flip as Paul's punning characterizations of Onesimus were and are. Some of the audacity of BDSM scenes is found precisely in the ways players in these scenes focus on the pleasurable effects of the bottom or "slave" participant. Unlike the kyriarchal slave systems of antiquity or the antebellum United States, respectively reflected in and then repeated from Paul's letter to Philemon, the bottom especially determines the dynamics of the scene in close and intense negotiation with the one playing the top or master role.[112] This aspect of BDSM is distinctive and important to reconsider.[113] Intimate, intense, and often messy relations are alternative places to begin from biblical foundations like Philemon, where Onesimus remains notably silent and mostly unaddressed, as Paul negotiates instead with the owner-users of this enslaved person and the larger assembly community there.

To be sure, this is a genuinely blasphemous use of Philemon (the letter, not the potential owner-user of Onesimus), but it is a use taken only because of the frightening, horrifying, and thus often disowned aspects of this letter. But, in proceeding queerly through BDSM relations, one can learn new habits about those bodies and body parts that have been viewed as base, attending to those parts, and those associated with them, and rearranging whose bodily pleasures matter. A reconsideration of Onesimus's body, his potential pleasures, rather than his use for others' pleasure and other, ostensibly elevated purposes, "backtalks" to the imperial slave ideologies infused in the letter.[114] Readers and users of these constructions have repeatedly tried to reassure themselves and others that these present eternal and unchanging truths, but the disconcerting juxtaposition of ancient slave and BDSM "slave" indexes the instability of both biblical and historical claims to power.[115] If the slave in a BDSM scene somehow *reconfigures* oppressive histories through some kind of resistant repetition or simulation of slavery, this slave's encounter with the enslaved Onesimus potentially *prefigures* the social arrangements changed from the ones reflected and reinforced in texts like Philemon.

In prizing bodily practices that resist, exceed, or are simply viewed as useless to exploitative economies, BDSM casts new light on claims about an enslaved person's (apparent) uselessness, as Paul claimed Onesimus once was: once *achrēston*, "useless" or "not-useful," to the you addressed in Philemon 11. By departing from heteronormative, and even heterocapitalist teleologies, BDSM potentially echoes those (other) resistant practices of enslaved people, where and when they subtly slowed or sabotaged economic processes that attempted to capitalize on their enforced limitation as living implements of labor.[116] When enslaved people resist the demands to be a productively embodied tool, they indicate the uselessness of their restraint at the hands of the owner-user, a uselessness that some find in the reuse of techniques of restraint in contemporary BDSM. Both signal alternate imaginaries for different kinds of communities than those that coincide with and contribute to exploitative economies.

Paul considers Onesimus less useful prior to the period the letter addresses, a time when Onesimus may have been resistant to his owner-users, possibly even including Paul, at least until Paul prevailed on him (or Onesimus just took a different tack) in a time (constructed by the letter as) between "before" and "now." Given the way the letter reflects the embodied utility of enslaved people, Onesimus's resistance could have been to particular erotic uses of his body. If so, and if this is the reason for Onesimus's absence from his owner-user(s), did something circulating among the assembly communities provide a spark? Did Onesimus hear of practices among these assembly communities that attempted to place (some) limits on sexual practices, at least with "prostitutes" (*pornē*, 1 Cor 6:15–17), a certain kind of enslaved person coerced into sexual use?[117] One cannot safely and responsibly argue that such condemnations extend the category of *porneia* to the sexual use of all enslaved people, including especially the use of a household slave.[118] To imagine such a scenario, one would have to differentiate between the arguments made in Paul's letters and the traditions or practices referenced by such arguments that might have been conceived or applied differently. After all, as in Philemon (and in Galatians, see chapter 3), Paul is comfortable using familiar slave images and practices in that very passage within 1 Corinthians, arguing that the audience member's body is not their own and that they have been bought by the divine through Christ's activity (6:19–20). Such arguments reflect a mentality displayed throughout this and the other Pauline letters where, as scholars are increasingly acknowledging, Paul never directly addresses the sexual use of

enslaved people, let alone condemns such use.[119] As Glancy's work continuously stresses, Paul's own arguments are evidence that he was not particularly concerned with this vulnerability.

Perhaps, then, Onesimus came into contact with the pre-Pauline baptismal formula—"there is neither Jew nor Greek, neither slave nor free, not
male and female; for you are all one in Christ Jesus"—that seemingly mitigated differences between free and enslaved people, and was circulating at
least among the Corinthian and Galatian assemblies (quoted in Gal 3:28 and
referenced in 1 Cor 12:13). Or had he heard about other embodied figures
imagined as strangely gendered (by some), those prophetic females who
seemed like *tribades* or the circumcising members cast as akin to eunuchs?
Of course, again, in each of these cases, Onesimus would have needed to
encounter or interpret them differently from how Paul's letters positioned
them, particularly in cases where enslaved figures were persistently situated as negative points of contrast. Is it possible that Onesimus was trying
to reverse the dynamics of use, as more recent BDSM practices have tried?
Given the Roman imperial context reflected in this letter, this potential resonance seems harder to imagine, unless he was ordered to act in a way that
scrambled the assumed isomorphism between sexual and social power by
his owner-user(s). If an enslaved male played the insertive role for either a
male or a female social superior (possibilities expressly considered by texts
and traditions of this time), this could create problems for the reputation of
the owner-users as properly in-control of themselves and their subordinates,
in accord with elite imperial norms of moderation (as well as tensions within
the elite imperial household). This could account for Onesimus's separation
from the household addressed by this letter.

Of course, as reflected by the ample use of qualifiers and conditionals in
these reflections, contemporary users of this text cannot know what pre-
cipitated the actions of Onesimus or Paul, presented, but often only dimly
glimpsed through this letter.[120] Even in a best-case scenario, we are dealing
with reflections of Onesimus's conflicted will, a will that one cannot quite call
agency, let alone consent. This, ultimately, may be the power of this juxtaposition, the manifest difference between Onesimus's context and more recent figurative practices within BDSM contexts. BDSM offers a set of sexual
practices that critique, in and through a range of embodied actions, the coercive, abusive, and nonconsensual use of enslaved people (like Onesimus or
those more historically proximate, who were themselves cast as akin to this
biblical slave), *even while* strangely repurposing the props of this coercive use.

Perhaps the strategic challenge enacted by BDSM practices can work *only through* the repurposing of these props and positions, resisting by denaturalizing their historical correspondence to certain dynamics of oppressive social power. In that case, if biblical epistles support just such exploitative uses of enslaved people (as I have argued), then, BDSM players in "slave" scenes are engaged in a provocative yet consequential blasphemy, one to which religious and not-so-religious people should attend.

Other Uses of History

This anachronistic juxtaposition of the enslaved figure Onesimus and the "slave" role reconfigured in BDSM could provide a queer alternative to the letter's oppressive continuities with slave regimes ancient and modern. But is such a juxtaposition worth the different kinds of trouble it can evoke, if BDSM practices do not satisfactorily acknowledge that enslaving practices persist as ongoing practices of nonconsensual mortification? There is good reason to hesitate at these configurations and then reconfigurations of the sexually available slave, for any and all of us living as "postslavery subjects." For, as BDSM practices do and do not acknowledge, enslaving practices structure and persist as ongoing practices of subjectification. Their effects are still most readable among and upon Black subjects, those racialized in ways akin to those who were more recently subjected to the visceral subjugation of slavery, those who are "said to have survived or to be surviving the pasts of slavery, that is not yet past."[121] Readers and users of biblical texts, including but beyond Philemon, have done damage to subjugated bodies, a heritage from which people have to recover, particularly (though not only) African Americans. Demetrius Williams, among others, details how and why African American church communities have responded to the letter of Philemon as bearing traces of this heritage:

> it played no essential role in the religious tradition and ecclesiastical life of African American churches most certainly because of the role it had played in supporting the Fugitive Slave Law and, perhaps even more emphatically, the role it played in endorsing slavery in general.[122]

As more African Americans have been (formally) trained in biblical and theological studies, this rejection or evasion has been increasingly supplemented by suspicious engagement or careful recontextualizations.[123] To engage a text that refers to slavery in such fraught ways is to participate in a scene that is already densely, yet dynamically racialized.[124]

As with their ancient predecessors, more recently enslaved people were (and are) racially characterized by a presumed promiscuity and availability for sexual uses.[125] Slavery has generated and deployed a range of figures in order to characterize bodies of color by their especially deviant sexuality, whether they were jezebels, breeders, and bucks (excessive and presumably willing), or mammies and Uncle Toms (asexual yet submissive), and these figurations persist, albeit in altered and even alternating forms into the present.[126] As Kelly Brown Douglas has demonstrated, contemporary forms and norms of Black sexuality have been shaped, but not entirely determined, by the legacy of white sexual assault supported and reflected by these racial-sexual types.[127] Since these racialized figurations have generated reticence, or even silence, for fear of confirming persistent stereotypes; it is no wonder that readers and users of letters like Philemon have also avoided the sexual use of enslaved people.[128]

Racially minoritized bodies have already been "queered" (so to speak) as departing from what was (or is) considered natural and normal ideals (occupied by only some of the people that one might classify as heterosexual).[129] These persistent dynamics signal, among many other things, that to chart and counter normalization and naturalization, one must contend with the dynamic histories of gender, sexuality, and embodiment intersecting, overlapping, and mutually influencing those of race, ethnicity, economy, and empire (among others). BDSM is often *only* a *partial* confrontation with such histories, and particularly the heritage of slavery (and those arguments that support, repeat, and reinforce this heritage). The manifest efforts to create and then play in BDSM scenes are a kind of work, work that can transform and even rework the social imaginaries we inherit, even as they are often not . . . quite . . . acknowledging their connections to these imaginaries. This is most especially the case when one attends (or does not) to the racialized resonances that are not quite repetitions in master-slave scenes and, perhaps, BDSM in general.

As much of the theoretical and even the recent ethnographic literature on BDSM reflects, participants in BDSM practices often insist on an essential dissonance, a central difference, or even an unbridgeable gulf between their practices of bondage, flagellation, or other forms of physical and verbal discipline and the practices of punishment found in "actual," "historical," or "real life" slaveholding societies.[130] Recall the aforementioned arguments that BDSM is a parody of authority, implicitly not an enactment of "real" authority. BDSM resituates seemingly stable roles, rather than shoring them up. Master-slave scenes are not like "actual" master-slave relations, because these roles can be reversed or switched in BDSM. Unlike the enslaving regimes historically reflected and then reinforced by letters like Philemon, such scenes are not making use of the subordinated bodies of enslaved people. If anything, the top's body is more clearly used for certain desired ends on the part of the bottom!

Within BDSM communities consent is the most frequently extolled factor that helps to differentiate slavery and "slave" scenes (or aspects to scenes). Indeed, as Paul's letter to Philemon exemplifies, whose consent is garnered was (and remains) no small matter, indicating this really can be a significant difference. Yet it is also common to appeal to the scripted or simulated quality of BDSM to explain this difference. Patrick Hopkins, for instance, argues: "SM sexual activity does not replicate patriarchal sexual activity. It simulates it."[131] Hopkins specifically addresses slave scenes, stressing the centrality of the notion of "scene"—"SMists do not enslave, they do slave scenes"—as a production and performance.[132] The way the scene is set does make a difference, though:

> In real slavery, the slave is commodity and possession; the master may need fear, but not approval. The slave is capital resource, and often a threat—to be purchased, or bred, and acted upon. In SM "slave" and "master" scenes, however, the "slave" may reject the "master" (or "mistress") because she is not dominant enough, not experienced enough, not skillful enough to satisfy the "slave's" desires.[133]

Here Hopkins repeats, yet specifies, claims described earlier, particularly around the consent, desire, even power of the "slave." But the language of simulation and the efforts at differentiation still indicate how these two different kinds of interactions with slaves are not entirely separated. Against what, after all, is this master-slave scene differentiated? What is being simulated here? Or is it a "when" that is being simulated?

Simulation often *refers back* to horrifying historical phenomena. Is it possible, then, that BDSM refers back, even to the biblical—to those rhetorical sites where Paul tried to negotiate his own authority with an enslaved person and an(other) owner? It is a peculiar, but seductive conception of freedom that holds that one's sense of self can be simply separated from the past, from one's own and others' (prior) practices. The simulative dynamic of BDSM tempers some of the utopic enthusiasm about BDSM inventing something new in relation to power.[134] Feminists and, or *as*, queer women involved in BDSM seem less likely to be overly celebratory about the ultimately liberatory, disruptive, or utopic possibilities within BDSM practices.[135] Their reflections on the sociopolitical significance of BDSM are frequently marked by ambivalence or qualification.[136] Gayle Rubin, for instance, notes:

> Of course, class privilege, race, and gender do not disappear when people enter the S/M world. The social power individuals bring to the S/M community affects their ability to negotiate within it, whether as tops or bottoms. But class, race, and gender neither determine nor correspond to the roles adopted for S/M play.[137]

I must admit my own ambivalence at this kind of ambivalent explanation. On the one hand, it seems right to me that the relation between tops and bottoms, even in instances where they adopt master and slave roles, could hardly be said to be a case of systematic oppression of the bottom or slave. On the other hand, I worry that Rubin, among others, was not grappling with certain correspondences and connections (though not equivalences) to histories and practices of slavery. Here, perhaps, is the virtue of introducing the rhetorical scenario of Philemon into this disconcerting juxtaposition with BDSM scenes, rather than vice versa (particularly considering the potential vice of the claims to virtue within the biblical verses)! The anachronistic juxtaposition of Pauline arguments about slave utility and owner-users' consent alongside BDSM help to highlight the connections, resonances, and inheritances from slave systems into the contemporary context. Previous encounters with the evasions of the biblical epistle and its interpreters prepare one to notice the kind of evasions of horrifying histories among interpreters of BDSM practices. These interpreters' arguments about bodily practices can present points of entry, but not final destinations when staging and then reflecting on this juxtaposition, as might prove to be especially the case when one grapples with the specifically racialized aspects of BDSM and its figurative reuses of slavery.

How Not to Race Past

Further reflections on more recent forms of slavery are important for rethinking these (potential) historical correspondences and the specifically racialized impacts on and through contemporary practices of gender, sexuality, and embodiment. As in the ancient Roman imperial context, enslaved people were objects and simultaneous sources of erotic and economic investment for the master class in the antebellum United States. Few scholars have historically situated and theoretically reframed these investments more than Hortense Spillers and Saidiya Hartman. Spillers particularly considers the impact of the Middle Passage on captive bodies conceived primarily as quantities.[138] In ways akin to ancient predecessors, the enslaved bodies' quantification dictated what would and would not be recorded about them, including in relation to their sexual use. As Spillers describes it:

> The loss of the indigenous name/land provides a metaphor of displacement for other human and cultural features and relations, including the displacement of the genitalia, the female's and the male's desire that engenders future. The fact that the enslaved person's access to the issue of his/her own body is not entirely clear in this historic period throws in crisis all aspects of the blood relations.[139]

Highlighting the natal alienation endemic to slave systems, Spillers surfaced the potentially queering effects of slavery (several years before the term "queer" gained a certain kind of critical and political momentum), as enslaved people were estranged not only from a people and a homeland but also from heteronormative kinship. Spillers's "displacement of the genitalia" even sounds like Foucault's and Halperin's characterization of BDSM, only now operating in a differently (which is to say explicitly) historicized and racialized register. Particularly in light of male masters' sexual uses of enslaved females (and the resulting offspring), enslaving practices unevenly undercut the naturalization of kinship, imagined as an innate affective bond founded on one's birth (rather than requiring material support and careful cultivation).[140] Both physical and psychic forms of dispersal generate modes of "disremembering" among people who might have otherwise been members of a family.[141]

Working in the wake of Spillers's problematization, Saidiya Hartman considers the more quotidian, even sentimentalized aspects of slavery, dynamics that enforce the subjugation of enslaved people as much as the more spectacular and horrifying practices.[142] Saidiya Hartman turns to "the terror of the mundane" and explicitly worries, from the very opening of her work, about our casual familiarity with the violence of slavery. The repetition of bloody scenes would just increase present-day habituation to this racialized past (that is not quite past), turning witnesses into voyeurs. Hartman asks:

> In light of this, how does one give expression to these outrages without exacerbating the indifference to suffering that is the consequence of the benumbing spectacle or contend with the narcissistic identification that obliterates the other or the prurience that too often is the response to such displays?[143]

Hartman's answer is to focus on the purported reciprocities and ambivalent pleasures projected by and even realized within enslaving institutions (including the law, family, and home). Because "sentiment, enjoyment, affinity, will, and desire facilitated subjugation, domination, and terror precisely by preying upon the flesh, the heart, and the soul,"[144] the supposed emancipation of enslaved people was a transitional continuation in modes of servitude, rather than a transformation or liberation.

While accepting the potential, or at least partial personhood of a slave could be seen as resisting or even undoing the quantification of enslaved bodies, Hartman demonstrates that slavery survives, even thrives in the confusion between person and thing, consent and coercion.[145] In the legal culture of the antebellum United States, "the dual invocation of the slave as property and person was an effort to wed reciprocity and submission, intimacy and domination, and the legitimacy of violence and the necessity of protection."[146] While the will of the enslaved is negated, since she or he cannot legally give (or withhold) consent, the wider legal and cultural discourse characterized the racialized slave body as lascivious and thus always already ready and willing to submit sexually. In fact, the only check on the (imagined) excess of the enslaved is the paternal feeling of the master(s), whose benevolent affection works in tandem with the enslaved person's willful submission.[147]

Situating desire and consent in this kind of context shows not the ways in which sexuality and slavery meet, but their already intimate acquaintance. This cultural, legal, and embodied intimacy facilitates subjugation, while also providing conflicted spaces to negotiate within it. Hartman, for instance, examines how the narrative of Harriet Jacobs depicts a complicated and compromised form of agency between, but also besides coerced compulsion and absolute and unhindered choice.[148] In her *Incidents in the Life of a Slave Girl*, Jacobs finds "something akin to freedom" in giving herself to another white male lover besides her master, arguing: "It seems less degrading to give one's self, than to submit to compulsion."[149] Hartman views Jacobs's deliberate calculation as troubling the always uncertain and unsustainable delineation of freely given consent, questioning whether Jacobs's act could be seen as a mode of resistance or just another kind of surrender.[150]

> After all, if desperation, recklessness, and hopelessness determine "choosing one's lover," absolute distinctions between compulsion and assent cannot be sustained. Yielding to another or giving one's self is no less subject to constraint, though it is certainly different from and preferable to being forced to submit.[151]

This subjection within seduction (or seduction within subjection) gives new meaning to Butler's formulation of gendered, sexual, and embodied subjectivity as "a practice of improvisation within a scene of constraint."[152]

These more recent figurations of slavery complicate the improvised relations within or between a range of contexts I have been considering so far in this chapter: Paul's letter to Philemon, its Roman imperial setting, and their correspondences to contemporary BDSM practices. Slavery's modes of embodied dispersal, sensate and social, could resonate with claims that BDSM can reterritorialize bodily pleasures, while also figuring slaves as troubling heteronormative kinship. Yet these denaturalizing estrangements are just one mode of maintaining social and political subjugation. These alienating practices are paired with "softer," more sentimentalizing strategies in the antebellum and Reconstruction periods in the United States, much as they were deployed in the ancient Roman empire and in Paul's letter(s). The coexistence of intimate reciprocity and violent subjugation in this American regime should, again, qualify any claims about the letter to Philemon softening enslaving practices in the assembly community or improving the situation of one particular slave. In this light, interpretive depictions of a benevolent Paul and a gratefully accepting Onesimus are a chilling replication of enslaving practices, across the centuries. The letter's language of love and affection (vv. 5, 7, 9, 10, 12, 14, and 16) are marks not of its difference from slave societies, but of its consonance with(in) them. Depicting Onesimus as Paul's own "heart" (v. 12) or the owner-user's "beloved brother in the flesh" (v. 16) echoes Hartman's descriptions of sentiment's facilitation of subjugation "precisely by preying upon the flesh, the heart, and the soul."[153]

Indeed, by admitting the (albeit constrained) humanity of the enslaved, masters found a way of maintaining the quantification of these living implements of their use. Slave systems exploit a "gray" area, not only between person and property but also between consent and coercion, unsettling certain pictures of both Philemon and BDSM. Unlike the owner-user addressed by Paul's letter's preference that "your goodness might be not according to constraint but according to a voluntary act" (v. 14), an enslaved person like Onesimus or Harriet Jacobs dwelled in a zone where actions, even if chosen, are taken within powerful constraints. Even if Onesimus "chose" to join this developing movement upon encountering Paul, or even if Onesimus "decided" to seek Paul as an intercessor between his owner-user and himself (two of the more common scenarios constructed by scholars), this action would have been more like the deliberate calculation made by Jacobs than a freely made, consensual choice. Whatever actions Onesimus took, they just might have been another kind of surrender, perhaps the least worst option, but an option that enslaving systems permit so that they might persist. Given this letter's congruence with the widely accepted sexual use of enslaved people, the characterization of Onesimus as now "good to use" could just reflect his calculated, but not-entirely-consensual acceptance that it is "less degrading to give one's self, than to submit to compulsion."[154] Whether this meant that Onesimus gave his self (or "stole" his self) to Paul, or learned from Paul to accept the giving (or taking) of his self to his owner-user(s), the rather modern distinction between compulsion and consent is difficult to maintain.

These enslaving dynamics throw not only kinship into crisis, but freedom, will, and consent as well—all concepts crucial within contemporary BDSM practices. Intensive modes of conversation and consent are cited as evidence of the more transgressive, even utopian possibilities present by BDSM. The idea of willed submission reflects neither distance nor difference from slavery, but a charged correspondence, even congruence with tops and bottoms in BDSM (and not only when playing in a master-slave scene). Tops show that they are taking good care of bottoms by playing in a way that reflects the bottoms' desires, negotiated and accepted in advance. Benevolent protection is matched by willful submission, cast as expressions of desire and pleasure. Perhaps this congruence accounts for why scenes with white tops and Black bottoms are so often avoided in BDSM. When players are considering the possibilities for interracial BDSM scenes, the fraught relationship to these histories of slavery and racism(s) threatens to come to the foreground, particularly for white players who imagine BDSM communities to be either not particularly racialized or especially nonracist. Black players, for instance, note and even complain that white players are uncomfortable topping for them, likely because such acts (even within a carefully negotiated BDSM scene) would too closely correspond to distinctively racialized historical practices.[155] As Tina Portillo notes, "especially for me as a *black woman* who plays with *white tops* (occasionally a white *male* top), people say that because of history I shouldn't be enjoying this, let alone wanting it."[156] Because of this history, then, the tendency within interracial scenes is to enact scenes that reverse rather than somehow mime or correspond to racial inequalities.[157] Such a tendency coincides with longer-standing BDSM arguments that its radicality is in its ability to switch codes of social power, even as it also clearly swerves away from too directly acknowledging and addressing the use of the past in such loaded forms of bodily contact. This tendency claims to counter social power, without quite confronting it.

Yet evasion is hardly the rule in other settings, particularly since there have been lively engagements of the impact of slavery on sexuality, particularly among womanist scholars in religious and theological studies. I cannot pretend to give an adequate survey of the breadth and depth of womanist work on sexuality, but the historical effects of slavery on gendered, sexual, and racial dynamics is a persistent and important topic.[158] BDSM practices have seldom been addressed in this work (thus far), except to critique the damaging effects of slavery and persistent racisms on the sexuality of racially minoritized people.[159] However, if one goal of to womanist or Black religious studies is to counter a politics of respectability or encourage the willful and outrageous connotations of the folk expression of "womanish,"[160] then there is some (albeit initial) space to reconsider a range of erotic practices on such terms.[161]

It becomes easier to enter this space if one learns more about and from a range of artists and scholars, working in antiracist, queer, and even queer-of-color modes of critique, who have addressed the specifically racialized aspects of BDSM in light of slavery and its aftermaths.[162] Admittedly, there has been a hesitance or even evasion to think about racialization in many corners of BDSM communities.[163] Yet, these aspects have been reframed and reconsidered by filmmakers, novelists, poets, and scholars in literary and cultural studies, often by and as people of African descent and as queers of color.[164] Thus, to counter the worldview presented within and perpetuated beyond biblical interpretations, one must confront a series of, in Christina Sharpe's terms, "monstrous intimacies"—not only between masters and slaves, between those racialized as whites and Blacks, but also between the past and the present, between sexual and (other) everyday practices.[165]

The materials and markers deployed in BDSM play, like whips and forms of bondage, carry a kind of historical baggage that is also racialized in the way they refer back (without ever absolutely belonging only) to slave systems.[166] By juxtaposing these depictions to biblical constructions, I am not importing race into an ancient Mediterranean context: the ancient and biblical contexts have already been enlisted in racist formations for centuries up to now.[167] These formations—those that have mediated the biblical for various "modern" or "contemporary" moments through the historical practices of slavery and racism—are explicitly what these artistic and scholarly interpreters are engaging, what at least some BDSM practices *could* make explicit. In the face of (or even within) the insistence, hesitance, or evasion of some, BDSM can make visible the traffic within and between various monstrous intimacies, particularly those mostly unacknowledged and disavowed in the everyday life of the present, by users of the biblical and other authoritative bodies. Ironically, these contemporary kinds of evasion or disavowal indicate how unremarkable this history's impact is to most, reflecting and even resembling prior dispositions that saw the sexual use of enslaved people as unremarkable or inconsequential, in either the ancient Roman imperial or the antebellum North American contexts.

Attending to the Past

To clarify, I am not suggesting that one condemns BDSM, and particularly interracial BDSM practices because of these intimacies and heritages, these resonances that are not quite repetitions, the kinds of connections and even correspondences that are hardly exact copies.[168] Still, given BDSM's fraught relationship to these histories of slavery and racism(s), one might not exactly want to wax poetic about its purely utopic or liberating effects either. This, frankly, is why I keep insisting on a juxtaposition of the past with the present, because of the persistence of the past despite (or even within) the resistance to confront it.[169] This insistence is inspired and infused by a similar, yet likely more audacious juxtaposition of BDSM and the history of slavery, in the work of Black British filmmaker Isaac Julien.[170] Julien's short film *The Attendant* (1993) confronts what has been obscured and disavowed in official versions of the history of slavery by calling attention to the unresolved desires in slave and postslavery economies. I have neither the space nor the ability to perform an adequate summary, let alone an adequate close reading, of this film, but in what follows I will do my best to articulate the most compelling and generative features of this eight-minute short.[171]

The film follows a male museum guard of African descent (the titular Attendant) working at the Wilberforce House Museum, a monument to Britain's collective imagination as an anti-slavery nation-state. The film features François-Auguste Biard's antislavery painting *Slaves on the West Coast of Africa* (1833), which depicts a slave market scene in which African bodies are variously inspected, bound, and whipped by bodies marked as European (likely French) in descent. Once the Attendant encounters a white male visitor to the museum and inspects his black leather bag (which holds a black leather whip),[172] a series of fantastic and possibly fantasized (by the Attendant) scenes attempt to pierce the somber setting, particularly by depicting interracial BDSM "scenes." The Biard painting, for instance, is transfigured into a group scene, with Black and white males striking poses that closely correspond to those found in the painting, only now wearing contemporary BDSM leather gear. Once these ghosts are queerly resuscitated, the Black Attendant and white Visitor (the latter now also in leather gear) take turns whipping each other's backsides (as depicted by two separate, semifrozen poses, midlash, with a soundtrack of the cracking of a whip signaling movement and action). Though the short is, in a way, dialogue free, the soundtrack features not only these sound effects, but also groans (of ecstasy?) and the Attendant singing an aria from the opera *Dido and Aeneas* which features the chorus: "Remember me, remember me, but ah, forget my fate."

The film is obviously rich and compelling, which is also to say that it is dense and occasionally even frustrating. Yet, its own set of anachronistic juxtapositions signals how BDSM can make alternate uses of the past.[173] *The Attendant* highlights the dynamics of embodied pleasure for the slave traders in the Biard painting as well as for the museum consumers of these images, those who might insist they inhabit a political space crucially distanced or different from that of the traders.[174] By (re)staging a correspondence between the painting and potential BDSM scenes, the film demonstrates the vein of disavowed desire running through the commemorative practices institutionalized by museums and the canonical versions of enlightened, modern, and free subjectivity they construct and uphold. Further, it also insists that the correspondence enacted by the juxtaposition of past and present is not just perpetuating or reinforcing these racialized historical practices, even as the impact of these practices persist into the present.

Though the meaning, not to mention the utility, of a representation cannot be reduced to the intentionality of its creator, Julien sees the film as explaining the possibilities for why Black queer folk choose to play with master and slave roles, asking: "Could not the fetish slave-band in the film, mimicking the metal collars worn by black slaves—which, for some readers, enacts this colonial memory—be read as something else . . . ?"[175] Indeed, Julien presses this point even further:

> For instance, if today a black gay man were to participate in such an act
> for sexual pleasure, could not the resulting "representation" of interracial
> s/m be read as a parody? . . . Alternatively, could not the representation of
> interracial s/m be read as a practice of a racial and sexual dynamic which,
> in displaying the codes of a (Fanonian) master/slave dialectic, presents a
> transgressive simulacrum, one which both parodies and disrupts the codes
> of societal and racial power?[176]

Here Julien alludes directly to claims of the parodic power of s/m, as explained by Califia, but extends and specifies the challenge of such parodying practices to the re-uses of the iconography and activities of the Atlantic slave trade.

Though the BDSM scenes in *The Attendant* seem to parody and disrupt power, including race's implications within formations of nation, gender, sexuality, embodiment, and ethnicity, they also confront the ambivalence of a desire to know the past and the present differently, precisely because of these intersecting implications. As Sharpe argues about the impact of this film:

> We cannot dismiss s/m as or reduce it to a "white thing," renounce interracial
> sex or desire as "sleeping with the enemy," nor can we reduce interracial s/m
> or a general desire to submit, to be the sadomasochist, to a *simple* repetition
> of the historical sadism of slavery that is archived but yet disavowed in the

Biard painting and in the Wilberforce House Museum. We also cannot dismiss forced submission and its everyday contemporary manifestations.[177]

On the one hand, the film clears a certain kind of playful space for representations of interracial desire and pleasures in interrelated BDSM practices, including those that evoke patterns or implements from slavery. On the other hand, it makes visible a haunting legacy that persists and thus must be recognized and remembered, in some ways insisting that one must encounter how slavery is internal to activities within both intimate and institutional domains.[178] In Elizabeth Freeman's reading of the film, then, Julien is "asking black and white men to examine the traumatic histories encoded in their interracial desires without demanding that they simply give these desires up."[179]

Beyond this critical impulse on the present (the use of the past in the present), Freeman argues that Julien's juxtapositions suggest different kinds of relations between parties of the past and the present. In reconsidering the combination of the various sound effects with the chorus imploring an audience to "remember me," Freeman posits:

These intertwined sounds seem to implore these men of the past and the present, asking them to move across time and take up their obligations to one another . . . they ask the dead slave to *release* any hold on their descendants that would deny later generations the capacity to recalibrate pain into pleasure . . . the sounds ask the living players never to confuse pleasure with historical amnesia.[180]

Though their conditions could hardly be seen as equivalent, the haunting connections between those players staged by the film indicate a set of mutual obligations between people in the past and the present. BDSM practices indicate that one might reuse, even remix those temporal materials typically frozen by practices of monumentalization. Yet, one must also remember the past while reconfiguring it for the possibility of a different present and future, times not entirely predetermined by the historical oppressions that nonetheless persist, but hopefully not finally and fully.[181] BDSM scenes, then, can operate as sites of combined temporalities, presenting histories that both correspond and clash, with the aim of reorganizing the possibilities of bodies in time.

Whipping Through Time

Anachronistically juxtaposing the sexual use of Onesimus, an oppressed figure from a biblically referred but obscured history, against these different uses of the materials and other markers of slavery in BDSM scenes does not cover over or evade the horrors and atrocities of embodied violence against enslaved people, as most biblical scholarship is still so prone to do. The ancient slave system still haunts contemporary sexual ethics and embodied practices, while also offering an alternative way to think and relate historically beyond more officially authorized versions of biblical interpretation, versions that whitewash the horrors and tamp the potential pleasures in encountering, but working contrary to, these worldviews. Rather than reinscribing the inequalities that accompany these histories, these juxtapositions negotiate with them explicitly, making traumatic histories and structures of oppression visible.[182] In a time and place one might want to call the present, queer-embodied practices can become critically rather than canonically historiographic or, as Freeman notes: "more than a cumulative effect of traumatic and/or insidious power relations, the body in sadomasochistic ritual becomes a means of addressing history in an idiom of pleasure."[183]

In what might be a first movement or moment, it is crucial to recognize the appalling ways Paul argues in the letter to Philemon. Confronting the rhetoric and potential realities of the *chrēsis*, the sexual use of Onesimus, is a necessary precondition for grappling with the letter's compatibility with the kyriarchal ethos of Roman imperial antiquity and the cultures that consecutively lay claim to this past as their own. Yet once one critiques the ideologies that inhere in these settings, one can be left with the distinct impression of rather limited options for next steps. Encountering the horrifying circumstances reflected and perpetuated in this sort of scriptural argumentation can have an overwhelming, even debilitating effect on interpretation. The starkness of the situation supported by systemic forms of oppression helps horror to morph easily into despair. In a second movement or moment, interpreters and other users of such authoritative argumentation must resist falsely totalizing oppositions that too often frame certain modes of response as appropriate. In the face of such uses of Onesmius, one should not be frozen into believing that one must either find a way to accept the worldview presented in these texts or abandon them. Given the ongoing impact and historical heritage amassed around the use of Paul's letters, an ethically and politically committed interpreter cannot accept the latter option. Yet acceding to the former option seems only to compound (or, at best, evade) the horror that created this impasse in the first place.[184]

The route of resistance I have chosen is this disconcerting juxtaposition between an ancient enslaved person and the BDSM "slave" role, between the sociosexual system reflected in the ancient biblical letter and the alternative erotic economies (some) BDSM communities aim to create. This anachronistic juxtaposition expresses and hopefully works through the proposition that, given the horrifying uses of human beings reflected in the biblical corpus, it would be far better to be inappropriate to and with these uses, imagining other uses of the body and of the past, unlike the previous uses, in reappropriating this biblical body. This might constitute a creative, even idiosyncratic form of remembrance, of Onesimus and others treated as embodied implements, a remembrance that confronts instead of evading their oppression, and counters instead of perpetuating the perspective that reduces the meaning of their embodiment to how a kyriarchal system arranged it. What would it mean to imagine a performer singing as Onesimus, rather than as Dido, repeatedly calling: "Remember me, remember me, but ah, forget my fate"? What forms of embodied remembrance can one enact that disrupt the oppressive impacts of this biblical heritage without forgetting, without slipping into a seductive, but falsely comforting amnesia?

One, likely unexpected guide can be The Attendant, by turns stark and playful, echoing but also imagining on and beyond the slave systems of the proximate and more distant past. The doubly imperial resonance of the aria from Nahum Tate's Dido and Aeneas, as a British adaptation of the Aeneid narrative justifying Rome's own origins and pretensions, demonstrates the historical and rhetorical traffic between these empires that themselves trafficked in various commodities, including humans debased to be owned, exchanged, and used.[185] Placing Isaac Julien's short film alongside Paul's shortest letter suggests different kinds of exchange, different potential uses of this fraught imperial heritage. Imagining the remembrance of Onesimus singing this aria would certainly be a catachresis of the imperial ideologies of use deployed against him and many others that were imaginatively constructed as embodying similar states of enslaved utility (and, thus, undeserving of commemoration). Yet another catachresis, or distinctly inappropriate use of Philemon, inspired by an exchange between these brief works, though, would require pivoting the letter's axis of exchange away from one between Paul and (another) owner-user to one between Paul and Onesimus, only now in another ritualized kind of power exchange, switching master and slave roles as the Attendant and Visitor did. Though patently improper, and likely to horrify and even outrage other interpreters and users of this letter, reimagining a different kind of relation between Onesimus and Paul along the lines of an interracial BDSM scene is likely to make this juxtapositional work so much more distasteful and objectionable (to some). Yet the kinds of rhetorical concerns around slave utility and owner-user consent found in the letter easily conform to the other props and positions of, to my mind, more offensive settings: the ancient Roman imperial and antebellum North American slave systems. When similar props and positions reappear in BDSM scenes, they are not divorced from this horrific historical heritage, but they can also move people to a negotiation and critical rearrangement of the elements persistently used to oppress those cast as others like Onesimus.

To be sure, such a theoretical strategy brings atypical reading partners together, while interrogating and challenging the boundaries for what theories are appropriate for use within biblical scholarship. Yet, BDSM practices and their role within Julien's *The Attendant* encourage scholars and other users to reconsider the relation between an important object from the past and the official and institutionalized kinds of commemorative work they are often made to do.[186] When Biard's painting springs to life in a transfigured scene of BDSM eroticism, it displays the desires of slavery's past evaded by official histories of this system and its abolition, as well as the present-day pleasures involved in the disavowing collective imagination that this past remains safely quarantined in the past. One can do similar work with the admittedly important object that is Paul's letter to Philemon. Thus, my present project's juxtaposition aimed to indicate the way confessional and canonizing tendencies have meant that most scholars and users of this letter have evaded the way enslaved people were implements used for the pleasure of their owners. It might further challenge the desires at work in the construction and maintenance of institutionalized narratives about Paul and other members of these ancient assembly communities as respectable or at least always recuperable. Both of these signal that the historical stories and present-day practices presented about fraught and multifaceted issues, like slavery or sexuality, can rarely, if ever, be free of the kinds of stickiness and complication that attend to our complicities and accountabilities to the past and in the present.

Perhaps audiences now can imagine, without exploiting, Onesimus similarly springing to life from the pages of this scripture. Recognizing that he likely dwelled, like others over the centuries, in a zone between coercion and consent can provide an alternative angle on this enslaved person, and account for the ambiguities and ambivalences of this brief letter (speaking coldly and warmly, punning on his name and status, but calling him beloved). Paul might have preferred that Onesimus remain with him to "serve me on your behalf" (v. 13), but in requesting the owner-user's consent, Paul also reveals that Onesimus "serves" with a term commonly used for specifically cultic, or religious roles—*diakoneō*—the verb at the root of the eventual leadership role of deacon![187] In such a role, Onesimus did more than serve Paul or any of his (prior?) owner-users, like Philemon, Apphia, or Archippus.

Breathing not a new, but a resuscitated life into this letter, one should recognize that Paul is trying to get Onesimus to serve him, but Onesimus's leading roles cannot and should not be reduced to how he could serve Paul's interests then or even our interests now. We should press the letter and switch roles some, to reconsider the perspective of Onesimus, an enslaved (or freed) member of this assembly, but also a leading figure. The letter provides the slightest glimpse of his difficulties (not Paul's or other owner-users') of a potential change of status, while still trying to live in a kyriarchal context that demands consent to coercion. Onesimus might need to make demands of those who seek to commune with him (then and now) to ameliorate or just simply negotiate this context. Deacon Onesimus would not serve, but make demands on us from below, from the bottom even. Looking, listening, even feeling for Onesimus can lead us out from underneath centuries of interpretation that enforce their own ambivalences and amnesias. If we remember Onesimus, remember, but not blink at his and others' fate, should he still haunt us, or can this ghost finally rest?

From where I presently stand in relation to this past that is not yet past, the letter's echo of a kyriarchal ethos requires that I must find other, ethically and politically accountable uses for letters that reflect (rather than evade) these kinds of *chrēsis*. If this attempt at an alternative use of this biblical body and appalling Pauline past exhausts those who encounter it, then perhaps we can take comfort that Onesimus may just be retroactively released from any demand to be useful (at least for the moment). For others, I hope this presents opportunities to take up obligations across

time, imagining and enacting other uses of and for pleasure, without confusing such other uses as alibis for historical amnesia.[188] If nothing else,
this inappropriate use of biblical epistle and interpretation demonstrates
that there is still much more one can do, still other uses for a letter that
argued over the use of Onesimus.

5

Assembled Gentiles

Terrorist/Barbarian

Everybody knows that the bible condemns homosexuality. One need never pick up the holy book to encounter and incorporate this common sense, given the frequency and intensity with which people have argued that the bible speaks clearly and authoritatively on such issues. Saint Paul's name is frequently invoked in these contexts, particularly since two passages from his letters, Romans 1:18–32 and 1 Corinthians 6:9–10, are among the most common texts enlisted for explaining the biblical stance toward homosexuality. Indeed, many a reader might be incredibly annoyed with me, waiting until this point to cover two texts so obviously relevant for thinking about gender, sexuality, and embodiment. How could a book on *Appalling Bodies* not start with these texts?!? To be honest, this delay was intentional, even strategic. Scholars have long demonstrated that both of these texts reflect very different concepts of gender, sexuality, and embodiment than those held by the people so loudly, repeatedly, and persistently citing them.[1] (This difference can be recognized in the worldviews described in the previous chapters.) A recitation of this difference can frankly become rather tiresome, and may do little to help the politically or ethically engaged interpreter of these texts in their efforts to take them elsewhere.

However, both texts do present certain figures as excluded and condemned, deserving of death. Even as homosexuality is not the target of either Romans 1 or 1 Corinthians 6, there is something to this image of a judgmental Paul. Yet, many people turn to Paul's letters for other reasons. To some the letters appear to be life-giving and transgressive sources for inclusion, given the way they depict the apostle's mission to the Gentiles. Paul has been described not only as the apostle to the Gentiles but also as the apostle of freedom (see chapter 3), the apostle of liberty, the apostle of the heart set free, and a man who changed the world.[2] This image persists. Popular British evangelical scholars believe Paul was erasing or transcending ethnic categories, casting his opponents as exclusivist, even nationalist.[3] Introductory texts stress that

Appalling Bodies. Joseph A. Marchal, Oxford University Press (2020). © Oxford University Press.
DOI: 10.1093/oso/9780190060312.001.0001

Paul preached a particularly inclusive gospel.[4] Even continental philosophers have lately turned to Paul as a promising figure of universalism and a source for organizing beyond "identity politics."[5]

There is, then, an obvious tension between these two popular images of the apostle. Some scholars point to these different ideas as evidence of contradictions within the letters themselves.[6] In previous chapters I have suggested dwelling longer in zones of confusion or indeterminacy in order to grapple with the strange ways figures and forms are deployed in these letters. In this chapter, however, there is a simpler route for comprehending what might seem like tensions or contradictions in these pictures of the apostle or his letters, and it can be found in more recent conceptualizations of sexual exceptionalism.

Exceptional Sexual

Sexual exceptionalism, in part, names the ways nationalist and imperialist formations deploy a set of interwoven perversities on the basis of gender, sexuality, race, and religion. Jasbir Puar's innovative and transdisciplinary work is focused on contemporary forms of sexual exceptionalism, particularly in the constructions of life in the United States.[7] Sexual exceptionalism in these sorts of (neo)imperial settings entails the compatibility of two claims about a territory or populace, deploying two meanings of the word "exceptional." They simultaneously claim their distinctiveness (they are *unlike* other peoples, even incomparably so) *and* they extol their own excellence (they can be compared to their Others, since they, after all, are now demonstrably *superior* to them).[8] Of course, such claims of exceptionalism by the United States (and other national-imperial-racialized groups) are not a particularly new phenomenon, and have been examined often.[9] Furthermore, there has been added attention to the "state of exception" element to governmental power because of the work of Giorgio Agamben, among others.[10] Puar notes, however, that *different* narratives of exception seem to be operating in the present regime's "war on terror"—narratives that explicitly deploy issues of gender and sexuality (those issues that many theorists, philosophers, and activists are still so prone to ignore).[11] The specifically sexual exceptionalism manages the life of a people by producing both properly normative citizen bodies and perversely racialized terrorist bodies. Puar's work recurrently identifies and describes "stagings of U.S. nationalism via a praxis of sexual othering, one that exceptionalizes the identities of U.S. homosexualities vis-à-vis Orientalist constructions of 'Muslim sexuality.'"[12] The imperial-national proclaims its excellence by claiming it manages populations correctly (and differently from others) by including the right kinds of sexualities, which can include *some* of those people and practices that were once considered perverse or improper.

Remarkably, then, in this instance, "the United States has investments in being exceptionally heteronormative even as it claims to be exceptionally tolerant of (homosexual) difference."[13] It is only under *certain* conditions that *some* sexualities (both homosexual and heterosexual) are folded into national and neoimperial life, through the "disavowal of *populations* of sexual-racial others," that is "through the proliferation of sexual-racial subjects who invariably fall out of its narrow terms of acceptability."[14] The conditions for select forms of inclusion (avoiding being homophobically demonized as sexual others) are based on alignment and complicity with nationalist and imperialist arguments, arguments that build on the "racialization and unnationalization of sexual others."[15] These forms of sexual exceptionalism operate through a doubled movement: an oscillation between (1) the celebratory liberal subject (queer as arrived, accepted, enclosed, and folded into life), disciplined as a subject, and (2) the pathological and perversely racialized groups (the south Asian, the Muslim, the terrorist as sexual, gender, racial, national, civilizational aberrant, who must be killed), controlled as a population.[16] These imperial forms of sexual exceptionalism offer dual and contrasting figurations: the homonationalist liberal subject is only acceptable because s/he functions as an alibi for the alignment against the monster-terrorist-fags.

Such dual figurations justify a dual move, then: incorporate some in order to quarantine others. Sexual exceptionalism explains which bodies to include and which to eliminate. Some bodies are targeted for dying because they are queerly raced bodies: in this context they only "come into being through their perverse sexual-racial attributes and histories."[17] The sexually exceptionalist imperial regime is the arbiter of proper and domesticatable differences, patrolling the lines that determine what is a disorderly kind of queer population (those who terrorize).[18] Terrorist populations are depicted as failed men, deviant and perverted sexually and racially, but also religiously: their religious difference is marked as part of the reason for their perverse activities.[19] Indeed, this recurs over the centuries in the United States, given the way a simultaneously legal and religious category of offense like Sodomy has consistently been viewed as an act of the racial and religious Other, associated with "Orientals," Hindus, and all manner of vagrants and foreigners.[20] Thus, these populations, seen as sexually perverse and pathological because of their religious, racial, national, and ultimately imperial difference, must be isolated and eliminated from the national body—killed—in order to maintain and manage the right kinds of life (necropolitics meets biopolitics).[21]

As Jacqui Alexander has noted about these formations and arguments: "The meeting place that collapses the enemy, the terrorist, and the sexual pervert is the very one that secures the loyal heterosexual citizen patriot."[22] Alexander's work, then, concentrates on these meeting places in the heterosexualization of nations and empires, recently and historically, in and outside of the United States. For instance, Alexander examines how women's political struggles in the Bahamas are linked with the doubled moves of heteropatriarchy to "protect" some good women by criminalizing others like sex workers, Sodomites, and lesbians as noncitizens.[23] Some belong because they are sexually exceptional, while others are removed to sanitize the state as a service economy. Such recurrences reflect not only how sexual exceptionalism travels to former colonies but also how it finds ways to fold the state into and as a neocolonial site for elite travel, incorporating subjects into serviceability.[24] Places and populations become "safe" for corporate uses, for heterosexuality and certain forms of homosexuality, only so long as they operate "in the service of service."[25]

A neocolonial site is "safe" once it "establishes a continuum of criminality in which same-sex desire is the apotheosis of a range of offenses including murder, robbery, dishonesty, lying, rape, domestic violence, adultery, fornication, and incest."[26] Certain expressions and acts of same-sex desire, cast spectacularly as the biblical and legal specter of Sodomy, become symptomatic of the threat that must be eliminated in the national and neocolonial scene.[27] Yet, simultaneously, the scene also only becomes serviceable to the extent that sexual consumption is available for the use of travelers to the Bahamas. While it is primarily conditioned in terms of white heterosexual capital, Alexander also notes that this serviceability extends, "foregrounding the imperial, for in the contemporary period the erotic consumptive patterns of white gay tourism follow the same trajectory as those of white heterosexual tourism."[28] Proper Third World subjects, in versions like the woman or the gay male, "get positioned as the objects of sexual consumption rather than as agents in a sexual exchange."[29]

Attending to the *histories* of such uses in racial and colonial formations, including but beyond the contemporary horizon, becomes important in countering their various, ongoing appearances and effects. In fact, Alexander attempts to demonstrate the simultaneity of multiple historical locales for heterosexualizations (what others might describe as sexual normativities), by herself juxtaposing three seemingly disparate historical and geographical sites.[30] Alexander aims to make visible the ideological traffic and proximity between these apparently segregated sites to "destabilize that which hegemony has rendered coherent or fixed" and "reassemble that which appears to be disparate, scattered, or otherwise idiosyncratic."[31] Thus juxtaposed and reassembled, each of these reflects and constructs "a composite ideological field that is interdependent and that can demasculinize, feminize, sodomize, and racialize as a way of producing a grotesque enemy."[32] Though not identical, the recurrence of these racially perverse and colonially gendered figurations shows their ongoing utility and availability, and underscores the need to persistently identify both their reappearance and their specificities.[33] Indeed, as Puar has argued, it also demonstrates the ways in which sexual, gender, racial, ethnic, national, colonial, and religious aspects slide and combine together in these sorts of argumentation and figuration, indicating the "stickiness" of these aspects to each other, but also how "sticky" as signifiers these kinds of claims and figures are, given their ability to attach and reattach, slide and then appear and reappear in different times, places, territories, and populations.[34]

In highlighting the white heteromasculine patriot and the demasculinized dark enemy in these sites,[35] Alexander joins Puar in examining the national, racial, and imperial uses of sexuality and gender. The persistent recurrence of certain forms of sexual exceptionalism alerts the careful critic to attend to the rhetorical pairing of an externalizing threat with internalized control in any sort of argument, whether in the twenty-first or the first century.[36] The threat of an internal enemy offers the options of compliant conformity or incarcerated criminalization and, in turn, is matched with an external enemy that justifies invasion and annexation "outside" and the narrative of "excellence" that reinforces the superiority of those who conform "inside."[37] Because what is sexually exceptional excels, it also claims how such an order should exceed its borders: even as this makes those "inside" *singularly* exceptional, it also paradoxically maintains that this order should be promoted *universally* over all.[38]

Overall, then, Puar and Alexander present a cluster of factors to consider when sliding to analyze still other historical sites like the biblically Pauline or the imperially Roman. *First*, their work indicates that it is common for imperial forces to argue in terms of exceptionalism, specifically in terms of gender and sexuality. *Second*, within this kind of argumentation, ruling groups construct different definitions of sexual propriety in order to claim their exceptionally superior status; those who belong only do the proper erotic things with their own and others' bodies. *Third*, in doing so, imperial regimes claim to be beneficently inclusive and orderly, offering two different destinations: life within this order or death due to one's disordered pathology. Even when such regimes find ways to temporarily "include" those who might otherwise have been cast as aberrant, this inclusion functions as an alibi and abettal: they incorporate some in order to quarantine those cast as pathological, perverse, and/or aberrant (at that point). This highlights, *fourth*, that the difference between these two fates is perversely racialized through both sexual and religious modes of identification. Once incorporated within this order, what makes a good racial/religious/colonial Other is their availability for sexual use/service/consumption. (Otherwise, they do not belong, they are excluded and propelled into death, likely because of their strange religious identities or activities.) *Fifth*, those enemies who cannot be incorporated are grotesquely and perversely embodied in and as a range of figures, like the savage Sodomite, the terrorist fag, and/or the gender-monstrous foreigner. This underscores that those deviants targeted for death are associated with a range of aberrant actions and identifications, but their sexual inferiority, even barbarism, is treated as exemplarily symptomatic of their enemy status.

Finally, these factors operate in multiple sites and trajectories, as both external threat and internalized control, claiming to be both singularly exceptional and universally applicable, within historically and geopolitically recurrent but contextually specific figuration and argumentation.

The Epistles' Exceptionalism

Though developed to trace contemporary discourses and practices, sexual exceptionalism provides a new angle on the tensions between some of the more popular images of Paul and his epistles,[39] most especially when one turns to those two passages that are most commonly enlisted in contemporary debates about homosexuality: Romans 1:18–32 and 1 Corinthians 6:9–10. These texts are about much more than sexuality, constructing a racialized difference that is established by and interwoven within intersecting gender, sexual, and religious perversities. Such constructions allow for a paired movement: offering a certain kind of inclusion, but only through the targeting of such perverse figures for exclusion.[40] A corrective incorporation for some, then, is matched by a violent quarantine of others, to be isolated and extinguished. Revisiting these "clobber passages" from Paul's letters, then, requires attention to more than the naming of two viceful people among others (1 Cor 6:9), more than the relatively brief citation of females and males leaving behind "natural use" (Rom 1:26–27).

The longer of these passages is Romans 1:18–32, an extended us-versus-them argument that focuses on what "they" have done so wrong so as to cause a divine response of judgment. Indeed, Paul opens this section by arguing that the wrath or anger of God is already acting against these figures (1:18). Though they have known about (this) God (1:19–20), they refuse to give proper honor or thanks (1:21), turning to images of humans or other animals (1:23). The originating problem in this passage, then, is misplaced or misapplied divine knowledge, an obstinate turn from this deity to polytheistic practices.[41] The argument maps a certain kind of religious difference onto figures, whose difference is also marked as unreasonable: "they became futile in their thinking and their senseless minds were darkened" (1:21).

This characterization gives rise to a three-pronged chain of cause-effect arguments (1:23–30). Each time the constructed "they" exchange or change from what Paul thinks they should be doing (1:23, 25, 26), they are met by divine judgment, as God "hands them over" (*paradidōmi*, vv. 24, 26, 28) to punishment. (Many standard translations, like the RSV and NRSV, assign too neutral or passive a role to the deity: God "gives up" on them.) This chain, then, is seen as one explanation for those condemned to be overtaken by passions of dishonor (1:24, 26): their unreasonable religious difference is the cause of a gendered and sexual perversity. This deity hands both females and males among this "them" to passions away from the "natural use" (*psychikēn chrēsin*, vv. 26, 27) and (at least the females) toward a use that is *para physin* (v. 26), something that is contrary to, even *beyond* nature.[42] "Their females" (v. 26) are excessive and uncontrolled by their males, males who are consumed, or enflamed by passion with other males (v. 27). Yet, the originating problem is stressed even after the description of this sexualized effect, since the unwillingness to recognize this deity (1:28) leads to a third and final effect: God handing them over to a whole series of vices (1:29–31) and, ultimately, to death (1:32).

Thus, a common defensive approach to this text insists that this passage is not about sexuality, since the main problem is one of idolatry: the worship of things that are not (the right kind of) God.[43] This is the cause of these figures' condemnation; their sexual activities are merely a side-effect of this main problem, a side-effect (curiously enough) caused by this deity.[44] Yet, the choice of such sexual side-effects is striking and harder to avoid than this approach indicates. The argument is considerably reinforced by the nature of this negative effect. One knows that these figures, "them," or the Others, with misplaced divine knowledge, are condemned because of their specifically sexual and gender perversity. They are failed men because they do not make proper use of "their females" (1:26), because they lack control, and are consumed with passion for other males (1:27). These behaviors stand out because the argument specifically pulls these improperly erotic and gender aberrant actions out from the vice list that follows in 1:29–31, stressing that the sexual is symptomatic of the overall perversity of these Others. Such claims demonstrate the "stickiness" of these qualities of the condemned (the sexual, gender, and religious, eventually also connected to the racial, ethnic, national, and colonial); they stick to each other, even as the sexual especially sticks out to convey an exceptionalist message.[45] The letter's version of "us" will need to exercise certain constrained forms of austerity in order to avoid association with these Others and the apparently originating offense of religious difference.

In developing arguments on such terms, the letter attempts to produce properly loyal members (so long as they conform to the norms proposed) by deploying a scare figure that is not only religiously and sexually different but also perversely racialized. As has long been acknowledged, Paul is making use of certain stereotypes of Gentiles, those who are nationally and ethnoracially different from ancient Jews, in Romans 1. Stanley K. Stowers, for instance, notes that this letter's Gentile figure is "what moderns would call an ethnic cultural stereotype."[46] When stressing a primarily sexual or religious significance to this passage, interpreters underplay the specifically racialized component of this kind of argument (wherever it recurs). Here, Paul evokes an excessively impassioned and gender-troubled Gentile figure by connecting misapplied divine knowledge (1:19–23, 25) as idolatrous polytheism to loss of control and erotic contact not according to natural "use" (1:24, 26–27). Recognizing these sticky, intersecting factors and the overarching sexual exceptionalist resonance of these claims, then, can lead us to interrogate under what conditions the letter constructs communal belonging.

One can see how such arguments about these Others, operating as an external threat and a scare figure, can also shift to discipline those who should internalize these views. This accounts for how the arguments switch from an us-versus-them argument in 1:18–32 to address the "you," who might just be doing those things deserving of death (in 2:1–3). The audience must learn to contend even against the "enemy within," if they seek the sort of living promised by such arguments (or threatened by divine wrath and death). After all, Paul is constructing the monstrous figure of those who have improper relations to divine knowledge and are, thus, handed over to uncontrolled embodiment, unnatural uses, and unreasoned actions in general, in order to claim that he and his vision of the community are *not* like them. Paul's "us" are distinctive and, thus, superior to these rhetorically constructed Others, on the basis of properly intertwined religious, racial, and sexual relations (*not* doing what "they" have done). Pushing further into the letter's argument, Paul is arguing that this particular group he is constructing is distinctively excellent and deserving of divine favor, including "eternal life" (2:7) of glory, honor, immortality, and peace (2:7, 10). This is, by no means, a universal fate for all of the nations under Rome's rule, as indicated throughout Romans 1–2.[47] Paul's message is not so much transcending differences as repeating or repurposing them. Paul's version of the assembly community is disaggregated from other nations. One can only be folded into this (version of) communal life if one avoids the decline of civilization narrated in 1:18–32. One belongs among such eternal living on the basis of death for these scare-figure Others: "those who practice such things deserve to die" (1:32). God's wrath has been stalking the gender-troubled Gentile since at least 1:18, but even as the argument begins to offer life for some, the violence of divisions spills over into the following chapter, where Paul's (version of the) deity is also repeatedly promising judgment, wrath, and distress (vv. 3, 5, 8–9). The biopolitics of a Pauline population is installed through the necropolitical acts of (this version of) the divine: only some can be incorporated so long as these Others are quarantined, to be excluded and eliminated.[48]

In some ways, then, Paul's version of this community would be singularly exceptional, yet the standard set through these arguments ostensibly applies to more than just his implied audience. The letter cycles between minoritizing and universalizing perspectives.[49] When it comes to the issue of divine knowledge (the source of the religious difference here), Paul operates with a historico-mythological view where once all humans had the proper understanding of the divine (universalizing), but now only some, those in

Paul's version of "us" who have not turned away to idolatrous polytheistic practices, act appropriately on this knowledge (minoritizing). Rhetorically, though, this argument functions to stress the outcomes of *not* practicing in accordance with proper divine knowledge: it is the stereotyped fault of Gentiles (minoritizing), but it also implicitly threatens and warns all in an audience of what could happen if "you" turn away to other practices, associated with idolatry (universalizing).[50] The improper use of divine knowledge can be effectively associated with gender troubling and excessively erotic Gentiles (1:18–32), but this section of the letter only serves as part of a set-up to demonstrate that all in the audience are lacking unless they commit to Paul's version of the divine, as revealed through Jesus (the point to which the letter builds in 3:21–25).[51]

Even more specifically, Paul's arguments about the effects of excessive erotics (ostensibly caused by the inappropriate practices of divine knowledge) reflect a further coexistence of the minoritizing and universalizing models. It is, of course, seen as one punishing outcome for this "them," only they have been handed over to passions and excessive desires by the deity (minoritizing). Yet, when the argument shifts to address the second person ("you"), this difference between "us" and "them" seems to dissolve, as even you "are doing the very same things" (2:1). Even if one were to argue these "things" refer back to the vice list (in 1:29–31) and not to the particular erotic practices (of 1:26–27), the outcome of deadly judgment (1:32) threatens all (universalizing).[52] These practices stereotypically belong to only some (ostensibly "outside" of the assembly community), but they function as a threat to all within the assembly, requiring immediate and vigilant policing (now and in the future).[53] This cycling between minoritizing and universalizing arguments, then, strengthens the way this passage combines an externalized threat and internalizing control.

Reconsidering the opening chapters of Romans, and especially Romans 1:18–32, in the light of sexual exceptionalism complicates the uses of this passage and the letter overall. If one seeks a condemnation for certain sexual practices, this text might seem like a good candidate, but only if one is not troubled by the ethnoracial[54] and even interreligious consequences of repeating such arguments. On the other hand, if one wanted to focus on Paul's message of inclusion to Gentiles, one would have to recognize and then try to bracket the fraught, stereotyped figuration of the opening chapter. Yet, this scare-figure slips into the following chapters, as is the promise of wrathful judgment first exercised against them, making it difficult to put significant distance between Paul's version of inclusion and the violent exclusion on which it was built. Paul implicitly and then explicitly claims to do the correct religious, ethnic, erotic, and even imperial things, in the face of Others' excess. Their behaviors are especially indicative, then, of their intertwined gender, sexual, racial, and religious perversity.

The next most commonly cited passage from Paul's letters is 1 Corinthians 6:9–10, which contains a vice list, like and unlike the one found in Romans 1:29–31. In these contemporary conversations, though, the focus is hardly even on this relatively short list, but narrowed considerably to two out of the ten kinds of viceful people named, the *arsenokoitai* and *malakoi* (v. 9).[55] Such selective reading requires bypassing not only the eight other vices (including greed and drunkenness), but even the immediate emphasis made in these verses, since the list is both introduced and reconnected to the letter's argument by stressing that all of these will be excluded from the kingdom (or empire, *basileia*) of God (vv. 9 and 10). As in Romans, Paul's argument proceeds on the basis of judgment and exclusion, indicating that there is more to these middle chapters of 1 Corinthians than the condemnation of those who practice these two, or even ten types of vices.[56]

Indeed, interpreters often note the opening of chapter 5 as the point at which Paul turns to discussing sexual matters with the Corinthian community. Here Paul is outraged by a report he has apparently received about the community: "there is *porneia* among you, and of a kind that is not found among the Gentiles (or nations); for a man has his father's woman" (5:1).[57] It is unclear whether Paul is more upset by the sexual offense (*porneia*, a malleable term for sexual impropriety), or the fact that the offending party has not been removed from the community (5:2–5). Like the already condemned Others in Romans (as early as 1:18), this member is already judged by Paul (5:3) *in absentia*. Now, Paul calls on the Corinthians to "hand over" the offending member to Satan for his fleshly destruction, using the same verb for God's threefold action of "handing over" the Gentiles in Romans 1 (vv. 24, 26, and 28). The passage continues to stress the danger to the community if they do not differentiate and distance themselves from such parties, since their effect is like yeast, leavening all the dough (5:6–7). Insider-outsider dynamics preoccupy Paul here as well, since those "of this world" are defined by an inability to separate themselves from (or as) sexually immoral, or *porneiac* people (5:9–11). This requires greater vigilance among Paul's construction of Corinthian "insiders," who are exhorted to drive out the wicked among them, while God judges those outside (5:13).[58]

The severity of the opening case of *porneia* is marked by its comparative excess—it is not even done by Gentiles! This rhetorical flash depends on an ethnoracial assumption that these other people are (more) associated with problematic sexual difference, strange practices that at least one member of the Corinthian assembly has managed to exceed. Yet, because the other Corinthian assembly members have not done anything about this, what typically lurks outside now threatens from within. Paul's construction of this Corinthian "us," then, operates through a differentiation from the strangely sexual and gender-troubled Gentiles. As in Romans 1, this figuration of the Gentiles is also structured by the combination of religious and sexual impropriety, since one initial set of vices links idolatry with *porneia* (in both 5:10 and 5:11).[59] Still, even as a range of vices stick to each other (in this and other instances),[60] the sexual continues to stick out as symptomatic, since it is *porneia* that preoccupies Paul, the problem he persistently returns to it in this and the following chapter (ten times, in all: 5:1, 9, 10, 11; 6:9, 13, 15, 16, and twice in 18).

It is in the following chapter that Paul deploys the second vice list, the one that many selectively, yet compulsively, cite or recite. The themes of the fifth chapter continue, as Paul argues that those inside the Corinthian assembly, the holy ones (6:1, 2) should not be going to the courts of this world (6:1–8), run by the unrighteous (6:1; cf. 6:7, 8), most especially because "the holy ones will judge the world" (6:2). It is these unrighteous who will not inherit the kingdom (or empire) of God, those Paul describes further by reference to a second, and slightly longer vice list. The removal of the offending party (5:4–5, 13) and the persistent contrast of those outside others "in the world" (5:10; cf. 6:2–3) from those insiders who can be/come the kingdom (6:9–10) builds an image of the communal outsiders as a potential contagion. The assembly identity forwarded by this argument requires separating the members from these religious, sexual, and ethnoracial Others, and purifying themselves. The interrelation of gender, sexual, religious, national, and racial perversities is solidified by the clustering of the first five kinds of viceful people in the second list (6:9): the *porneiac*, the idolaters, the adulterers, the *malakoi* (morally soft or effeminate), and the *arsenokoitai* (rather uncertain, but potentially combining sexual and economic exploitation).[61] As with the previous vice list (5:10–11) and the more elaborate argument in Romans 1:18–32, idolatry as a religious problem also characterizes a national or ethnoracial group, the Gentiles, who are in turn figured as practicing other gender and sexual vices. Indeed, the vice of idolatry is sandwiched between the two vices with the clearest sexual connotations—*porneia* and *moicheia* (adultery). Fredrik Ivarsson convincingly argues that this distinctive association, "stereotypes the deviants as Gentiles, Paul's regular rhetorical scapegoats used for frightening his audience."[62]

While the vice list of 1 Corinthians 6:9–10 is a less developed, and perhaps less referenced, text than Romans 1 is, it reflects a similar cluster of factors for sexual exceptionalism. The text is clearly situated in a set of reflections and exhortations about how Paul wants the Corinthians to be unlike others, and differentiates again on the interrelated basis of sexual, gender, ethnic, racial, national, and religious difference (1 Cor 5–6). Their distinctiveness will mean an excellence that means entry into the kingdom (or empire) of God (6:9). Paul employs two vice lists (6:9–10 and 5:11) to contrast his version of us from these Others, to develop a boundary between those inside and outside the Corinthian assembly/ies (esp. 5:12–13). Since it is impossible to avoid these vices among outsiders, this construction of the compliant Corinthians underscores how much they would be quite the religious, racial, ethnic, ethical, and sexual exception from all others. The Corinthians should separate, disaggregate, not associate with these Others—whether they are Gentiles or even worse than them (5:1). The difference of these Others is exemplified by the symptomatic stickiness of the sexual to all other vices, but also the way the sexual again sticks out in the elaboration on *porneia* after the second vice list (6:12–20). This separation is one element of the incorporation of some in order to quarantine others: those who belong will have a resurrected life (6:14) in the divine *basileia* (6:9), but only if they drive out and hand over some, cast as too much like their Others (5:5, 13), for destruction and divine judgment (5:3, 5, 13; 6:9–10, 13).

Further, the vice lists in both Romans 1 and 1 Corinthians 6 are deployed to stress the potential dangers of slipping and sliding across the border and becoming (again) these Others. As noted previously, after its appearance in Romans 1:29–31, the argument turns to the "us" and suggests that "you" do the same things (2:1–3). After the list in 1 Corinthians 6:9–10, the argument recalls that "some of you were" these kinds of vice-ridden people before a cleansing and sanctification (6:11). Both of these texts set and remind the audience of the terms of their vulnerable, even precarious "inclusion," the specific ways in which they can be folded into the life of the assembly community and the promise of the kingdom or can be handed over for judgment and destruction. Such argumentation and figuration reflect how narrow the terms of acceptability are, posing threats internally and externally to the sexually exceptionalist regime. This underscores the paradoxical way in which this system reflects a singular and specific group (Paul's concept of the assembly community) and yet, based on this singularity, claims a certain universal jurisdiction for this deity and his earthly emissaries (Rom 1–3; 1 Cor 6:2–3). On the one hand, the scare-figure of the sexually strange and gender-troubled Gentile constructs and reinforces an exceptional identity for those not practicing such vices. On the other hand, the boundary between "us" and "them" is less permanent and more permeable than this apparent distinction posits.[63] After all, some in the Corinthian community do worse things than the Gentiles, at least some of the Gentiles "in Christ" were once like these viceful people, and, thus, everyone is in danger of slipping into a similar sticky association now or in the future!

More recent conceptualizations of sexual exceptionalism help interpreters trace these interrelated factors in both of these common "clobber" passages from Paul's letters. Both passages deploy a sexually exceptionalist stereotype of the Gentile, figured as an ethnoracial and religious foreigner, susceptible to gender and sexual trouble. This type of argument constructs both an externalized threat and an internalized discipline, a scare figure that encourages conformity to a constrained order of belonging. On the one hand, this demonstrates how these texts are about much more than sexuality, constructing a racialized difference that is established by and interwoven within intersecting gender, sexual, national, and religious perversities. On the other hand, the threat of judgment, exclusion, and death looms, within and without, because those deviant outsiders are targeted not just for a variety of aberrant practices but also for their sexual inferiority, even their barbarity. The sexual sticks to other practices and qualities, but it also sticks out.

This sort of argumentation certainly troubles the use of these letters for promoting a message of "inclusion," given its dependence on the exclusion of perverse figures. From this angle inclusion looks more like a corrective incorporation, a way to avoid the violent quarantine of Others who will be isolated and extinguished. However, if Paul is working so hard to get his audiences to dissociate themselves from other people, and used such stereotyped figurations of the barbarous foreigner, then what should one do with some of his more explicit claims, not only about Gentiles as Others, but also about barbarians? For instance, just a few breaths before breaking out this stereotype, invoking the wrath of God against such people in Romans 1:18–32, the letter describes him as in debt to both Greeks (Hellenes) and barbarians

(v. 14), and connects this obligation to his hope to evangelize among this audience in Rome (v. 15)! Paul's letters appear to adapt representations of ethnoracial Others as outsiders, foreigners, and even barbarians. It seems important, then, to clarify exactly what makes someone a barbarian anyway.

Barbarians, Among Other Perverse Figures

In many ways "barbarian" (*barbaros* in Greek, *barbarus* in Latin) is a relatively simple term, defined by a negation: barbarians are the foreign outsiders, the people "we" are not, for both Greek and eventually Roman imperial populations. In Thucydides, for instance, the barbarians were everyone but the Hellenes (or Greeks), once they were united (*History of the Peloponnesian War* 1.6.1, 5–6). This unification is actually a key aspect to the definition or, rather, the invention of the barbarian; constructing the polar opposite of the Greek helped to define a common Greek culture.[64] The Greek wars with the Persians earlier in the fifth century BCE were crucial in developing this stereotyped Other; it helped to justify unified military action among the many Hellenic peoples. In works like Aeschylus's *Persians*, then, barbarian meant Persian, even as "Persian" included all of the peoples subjected to the Persian Empire (see also Herodotus, *Histories*, 1.4.4). Barbarian was developed as a totalizing, oppositional category: barbarians were more than just non-Greeks, they were anti-Greeks.[65]

At first it was language that helped to define this fundamental difference between Greek and barbarian.[66] The term *barbaros* has this linguistic emphasis, since it conveys through onomatopoeia how a foreign and inferior speech sounds—*bar, bar*—like gibberish or what more recent people might call "baby talk."[67] Over time, however, the term was about more than language, as the Greeks applied it to people throughout the world. Other factors influence the development and maintenance of ethnic boundaries, including claims about common territory, shared descent, or religious practice.[68] Rituals played an important role in uniting members of a group, as Greeks emphasized the difference of their religious practice from the (even more) heterogeneous practices of barbarians.[69] These other elements could help mitigate the relative flexibility built into language as an ethnic marker. After all, if it depends primarily on language, ethnic difference could not be nearly as absolute or totalizing as many Greeks insisted, since the Greek language could be learned (as Herodotus recognizes in *Histories*, 1.57.1–3).

The Romans, of course, adapted this Greek concept of ethnoracial difference, particularly as their empire grew.[70] Cicero, for example, divided the world into *Italia, Graecia*, and *omnis barbaria* (*De finibus* 2.49; cf. *De divinatione* 1.84). As with the Hellenes, though, there was no one clear factor that differentiated the barbarian from the Roman.[71] While there were signs that both the Greeks and the Romans were aware of how flexible a category the barbarian was, the expanse and ideology of the Roman empire created special problems for the use of this category. In their efforts to conquer and their accompanying claims to incorporate those conquered within a larger hierarchical order, the Roman system involved routes for barbarians to become Roman, as subjects and even (occasionally) citizens.[72] Barbarians, then, are a source of Roman anxiety.[73] Many of their imperial cities, and Rome in particular depended on the traffic in people and/as goods between their center(s) and their various territories and peripheries. Barbarians are at once Romans' external and internal other. Roman-barbarian difference was constantly posed, negotiated, and transformed. The word "barbarian" had strong and clear connotations, but its points of reference were flexible, capacious, and at times ambiguous to the point of contradiction.

Such definitions were constructed, and anxieties managed, by reference to a range of embodied features and practices attributed to the barbarian peoples. Once again, gender and sexual difference stands out and sticks to such figures. Starting with the Greeks, other cultures were sexually deviant, characterized as promiscuous and incestuous.[74] For both the Greeks and the Romans, the barbaric east was persistently portrayed as effeminate.[75] Their gender and sexual difference, as evidenced by their servile, despotic, luxuriant culture, virtually mandated, at first Greek resistance to Asiatic peoples, but in time Roman imperial conquest and order. What once applied primarily to "the east" will be extended in Roman depictions of the northern barbarians, confirming the importance of sexual promiscuity to Roman stereotypes of their Others.[76] Yet, it was to the east that both Greeks and Romans repeatedly looked for barbarian figures of contrast, and dynamics of gender and sexuality marked their difference.

More recent discussions of sexual exceptionalism are relevant for rethinking the ancient figures in Paul's letters, in part, because ancient concepts of foreign barbarity have been important for analyzing historical patterns of racism and colonialism. Edward Said's best-known intervention into the latter traced elements of Orientalism back to Aeschylus's depiction of the Persians.[77] Scholars in classics have picked up on such interventions, similarly linking the past to the present. Edith Hall, for example, describes Aeschylus's *Persians* as "the first unmistakable file in the archive of Orientalism, the discourse by which the European imagination has dominated Asia ever since by conceptualizing its inhabitants as defeated, luxurious, emotional, cruel, and always as dangerous."[78] Here and elsewhere, Hall foregrounds the lasting influence of this conceptualization by foregrounding the operation of sexual and gender deviance in the characterization of foreign figures as barbarian. These dynamics will be adapted and perpetuated by the Romans. Thus, Iain Ferris also considers

> the possible linearity of Edward Said's concept of Orientalism as having its origins in the Greek world, with Roman attitudes towards the eastern barbarians again being part of the same rhetoric of power relations, mediated through the creation and manipulation of cultural, national and regional stereotypes. The negative qualities attributed to the Persians by the Greeks—their love of luxury, their effeminacy and so on—were subsequently redeployed by the Republican Romans.[79]

As with the Greeks before them and the Europeans and Americans much later, the Romans constructed the foreign Other as barbarian through a range of stereotypes that included problematic forms of gender and sexual variation.

These features of barbarians, then, can be fleshed out by their depictions with or as gender-variant females, effeminized males, eunuchs, and/or enslaved—precisely the figures Paul's letters have redeployed (and considered at greater length in the three previous chapters). Powerful or transgressive females are repeatedly associated with barbarians. Medea, for instance, is often depicted as a paradigmatic barbarian, not because she is from Colchis (east of the Black Sea), but because she is an out-of-control woman, enacting murderous and matricidal vengeance against her husband, the Greek hero Jason.[80] Indeed, as Hall stresses, whenever women get "out of hand" in Greek tragedies (as with Medea, Clytaemnestra, and Helen), they are associated with or identified as barbarians.[81] As I discussed earlier (in chapter 2), elite Romans carried similar anxieties about androgynous, gender-variant, or otherwise active or excellent females. Romans frequently insist on the foreignness of different gender and sexual practices, casting them as belonging to the east.[82] This, in part, accounts for why Romans borrowed Greek terms in depicting *tribades* and *cinaedi* as scare-figures: their gender and sexual difference are intertwined with their racial and regional difference. The female version of these transgressive sexual figures, the *tribades*, are depicted as non-Roman gender monsters, a way to define Roman imperial gender through those ethnoracial Others who are excessive and do the improper things in their erotic behaviors.[83] Though only certain, occasional gender variations are permitted among elite Roman females, for the most part female practices of androgyny or gender variation are cast in profoundly negative ways, and particularly as signs of the creeping influence of Rome's imagined Others from the east.

From the Roman imperial perspective foreign peoples were like women, in a subordinate gendered position.[84] Ferris traces the impact of this perspective on the visual culture of the empire, especially through the use of female barbarian figures. While these depictions were meant to demonstrate elite Roman imperial male potency, they also reflected a doubled anxiety, from within and without, as they "testified to a fear of female transgression and unsuitable behaviour, both by barbarian women and by the women of Rome and the empire."[85] Barbarian figures and practices could penetrate and infect those inside and ostensibly under the control of the empire. Yet, as Davina Lopez stresses, the empire did persistently personify the conquered and incorporated barbarian peoples as ethnoracially specific female or effeminized bodies.[86] The bodies on these statues and reliefs, then, reveal and display the barbarism of Rome's Others by their effeminacy and gender transgression, a barbarism that begs for Roman military intervention. Parthian males are depicted as eastern girlymen, while Gauls, Celts, and Galatians are quintessentially barbarian because they are gender outlaws.[87] When not represented as males, these nations are repetitively represented as women, sexually humiliated and used, and on the verge of being violently killed by the genuinely virtuous masculine Romans. These people, of course, are not permanently wiped out but, given the divine potency of the Roman empire, they are revived as subjects and incorporated into the extended family, the pious head of which is Augustus (and his various successors).[88] The dominated peoples will belong within this imperial order, so long as they acquiesce to its terms, generated by a specifically Roman imperial form of sexual exceptionalism. Transgressive or gender-troubled females (or whole, feminized peoples) are transformed and domesticated by and within the empire as family.

These barbarians were seen as like (problematic) women, not only because of their females but also because of their effeminized males. The Greeks repeatedly associated their eastern others as effeminate and luxurious. Problems with their transgressive women can even be explained by their relationships with effeminized males, as when Helen brings eunuchs back from Troy.[89] As I discussed earlier (in chapter 3), elite imperial Romans made similar associations with castrated males, as evidenced by their ridicule of *galli*. The *galli*, as castrated ritual figures connected to various mother goddess cults in Asia Minor and elsewhere, reflect a monstrously gendered figure: a body softened and opened to penetration, now a "half-man," *semivir*, as a result of a distinctive act of violation, a violation representative of their regional and religious difference. From the Roman imperial perspective these half-men embody such sexual and gender difference because of their specific religious behavior, the sort of behavior that typifies Rome's ethnoracial Others to the east. Indeed, to voluntarily undergo such an effeminization seemed barbaric to elite Roman males, even as the cult of Cybele reached the very center of Rome. Still, castration was widespread and well known, and the demand for enslaved eunuchs rose, despite various emperors' attempts to prohibit the operation. Such laws only reinforced claims that castration was distinctly non-Roman, happening outside of the empire, so that eunuchs could only be "foreign" exports in the larger slave trade. When combined with this association with "eastern" religious practices and stories, such claims cemented the notion that eunuchs are particularly foreign and barbarian.

The eunuch's altered and often ambiguous genital capacity confounded elite Romans: did their loss of "masculinity" make them asexual, or desirable for penetration, or capable of surreptitious penetration? The last of these options indicates a worrisome possible similarity with elite Roman women: their desire for and ability to have improper and undetected sex.[90] Thus, they remain a constant source of anxiety and explicitly sexualized ridicule. They are commonly associated with *cinaedi*, stereotypically effeminate dancing easterners who play receptive sexual roles; the unmanning castration of the *galli* is often cast as the eventual destination for the *cinaedi*. This sort of slippery-slope argument—comparing effeminate and/or sexually receptive males as *cinaedi*, and then *galli*—has led Craig Williams to suggest that the castrated *gallus* was "the ultimate scare-figure of Roman masculinity."[91] Indeed, the three scare-figures of the *galli*, *cinaedi*, and *tribades* share several things in common, most especially the way they figure perversities that weave gender and sexual difference with ethnoracial and regional difference. All three are persistently associated with or as the foreign and barbarian Other. Like the *tribades* and *galli*, the *cinaedus* intertwines multiple aspects as a term of insult and ridicule (or threat and warning), condemning its target for being foreignly Eastern, effeminately penetrable, and disgracefully gendered (as a dancer).[92] Like *tribas*, the Latin term *cinaedus* was borrowed from the Greek *kinaidos*, with additional potential etymological connections to Asia Minor. Williams stresses how all of these qualities "stuck" to this derogatory term: "the image of an effeminate Eastern dancer lurked behind every description of a man as a *cinaedus* in the transferred sense, and that behind the Eastern dancer in turn lurked the image of the *gallus*."[93]

Eastern, foreign, barbarian cultures and their influences are typified by these kinds of figures. Enslaved people might be less obviously associated with the barbarian or foreign Other to Greeks and eventually Romans, but the stereotype that other people are best suited for enslavement is a persistent one. Aristotle, for instance, maintained that the barbarian and the enslaved have the same nature, thus demonstrating that barbarian peoples should serve as slaves to Greeks.[94] Indeed, when free and Hellenic became synonymous, so too did servile and barbarian.[95] The other, typically gendered, sexualized, and racialized faults of the barbarian foreigner can be related back to their inability to master or control themselves.[96] They are enslaved to their bodies and their passions. This is why their women are out of control, why some would castrate themselves, or ultimately, why they cannot keep others from castrating them. In this last instance they may have had no legal right to control their own body. Indeed, many of the eunuchs discussed earlier would also have been enslaved, made by or acquired for owner-users for a variety of purposes including sexual uses (described in chapter 4). This extended in the Roman imperial period, when enslaved people were associated with their wars of expansion and incorporation. Conquered peoples were one of the main sources for the slave system, and Romans often depicted these subject peoples as enslaved. Cicero, for instance, describes Syrian Greeks and Jews as "nations born to slavery" (*On the Consular Provinces*, 5.10). Peoples who opposed them militarily were often imagined as mostly slaves, as the Romans claim about the Parthians.[97] These associations were typically not based on any kind of military intelligence or ethnographic knowledge beyond the kinds of stereotyped notions about barbarian figures I have briefly surveyed. Roman victory, imperial rule, and penetrating power were evidence enough that the foreign outsider, now mostly incorporated inside the empire from below or on the bottom, was a gender, sexual, racial, and imperial inferior.

Exceptionalism Rules

This ancient barbarology is also, anachronistically, an ancient kind of sexual exceptionalism. Barbarians in all of their various, yet intertwined gender, sexual, ethnoracial, regional, and even religious difference are key figures in a Greco-Roman and ultimately Roman imperial form of sexual exceptionalism. These are the figures that help to prove that the Romans are the exception who should rule. The foreigners' sexual, gender, and racial inferiority are the flip side of the Roman imperial elite who maintain their own exceptional superiority on the basis of their sexual standards and gendered activities.[98] The Romans justified their empire through arguments about their distinctive excellence in the areas of erotic conduct and, thus, ethnoracial status. Their conduct was directed by a Priapic protocol, where Romans demonstrate that they are real men by only playing the insertive, or penetrative role in erotic activities.[99] This prime directive of penetration is exercised by making use of proper receptacles, on which there were very few limits, particularly if the elite Roman used enslaved people, prostitutes, or noncitizens of either sex. With the rise of the Roman empire, these groups were often composed of populations from outside of the Italian peninsula, outsiders yes, but also foreigners. Among the less problematic receptacles for sexual use, then, were the kinds of figures I have considered in successive chapters: foreigners, enslaved, eunuchs, and women.

A good Roman (free, adult, male, citizen, and elite) demonstrated that he was unlike these imperial subjects and social inferiors because he was the kyriarchal exception, part of a relatively small group of people who can be, in the words of Jonathan Walters, "the impenetrable penetrators."[100] Such ruling groups are protected from any "invasion of the boundaries of the body," because they exercise such invasions and boundary-crossings not only on the bodies of Others, but also on larger, geographical bodies (pornotropics).[101] As Amy Richlin has argued, such a worldview constructs a particularly gendered and sexualized image for the empire as a whole: "the Roman projection of Rome as a male fucking the rest of the world."[102] The Romans are an empire, because they are hard, impermeable, impenetrable, and inviolable.[103] Within this context they are sexually exceptional; they are unlike all Others who cannot protect and keep their own boundaries, on their persons and in their places.

This inability to exercise the particular imperial sexual comportment is what marks barbarians, or really all but the Roman imperial males as "non-men," or "unmen."[104] Not all males are men, since the Priapic protocol reflects and maintains a kyriarchal sociopolitical order.[105] As Stephen Moore describes it:

> In the centre of the circle or at the apex of the pyramid, were adult free males, supremely, though not exclusively, those of high social standing (rulers, magistrates, heads of elite households, patrons, etc.), while around them, or below them, were others who, each in their own way, were conceived as *unmen*, or at least as *not fully men* (women, youths, slaves, "effeminate" males, eunuchs, "barbarians," etc.).[106]

Thus, the colonizing (mostly) male authority can claim his superiority, virtue, and civilization by extolling sexual norms (of his own establishment) that the sexually savage or debased colonized people apparently do not embody.[107] Their aberration proves the necessity, even the elevated benefit, of imperial-colonial forces. Their rule claims to bring order by incorporating these Others into their imperial-colonial system. An ethics and politics of "hardness" are paired with the claim that other peoples were soft, strange, and even savage, sexually aberrant and uncontrolled—manifest signs of Roman superiority. These contrasts in bodily comportment coincide with ethnoracial and religious differentiations: by showing that they are the right and righteous people, guided by the right gods in their conduct, then, the Romans claimed a religious and cultural right to bring the progress of their own civilization to other lands and peoples.

The Roman imperial sexual exceptionalism maintains itself, then, through claims about "themselves" *and* their "Others." Those who were "outside of" the Roman imperial order, but are eventually folded within this order, but as those below, or on the bottom (in more than one sense of that word), are characterized as backward and perverse. Peoples from the Romans' east are seen as particularly soft and effeminate, so much so that it is commonplace to associate these elements (foreignness, the East, and effeminacy) as one rhetorical complex.[108] Indeed, one way a Roman orator might try to rally fellow Romans against potential decadence would be by arguing that they have begun to decline due to too much contact with those from the East.

Thus, this imperial sexual exceptionalism operates by calling on various scare-figures of barbarian or foreign difference, again, much like the figures I have been considering throughout this book. These figures justify Roman imperial superiority, but also work to discipline both ruling and subject populations (in different, and hierarchically differentiated ways). This imperial-erotic protocol explains how the Romans can incorporate these Others, while providing key rationales for maintaining internalized modes of control over these subjects. Such figurations provide, then, not only their favorite ways to portray distant Others, the barbaric peoples they "save" by killing and enslaving them, but also the stock elements within their own rhetorical and political struggles over who resides at the exceptional apex of the empire.[109] That Julius Caesar was insultingly portrayed as a *cinaedus*, Augustus a *gallus*, elite Roman matrons as *tribades*, and countless emperors and elite figures baited as excessive and effeminate in some way or another, using castrated and (or as) enslaved bodies too much (among other things), all indicate the centrality of the specifically gendered and sexual exceptionalism at the heart of Roman imperial ideology.[110] It was exceptionally difficult, then, to demonstrate an exceptional mastery of self and Others, to guard against the influence of so many unmanly, feminine, receptive, and barbaric figures.

An Unexceptional Paul

One can find places where Paul's letters are attempting to displace Roman imperial views, perhaps especially their claims of ethnoracial and religious superiority. However, Paul's (albeit minoritarian) challenge to his imperial setting shows far more signs of the influence of these barbarologies on his letters' sexual exceptionalism. As I argued earlier, Paul's letters reflect their own kind of sexual exceptionalism, but I have now shown that they were hardly distinctive or exceptional in this regard in the ancient Mediterranean setting.[111] These letters inherit a common ethnoracial, gender, and sexual heritage that can be traced back to the Greeks and most especially Roman imperial adaptations. His persistent deployment of Gentiles as ethnoracially sexualized scare-figures reflects how much his rhetorical tendencies are steeped in this rather dominant and relatively common background. Reflecting primarily on the vice lists in 1 Corinthians, Ivarsson is right to highlight how this figuration "stereotypes the deviants as Gentiles, Paul's regular rhetorical scapegoats used for frightening his audience."[112] This characterization of Paul's rhetorical habits fits not only 1 Corinthians 5–6, and not only the other "clobber passage" of Romans 1:18–32, but also several other passages in these and in other letters.[113]

In Galatians, for instance, Jews and Gentiles are juxtaposed to each other with a formulaic allusion to "Gentile sinners" (2:15), before Paul frets about the possibility of the Gentile audience turning back to their prior enslavement to elements that were not gods (4:3, 8–9). As discussed in chapter 3, this return is intertwined with how Paul persistently returns to his anxieties about flesh, as the location of desire (5:13, 16) and seat of many vices, again including both sexual immorality (*porneia*) and idolatry (5:19–20). Indeed, he claims to have warned the Galatians about this previously (5:21), suggesting that they have long been susceptible to such vices, practices that would (again) exclude them from the kingdom (5:21). In 1 Thessalonians, the audience had also turned to God from idols (1:9), but must make efforts to abstain from *porneia* (4:3) to demonstrate their belonging. The male audience members, then, should acquire an appropriate vessel (or receptacle) for their penetrating practices (4:4). The importance of these patterns is driven home by a now familiar negative point of contrast, to behave "not with lustful passion, like the Gentiles who do not know God" (4:5). The Gentiles' sexual and gender disorder are directly related to their religious difference (ignorance of God).

Concerns about passion, flesh, and the assembly members' prior lives recur in other sections of both Romans and the Corinthian correspondence.[114] Later in his letter to the Romans, Paul describes how Jesus altered the "old self," a sinful body, once enslaved to sin, but now destroyed (Rom 6:6). Still, a certain weakness in the flesh persists, akin to the time when these Gentiles presented "their body parts as slaves to impurity" (6:19; cf. 6:13). When they were slaves to sin (6:17, 20), they were destined for death (6:21).[115] This sin regularly reflects an embodied lack of control: obeying the passions of their bodies (6:12), when they were living in the flesh and led by their sinful passions (7:5). It is only by their current enslavement to (Paul's version of) God that they will have eternal life (6:22). As in 1 Corinthians, they were not always this way: once they were low and despised (1:28). Now, however, they must attend to examples that link idolatry and sexual immorality (10:7–14). Paul implores his Gentile audience to not become idolaters (10:7), whose most obvious sign is engaging in sexual immorality (the verbal form of *porneia*, 10:8), and leads to the immediate death of tens of thousands. In case it is at all unclear to whom these warnings were directed, Paul again reminds the audience: "when you were Gentiles, you were led to idols" (12:2). In his second letter to the Corinthians, Paul still worries that those who sinned previously will not have turned away from sexual immorality

(2 Cor 12:21). This *porneia* is a characteristic part of the Gentile assembly member's past, always threatening to break back into their present.

Thus, these two passages (ostensibly "about homosexuality," Rom 1 and 1 Cor 5–6) are themselves far from exceptional, even within these letters. They may stand out in citational practices now, but they do not stand apart from these repeated rhetorical tendencies. Indeed, all of these letters reflect a troubling tendency to figure Gentiles as barbarian foreign Others, their barbarity typified by the interlocking marks of their gender, sexual, ethnoracial, and religious difference. One can notice disturbing echoes of this pattern in more recent figurations of the monster-terrorist-fag. As one potential set of ancient predecessors, then, Paul's letters reflect and perpetuate this worldview, expressing an anxiety, even fear that the Gentiles (in Christ) are particularly prone to fall back into such practices. Paul's letters grapple with, but also maintain the specter of, this past, a past that is not yet past for all of the other Gentiles who live alongside and all around the Jews and Gentiles (in Christ) in these assembly communities.

The ancient figures considered throughout this book—gender-variant females, castrated males, sexually available slaves—fold into and fill out figurations of the barbarian and foreign Other. By this point these figures are overlapping and even piling up, but so have some alternative angles on those people addressed by such rhetorical practices in Paul's letters. In short, we are not left with these dominant images. It is important to resituate these oft-cited texts in an ancient Roman imperial setting that is shaped more by concerns about sexual exceptionalism than more recent notions of sexual orientation. Yet, to stay there would mean leaving the fraught ethnoracial, religious, sexual, and gender claims about Rome's and then Paul's Others as barbarian uncontested.[116]

Thus, the value of the preceding chapters for this one is demonstrated not only by the range of ancient figurations considered, but also by the alternative angles proposed for approaching these letters and the people addressed by them again. Indeed, the first chapter to consider one of these figurative practices in greater depth treated another flashpoint passage in one of the letters examined here—1 Corinthians. At first glance, one might be inclined to think a discussion of the role of women's speech and their head hair practices (in places like 1 Cor 11, as well as 1 Cor 14) is somewhat distanced from claims about Gentile gender trouble, sexual sin, and ethnoracial difference.[117] Yet, backtracking to those middle chapters of the letter, *porneia* is the persistent vice that stalks and sticks to the Gentile addressees of the letter.

The arguments that follow the second vice list focus especially on *porneia* as a problem of contact with sexually immoral females (often translated as prostitutes, 6:15, 16). Moments later in the letter, Paul tries to manage a situation in which females have withdrawn from sex and marriage (with males) (7:1–11, 25–40).[118] On the one hand, this could be one indication of how much these (Gentile) females sought to avoid or even counteract the association of sexual misconduct with (their) ethnoracial and religious difference. On the other hand, this kind of effort could only strengthen the gendered components of the stereotyped barbarian figure from an elite Roman imperial perspective: these females are out of control, because they are not under the control of the males.

This withdrawal from sex, then, could be rhetorically linked to the depiction of prophesying females as engaging in a negative type of androgyny, in gender-variant activities that need to be condemned and controlled. The letter focuses on the role of women's speech in both 1 Corinthians 11 and 14. The former I have considered at length in chapter 2, but the latter specifies limits to female speech in the assembly community, enjoining females to be silent in assembly gatherings (14:34) and to ask their men (or husbands) in their own homes if they have any questions (14:35). These arguments strengthen the previous limits on their speech (made in 11:2–16), by linking it with the advice to be married and sexually available (7:2–5, 9–16, 28, 36, 38). In this instance, though, Paul emphasizes the importance of a gendered "order" that limits confusing or just enthusiastic participation in the assembly community (14:26–40).[119] The entire chapter attempts to reclassify prophecy and speaking in tongues into a particular hierarchical order (14:1–40), ostensibly to promote good order and prevent uncertainty, chaos, and confusion.

It should come as no surprise, then, that Paul turns explicitly to the figure of the barbarian in asserting these claims of a gendered order and the proper place of sexually strange females in an assembly with Gentiles (in Christ). From this point of view, the problem with inspired speech, as with speaking in tongues, is ignorance about the meaning of such speech, with the result that "I will be a barbarian (*barbaros*) to a speaker, and the speaker a barbarian (*barbaros*) to me" (1 Cor 14:11).[120] In the frame set by the letter and the ancient figurative practices it redeploys, it would be horrifying for Paul and any acquiescent assembly member to become a barbarian (again). It is precisely this fate, a lapse back to their previous state, that Paul has evoked as a scare tactic for his Gentile audience members, often through allusions to an interlocking gender, sexual, ethnoracial, and religious difference. The barbarian has its roots in claims of linguistic and thus intellectual inferiority, but this hierarchical difference was strengthened and maintained by its intersectional qualities.[121] In isolation this sentence might appear only as a fleeting reference to the former, but in the larger setting of this section of the letter (14:1–40), and in its reliance on arguments from previous sections, this barbaric speaker hearkens back to a figure that haunts audiences for these interwoven reasons.

Paul's letters persistently redeploy a figuration of the Gentiles as barbaric and foreign Others, particularly through their inclinations toward gender trouble and sexual sin, but they also explicitly use the Greek term *barbaros* in two passages. Indeed, the only two letters in which Paul uses this term are those I have been treating in this chapter—Romans and 1 Corinthians! This might be coincidental, but it could be more important for understanding these letters, the figures deployed within them, and those addressed by them, as this link is certainly clearer than more recent claims that these two letters can be combined to provide people a coherent Pauline "stance on homosexuality."

One finds the other explicit reference to barbarians, then, by returning to the opening chapter of the letter to the Romans. In a somewhat typical thanksgiving section, Paul apologetically explains how he has often hoped to come to the Roman assembly community (1:13). (This feature is one thing that makes the letter atypical, since it is written to a community Paul has not previously visited.) The audience is at least partially identified by his desire to reach them as a group "among the rest of the Gentiles" (1:13). It would be hard to claim, then, that the following deployment of the Gentile scare-figure in 1:18–32 would have nothing to do with the community there (as Paul understands, or at least imagines them). This desire to evangelize among them as Gentiles and specifically as those who are in Rome (1:15), then, is tied to a debt to both Greeks (*Hellēnes*) and to barbarians (*barbaroi*), both the wise and the foolish (1:14). This division of people was not only a Greek product but also a common Roman way of thinking. Cicero, for instance, divided the world into the Roman homeland (*Italia*), *Graecia*, and *omnis barbaria* (the barbarian world).[122] Thus, other Roman imperial-era Jewish writers used a similar tripartite distinction between Jews, Greeks, and barbarians.[123] Paul's seemingly straightforward division of a "them" to whom he must reach and preach into Greeks and barbarians reflects a common ethnoracial and imperial worldview. As I noted earlier, Paul's letters might seek to contest the religious primacy and ethnoracial superiority claimed by the Romans, yet they repeat and reuse these terms for their own sexually exceptionalist purposes. It is no coincidence, then, that Paul launches into his extended us-versus-them argument moments later by highlighting Gentile religious difference (idolatry) and their corresponding gender and sexual difference as divine punishment (1:18–32).

In returning to this passage, it is also helpful to have briefly recalled the gender-variant females reflected in the arguments of 1 Corinthians. Indeed, for those currently seeking a condemnation of both male *and female* same-sex conduct, Romans 1:18–32 is an essential text (since none of the other most common "clobber passages" allude to female–female behavior).[124] The punishment these idolatrous Gentiles receive is that "their females exchanged natural use [*chrēsis*] for (use) contrary to (or in excess of) the natural" (Rom 1:26). There are several things to notice about this brief clause, but the first is the identification of "their females," the possessive adjective emphasizing that *those* females are not *our* females, but they belong to *them*. Further, as one might recall from the discussion of the term *chrēsis* (in chapter 4, earlier), what counts as proper sexual activity, a natural kind of "use" of another, is how much it corresponds to the larger kyriarchal order that places elite, free, imperial males over women and (or as) enslaved, and (or as) conquered, and (or as) castrated, and (or as) barbaric foreigners. Leaving behind a "natural use," then, would mean that these females, these social inferiors, are once again out of control, most especially because they are not under the control of their social superiors, certain kinds of males. "Their" in "their females" reminds that they are an ethnoracial group characterized by the inability of their males to control their (supposed) inferiors. This echoes with the kinds of arguments deployed about and against females in 1 Corinthians, especially since both Romans 1 and 1 Corinthians 11 rely on ancient ideas of "nature" (Rom 1:26; 1 Cor 11:14), in order to naturalize a hierarchical difference.[125]

Paul's letters, then, reflect a particular anxiety, even defensiveness, about female participation and leadership; but it might also be time to consider this anxiety as intersecting with claims about Jews and Gentiles (in Christ) in these assembly communities. Do these repeated figurative practices indicate that this is an accusation or just a stereotyped figuration that these assembly communities have encountered before?[126] As my previous reflections on gender-variant females (in chapter 2) demonstrate, even having active or otherwise prominent females could draw just such attention from audiences conditioned by such rhetorics. The overlapping ways in which such claims operate in figurations of the barbaric and foreign Other indicate that this may not be an issue only for those letters (like 1 Cor) that discuss female leadership in prophecy, prayer, and austerity.

Some Alternative Assembly Required

It may not be coincidental, then, that Paul opens his letter to the Romans with allusions to his audience including barbarians, before developing a sexually exceptionalist scare-figure of troubled Gentiles, and claiming that his audience were once enslaved to their sinful flesh and passions, before closing with a lengthy set of greetings for or about specific females in the assembly community at Rome.[127] In the first sixteen verses of chapter 16, Paul cites no less than twenty-five community members by name and several more (indicated explicitly as one's mother or sister [vv. 13, 15] and implicitly in groups of assemblies, households, brethren, and holy ones [vv. 5, 10, 11, 14, 15]).[128] Among them, there are at least ten women, a number of solitary figures, six pairs, and several groups.[129] The sheer number of people greeted or named in this section indicates how much Paul needs to show his ties to such figures (better) known in the assembly community at Rome, a number that reflects not only Paul's potential anxiety (about his position, the authority of women, and any association with eastern or barbaric difference) but also an opportunity to take an alternative angle to the figures addressed by Paul's ethnoracial repetition of a sexualized scare figure.

Feminists have long noted the number and prominence of women in this section of greetings. Though the details about these women are often rather slight, they provide glimpses of other perspectives, and serve as specific reminders that the arguments in these letters represent the views of only one person out of many in these networks.[130] Indeed, Paul would have depended on so many of these other people in order to do his work, something the letter cannot avoid in noting in sections like these. For instance, the greetings section begins with his commending Phoebe, the likely carrier of this letter to the Romans. Paul describes her as a benefactor (*prostatis*) to many in the movement, including himself (16:2).[131] When she is first introduced, though, he stresses that she was a *diakonos* ("deacon") of the assembly at Kenchreae. In another link to the community at Corinth, then, Phoebe is a leader in the community at Corinth's eastern seaport. This leading female figure would not have been the (primary) audience for this letter, though she could have been the one who delivered and even recited it to (some of) its first recipients in Rome.

The letter anticipates that plenty of other people will be in the assembly community at Rome, starting with greetings to Prisca and Aquila (16:3–5). Given the patriarchal tendency to name males before females in such pairings, it is striking that Prisca is named before her (presumed) husband and partner in evangelizing here (16:3, and elsewhere, in Acts 18:18, 26). This suggests that she is of greater importance in these communities than Aquila. Paul presumes multiple assembly communities will know both Prisca and Aquila, since he also sends greetings from them and the assembly in their house toward the end of 1 Corinthians (16:19). It is possible, then, that he starts these greetings with them because he already knows them. Indeed, he stresses their history together by describing them as coworkers (16:3) "who risked their necks for my life, to whom not only I but also all of the assemblies of the Gentiles give thanks" (16:4). This brief narration about Prisca and Aquila highlights the risk involved in working within this movement. As with Phoebe's benefaction, though, the letter stresses more than just a connection to Paul, since many more besides Paul apparently give thanks to Prisca and Aquila. Indeed, given the previous discussion of how Romans and other letters characterize Gentiles, it is particularly intriguing that Paul claims here that "all of the assemblies of the Gentiles" also give thanks to them.

In reintroducing this ethnoracial difference within the assembly communities, Paul aims to position Prisca, Aquila, and ultimately himself in specific ways. Given the brevity of these greetings, though, it is relatively difficult to situate Prisca and Aquila without reference to later texts, like Acts 18, with their own, distinctive, even unreliable rhetorical aims.[132] Acts, for instance, describes Aquila as a Jew from Pontus (18:2), a region in Asia Minor, a description many biblical scholars follow.[133] From a Roman imperial perspective, then, Aquila comes from the east, living among the barbaric subject peoples. Yet, Acts also claims that Prisca and Aquila came to Corinth because they had been expelled from Rome when the emperor Claudius ordered that all Jews must leave the city (in 49 CE). According to Suetonius the proximate causes of this order were "the disturbances at the instigation of Chrestus" (*Claudius* 25), a likely reference to Christ (or *Christos*, in Greek). According to Acts 18, then, Aquila is from an eastern Roman province and has returned to a different Roman *colonia* in the east. Though Acts is not exactly dependable, Paul's greetings in both Romans 16 and 1 Corinthians 16 indicate that he knows Prisca and Aquila from his own prior experiences in the east, that many others in the east know them, and that the pair have since traveled (or returned) to Rome from the east and are (already) recognized in the assembly communities there.[134]

Still, Prisca's own ethnoracial status or origins are moderately difficult to establish. It is unknown if she was Jewish (as is presumed about Aquila), but Prisca is a common Latin name, with ties to the noble Roman clan *gens* Acilia. The name only tells interpreters so much about Prisca's economic status, though, since it could indicate that she was a freedperson from this Roman family.[135] Yet, even with these sketchy details about the people in this pairing, there is a hint of a Jewish-Gentile partnership within these early assembly communities.[136] If they were a wife and husband team, this partnership also combined gendered, sexualized, and evangelizing (or religious) aspects. Even if one presumes that Prisca must have been Jewish (because her husband Aquila was), Paul describes them as important to all of the assemblies of the Gentiles, indicating the relational ties between Jews and Gentiles (in Christ). Paul briefly greets the assembly in their house (16:5), indicating the possibility that they assembled Gentiles alongside (at least some) Jews in whatever space they had in their quarters.[137]

After two brief greetings to Epaenetus and to Mariam (whose names likely reflect Greek and Jewish backgrounds, respectively), Paul sends slightly longer greetings to another male-female pair, Andronicus and Junia. Here, Paul describes them as "my kin and my fellow prisoners, they are outstanding among the apostles, and they were in Christ before me" (16:7). Since the time of Martin Luther, mostly malestream interpreters have been anxious about the second clause in this greeting, since it names the female Junia as an apostle—and distinguished, or outstanding among them at that! Many modern translations have tried to correct this "mistake" by masculinizing her name to Junias, but starting with Bernadette Brooten, scholars have demonstrated quite simply, yet pointedly, "that we do not have a single shred of evidence that the name *Junias* ever existed."[138] Indeed, the Latin female name Junia is extraordinarily well attested, within and beyond Rome. Though it may stand out in the kyriarchal Christian imagination, the passing reference to this woman as a distinguished apostle very much fits within this series of greetings in which other women have already been commended as deacons, benefactors, coworkers, and assembly leaders.

Yet, this reference to the apostle Junia is not the only interesting aspect to this sentence. As with Prisca earlier, Junia is a prominent Latin family name, so Junia was possibly also a freedperson, or perhaps a descendant of someone freed by a Roman of this clan.[139] Paul's description of Andronicus and Junia as kin or relatives likely meant that they were also Jews.[140] Paul also knows them from their prior experiences in captivity together, an imprisonment that must have happened in the east. Last, but certainly not least, Paul explicitly admits that they preceded him in this movement. If the tradition behind Acts 18 is at all reliable, then both of these couples—Junia and Andronicus, and Prisca and Aquila—were members of these assemblies before Paul. These names are brief reminders that this movement and these assemblies preexist Paul and his letters. When looking for alternative angles on those people addressed by figurations like that of the sexually barbaric Other, it is vital to remember that people likely assembled and organized in ways besides those Paul promotes. This possibility is easier to imagine when the priority and preexistence of people beside Paul are plain to see in passages like Romans 16, precisely because he writes to so many people in the community at Rome, a place he still only anticipates visiting.

It is also striking that Junia and Andronicus are also described as being prisoners with Paul in the past. The dangers of life in these assembly communities are reflected in these experiences of imprisonment. Discussion of imprisonment and Paul's letters often focus on Paul's imprisonment, Paul's risks, Paul's precariousness,[141] but the brief allusions to Junia and Andronicus in prison, and Prisca and Aquila's risk help to decenter and pluralize the significance of precariousness in these assembly communities. Paul uses a clear colloquialism for risking execution by decapitation when he argues that Prisca and Aquila "risked their necks for my life" (16:4).[142] Even if exaggerated, such a strong image indicates the mortal risks involved in active and prominent participation in this movement.[143] Both of these pairings, then, are greeted with indications of the necropolitical precarity of life for leading figures in these assembly communities.

This initial survey of just a few of the women named in the greetings indicates both their prominence and precarity.[144] These qualities might be conceptually linked—these women might have been regarded with suspicion by anyone influenced by the Roman imperial mindset toward women from the barbaric east acting in gender-variant fashion. This suspicion could have been reinforced by the way these communities assembled members from a variety of positions and backgrounds with lower status. Indeed, after the greetings to Andronicus and Junia, the references to other named and unnamed figures in the assembly community at Rome pick up in pace, most receiving only a clause or two of attention (16:8–13) before Paul simply begins listing groups of five (or more) at a time toward the end (16:14–15). Two groups are identified as "those belonging to Aristobulus" (16:10) and "those belonging to Narcissus" (16:11), demonstrating that two sets of enslaved (or freed) people, but not their named owner-users, were recognized in the assembly community at Rome.[145] Indeed, after Prisca and Junia, quite a few of the figures in this section bear names associated with enslaved (or freed) people, including Ampliatus (v. 8), Herodion (v. 11), Tryphaena and Tryphosa (v. 12), Persis (v. 12), Hermes (v. 14), Julia (v. 15), and Nereus (v. 15).[146] As previous chapters have discussed, in a kyriarchal household these assembly members would have been vulnerable to their master-owner's uses, including sexual uses. Given such uses, some of these enslaved males could also have been castrated, a possibility strengthened if their names reflect an eastern origin (since Romans often claimed castrations were not performed in the imperial center, see chapter 3). We cannot know if their owner-masters made such uses of them, but these also cannot be ruled out—a stark reminder of the kyriarchal structures in which these people lived.

While most of those listed after Andronicus and Junia are greeted individually, three pairs are mentioned: Tryphaena and Tryphosa (v. 12), Rufus and his mother (v. 13), and Nereus and his sister (v. 15). If one dwells over these for a moment, the first stands out from the other pairings since they link two women together. Interpreters typically assume that male-female evangelizing pairs are partners in marriage and in mission (as with Prisca and Aquila, and Andronicus and Junia, earlier), unless otherwise specified (as with Rufus and his mother). Is it reasonable to infer that Typhaena and Tryphosa are more than just "workers in the lord" (v. 12) together? Mary Rose D'Angelo has considered precisely this question by closely examining them, and two other female-female pairs, in the context of re-cut funerary reliefs in the Augustan era.[147] If these women were both freedwomen,[148] they may have been *conlibertae*, freed together, and bound together in this process.[149] Their similar names could be a marker of the same owner-user. Indeed, the voluptuous or luxurious connotation of their names (derived from the same Greek verb, *tryphaō*) could even indicate the sexual tasks they were given when enslaved, possibly even as sex workers.[150] Their choice to stay together and work together after manumission may have also been a sexualized choice.[151]

If one focuses only on the potential homoeroticism of this female-female pair in the assembly community at Rome, then one might consider the condemnation, embedded in the letter's opening, of "their women" for departing from "natural use" (1:26) as a defensive or apologetic gesture, an attempt to dissociate his audience from this commonly denigrated practice.[152] Yet, both the opening and the closing of this letter demonstrate something even more complicated, if still related to this inference. The first chapter deploys an ethnoracial stereotype of a barbarically sexualized Other, and this final chapter refers to a range of women and men, who were free, freed, and enslaved, Jews and Gentiles, most of whom were from the east. The assembly communities at Rome are characterized by the intertwining of their gender, sexual, economic, ethnoracial, regional, and religious difference. Just as the ancient image of the barbarian is, in part, constituted and reinforced by images of gender-variant females, castrated or otherwise effeminized males, and enslaved peoples, so this mostly-Gentile audience was composed of people who lived on the lower ends of a range of kyriarchal hierarchies. It is no wonder, then, that participation in this sort of movement involved serious risks, including incarceration and execution. Indeed, it would account for why a sexualized scare-figure of barbaric difference is deployed, but it is difficult to reduce this simply to an argument about sexuality. Some of the figures targeted by such argumentation are starting to sound, anachronistically, like those monster-terrorist-fags operating especially since the dawn of the "war on terror."

This assembly of people might also provide an opening on perspectives besides those Paul repeats in this letter. The connections between the opening figuration and the range of people cited in these concluding greetings indicate that they likely already knew of this stereotyped figuration of the barbarian Other, but they may not have accepted the terms of this figuration in their own views of communal life together. If Paul is, in fact, trying to redeploy this barbarian figure to address Gentiles in the assembly communities (at Rome and at Corinth),[153] the eccentric assemblage of figures along the edges of these letters makes me wonder: how would the Gentiles (in Christ) and the Jews in community alongside them have responded to Paul's figuration? To be sure, constructions of ethnic groups (like Roman, Greek, or Jewish) depend on constructions of a different, even opposed ethnic group. Yet, the indicators for these ostensible differences vary and shift, and the boundaries they purport to describe are never as definite and as fixed as they claim.[154] The apparent distinctions between Jew and Gentile appear to be no different. Paul's redeployment of this sexualized scare figure of the barbarian foreigner to address Gentiles cannot be described as a simply Jewish practice, then.

It is important to not let later, mostly Christian stereotypes dictate the picture of the potential relations between Jews and Gentiles in the Roman imperial context. One might think that Jews and Gentiles were diametrically opposed and thus easily separated groups in this context. Yet, a more careful reading of the sources shows that Jews and Gentiles for the most part lived alongside each other and, perhaps most surprisingly to the traditional (Protestant) interpreter of Paul's letters, one simply could not be sure who was Jewish or non-Jewish in most contexts.[155] There were certainly Roman imperial stereotypes of the Jews as a collective and specifically as a conquered people, but many social mechanisms for distinguishing Jews from Gentiles simply did not work in this era: Jews did not have distinctive looks, clothing, language, names, or occupations.[156] Even circumcision fails to be a particularly useful marker of Jewish-Gentile difference: it is irrelevant for (at least) half of the people (because they are women and/or lack a penis), it requires public nudity to be used, and it was common among many peoples in the east.[157] One might be able to infer that someone was Jewish if they spent time with (other) Jews, but this observation would be incredibly unreliable given the variety of ways Jewish sources describe Gentiles living among, interacting with, and participating in the ritual lives of Jewish communities.[158] Gentiles could and did show respect for or interest in Judaism(s) in a number of ways, and the elements necessary for "conversion" themselves shift.[159]

The relationships between Jews and Gentiles were not structured by a concrete or absolute division in the first century CE. It was a difference that needed to be constructed, and thus was constructed and then lived in different ways. If one was too stringent with certain assumptions, a Gentile could be mistaken for a Jew, and a Jew could pass as a Gentile.[160] To the extent that there were boundaries between Jews and Gentiles, they were porous, and whatever lines they drew could move. Interaction with Gentiles was not a particularly strong source of anxiety for ancient Jews; synagogues in the diaspora welcomed Gentiles, and Jews and interested Gentiles observed the Sabbath together.[161] This more nuanced picture should change common views of the assembly communities (in places like Rome) and of the author of the letters to these communities. The members of these communities and the wider sets of early Jesus movements were not special innovators in the matter of Jewish and Gentile relations. By the time Paul writes these letters, Jews were *already* living among Gentiles, and Gentiles could *already* be found in synagogues. Indeed, some interpreters of the letter to the Romans start from this recognition: though the assembly community at Rome is primarily composed of Gentiles, they had already been involved in Jewish communities before joining this specific and small movement within Judaisms.[162]

Plenty of people preceded Paul in these assembly communities, as even he admits in the concluding greetings in Romans. Similarly, plenty of Jews and Gentiles were living with each other and interacting in Jewish communities within predominantly Gentile cities in the Roman empire, before the time of Jesus and of the movements that take his name. Once one gets past the stereotypes of Jewish exclusivism, then one has a harder time depicting Paul as a particularly radical or transgressive apostle to the Gentiles.[163] The "inclusion" or acceptance of Gentiles (in Christ) would not particularly stand out in this context, and it cannot be attributed especially to the efforts of Paul. In his willingness to interact and work with Gentiles, Paul would have been far from exceptional among other first-century Jews. This context makes the repetition of a sexualized stereotype about Gentiles all the more stark.

It also does not seem particularly productive, or even interesting, to "blame" Paul for the redeployment of this stereotyped figuration. It is important to acknowledge the operation of these figures in Paul's letters, especially if one is interested in seeking those targeted by such argumentation. Situating these letters in the larger Roman imperial setting helps me to identify and trace the use of the barbarian Other as a figure of gender, sexual, ethnoracial, regional, and religious difference, in and outside of these letters. The repetition of this figuration, then, seems more like the work of a colonized consciousness,[164] a colonized Jew who figures difference this way not because he is Jewish (fitting a stereotype of the exclusivist Jew), but because he is a colonized subject of the Roman empire, suspiciously coming from the east in a movement that features gender-variant females, effeminized males, and (formerly) enslaved people, often in leading roles. As Tat-siong Benny Liew has demonstrated, the abjection and stigmatization of colonized people does not prevent these kinds of arguments; rather, their colonized mindset explains how people like Paul would duplicate and displace Roman imperial figurations of sexually barbaric Others, away from themselves and onto their own Others.[165] This explains, without excusing, the redeployment of various figures of vilification in Paul's letters.

However, Paul's perspective is far from the whole story. One cannot avoid that Paul's letters repeatedly depict Gentiles as prone to an interlocking set of gender, sexual, ethnoracial, and religious perversities.[166] Yet, given the range of ways Jews and Gentiles lived among or alongside each other, this depiction of barbaric Others is not an inevitability. Further, given the number of figures addressed by the concluding greetings in Romans (and other sections of these letters), one can see that there are plenty of other people who negotiated this same set of differences, people who may not have cast them on the same stereotyped terms, or people who knew them, but evaluated them differently than the kyriarchal context of the Roman empire did. Indeed, the assembly communities at Rome are characterized by the intertwining of their gender, sexual, economic, ethnoracial, and religious difference. Instead of following the trajectory of one, particular, colonized, Jewish writer, one should start imagining what other colonized subjects, those who were Jewish and non-Jewish, female and often effeminized, enslaved and freed, living in the lower reaches of several intersecting kyriarchal systems, did as they negotiated this same context, particularly if their ways of life looked especially vulnerable to such stereotyped charges.

This vulnerability was likely reflected in the passing references to the precariousness of living and working in such assembly communities.[167] Other apostles like Andronicus and Junia were imprisoned (16:7), and Prisca and Aquila risked their own lives for their work among the assemblies of Gentiles (16:4). These communities included well-known and often-named (formerly) enslaved members, some of whom were bonded in female–female partnerships (16:12), and still others who could not be named and belonging to master-owners who were not members of these assemblies (16:10, 11). By encountering these named and unnamed members of the assembly communities as targets of ethnoracial figures of gender and sexual variation, subject to violent punishment, incarceration, and death, they increasingly make contact across the centuries with those who have been monstrously gendered and perversely racialized as terrorizing bodies, criminalized, quarantined, and killed, with Muslims imagined as the savage Sodomite, the terrorist fag, and/or the gender-monstrous foreigner.

Such an anachronistic juxtaposition with more recent figurations of monstrously foreign, strangely gendered, and perversely racialized barbaric Others provides an alternative angle on those targeted by similar argumentation in the ancient settings of the assembly communities in places like Rome and Corinth. Some of this is aided by recognizing the greater variety and complexity within Jewish communities and in the relationships between ancient Jews and Gentiles. Indeed, Jewish interpreters often notice that this ancient complexity is not entirely unlike the variety of practices around ritual observance and Gentile affiliation found in the present day.[168] The traffic between these eras could spark still more daring alliances and remembrances.

Instead of starting with the sexual exceptionalism of ancient and more recent empires, one could remember that these systems cast all of their subject peoples, whether they were Jewish or not, as strangely gendered, female or effeminized, often enslaved peoples, eliminated or incorporated and controlled toward the bottom.[169] Indeed, it is only very recently that Western powers have shifted Jewishness to the "civilized" side of the Manichean dualism of barbarism versus civilization.

How would an alternative politics of alliance, of assembly, look if one resisted the sexualized and racialized figuration of barbarian foreignness, but somehow retained the term "barbarian"? Indeed, the decolonizing writer Albert Memmi appears to have considered just such an option when he declared, "I am an incurable barbarian."[170] The Argentinian Jewish scholar Santiago Slabodsky has taken these words from Memmi, himself a Tunisian Jew living under French colonial rule (who, in turn, mastered French literary culture), as the inspiration for a positive counternarrative of barbarism.[171] Decolonial Jewish thinkers like Slabodsky signal the possibilities for rethinking barbarism, not according to imperial-colonial narratives, but in conversation with other barbarians. What if the many people addressed in the concluding greetings of Paul's letter to the Romans recognized that they were supposed to be targeted by the sexualized scare-figure in the letter's opening, but saw their assembling as and with barbarian peoples, in all of their gender, sexual, and ethnoracial variation, as a resource worth the risk of expulsion, incarceration, and execution at the hands of those who used such imperial figurations? Might Tryphaena and Tryphosa have more in common with more recent terrorizing bodies? Is it useful to imagine Prisca and Aquila detained and deported from states with their own imperial histories and aspirations? Are Andronicus and Junia prominent in their return to the field because they somehow survived their own detention, as some have at Abu Ghraib or Guantanamo?[172] (Who else has been disappeared from the archive of the ancient assembly and more recent wars against barbarian forces?)

It is my hope that such admittedly anachronistic questions highlight the persistence of such figurations of gender, sexual, racial, and religious perversity across the centuries. Those targeted by sexual exceptionalism as figures of barbarian difference share certain kinds of necropolitical vulnerabilities: their lives are conditioned by risks and precarities that others who have been folded into the political order do not face. The strange traffic, the queer proximities between these people across time, foreground that the aims of sympathy and solidarity are far more complicated than more popular narratives about inclusion can typically handle.

Analogy, Anachronism, Assembly: A Contingent Conclusion

In some liberal or progressive settings, particularly among Christians, Paul has been used as an example of how and why people can and should be inclusive now. The thinking in this redeployment of Paul emphasizes his (self-appointed) status as the apostle to the Gentiles and presumes that he is especially transgressive in crossing boundaries between Jews and Gentiles in his mission. By way of analogy, then, since Paul transgressed ancient norms to include an unexpected group in the first century, Christian communities should transgress more recent norms to include LGBTIQ believers, contrary to common expectations and assumptions about condemnation. The message is that people should be more like Paul now. Of course, this narrative presupposes its own forms of exceptionalism: that Paul was an exception in the ancient world, singularly transgressive at least in terms of Jewish-Gentile difference. Further, this narrative presupposes that these "accepting" or "inclusive" Christian communities could be exceptions themselves to the ambient homophobia or heterosexism, often taken to be characteristic of Christianity in recent history.

The picture of Christian communities on the ground is, of course, much more complicated than these narratives, but so also was the context in which Paul's letters circulated to audiences that included both Jews and Gentiles. As I have already highlighted, this more recent narrative of exceptionalism cannot rely on an ancient analogy with Paul. This apostle is not so very different from other ancient Jews interacting and working with Gentiles; he fits within the range of ancient Judaisms of the first century. Far more disturbing for many more recent pictures of Paul are the ways his arguments fit with the Roman imperial setting—in recirculating an ancient version of sexual exceptionalism and an accompanying sexualized stereotype of the barbarian Other. Indeed, Paul uses this racialized figuration of regional, religious, gender, and sexual perversity to specifically speak of those his letters ostensibly "include"—Gentiles. Paul's letters fit in surprising ways with the types of sexual exceptionalism examined in more recent queer studies (where it intersects with race-critical, feminist, and postcolonial studies): the letter's version of inclusion, built on a violent exclusion of perverse figures, looks more like a form of disciplinary incorporation.[173] It is just a way to avoid the quarantine aimed at Others, who will be isolated and extinguished, a fate to which one might still fall (if one does not assent to the arguments of these letters).

Still, this analysis remains too focused on Paul, a tendency with which I have struggled mightily here and throughout this book. It is important to identify how these letters repeat ancient figurations of perverse Others, but the consequences of the juxtapositional work of this chapter are greater than what they might tell us about Paul. First of all, I have tried to pursue those Gentiles, and the Jews who live among them, those addressed in the letter and targeted by these figurative practices. Though it is hard to be certain about some of these identifications, collectively it appears that the assembly communities at Rome gathered together prominent females and males, enslaved, freed, and free people, Jews and Gentiles, most of whom were from the east. This assemblage may just be a more concrete instantiation of the baptismal formula circulating in these communities, where they are no longer Jew or Gentile, slave or free, male and female (Gal 3:28). This collective pulled together people living through the range of those intersecting positions that result from the combination of these three more simplified dyads (not just Jews and Gentiles, but enslaved Gentiles, freed Jews, a freed woman apostle, Gentile women living together, Jewish couples hosting Gentile assemblies, and enslaved people still subject to masters outside of the community, among many others). It is, in short, a motley crew, an eccentric assemblage of figures. In a manner not unlike Carolyn Dinshaw's queer historical impulse (see chapter 1), I wonder who might these people be, and, further "How can we know them? And thinking we know them, what do we know?"[174] Does this open up the possibilities for that elusive "touch across time" between people positioned queerly in, by, and perhaps partially against the marginalizing arguments?

Second, this potential touch across time opens my consideration back to the twenty-first century, to critically reconsider my present-day project in light of queer theory. I have often taken as my starting point how much of queer studies and politics, in and outside of religious studies, has used the term "queer" as a reclamation and ethical reversal of the word's association with the abnormal, strange, perverse, or odd. In doing so, there is an at least implicit claim of the distinctive, even unique vantage point of queer, precisely because it revalorizes its (or even our) oddness, departures and differences, abnormalities. The use of "queer," then, can indicate a challenge to regimes of the normal, a desire to resist and contest such a worldview. Queer as a mode (and occasionally an identity, or anti-identity, of sorts) casts itself, then, as inhabiting an ethos and praxis especially useful for interrogating regimes of the normal and the natural. Described thusly, queer is an oppositional, resistant, transgressive movement, contrary and troubling to what surrounds and precedes in normalization.[175]

What scholars like Puar have demonstrated, though, is that "queerness has its own exceptionalist desires."[176] The use of "queer" I have been describing depends on queer as especially, possibly even *uniquely* transgressive, the exception to the world constituted by the dynamics of normalization and naturalization. This oppositional conceptualization of queer may even obscure the operations of sexual exceptionalism, particularly in moments where some domesticatable queer subjects are offered opportunities to be "included," incorporated in an order that disaggregates them from other perverse groups.[177] This raises potentially unsettling questions about more recent religious modes of assembling and arguing. On what terms are so-called progressive religious communities offering inclusion, tolerance, or affirmation of (at least some) forms of queerness? Does it depend on a continued politics of respectability and/or the exclusion of certain perversely pathologized figures (even if the targets of these figures shift)?[178] Does belonging depend on homonormative measures around marriage, money, or the military? Or do recent claims about American exceptionalism and thus entitlement to isolate, expel, or invade exploit similar claims of our (only very recent, even sudden) openness to sexual minorities?

Can queer refuse to play along as an alibi in any of the figurative practices? Sexual exceptionalism can be used to demonstrate how *incompletely* queer studies and movements challenge a range of normalizations, including those ways some LGBTIQ folks are folded into late turbocapitalist and neoimperial life, while others are perversely racialized as estranged to this life. The problem, then, may just be that some LGBTIQ folks have claimed a uniquely transgressive site from which to argue, which is not actually *that* transgressive, given the way it obscures some forms of normalization and naturalization, including specifically racialization and nationalization. The problem may be with defining queer in relation to transgression, or it may lie with how reflexively this mode is used.

Sexual exceptionalisms peel people away from each other for the chance to be folded into an overarching order, dividing subjects into distinctive biopolitical and necropolitical fates. It is my anachronistic aspiration, though, that these chapters have pulled together a counterassembly: one in which twenty-first-century bodies reach back in order to critically reflect on which monsters, which perversities, which pariahs, which Others do we continue to create. This series of juxtapositions might offer different conditions for queer as coalitional, for anachronism as a form of assembly: gender-variant females, Corinthian women prophets, and drag kings, eunuchs, circumcised and other effeminized peoples, alongside people with intersex conditions, enslaved and freed people, including Onesimus, and those they haunt, even in their sexual practices, Gentiles and Jews, with Muslims and South Asians, migrants and "foreigners." Named and unnamed figures only partially lost to us, Phoebe and Onesimus, Prisca and Junia, Tryphaena and Tryphosa, might still choose to ally with Philemon or Aquila or Andronicus, and possibly even Paul after all. All of these "barbarians" of one kind or another coalesce, crashing gates together across time, not transgressively, but contingently, temporarily, not building new gates, but turning around to see who else has been targeted, and reaching . . . .

Epilogue

Biblical Drag

It's about time.

The preceding juxtapositions of ancient and more recent figures raise questions about how much "our" time connects with other times, often just called the past. I have tried taking queer angles on temporality, historicity, anachronism, and spectrality. Perhaps some readers have been following, preparing a comprehensive list of such angles as offenses, so as to better lodge their objections to such (admitted) anachronisms. These readers might even consider themselves religious defenders of these texts and traditions, as well as their proper contexts and communities. Still, religious beliefs and practices, ideas and institutions are most certainly shaped by various struggles over whether and how one can draw on the example of the past. Often, the assumption is that divides of space and time can be crossed, or already have been by supernatural forces. How else can the very contemporary question—which is really more an instruction, even a demand—"What Would Jesus Do?" make sense? Such religious figurations cannot only be relics of the past; they must live on and be reenacted in everyday lives. Indeed, whether you or I practice it, whether you or I believe in it, the biblical in particular persists. One cannot just leave the biblical behind. Biblical images and arguments, figurations and formations have potently, if still often problematically and even oppressively, crossed time and exceeded periodizations. This is one way that scriptures persist as scriptures. This could also be the way to trace the temporally queer dynamics of "the biblical."

To think seriously about the strange temporality of scriptures,[1] I have considered a cluster of queer approaches, including what Carolyn Dinshaw describes as the desire to "make relations with" elements of the past, seeking a "touch across time" (first discussed in chapter 1).[2] Dinshaw posits that "queers can make new relations, new identifications, new communities with past figures who elude resemblance to us but with whom we can be connected partially by virtue of shared marginality, queer positionality."[3] Those voices

Appalling Bodies. Joseph A. Marchal, Oxford University Press (2020). © Oxford University Press.
DOI: 10.1093/oso/9780190060312.001.0001

who barely leave a trace, if any, like and unlike the Corinthian females, the circumcurious Galatians, the alternately remembered Onesimus, or the gender-troubled Gentiles, each addressed by Paul's arguments, might only resemble some contemporary groups because they were marginalized by the prevailing forces of their own times and places. The effort to reconstruct such people and practices might, in fact, link up with efforts to make "connections across time between, on the one hand, lives, texts, and other cultural phenomena left out of sexual categories back then and, on the other, those left out of current sexual categories now."[4] The juxtaposition of these figures alongside more recent figures of vilification or stigmatization presents a series of such efforts. These improvised queer communities or coalitions are made by partial connections across time, echoing the never-perfect aspects of identification, the never-foreclosed dynamics of imitation, the alterity embedded within performativity (especially discussed in chapters 1 and 2).

Judith Butler famously highlighted the embodied practices of drag as one potential example to highlight the function of performativity.[5] With the help of Jack Halberstam, I described the practices of drag kings (in chapter 2) as one of several, subversive possibilities involved in female masculinity. Yet, drag also connotes a crossing, or even dredging across space and time. This is why Elizabeth Freeman suggests that temporal drag is a helpful way to reconsider our potential relations with the past. Freeman coined the term "temporal drag" to reflect "the pull of the past on the present" in all of its ambivalent qualities.[6] She notes how the past exerts pressure on the present,[7] stressing the haunting ways in which the specters of the past can make demands on us.[8] The past drags us to look and even feel backward, but the present also reflects how the past drags on, continues, keeps showing up, even in surprising fashion.

Temporal drag can be just one process that explains the coexistence of different chronologies or temporalities. It reflects the possibly energizing functions of the past,[9] like those partial connections between parties conceived as "then" and "now" on the basis of their "shared marginality, queer positionality." Certainly, such partial connections, viewed as anachronistic citations, would be one set of ways to rework normative uses of the past. Yet, the difference of the past must somehow also be preserved; false idealism or naïve utopianism could even prevent these connections, these reconfigured repetitions. Hence, Heather Love warns: "Taking care of the past without attempting to fix it means living with bad attachments, identifying through loss, allowing ourselves to be haunted."[10] The past requires recognizing

differences and losses, but many queer scholars do not give up on the potential pleasures of reflecting historically. Thus, Freeman imagines temporal
drag as "a way of connecting queer performativity to disavowed political histories" and then asks,

> Might some bodies, in registering on their very surfaces the co-presence
> of several historically-specific events, movements, and collective pleasures,
> complicate or displace the centrality of *gender*-transitive drag to queer
> performativity?[11]

In looking back, reaching past, around, and through, for these before-and-
after figures, then, these appalling bodies could be pleasurable, yet complicated registers of temporal co-presence.

These letters often reflect on the readable surfaces of bodies, or more
plainly, they register their disdain for all kinds of bodies marked by specific histories. Consider, for instance, baptism; or, more specifically, what
the preservation of an ancient baptismal formula within Paul's letters could
register. The clearest appearance of this formula is within Galatians 3:28 (as
discussed in chapters 2 and 3), but this formula was cited to do many things
in the first-century assembly communities, two of which Paul attempts at different occasions. In Galatians he cites the tradition to talk about the relations
between Jews and Gentiles and whether to circumcise bodies. The focus here
is on just one of the three "no longer" pairs, "Jew or Greek," rather than "slave
or free, not male and female." Yet, the letter's citation demonstrates that Paul
assumed the Galatians already knew this formula. His strenuous efforts to
convince them of his point of view reflects the likelihood that the formula
was used in ways differently than he tries to use it in the letter. Indeed, this
formula could be deployed to imagine gender, status, ethnicity, and embodiment in more capacious ways than the vision shaped by those anxious about
such dynamics in the Roman imperial ambience of the letters.

The baptismal formula's capacity is underscored by its own drag qualities, its temporal co-presences. Since the last pair, in particular, "not male
and female" appears to break the "Y or Z" rhythm of the two previous pairs,
it looks like a pointed citation of the creation story that depicts humans as
made "male and female" and "in the image of God" (Gen 1:27). When people
in these ancient assemblies cite or recite this baptismal formula in the first
century, their own "present day" (which is our past) practices of baptism call
on an even more distant, primordial past so that their bodies might register

an altered order for creation. The baptized body's relation to its present time is reorganized by the formula's own negating citation of another time—*not male and female*. These bodies now reflect multiple moments—they move through their lives with bodies marked by a proximate past when they "clothed themselves in Christ" at their baptism (in Gal 3:27) and a prior moment that echoes and renegotiates a more primordial past of creation.

Galatians is not the only place Paul's letters engage creation accounts in order to argue about clothing practices in these communities. Recall that the aim in 1 Corinthians 11 (discussed in chapter 2) was to convince females to cover their heads in prayer and prophecy. Paul again alludes to creation, and partially recites this tradition, when he claims that man is made "in the image of God" (in 11:7). This argument excludes that these humans were made "male and female" in this divine image in the first account (Gen 1:27), in order to assert a hierarchical difference between males and females. Such an exclusion looks all the more purposeful when Paul again alludes to the baptismal formula in the following chapter ("Jews or Gentiles, slaves or free"), but drops the male and female pair (in 1 Cor 12:13). Feminist scholars like Antoinette Clark Wire have tracked such elisions, and posed them as Paul's probable response to the prophetic females' own citations of these traditions. Restoring the missing female in citations of both creation and baptism underscores the Corinthian females' likely emphasis on a creation reordered in the assembly community, a prophetic realization and proclamation, where they are no longer male and female.[12]

Thus, 1 Corinthians partially re-cites the formula that also appears in Galatians 3:28, but tried to run away from the "male and female" pair, probably because of its use in the assembly community. Yet, this baptismal formula calls up a poetic story about a primordial past, in order to claim that this ritual initiates a new creation.[13] Competing views of multiple times, times in relation to each other at that, start to cluster and pile up. Paul's concept of temporal co-presence is clashing with other concepts of temporal co-presence within these audiences. Among the prophetic females, then, some of the uncovered surfaces of their bodies register different ways of relating to a past. Among the circumcurious Gentiles as well, these Galatian members were considering adding another moment to mark their bodies, a practice shaped in part by citations of other ancestral traditions, also from Genesis, around Abraham, for instance (17:1–27). As I considered in previous chapters, if this formula was recognizable to some assembly audiences, then it could have circulated in still other places and times. We could add still other temporal co-presences, unlike those proposed by Paul's letters. Their co-presence elsewhere would signal a change, or at least a troubling negotiation for the enslaved Onesimus (in chapter 4), while the formula's pairs possibly echoed and combined in the motley assemblage of people named toward the end of Romans (in chapter 5).

The previous chapters' juxtapositions present us with the dense meeting of multiple temporalities in various first-century moments. Yet, of course, this presentation of temporalities is further layered and fraught by the way some of these arguments have prominently crossed time, and others were nearly lost, elided, marginalized, and potentially even disavowed. Strangely enough, dredging up the pasts evoked in these epistles from the past highlights the queer potentiality of biblical citationality, in general. The repetition, citation, and circulation that make the biblical, well, biblical not only are performative (see chapter 2) but are also drag!

It's about time, then, again and again. In reaching toward the figures within these letters, we encounter temporal co-presences that are promising and problematic. Paul remains persistently anxious, for example, about the past of the Gentiles crashing back into the present. When Paul disapproves of certain people and practices, they are presented as a threatening kind of regression. This past which should remain in the past (but never quite does, at least in Paul's eyes) is characterized by the Gentile's enslavement on several occasions. This argumentative approach is plainly about time, but the deployment of the enslaved figure here also reminds us that the ancient figures considered through the last four chapters also reflect and perform temporal functions. Enslaved and barbarian peoples were both cast with specific pasts and destined for circumscribed futures. Eunuchs bore the physical marks of particular surgical events from their past. The vulnerability of all of these figures to invasion, possession, and penetration was imagined as demonstrating a temporality that prevails because it persists—the past, present, and future of Roman imperial power.

Before and after these letters, then, the crack of a whip or the cut of a knife demonstrate that not all touches that drag on bodies across time can or should be valorized. Indeed, intersex theorist Iain Morland engages the limitations of both Freeman's conception of temporal drag and Dinshaw's touches across time along these lines. Surgically altered bodies, like those of both the ancient eunuch and the more recent intersex person, are bodies marked (and re-marked) by a prior moment, a bodily intervention that cut off a set of social and temporal relations, foreclosing other futures. Morland notes that such bodily treatments are never quite over: "genital surgery is a drag act that performatively produces gender by 'dragging on' in the life of the postsurgical subject."[14] The bodily surfaces of surgically modified people register different, historically specific events in some of the ways that Freeman argued would complicate queer concepts and practices of performativity.[15] Yet, such work highlights that there are many different types and impacts of temporal drag; this kind of pull of the past on the present could be subversive and destabilizing, as well as scarring and stigmatizing. Ancient and more recent slave regimes marked bodies in similarly scarring ways, not always through castration, but often through tattooing, branding, whipping, and other scarring and stigmatizing practices. It is precisely such violent practices that give Saidiya Hartman pause about our own practices of looking back and the potential habituation to a racialized past (that is not quite past).[16] These practices reinforce the natal alienation that swaps the slaveowner's temporality in for the enslaved person's previous temporality. As Hortense Spillers noted, the temporality of normative kinship may be undermined by slavery, but it is an estrangement easily exploited by enslaving systems.[17]

These practices all drag on, can be registered on the surfaces of bodies, and thus reflect temporal co-presences. Not all modes of temporal drag are to be immediately idealized or celebrated. Furthermore, since surgeries so often damage or even eliminate sensation, the bodily conditions of these figures interrogate Dinshaw's emphasis on a "touch across time." Surgical and (or as) enslaving touches, after all, drag in time on and across bodily surfaces and even interiors by altering, deadening, delaying, or destroying capacities for tactility; the value of touch is complicated, as are the potential relations between touch and tactility.[18] As more recent work on slavery stresses, touches can range between coercive and consensual, demonstrating the mundane, if still monstrous intimacies in the contact between bodies and histories. These times drag on and touch too, still haunting contemporary sexual practices. As these chapters increasingly recognize, these figurations of vilification and stigmatization are distinctly racialized, they especially stick to certain bodies cast as perverse and terrorizing. In such contexts the past is most definitely not yet past, which means we should not swerve away from grappling with these charged historical correspondences. Instead, I hope that each of the preceding chapters presents a distinct effort to swerve into what touches and drags.

Indeed, this entire project could retrospectively be described as a multilayered exercise in temporal drag. In tracing how the letters dredge up and deploy figures already circulating in the kyriarchal ambience of the Roman empire, they reflect the pull of prevailing views of that past. The imperial period is one riven by sexual-temporal anxieties as to whether they measure up to or significantly depart from their republican past and the persistent influence of Hellenistic culture. This set of insecurities underscores that drag is not only temporal but also spatial: to drag is to move, particularly in pushing and pulling directions. Their kyriarchal directions are moved by attitudes and assumptions about the inferiority of a variety of "eastern" figures, themselves dragged across and all around the empire (including within these letters).

These letters, however, cannot help but be moved by still other possibilities; they are pushed and pulled to respond to plenty of other people beside Paul. More than twenty-five named people are dragged into just one chapter of these letters (Rom 16), a fairly explicit push to remind readers that these people and the assembly communities they created preceded Paul and his epistles. In trying to reach them, these letters cannot help but reflect on a past, only occasionally shared by the assembly and author. Danger and death may stick to and drag on, even drag down, some of their bodies. Thus, the risks of the past and present marked these bodies, particularly whenever they were targeted with or as figures of vilification and stigmatization. The letters may be trying to push the rhetorical figures of androgynes, eunuchs, slaves, and foreign Others in order to address certain historical figures, alternately pulling them together and apart so that Paul might be co-present in bodies that assent to such arguments. Yet, I find that these figures pull on me and a few other interpreters, pushing us to reach out and try for a contingent touch. This might just be because such letters are pulled into debates today . . . or is it that the biblical persists so much that it was already there? More likely, in my case at least, is that I see glimpses and specters of such ancient figures in more recently targeted figures . . . or is it just that it is easier to see, feel, and reach for all of these figures once I have tried to bring them into partial contact through anachronistic juxtaposition?

If this book has come alive for any of you, it is likely because it has registered on its own surfaces these co-presences: of bodies marked by histories, of our histories haunted by bodies, of embodied figures up alongside each other, pushed and pulled closer together, in order to get another angle on disavowed possibilities. In juxtaposing such figures, I have refused to swerve away from the potential for partial, if still particular historical correspondences, references, or echoes out of fear of anachronism.[19]

Anachronism may be imagined as a cardinal sin of history, but in this project I do not find anachronism to be particularly worrisome, because times always relate to each other, embedded or "in bed" with each other, right there with us. "Anachronism" itself could even work as a kind of insult or brush-off, an alibi for not attending to certain people or practices. Such dismissive attitudes hardly rise to the level of insult and anxiety directed toward figures like androgynes, eunuchs, slaves, and foreigners, but I am curious if certain disavowed techniques keep us from trying to reach out and follow alternative angles toward such figures.

"Drag," too, can connote undesirable sensations or activities. If it's such a drag, it may be unwelcome or disappointing, something that brings you down. In some circles drag is colorful slang for thoroughly insulting, ripping, or ridiculing someone. Dragging, then, could be akin to "reading" someone (as found in some drag ballroom, queer, and/or trans spaces), criticizing, cutting down to size, or exposing them. Anachronistically, then, one could say these letters drag figures up and out, to call people out, and to read the potential audiences as akin to these figures, *if* they do not follow what Paul prescribes for them. Perhaps, some readers of this book's chapters find them to be piling up and on these letters, dragging and "reading" them, fairly or unfairly. To be sure, I have courted anachronism, risked drag, and possibly even encouraged being read (or is it "read"?) through these juxtapositions. The book has been dwelling in appalling territory for a while now.

I think these anachronistic juxtapositions are worth the risk. Anachronism may not be so appalling after all. Anachronism is not ahistorical, let alone antihistorical. It is neither the absence of temporality nor the negation of a particular temporality. Rather, exchanges like those reflected before, after, and through Paul's letters are already anachronistic, in that they bring times into touch with each other. Anachronisms, like these epistles, do not feature times against or contrary to other times, that would be contra-chronistic. Ana-chronisms are times moving up, naming time on top of time, time up along time. Anachronism, then, is a distinctive kind of historical co-presence, a pull of the past still in the present, persisting, partially lost, but haunting. Both lost and found, anachronism stages juxtapositions to affects both appalling and appealing.

As I suggested toward the conclusion of the previous chapter, anachronisms are a kind of assembly. Through a series of willful juxtapositions,[20] I have assembled some appalling bodies. But different readers are certain to find different bodies appalling. Are the Pauline epistles themselves the appalling bodies, given the way they argue and address some through figures of gender, sexual, ethnoracial, and imperial perversity? Perhaps just those figures—and those they purport to describe—are appalling, given their appearance before and after the letters? Or are those who construct and circulate such figures appalling? Do those who receive and accept such a worldview or those who deny and try to negotiate them deserve our dismay or horror? Who among the gender-variant females, Corinthian women prophets, and drag kings; the eunuchs, circumcised, and other effeminized peoples, alongside people with intersex conditions; the enslaved and freedpeople, including Onesimus, and those they haunt, even in their sexual practices; the Gentiles and Jews, with Muslims and South Asians, migrants and "foreigners," deserve our affective and argumentative responses as appalling or appealing?

They may be appealing because they are appalling, or appalling because appealing, but I remain haunted and queerly energized by them all. We may never quite touch across time, but if these times are trying, it's also well past time to try.

Notes

Prelude

1. Rubin, "Thinking Sex," 283.
2. Rubin proposes that a more radical theory of sexuality must interrogate this hierarchy, the accompanying fallacy about scale, and its domino theory of sexual peril, with a more pluralistic, sex-positive ethic of benign variation ("Thinking Sex," 279–83).
3. Rubin, "Thinking Sex," 278.
4. Most especially Brooten, *Love Between Women* (which will be discussed in greater detail in the first chapter); and, then, Martin, "Heterosexism and the Interpretation of Romans 1:18–32"; and Martin, "*Arsenokoitēs* and *Malakos*." Even the electrifying exegesis performed queerly on Romans 1 by Moore is focused on Paul's position, albeit as a bottom to the deity his own argumentation constructs (*God's Beauty Parlor*, 133–72). More recently, Liew develops a particularly convincing explanation of Paul's "position," specifically his gender, sexual, and racialized arguments, in light of Paul's colonized consciousness (*What Is Asian American Biblical Hermeneutics?*, 75–97, 175–88).
5. For different strategies of juxtaposition, see Runions, *The Babylon Complex*; Townsley, *The Straight Mind*, 193–252; and Blanton, *A Materialism for the Masses*.
6. Richlin, *The Garden of Priapus*; and later attempts at systematizing the protocols of masculinity, like Williams, *Roman Homosexuality*. On Roman sexualities, in general, see Hallett and Skinner, eds., *Roman Sexualities*.
7. Here, I borrow the notion of Romosexuality (from Ingleheart, "Introduction: Romosexuality"), in order to highlight not only the potential distance in ancient Roman imperial conceptualizations of sexual practices but also the ways these conceptualizations move "backward and forward" between the first and the twenty-first century.
8. For the once-popular "one-sex model" (that male and female bodies are different not in kind, but in their hierarchical perfection or imperfection), see Laqueur, *Making Sex*; and the important critique and complication in King, *The One-Sex Body on Trial*.
9. For example, Halperin, *One Hundred Years*, 29–30.
10. Walters, "Invading the Roman Body," 41, cf. 36–37.
11. Walters, "'No More Than a Boy.'"
12. For religious and theological studies, start with Cornwall, *Controversies in Queer Theology*; Schippert, "Implications of Queer Theory," and Brintnall, "Queer Studies in Religion." For biblical studies, see Stone, "Queer Theory and Biblical Interpretation"; and Moore, *God's Beauty Parlor*, 7–18. For my own attempts at the task, see Marchal, "Queer Approaches"; Marchal, "Homosexual/Queer"; and Moore, Brintnall, and Marchal, "Queer Disorientations."

13. Key works from this phase include: Butler, *Gender Trouble*; Butler, *Bodies That Matter*; Foucault, *The History of Sexuality, Volume 1*; Sedgwick, *Between Men*; and Sedgwick, *Epistemology of the Closet*.

14. Foucault surveys aspects of Greek and Roman culture in the next two volumes of *The History of Sexuality*.

15. McIntosh, "The Homosexual Role"; and Weeks, *Sex, Politics, and Society*.

16. For example: Cohen, "Punks, Bulldaggers, and Welfare Queens"; Muñoz, *Disidentifications*; Ferguson, *Aberrations in Black*; Holland, *The Erotic Life of Racism*; and Weheliye, *Habeas Viscus*.

17. For just a small sampling of this work, consider: Anzaldúa, *Borderlands/La Frontera*; Smith, *Toward a Black Feminism Criticism*; Lorde, *Sister Outsider*; and Spillers, "Mama's Baby, Papa's Maybe"; as well as edited collections like Moraga and Anzaldúa, eds., *This Bridge Called My Back*; Hull, Scott, and Smith, eds., *All the Women Are White, All the Blacks Are Men, But Some of Us Are Brave*; and Smith, ed., *Home Girls*.

18. Some of the most prominent queer projects on desires and death drives include Bersani, "Is the Rectum a Grave?"; Bersani, *Homos*; Dean, *Beyond Sexuality*; Dean, *Unlimited Intimacy*; and Edelman, *No Future*.

19. Dinshaw, *Getting Medieval*, 3, 12, 21.

20. Dinshaw, *Getting Medieval*, 1.

21. For one, more traditionally historical interpreter's objections to anachronism in the study of Paul's letters, see Fredriksen, "How Later Contexts"; and Fredriksen, "Mandatory Retirement." For another, innovative approach to the afterlives of these letters, in ways that my present project does not pursue, see Twomey, "The Pastor." On the various pictures of Paul over the centuries, see Seesengood, *Paul*.

22. Especially Schüssler Fiorenza, *Rhetoric and Ethic*; Schüssler Fiorenza, "Paul and the Politics of Interpretation"; and Wire, *The Corinthian Women Prophets*.

23. For further examples of this approach, see also Kittredge, "Rethinking Authorship"; Kittredge, "Feminist Approaches"; and Schüssler Fiorenza, *The Power of the Word*, 69–109.

24. Schüssler Fiorenza, "Paul and the Politics of Interpretation."

25. Especially, Wire, *The Corinthian Women Prophets*, 4–11.

26. For further reflections on queer studies as a kind of feminist project, see Marchal, "Queer Studies and Critical Masculinity Studies."

27. For initial definitions and elaborations on "wo/men," see Schüssler Fiorenza, *Rhetoric and Ethic*, ix; and *Wisdom Ways*, 55–59, 107–9, 216.

28. For example, Schüssler Fiorenza, *Wisdom Ways*, 1, 118–24, 211.

29. "Kyriarchy" also happens to be a concise, perhaps more convenient term (like "queer") for describing multiple dynamics that become increasingly cumbersome to name and narrate (like the sequence of descriptions free, elite, adult, Roman imperial male).

Chapter 1

1. The phrase "making history" alludes to and is inspired by (with both debts and apologies to) the work of Weeks, *Making Sexual History*.

2. For an understanding of the rhetoricity of any form of historical reconstruction, see Schüssler Fiorenza, *Rhetoric and Ethic*, especially 129–48.

3. For more on this divide between altericist or historicist differentiating and continuist or transhistoricist mirroring, see the arguments that follow. For some of the general contours of this tension as it relates to historiography and gender, sexuality, and/ or embodiment, see Fradenburg and Freccero, "Introduction"; Dinshaw, *Getting Medieval*; Goldberg and Menon, "Queering History"; McCabe, "To Be and to Have"; Freccero, *Queer/Early/Modern*; and Love, *Feeling Backward*, especially 1–30. Love adeptly discusses both the pull to look backward and the impulse to imagine another future, especially considering a fraught past and present for queer populations. Just as I tend to argue for how biblical arguments are part of a "mixed heritage," Love discusses the "mixed history" of queer subjectivity (in *Feeling Backward*, 18). For further reflections on looking backward and/or feeling behind, as it relates to biblical studies' potential relationship to queer approaches (especially in literary studies), see the contextualization above and Moore, *God's Beauty Parlor*, 7–11, 17–18.

4. For some further reflections on the binds and bonds of reflecting on sexual histories (or the chronopolitics of eroticisms), see Freeman, "Time Binds"; as well as Freeman, "Still After."

5. Indeed, the "straight-forwardness" is perhaps specifically part of this tension, as many modernist historical approaches (in and outside of biblical studies) presume a linearity and a teleological trajectory up to a "now" that is an indicator of an assumed forward, even ascendant progression to this point in human history. Queer theories might be especially poised to interrogate such a view of history, suggesting one potential tension between the queer and the historical apart from the methodological divides or departures in biblical studies. Furthermore, many queer subjects and/or practitioners assume a default opposition to any biblical reference, while (or perhaps because) many who refer to biblical materials in various publics do so to counter or quash queerness. The complex negotiation of what could be called the queer/biblical/ historical, then, reflects this context of ostensible oppositions while offering another way to operate by sorting, borrowing, relating, and assembling promiscuously from all three. For further reflections on the perils of and responses to certain forms of linearity, see Freccero, *Queer/Early/Modern*, among others. Clearly, my posing of these tensions and negotiations reflects Freccero's titularly similar threefold juxtapositions. For how something like a "queer commentary" on biblical materials represents both continuities and discontinuities (and additional puns on straight-forward), see Stone, "Queer Theory and Biblical Interpretation," especially 12–14.

6. Not very many biblical interpreters acknowledge the influence of Sedgwick's or Butler's work to their interrogations and assessments of biblical materials, thus the impact of such queer analytics is potentially delayed (a lag that this present study at least partially attempts to bridge or cross). The few most prominent cases of queer biblical interaction with either figure's work include, for Sedgwick, Moore, *God's Beauty Parlor*, and, for Butler, Stone, "The Garden of Eden and the Heterosexual Contract"; and Hornsby, "The Annoying Woman."

7. In describing normalization thusly, I follow Halperin's instructive effort to highlight and retranslate a portion of Foucault's *Discipline and Punish* (182–84), stressing the

function of normalization as it "compares, differentiates, hierarchizes, homogenizes, excludes. In a word, it normalizes" (in Halperin, *How to Do the History*, 195, n. 68; cf. 136). My own efforts to think through the figuration and function of "the biblical" at least partially derives and departs from Dinshaw's consideration of "the medieval" and "the middle" in *Getting Medieval*. Indeed, often the biblical and/or the ancient (especially Greco-Roman antiquity) can function similarly to characterizations of the medieval or the Middle Ages when they are "made the dense, unvarying, and eminently obvious monolith against which modernity and postmodernity groovily emerge" (Dinshaw, *Getting Medieval*, 16). One difference for the biblical (and frequently the ancient), though, lies in the ways in which it is evoked and cited as a root or foundation for "today," deriving authority by dint of either its "timeless" quality (simultaneously and contradictorily outside of time, yet also locatable from the start, as it has been "with us since the beginning of time") or its attributed ethical and moral significance. For further strategies for how to use something seen as "middle," see Dinshaw, *Getting Medieval*, 219, n. 56, where she follows Haraway, "The Promises of Monsters," 304.

8. For example the descriptions in Brooten, *Love Between Women*, 9–26. This is a task she continues even today, as she leads a research project on the history of slavery and sexual ethics.

9. Brooten, *Love Between Women*, 25. Feminist biblical scholars like Schüssler Fiorenza argue that one can "read against the grain" of constructions, so as to reconstruct the roles of women and/as others subordinated and dominated by the powers that generate these constructions. See, for example, Schüssler Fiorenza, *Rhetoric and Ethic*. In her response to the *GLQ* forum to *Love Between Women* ("Lesbian Historiography," 610–11), Brooten highlights her methodological connections to and the impact of Schüssler Fiorenza's work.

10. Brooten's ongoing work (with Hazelton, ed., *Beyond Slavery*) continues to focus on the "Others" of such constructions as they relate to sexual relations, not only in the instance of the *tribas*, but also (and now especially) in the sexual uses of enslaved people.

11. Halperin, *How to Do the History*, 16–17, 92. Haunting presents another way to interrogate the supposed "ruptures" between past and present. See more in what follows, but in biblical studies, start with the work of Buell, "God's Own People"; Buell, "Cyborg Memories"; and Buell, "Hauntology Meets Post-Humanism."

12. This insistence (or persistence) in demanding discontinuity might bear striking resonances (even continuities) with Paul's ascetic impulses, as Fradenburg and Freccero argue: "the argument that modern desires and perspectives can and must be set aside if we are to read the past properly is itself revealing, for it suggests that historical knowledge is often founded on the renunciation, the *ascesis*, of 'self.' And to the degree that this renunciation tries to hide its own narcissistic investments, it begs for queer scrutiny" ("Preface," viii). For some interrelated queer concerns about desire and temporality, see also Menéndez-Antuña, "Is There a Room?"

13. Halperin, *How to Do the History*, 63.

14. Here, one could note both that Halperin's more recent work adds a concern with contemporary effects (in the third task earlier), even as it preserves and continues

to prioritize his previous efforts at stressing historical discontinuities (as reflected by the simple, if not word-for-word repetition of two similar tasks from the previous work). Contrast and connect the above with Halperin's delineation of priorities in *One Hundred Years*, 29.

15. For some introductions to recent approaches to historiography, see Burke, ed., *New Perspectives*.

16. Halperin, *How to Do the History*, 175–76, n. 46. Though Halperin's tendency is to see difference and to frame the history of sexuality's connection to antiquity as structured by rupture, his method nevertheless manages to reinforce the idea of the past as transparent to us (if only the discourse that can be reconstructed, but not the subjects, especially those subordinated by the discursive constructions). Thus, for Halperin the historical pursuit still functions mimetically.

17. For critiques and concerns about how Halperin's approach operates and its relation (if tenuous or tensive) with Foucault's project(s), see Freccero, *Queer/Early/Modern*, 31–50; and Goldberg and Menon, "Queering History," especially 1610.

18. Halperin, *How to Do the History*, 110. Halperin continues: "though it is not entirely limited to them, as such it will be admittedly partial and incomplete. A fully realized genealogical inquiry would need to overcome, to the greatest possible degree, such limitations" (110, cf. 77). Halperin's (at times casual) disposition to those subjugated in and by these constructions indicates how much less he is haunted by the ghosts of those unrepresented in his historical work. For the emergence of haunting and spectrality as it relates to ethical forms of historiography (and its intersections with queer forms of history), see Freccero, *Queer/Early/Modern*, 69–104; Love, *Feeling Backward*; Brown, *Politics Out of History*, 138–73; Gordon, *Ghostly Matters*; and Derrida, *Specters of Marx*. Freccero's critique of Halperin follows on the concerns raised by Sedgwick (see more earlier), while Freccero's concern with those who might haunt present efforts echoes Sedgwick's opening meditation in *Tendencies* (1 and 3) on motive for queer (or gay and lesbian) studies: "I think everyone who does gay and lesbian studies is haunted by the suicide of adolescents." "Seemingly, this society wants its children to know nothing; wants its queer children to conform or (and this is not a figure of speech) die; and wants not to know that it is getting what it wants."

19. This is indeed ironic considering how suppressed and silenced was the knowledge of sexuality by scholarly propriety and circumscription until the recent surge in sexuality studies, lesbian and gay studies, and now queer studies (a surge in which Halperin has been no minor player or inert bystander, but a vocal advocate). In addressing "religious" dynamics from biblical and ancient materials, however, one should not narrow their potential functions to a legally prescriptive quality alone. Freccero has highlighted how Foucault's work exhibits "a symptom of a modernist desire to simplify premodern discursivity by privileging the juridical over other discourses perhaps more obscure and less legible for being less assimilable to modern institutions and discourses" (*Queer/Early/Modern*, 34). Halperin's narrowing of focus partially follows this trend, yet paradoxically also reverses it by excluding the "religious" (often received as juridical, but perhaps also as assimilable to recent formations). Nevertheless, in reading biblical materials and their claims to authority, one must

guard against too neatly assuming it as reflecting a transparent and fulminous ancient reality. (Freccero wonders: "It would be interesting to ask whether the availability of certain documents and not others from premodernity produces the impression that the primary discourses governing sexuality were legal *and religious*" [*Queer/Early/ Modern*, 42, emphasis added].)

20. Halperin, *How to Do the History*, 16. Note here how Halperin, despite his claims and protestations otherwise, might be closer to Brooten's stance of redeploying terminologies of the present to suggest continuities in nonheteronormativities.

21. Lochrie's tracing (in *Heterosyncracies*) of the category of the normal and the "quite unheterosexual" forms of female sexuality in medieval texts are instructive in this regard. My current projects persist in deploying terms like "norms" and "normalizing" in analyzing premodern arguments like Paul's since they tend to function in ways analogous or akin to what these terms signify: they compare, prioritize, valorize, regulate, hierarchize, and prescribe in terms of proximity and propriety to a standard. Though Lochrie (and others) are right to note the axial difference between how the premodern "natural" and modernist "normal" are organized vertically and horizontally, respectively (see *Heterosyncrasies*, xxii–xxiii, 1–25), such arguments do still function similarly, particularly in Paul's letters, where the supposed ideal (vertical) is also a kind of prescribed communal standard (horizontal) that aims to establish boundaries for excluding deviant "outliers" who have inappropriate dispositions or practices and policing insiders who stray too far (for figures like Paul, at least). Several other core concerns of Lochrie's work persist in this book, including the flattening or disappearance of female sexualities in queer studies and the potential stabilization of heteronormativity in the present (because one uses it for the past). I share a similar commitment to counter both such practices, particularly in aiming to find, in Sedgwick's words "unexpectedly plural, varied, and contradictory, historical understandings" (Sedgwick, *Epistemology of the Closet*, 48; also cited in Lochrie, *Heterosyncrasies*, xix). The difference between Lochrie and me, though, at least partially lies in my willingness to deploy an anachronistically promiscuous use of normalization to such ends.

22. On how representative (if not also influential) this view of Halperinian discontinuity is, Fradenburg and Freccero note: "Diverse as such projects may be, many of them share, to borrow Suleri's term (1992, 12) an 'alteritism'—a belief in the absoluteness of cultural and/or historical difference—that has, for many students of modernity, come to signify the essence of our contemporaneity" ("Introduction," xv; quoting Suleri, *The Rhetoric of English India*, 12).

23. Fradenburg and Freccero, "Introduction," xix.

24. Fradenburg and Freccero, "Introduction," xvii.

25. This suggestion of a Foucauldian strategic resonance (in terms of the unanticipated directions of power-knowledge formations) with Brooten's presentation is, indeed, ironic given her own objections to Foucault (particularly, but not only, as he is enlisted as straightforwardly evangelizing a "Great Paradigm Shift" in the history of sexuality). See, for example, Brooten, *Love Between Women*, 8–9, 21–22, 143–46, 361. (Some of these also serve as Brooten's response to Halperin.) While some critical

theorists focus greater energies on Foucault's conceptualization of power (evident especially in the latter portion of *The History of Sexuality: An Introduction*), (too?) many scholars in lesbian and gay and/or queer studies have intensively (re)read his claims about sodomy and homosexuality into a range of contexts: "The sodomite had been a temporary aberration; the homosexual was now a species" (*The History of Sexuality, Volume 1*, 43). Sedgwick's critique of Halperin might be as much a critique of a particular reading (or misreading) of Foucault deployed by Halperin, yet not necessarily practiced by Foucault.

26. Dinshaw, *Getting Medieval*, 34.

27. Halperin most clearly claims his association with a range of Foucauldian arguments and practices (even as it was once foisted on him in ways unanticipated). See also his *Saint Foucault*. Halperin links Brooten with Boswell's "realist" approach to historiography (in *How to Do the History*, 58), but Brooten specifically criticizes Boswell, however, and distances her project from his in several instances, including: *Love Between Women*, 10–14, 21–22, 361.

28. For one such connection that Foucault drew from Boswell's work (especially *Christianity, Social Tolerance, and Homosexuality*) regarding the historical contingencies of collective self-fashioning in and as sexuality, see Dinshaw, *Getting Medieval*, 32–34. For suggestions about Foucault's tactical use of historical arguments, see also Dinshaw, *Getting Medieval*, 194–206.

29. Yet, for critical interrogations of the way terminologies of time rely on certain imperial-colonial conceptions of space (and how these views of space also exploit "pastness" and progress), see, for example, Latour, *We Have Never Been Modern*; McClintock, *Imperial Leather*; Fabian, *Time and the Other*; and Halberstam, *In a Queer Time and Place*.

30. Dinshaw, *Getting Medieval*, 167.

31. Pellegrini, "Touching the Past," 188.

32. Dinshaw, *Getting Medieval*, 39.

33. Halperin, *How to Do the History*, 16 and 158, n. 24 (specifically referencing Dinshaw's *Getting Medieval*).

34. Halperin's inability or unwillingness to develop strategies beyond the altericist inclination cannot be based on an ignorance of Dinshaw's work, not only because he cites her (if but momentarily), but also because the two of them cofounded *GLQ: A Journal of Gay and Lesbian Studies*.

35. Sedgwick, *Epistemology of the Closet*, 45. Brooten refers and somewhat responds to Sedgwick's critique in *Love Between Women*, 21. Halperin's recent work (*How to Do the History*, especially 10–13, 21–23) seems meant to alternately address, accept, adjust to, and allay some of Sedgwick's points, but it often does so inadequately (as argued here and at several points in the body previously).

36. Sedgwick, *Epistemology of the Closet*, 47. Even after addressing Sedgwick's critiques of his uses of and departures from Foucault in delineating a rupture in the history of sexuality (*How to Do the History*, 10–13), Halperin continues to refer to a stable present through the use of the term "nowadays" or "what we now call homosexuality" (see, for instance, *How to Do the History*, 118, 121). See also Freccero's critique in *Queer/*

Early/Modern, 38–39. Goldberg similarly critiques the altericist *and* the continuist viewpoints, as they "prove identical in several respects. For one thing, they can imagine the past under the sign of difference, but not the present. In that way both of these narratives remain devoted to a historical positivity that seems anything but the model offered by queer theory or even by its instantiation in the historical project represented by Foucault's introductory volume" ("After Thoughts," 502). Sedgwick's "unrationalized coexistence" of two models for sexuality (minoritizing and universalizing) will be discussed further in what follows.

37. Sedgwick, *Epistemology of the Closet*, 10.

38. For further reflections on the political potency of claims to alterity or similarity, see Fradenburg and Freccero, "Introduction," xix.

39. While Dinshaw's examination of the archive of letters Boswell received indicates a definite impact on those who read, or simply heard of, Boswell (*Getting Medieval*, 31–32), the potential impact is perhaps better registered in the move toward a more conservatizing (or reformist) apologetics for gays and lesbians. Indeed, this movement might also be recognized in the celebratory narrative about history's (or historians') impact on the US Supreme Court deliberations in *Lawrence v. Texas*. I (among others) am suspicious as to whether the court was swayed as much by historical claims about discontinuity as they were by an appeal to extend other kinds of normalizing arguments and dynamics, like the claim to "privacy" (the decision at least functions in this way, despite any particular read of certain justices' intent). What strikes me in this case (and others) is the persistence of the moralizing logics of differentiation and condemnation: the target of the "sodomite" figure persists, even if sodomy legally does not (at least exactly, as if it ever did so exactly). Here, I would highlight Lochrie's critique of those who see heteronormativity as stable in the present (and, then, in the past) unwittingly reproducing and naturalizing its normalizing force (*Heterosyncrasies*, xii–xxvii). Of course, the phenomena of the homonormative and the homonational indicate how unstable, flexible, yet still variously effective and agile normalizing dynamics can be. See, for example, Duggan, "The New Homonormativity"; and Puar, *Terrorist Assemblages*. Indeed, Puar's work suggests several ways to reevaluate this particular court case (in *Terrorist Assemblages*, 115–65). For further meditations on concepts of privacy and property as opposed to freedom, see also Jakobsen and Pellegrini, *Love the Sin*.

40. Sedgwick, *Epistemology of the Closet*, 11.

41. For a queer critique of the shift toward claiming "normalcy" among some in lesbian and gay (and perhaps also bisexual, trans, and intersex) circles, see Warner, *The Trouble with Normal*.

42. Sedgwick, *Epistemology of the Closet*, 43. Brooten argues to defend her use of "lesbian" in discussing the depictions of female-female erotic contact (in *Love Between Women*, 7–9, 18–23), insisting that even in suggesting continuities, "I will not use the term 'lesbian' in a way that could obscure the historical discontinuities" (*Love Between Women*, 18). Yet, her work does not take the additional step to argue that the existence of or prior continuities with ancient "lesbians" should be the basis for endorsing or supporting contemporary lesbian communities. In short, her argument is that the biblical and ancient materials should *not* be used for such purposes.

43. Sedgwick, *Epistemology of the Closet*, 90.

44. For example, Butler, *Undoing Gender*, 1, 15.

45. Butler, *Undoing Gender*, 54; cf. 253, nn. 14–15. Butler and Sedgwick depart on the degree to which it is preferable conceptually and strategically to treat gender and sexuality together. In at least this sense, Halperin and Sedgwick tend to agree in viewing gender and sexuality as separable, whereas Butler maintains that any such separation obscures the conditions of their functioning. Freccero highlights that this separation "may, at least potentially, present obstacles to understanding the particular struggles of queer sexual communities that centrally concern gender, such as movements for intersex, transgender, and transsexual rights and recognition" (*Queer/Early/Modern*, 41). One of Brooten's main critiques of Boswell involves the lack of attention to gendered difference in his constructions of ancient erotic practice and identification (*Love Between Women*, 11–12). For Butler's and Sedgwick's views, see Butler, "Against Proper Objects," and Sedgwick, *Epistemology of the Closet*, 27–35.

46. Butler, *Undoing Gender*, 179.

47. Butler, *Undoing Gender*, 37.

48. Butler, *Undoing Gender*, 214; cf. Butler, *Gender Trouble*.

49. In their proposal for an *un*historicist approach to historiography, Goldberg and Menon offer "idemtity" (as an alternative to identity) in order to stress "proportionality, likeness, or similarity that is more an approximation than a substantialization" ("Queering History," 1609–10).

50. Here, Butler argues that humans often or at least can "fail to repeat loyally" (*Bodies That Matter*, 124).

51. Butler, *Undoing Gender*, 217.

52. Butler, *Undoing Gender*, 216, 231. Here, Butler's work also links up with Spivak's injunctions toward a kind of "persistent critique."

53. Such a partial connection or negotiated identification works like what Dinshaw might call queer relations. For some of Dinshaw's specific negotiations of queer theory's "never-perfect aspect of identification," see *Getting Medieval*, 35. Connecting as much with the difference as with the similarity and, thus, transforming or parodizing the focus of identification has clear resonances with the critical interventions in Muñoz, *Disidentifications*. For example, Muñoz argues: "Disidentification is the third mode of dealing with dominant ideology, one that neither opts to assimilate within such a structure nor strictly opposes it; rather, disidentification is a strategy that works on and against dominant ideology. Instead of buckling under the pressures of dominant ideology (identification, assimilation) or attempting to break free of its inescapable sphere (counteridentification, utopianism), this 'working on and against' is a strategy that tries to transform a cultural logic from within, always laboring to enact permanent structural change while at the same time valuing the importance of local or everyday struggles of resistance" (11–12).

54. Fradenburg and Freccero, "Introduction," xviii.

55. Butler, *Undoing Gender*, 10.

56. Butler, *Gender Trouble*, vii.

57. As highlighted earlier, one might try to map the two scholars under the signs of "difference" (Halperin) and "continuity" (Brooten), but the potency and priority of such a divide between these views of history begin to collapse and deflate in the face of the foregoing arguments. Certainly, as Fradenburg and Freccero maintain ("Introduction," xix) and Dinshaw affirms (*Getting Medieval*, 35), pleasure can be found in both claims to historicist difference and transhistoricist similarity. Further, even as Brooten posits some continuities between ancient and more recent views of female-female erotics and between Paul and his historical context, the ethical-political impulse of her work presumes that there is (and should be) a significant discontinuity between antiquity and today (given the evident misogyny and gender asymmetry of the ancient contexts). For some opening and closing reflections on these kinds of continuities and discontinuities (and their contemporary significance), see Brooten, *Love Between Women*, 2–4, 18–24, 302, 361–62. Halperin's own (partial) attempts to account for continuities and his stabilization of an undifferentiated present have already been discussed earlier.

58. Halperin maintains that: "We might have expected her to foreground the opacity of the ancient sexual discourse and, instead of trying to see through them to the 'real women' who are so bizarrely represented in them and whose own experiences of same-sex desire and same-sex eroticism have left only exiguous traces in the surviving record of classical antiquity, to make those discourses reflect on the men who produced and maintained them" (*How to Do the History*, 77). Though Halperin stresses these traces as "exiguous" (meaning scanty and insignificant), the Latin root of this term also connotes exactness. The traces, though slight, might also be precise in their focus (and thus worth the historian's focus). The relation of the same root to the term "exigence," the occasion in and to which a rhetorical act addresses, also indicates the especial relevance of seemingly minor details or figures. If something contributes to an exigence, it is especially relevant for understanding a rhetorical act, whether one wants to consider the act as dissonant from or consonant with a now, then, or future. Even if scant, the continuing acts of their citation contribute to a current exigence: the citation and use of biblical texts in multiple contexts to discuss sexual norms and forms. If not yet apparent, this dismissal or at least diminution of the study of women as well as the continued impact of biblical arguments and images (by Halperin and others) strikes me as strategically shortsighted. Such responses ignore ongoing and variegated potencies and cede a vital ground of contestation, improvisation, and disidentification.

59. Dinshaw, *Getting Medieval*, 1.

60. The forms of temporal coincidence that recur in many ruminations on queer temporalities or historicities often directly or indirectly echo Sedgwick's observations about the "unrationalized coexistence of different models" (*Epistemology of the Closet*, 47). Dinshaw, for example, responds to concerns about distorting anachronisms by insisting on investigating the potential productivity of "the simultaneous copresence of different chronologies, to explore the power of multiple temporalities in a single moment" ("Got Medieval?" 209, n. 8). Goldberg and Menon seek to counter an insistence on "determinate sexual and chronological differences"

through a model of unhistoricism that "should not sacrifice sameness at the altar of difference nor collapse difference into sameness or all-but-sameness. In keeping alive the undecidable difference between difference and sameness it would refuse what we might term the compulsory heterotemporality of historicism" ("Queering History," 1609, 1616).

61. In this sense, my approach is inspired and provoked by the seven-stepped "dance" of interpretation that Schüssler Fiorenza has continuously generated, shaped, and revised, particularly in its use of suspicion, critical evaluation, historical remembrance, and an ultimate goal of transformation (for example, *Wisdom Ways*, 169–89; and *Rhetoric and Ethic*, 48–54). Though all the steps are vital, the emphases and rearrangements of my present approach are one attempt to suggest how the feminist hermeneutical process deserves and requires constant (re)evaluation and assessment as to the effects and affects desired from this process. For further considerations and qualifications of a priority on the historical horizon in biblical interpretation, see Marchal, *Hierarchy, Unity, and Imitation*, 192–202; and Marchal, *The Politics of Heaven*, 91–109.

62. See especially Wire, *The Corinthian Women Prophets*; Schüssler Fiorenza, *Rhetoric and Ethic*; Kittredge, "Rethinking Authorship"; and Marchal, *The Politics of Heaven*, especially 91–110.

63. For more of Dinshaw's reflections on and arguments for a queer kind of community or coalition across time, see *Getting Medieval*, 136–42, 170–82.

64. On proximity and approximation with identity and identification in historical processes, see Goldberg and Menon, "Queering History," 1609–10.

65. Recall Goldberg and Menon's charge for a queer unhistoricism not to repeat, but to transform normative sexual and chronological logics of difference away from "compulsory heterotemporality" (in "Queering History").

66. Butler, *Undoing Gender*, 231.

Chapter 2

1. For instance, Scroggs, "Paul and the Eschatological Woman," 297; Schüssler Fiorenza, *In Memory of Her*, 227; and Horrell and Adams, "Introduction," 34.

2. Beyond the treatment of gender performativity in *Gender Trouble* (often viewed as one of the more dense explications of this concept), see also Butler, "Imitation and Gender Insubordination"; *Bodies That Matter*; and *Undoing Gender*.

3. Butler, "Imitation and Gender Insubordination," 21.

4. Butler, *Bodies That Matter*, 124.

5. On the potential ambiguity of where this passage begins, see also Wire, *The Corinthian Women Prophets*, 116. Much of my analysis of this section of argumentation is directly influenced by or just following the insightful feminist rhetorical work of Wire and Schüssler Fiorenza (see then the essays in her *Rhetoric and Ethic*).

6. On this point, see also Castelli, *Imitating Paul*, 112–13; and Økland, *Women in Their Place*, 176–77.

7. Townsley, "*Gender Trouble* in Corinth." Townsley's preliminary analysis rarely (or even barely) considers the imitative, repetitive, and citational qualities I have stressed (reflecting similar tendencies within biblical scholarship in general).

8. This focus on the males in Corinth, in fact, persists across Townsley's work, even when it seems like such work would find closer connections with females who are engaging in certain kinds of gender variant practices: Townsley, "*Gender Trouble* in Corinth"; Townsley, "*The Straight Mind* in Corinth"; and now also Townsley, The Straight Mind *in Corinth*.

9. On the confusion of possibilities or even a deadlock in the options, see for instance, Conzelmann, *1 Corinthians*, 185; and Vander Stichele and Penner, "Paul and the Rhetoric of Gender," 300–302.

10. Jervell, *Imago Dei*, 293–312; Meeks, "Image of the Androgyne," 165–208; MacDonald, *There Is No Male and Female*; and MacDonald, "Corinthian Veils."

11. MacDonald, "Corinthian Veils," 276 (but see also 282, where MacDonald describes trying to understand the women's motivation for their actions). Feminist readings of this passage, like Wire's, explicitly take up this question as well. Scholars' refusal to seriously engage feminist work on this passage often leads to a corresponding inability (or unwillingness) to conceptualize what, how, or why the female Corinthians in this assembly were engaging in specifically embodied practices. Martin's failure to consider Wire's analysis (particularly from *The Corinthian Women Prophets*) more carefully (or his absolute lack of curiosity about them, despite their importance for treating this argument in *The Corinthian Body*, particularly 229–49), for instance, is symptomatic in this regard. For further reflections on the·potential motivations (of both scholars and of prophetic females in Corinth), see Matthews, "A Feminist Analysis of the Veiling Passage."

12. For instance, the conclusions in Meeks, "Image of the Androgyne," 206–8.

13. MacDonald, "Corinthian Veils," 285. Meeks's view is conveyed in the past tense, due to the report of Martin: "Meeks has since changed his mind and now recognizes that androgyny does not imply equality in Paul's conception (private conversation)" (*The Corinthian Body*, 294, n. 4).

14. For instance, Williams, *Rethinking "Gnosticism"*; and King, *What Is Gnosticism?*

15. For instance, the discussion in Schüssler Fiorenza, *In Memory of Her*, 205–7.

16. Wire, *The Corinthian Women Prophets*, 281, n. 16.

17. This is, in part, one of Brooten's objections (or perhaps simply cautions) about MacDonald's arguments, in "Response to 'Corinthian Veils,'" 291–96.

18. For instance, the discussion in Martin, *The Corinthian Body*, 230–33. For further reflections on the "spiritual androgyne," particularly as it relates to both Philo and Paul, see Boyarin, *A Radical Jew*, 180–200.

19. Martin, *The Corinthian Body*, 231.

20. On the predominant politics of identification in the study of Paul's letters (with Paul as the primary point of identification among scholars), see Schüssler Fiorenza, "Paul and the Politics of Interpretation"; and Johnson-DeBaufre and Nasrallah, "Beyond the Heroic Paul." (However, in the case of the latter, I cannot agree with their estimation that my own work remains focused on the figure of Paul. Even a brief survey of

the contents of the particular work in question [*The Politics of Heaven*] reflects the persistent efforts to consider and [re]construct perspectives besides Paul's, especially [but not only] those of female figures like Euodia and Syntyche.)

21. Martin's identification with Paul's perspective and incurious disposition toward these women persists throughout his examination of this passage. Notice, again, whose perspective is adopted in the question: "if veiling was understood in ancient culture to protect vulnerable women from the penetrating gaze and from dangerous invasion, who or what were those forces thought to threaten the Corinthian women prophets?" (*The Corinthian Body*, 242). Martin's method proceeds by posing an elite male perspective (about "protection" of women cast as "vulnerable") as the background, in order to explain (away?) why it was necessary for Paul to argue in a comparably "protective" way.

22. For instance, Collins, *1 Corinthians*, 409; Horsley, *1 Corinthians*, 155; and Fitzmyer, *First Corinthians*, 414.

23. Wire, *The Corinthian Women Prophets*, 118.

24. Thistelton also depicts Paul's intention "to enact a rhetorical shock" with this portion of the passage (*The First Epistle*, 832).

25. Conzelmann's commentary, for instance, spends only two sentences on verse 6 (*1 Corinthians*, 186). Even in an article that focuses on this passage, Scroggs skips over verses 5b–6 when explaining the predominant "thought structures" of this passage ("Paul and the Eschatological Woman," 298–302). The arguments in these two verses (11:5–6) are treated directly nowhere in a collection of essays specifically aimed at reconstructing the practices of Corinthians (and selecting the most influential scholarly work that [ostensibly] has such aims): Adams and Horrell, eds., *Christianity at Corinth*. In fact, these two verses are only noted in passing on four occasions in an entire volume dedicated to picturing the "Corinthian Christians"! The studied marginalization of these arguments is only increased if this passage on women's prayer and prophecy is treated briefly, as in other influential works on the letter like Mitchell, *Paul and the Rhetoric of Reconciliation*.

26. Horsley, *1 Corinthians*, 154.

27. Wire, *The Corinthian Women Prophets*, 119.

28. Økland, for example, traces just one set of ways in which it was possible to become male (*Women in Their Place*, 51–57). Indeed, it is on this point where my analysis of this passage departs from that of Wire, as well as Townsley. In what follows, I aim to show that the capacious, if confused category of ancient androgyny has at times rather precise ways to think about females with short or shaved head hair (contra Wire, earlier) and males deemed effeminate (contra Townsley, *The Straight Mind in Corinth*). For further compelling options beyond those I trace, see especially Matthews, "A Feminist Analysis of the Veiling Passage"; and Matthews, " 'To be one and the same.' "

29. All three of these terms are not found in Paul's letters, besides in 1 Corinthians 11:1–16; the last of them (*katakalyptomai*) is not found in any other New Testament passage.

30. Vander Stichele and Penner have argued that this claim could even be the "critical lynchpin of Paul's argument in 1 Cor 11" ("Paul and the Rhetoric of Gender," 292).

31. See the discussion in (and around) Laqueur, *Making Sex*, 25–27.

32. Dover, *Greek Homosexuality*, 144–45. There Dover notes: "Eupolis' comedy *Astrateutoi* ('men who have not been on military service') had the alternative title *Androgunoi* ('women-men')" (*Greek Homosexuality*, 144). See also Brisson, *Sexual Ambivalence*, 61–62.

33. See Polemo 51, 1.264F, as discussed in Gleason, "The Semiotics of Gender," 394.

34. Brisson, *Sexual Ambivalence*, 1–5.

35. Brisson, *Sexual Ambivalence*, 1. He elaborates and specifies, slightly differently, in the following sentence, "we will use the term 'dual sexuality' to refer to the possession of both female and male genitalia, whether successively or simultaneously" (1).

36. Hippocratic corpus, *Regimen* (*Peri diatēs*) 1.28; 6.500–502. For some brief discussion, see Brooten, *Love Between Women*, 157–58.

37. Brisson, *Sexual Ambivalence*, 38; from Pliny, *Natural History*, but see also Aulus Gellius, *Attic Nights*, 94, 16.

38. Hallett, "Women as *Same*," 76.

39. Brisson, *Sexual Ambivalence*, 23–31; see also MacBain, *Prodigy and Expiation*, 127–35.

40. Cicero, *De Divinatione* 1.43.98: *ortus androgyni none fatale quoddam monstrum fuit.*

41. Livy, 27.11.4–5: *et Sinuessae natum ambiguo inter marem ac feminam sexu infantem, quos androgynos volgus, ut pleraque, faciliore ad duplicanda verba Graeco sermone appellat*; see also 27.37.5f.; 31.12.6f.; 39.22.

42. On such "Hellenizing" tendencies in Roman imperial depictions of different gender and sexual practices, see Hallett, "Female Homoeroticism"; as well as Swancutt, "*Still Before Sexuality*."

43. Suetonius, "Greek Terms of Abuse," 61, and the discussion in Gleason, "The Semiotics of Gender," 394–95.

44. *Anon. Lat.* 98, 2.123F: *qui inter virum est et feminam.* (The translation is from Gleason, "The Semiotics of Gender," 396.)

45. Throughout Gleason, "The Semiotics of Gender," but especially the discussion in 396–97.

46. For an overview on *cinaedi*, see Williams, *Roman Homosexuality*, 172–224, which differs from and complicates the frequent scholarly emphasis on the *cinaedus*'s specifically sexual role (as found, for instance, in Gleason, "The Semiotics of Gender," 396).

47. Valerius Maximus, 8.3.1. See discussion in Hallett, "Women as *Same*," 66–67.

48. Williams, *Roman Homosexuality*, 127.

49. Again, the Hippocratic corpus, *Regimen* (*Peri diatēs*) 1.28; 6.500–502. For Seneca, see his *Dialogi* 12.16.5 and brief discussion in Williams, *Roman Homosexuality*, 133.

50. Plutarch, *Lives, Life of Cato the Younger*, 73.4; cf. *Life of Brutus* 13 and 53. As the wife of Brutus, Porcia was privy to the conspiracy against Julius Caesar and is thus depicted, first, as stabbing herself (to show she can keep the secret), and second, when under surveillance, finding a way to kill herself, further demonstrating the courage attributed to her own noble background (as Cato's daughter).

51. Valerius Maximus, 4.6.5: *muliebri spiritu virile patris exitum imitate.* Briefly discussed in Williams, *Roman Homosexuality*, 133.

52. Valerius Maximus, 6.1.1 (on Lucretia): *cuius virilis animus maligno errore fortunae muliebre corpus sortitus est.* Also briefly noted in Williams, *Roman Homosexuality*, 133.
53. Hallett, "Women as *Same*," 61–69.
54. Cicero, *Epistulae ad Quintum fratrem* 1.3.3: *effigiem oris, sermonis, animi mei*, as discussed in Hallett, "Women as *Same*," 62.
55. Valerius Maximus describes Hortensia's speaking in this way, in 8.3.3: *revixit tum muliebri stirpe Q. Hortensius verbisque filia aspiravit*; as discussed in Hallett, "Women as *Same*," 62.
56. Hallett, "Women as *Same*," 62. See Pliny, *Epistles* 5.26: *quae non minus mores eius quam os vultumque referebat, totumque patrem mira similitudine referebat.*
57. Hallett, "Women as *Same*," 64.
58. As Hallett notes, there are no male counterparts to these females seen as similar to their male kin; there are no "corresponding depictions of actual elite Roman men who merit special distinction for displaying . . . traits regarded in their milieu as specifically feminine and as publicly manifested in blood kinswomen" ("Women as *Same*," 64).
59. Skinner, "Introduction," 9; Hallett, "Women as *Same*," 67; and Skinner, *Sexuality in Greek and Roman Culture*, 201. See also Cornelius Nepos, 6–7.
60. Treggiari, *Roman Marriage*; Cantarella, *Bisexuality in the Ancient World*, 148–52. On remaining members of her natal family, see Gardner, *Women in Roman Law*, 162–203; Skinner, "Introduction," 10; Pomeroy, *Goddesses, Whores, Wives, and Slaves*, 154–55; and Garnsey and Saller, *The Roman Empire*, 130–36.
61. Hallett, "Women as *Same*," 67.
62. See especially Brooten's magisterial discussion of *tribades* in *Love Between Women*.
63. Martial, *Epigrams*, 7.70; see the discussion in Hallett, "Female Homoeroticism," 261–63.
64. Pseudo-Lucian, *Erotes* 28. Interestingly, the debater who brings Philaenis up as a recognizable example is described as a Corinthian.
65. Brooten, *Love Between Women*, 55.
66. Valerius Maximus, 6.1.1.
67. Brooten, *Love Between Women*, especially 61–70.
68. Especially Pintabone, "Ovid's Iphis and Ianthe."
69. Ovid, *Metamorphoses* 9.758 reads: *non vult natura.* See also 9.730.
70. Under the classificatory schema of scholars like Brisson (*Sexual Ambivalence*, 42–45), then, Iphis becomes an example of androgyny as a successive, rather than a simultaneous "dual sexuality."
71. On the complexity of Ovid's presentation of this story in this light, see Pintabone, "Ovid's Iphis and Ianthe," 264–67, 278–81.
72. Brooten, *Love Between Women*, 162–71.
73. For a different assessment of Lucian's aim in this dialogue (to be discussed further, in what follows), see Haley, "Lucian's 'Leaena and Clonarium.'"
74. On adultery, see Edwards, *The Politics of Immorality*, 34–62.
75. Elsewhere, Martial describes with disapproval the way a man becomes the wife, is unmanned by a rich wife as husband (8.12).

76. On the proximate threat of Roman matrons, see Swancutt, "*Still* Before Sexuality," 13.

77. Skinner, *Sexuality in Greek and Roman Culture*, 254.

78. The same verb, of course, is used in the preceding half of verse 6: "For if a woman will not cover, then she should shortly cut (*keirasthō*)." (Both clauses likely imply head hair as the object of the verbs.) For a brief discussion that links both of these passages, see also Knust, *Abandoned to Lust*, 82–83.

79. Wire, *The Corinthian Women Prophets*, 118–19; and Vander Stichele and Penner, "Paul and the Rhetoric of Gender," 292.

80. For instance, Schüssler Fiorenza, *In Memory of Her*; and Kraemer and D'Angelo, eds., *Women and Christian Origins*.

81. Just in 1 Corinthians, Paul casts himself in the paternal role to the Corinthians as "children" (in 3:1–2; 4:14–15, 21; see also 14:20) and uses the term *adelphoi* repeatedly (1:1, 10–11, 26; 2:1; 3:1; 4:6; 5:11; 6:1, 5–6, 8; 7:12, 15, 24, 29; 8:11–13; 10:1; 11:33; 12:1; 14:6, 20, 39; 15:1, 6, 50, 58; 16:11–12, 15, 20).

82. This would, for example, fit with Butler's conceptualization of gendered performativity, since one cannot exactly get outside the categories of sex-gender, but one can repeat their practices differently.

83. Wire, *The Corinthian Women Prophets*, 119–25. Jervell (*Imago Dei*, 295) has also posited that Paul's use of the Genesis creation stories and his own changed ideas about divine image were specifically in response to an alternative interpretation in the Corinthian assembly community.

84. Elite Romans like Cicero worried over infants as monstrous prodigies, Iphis narrates her love as monstrous, Martial claims Bassa's lust was monstrous, *tribades* in general are viewed as a certain kind of gender monster. For more on the potential of the monstrous in interpretation of this passage, see Townsley, The Straight Mind *in Corinth*, 193–252.

85. The horror Paul might be trying to evoke through this argument should not be mistaken as the "horror of homosexualism" (Barrett, *A Commentary*, 257). Beyond the anachronism it presents, it needlessly reduces and specifies forms of gender variation, often known as androgyny, as homoerotic sexual practices.

86. For some discussion of Paul's difference in perspective (from both ancient surroundings and more recent "followers"), see Martin, "Paul Without Passion."

87. Brooten, "Response to 'Corinthian Veils,'" 295.

88. As discussed earlier, this is the question about which most biblical scholars remain studiously aloof, but that feminist scholars (like Wire and Matthews) persistently pursue.

89. For further reflections on the disciplinary effects of certain accepted narratives for trans people to gain access to specific psychological endorsements for medical attention or care, see Marchal, "The Corinthian Women Prophets and Trans Activism."

90. Haley, "Lucian's 'Leaena and Clonarium,'" 297. On the use of the mannish lesbian for texts like these, see also Gordon, "The Lover's Voice."

91. For further reflections on terminologies, their origins, and their uses, see Stryker, "(De)Subjugated Knowledges"; as well as Stryker, *Transgender History*. Stryker notes

that transgender "most generally refers to any and all kinds of variation from gender norms and expectations" (*Transgender History*, 19).

92. Stryker, "(De)Subjugated Knowledges," 2–4; Halberstam, *Female Masculinity*, 161. Elsewhere Halberstam explains: "Transgender is for the most part a vernacular term developed within gender communities to account for the cross-identification experiences of people who may not accept all of the protocols and strictures of transsexuality. Such people understand cross-identification as a crucial part of their gendered self, but they may pick and choose among the options of body modification, social presentation, and legal recognition available to them" (*In a Queer Time and Place*, 53).

93. Feinberg, "Transgender Liberation," 206.

94. For some preliminary indications of the debts, links, differences, and overlaps between feminist, queer, and transgender studies and movements, from a set of explicitly transgender studies' perspectives, see Hines, "Feminism"; Murib, "LGBT"; and Love, "Queer." For some of the tensions and connections between lesbian, gay, and trans communities and activisms, see Bornstein, *Gender Outlaw*, 67–68. (For a brief reflection on the same groups, as well as bisexual and BDSM communities, see *Gender Outlaw*, 159.)

95. Bornstein, *Gender Outlaw*, 121.

96. Bornstein, *Gender Outlaw*, 69.

97. Bornstein, *Gender Outlaw*, 134–35. Bornstein imagines (and builds) such alliances under a provocative, yet provisional banner, "a banner that would include anyone who cares to admit their own gender ambiguities" (*Gender Outlaw*, 98).

98. This accounts for the capaciousness of transgender studies, as Stryker describes it ("(De)Subjugated Knowledges," 3). As with ancient figures and forms of androgyny, this appears to indicate that there is no brief, pithy, accurate, and adequate definition of transgender (studies). Transgender studies has developed so quickly (and in such a rich variety of directions) that my chapter cannot begin to do justice to, or pretend to offer a comprehensive overview of, this transdisciplinary field. One sign of its impact is the successful launch of a journal solely dedicated to such work: *TSQ: Transgender Studies Quarterly*. Indeed, the first edition of this new journal (*Postposttranssexual*) provides a helpful entry point into the field.

99. Stryker, "(De)Subjugated Knowledges," 13.

100. Weismantel, "Toward a Transgender Archaeology," 321.

101. Stryker, *Transgender History*, 23–24. In this discussion Stryker also admits the difficulty in using terms that subjects (like butches or transsexuals) might not always accept for themselves: "There is no way of using the word that doesn't offend some people by including them where they don't want to be included or excluding them from where they do want to be included" (*Transgender History*, 24).

102. Halberstam, *Female Masculinity*, 1; and Halberstam, "The Good, the Bad, and the Ugly," 345.

103. Halberstam, *Female Masculinity*, 240–41; as well as entire section of essays on transgender masculinities in Stryker and Whittle, eds., *The Transgender Studies Reader*, 469–544.

104. Rubin, "Of Catamites and Kings," 467.

105. Rubin, "Of Catamites and Kings," 469.

106. Halberstam, "The Good, the Bad, and the Ugly," 345.

107. Halberstam, *Female Masculinity*, 1.

108. Bornstein expresses a set of concerns with contemporary claims about androgyny, given how it can stabilize specific gender roles and present them as if they are on a continuum: "Androgyny could be seen as a trap of the bi-polar gender system, as it further establishes the idea of two-and-only-two-genders" (*Gender Outlaw*, 115).

109. For instance, Green, "Look! No, Don't!," 502; and Cromwell, "Queering the Binaries," 513.

110. Volcano and Halberstam, *The Drag King Book*, 120, 125.

111. Volcano and Halberstam, *The Drag King Book*; as well as the overview and analysis in Halberstam, *Female Masculinity*, 231–66.

112. Halberstam, *Female Masculinity*, 30–39. See also some of Volcano's additional and overlapping portraits of masculine women, in *The Drag King Book*, 33, 37, 38, 151; and Volcano, *Sublime Mutations*.

113. For instance, Halberstam, *Female Masculinity*, 109.

114. Rubin, "Of Catamites and Kings," 473.

115. For example, the arguments in Raymond, *The Transsexual Empire*. Raymond's view (though influential in some circles at certain points) should not be treated as representative of the whole of feminisms, particularly given the ways transgender studies and movements are rooted in feminist principles and include feminist participants. For just a few of the reflections on feminisms and trans politics and practices, see the work of Feinberg, Bornstein, Halberstam, and many of the other scholars examined within this section, as well as Wilchins, *Read My Lips*; Scott-Dixon, ed., *Trans/ forming Feminisms*; Serano, *Whipping Girl*; and Enke, ed., *Transfeminist Perspectives*.

116. Halberstam, "F2M"; and "Transgender Butch"; revised and expanded in *Female Masculinity*, 141–73.

117. Halberstam, *Female Masculinity*, 143–44.

118. For instance, Rubin, "Of Catamites and Kings," 469–70.

119. Halberstam, *Female Masculinity*, 156; as well as Spade, "Mutilating Gender," 323.

120. Spade, "Mutilating Gender," 323.

121. APA, *DSM-IV* (1994), 533. Of course, hair-cutting can be represented in a range of pleasurable, affirmative, and ambivalent fashions for butch and trans practices. See the discussion in Halberstam, *Female Masculinity*, 224–25, 268; and Spade, "Mutilating Gender," 322.

122. Rubin, "Of Catamites and Kings," 477.

123. Halberstam, *Female Masculinity*, 144.

124. Such a model of masculinity can reinforce claims that trans men have crossed a line and "taken masculinity too far," or that butches are really just "aspirational" trans men.

125. As described in Cromwell, "Queering the Binaries," 512.

126. Cromwell, "Queering the Binaries," 512. Over the years Halberstam has increasingly adopted masculine pronouns (and the first name Jack), but still uses terms of

variation in self-description: "I identify as a trans-butch or a drag butch, in other words, a butch who is at the transitive edge of female masculinity." Halberstam, "Preface," in *The Drag King Book*, 1. This book used Jack as an intermediate name, as does the more recent *Gaga Feminism* (J. Jack Halberstam), whereas the first name Judith was used and occasionally still appears in other publications (including *Female Masculinity, In a Queer Time and Place*, and *The Queer Art of Failure*). In short, publication history offers no straight-forward, linear "transition" for patterns of identification.

127. Volcano interrogates the construction of contemporary forms of androgyny in a series of self-portraits in *Sublime Mutations*. See also the discussion in Singer, "From the Medical Gaze," 601–20; and Bornstein, *Gender Outlaw*, 165.

128. Halberstam, *Female Masculinity*, 232.

129. Volcano's definition can be found in Del's "Foreword: A Kingdom Comes," *The Drag King Book*, 10–28, 16.

130. Halberstam, *Female Masculinity*, 232.

131. The overlaps between trans, butch, lesbian, and drag king codes and communities are discussed in both *Female Masculinity*, 231–66; and *The Drag King Book*. While Halberstam often describes the drag kings as lesbian performers, Volcano sees drag kings as "part of the transgendered spectrum but not everyone who does drag is transgendered or wants to be" ("Foreword," 27).

132. Halberstam, *The Drag King Book*, 150.

133. Stryker, "My Words to Victor Frankenstein"; reprinted in *The Transgender Studies Reader*, 244–56. Though the editors of the latter stress the unique way in which Stryker's article links transgender studies to queer theories, it should be noted how much queer theoretical materials attended to transgender practices and people even in its "beginnings" (as reflected in this article's appearance in the first year of the journal, *GLQ*). For a critical, if occasionally misdirected appraisal of the appearance of trans figures in queer scholarship, see Prosser, "Judith Butler"; reprinted in *The Transgender Studies Reader*, 257–80.

134. Stryker directly references both Raymond, *The Transsexual Empire*, 178; and Daly, *Gyn/Ecology*, 69–72.

135. Stryker, "My Words to Victor Frankenstein," 240.

136. Sullivan, "Transmogrification," 553.

137. Stryker, "My Words to Victor Frankenstein," 247.

138. This problem of access to the perspectives of those who engage in such practices is foregrounded by Brooten in her response to MacDonald: "We should not assume that those who wrote about transvestism and same-sex love in antiquity held the same views of these phenomena as those who practiced them. I am not convinced that women who dressed as men or who loved women perceived themselves as masculine or that men who wore long hair or who loved men perceived themselves as being like women" (Brooten, "Response," 295–96). I agree in principle with Brooten's concerns about the specifically kyriarchal perspective of many sources, even as I am not yet convinced that one can entirely rule out the possible reuses of conceptions of masculinity among the prophetic females in the Corinthian assembly. In later work,

228   NOTES

Brooten is (at least briefly) willing to consider some of the different ways women can deploy masculinely coded behaviors.

139. Murphy-O'Connor, "Sex and Logic."

140. Barrett, *A Commentary*, 257; Scroggs, "Paul and the Eschatological Woman," 297; as well as Murphy-O'Connor's specific citation of their (brief) precedent to this reading in "Sex and Logic," 487, n. 25.

141. Meier, "On the Veiling of Hermeneutics," 219, n. 15.

142. Murphy-O'Connor, "Sex and Logic," 485.

143. Murphy-O'Connor, "Sex and Logic," 490. (In the article, though, his suggestion of a parallel mistakenly attributes the teaching about male hair length to v. 15, rather than v. 14.)

144. Murphy-O'Connor, "Sex and Logic," 489.

145. Fitzmyer, for instance, objects: "it is wholly gratuitous to introduce into the interpretation of this pericope a consideration of male homosexual styles of wearing hair" (*First Corinthians*, 406).

146. Thistelton, *The First Epistle*, 833. Just prior to this, Thistelton notes the importance of Murphy-O'Connor to this reading: "Classical literature contains examples of the blurring of gender complementarity in lesbian relations in the context of 'cropped' or 'shaved' hair, which coheres with arguments above, including Murphy-O'Connor's allusion to male homosexuality in v. 4" (*The First Epistle*, 832).

147. MacGregor, "Is 1 Corinthians 11:2–16 a Prohibition," 213. Beyond just the agreement about the significance of hair length for sexed differentiations, in many places MacGregor uses the same roster of ancient texts and traditions and simply repeats Murphy-O'Connor, often without citation.

148. Writing more than a decade after Halberstam's *Female Masculinity* (1998), MacGregor names "female masculinity" (again, without citation) as the problem Paul has with the Corinthian audience three times, once each on the three final pages of his article, "Is 1 Corinthians 11:2–16 a Prohibition," 214, 215, 216. (The first such occasion is quoted earlier.)

149. MacGregor, "Is 1 Corinthians 11:2–16 a Prohibition," 214.

150. For the best examination of what is known and not known about the meaning of these two words, as well as the baldly heterosexist impact of their recent translation(s), see Martin, "*Arsenokoitēs* and *Malakos*." MacGregor regularly appears to exaggerate claims about both the epistle and the state of its interpretation, while also demonstrating a thorough lack of knowledge about contemporary lesbian or gay practices (by, for instance, twice claiming the letter's condemnation of the "full range" or "full scope" of "homosexual behavior" ("Is 1 Corinthians 11:2–16 a Prohibition," 203, 214), again, via a reference to just two contested words quoted from a vice list).

151. MacGregor's perspective is made clear by his conclusion: "Proponents of inerrancy should proceed to a straightforward application of this text which forbids homosexual practice, male effeminate and female masculine behavior, and dress indicative of the opposite sex" ("Is 1 Corinthians 11:2–16 a Prohibition," 216).

152. These sorts of arguments are one reason (among many) for the kinds of alliances forged between these groups, because they are often targeted together for either identical or related reasons (however misconceived, mistaken, or even occasionally correct about the challenges such people or practice could pose).

153. Rubin, "Of Catamites and Kings," 469. Further, D'Angelo ("Veils, Virgins,") argues that Paul may be insisting that women cover their heads and their hair because he sees these as analogous to their genitals, body parts that should signal their belonging to husbands (or others with authority over women), some of the parts stressed in negative characterization of female androgyny.

154. Halberstam, "The Good, the Bad, and the Ugly," 345.

155. In introducing *Female Masculinity* (the book, the concept, and the practice), Halberstam asserts the book "describes the details of masculine difference by comparing not men and women but butch lesbians and female-to-male transsexuals" (*Female Masculinity*, 3).

156. On the difficulties gender and/or sexual difference presents to theological systems of anthropology, in the wake of Paul's letters, see Dunning, *Specters of Paul*; and Dunning, *Christ Without Adam*.

157. Haley, "Lucian's 'Leaena and Clonarium,'" 297.

158. Halberstam, *Female Masculinity*, 144. For another valuable adaptation of Halberstam's for a trans reading of biblical masculinities, see Guest, "Modeling the Transgender Gaze."

159. In contrast to my present reading of this passage, even a scholar attentive to bodies, like Martin, is mostly concerned with demonstrating why Paul (among others in the ancient world) would have objected to females engaging in uncovered prophecy, not in considering how such an action potentially resonates with other patterns of gender variation (evaluated positively, negatively, and otherwise). In short, Martin remains remarkably incurious about the Corinthian females themselves and uninterested in their own interests or rationales for participating in assembly life in this way. This disinterest, even occlusion, is stark given the careful rhetorical analysis of the letter performed in light of these women by Wire (in *The Corinthian Women Prophets*, preceding Martin's *The Corinthian Body* by several years).

160. Wire, *The Corinthian Women Prophets*, 119 (cf. 122).

161. For instance, Wire's characterization of the prophetic females here: "Rejecting all social privilege and social disadvantage, they take on a single common identity in Christ and practice gifts of prayer and prophecy without regard to gender" (*The Corinthian Women Prophets*, 126). Wire frequently discusses their different negotiations of gender, changed basis of respect or honor, and the potential disruption they attributed to divine actions in their lives (but just a few examples can be found in *The Corinthian Women Prophets*, 129, 176, 184).

162. Stryker, "My Words to Victor Frankenstein," 240; and Sullivan, "Transmogrification," 553.

163. Stryker, "My Words to Victor Frankenstein," 247.

164. Namaste, "Genderbashing"; reprinted in Namaste, *Invisible Lives*, 135–56; and Stryker and Whittle, eds., *The Transgender Studies Reader*, 584–600.
165. Love, " 'Spoiled Identity,' " 498.
166. Dinshaw, *Getting Medieval*, 167.
167. For further consideration of these people on the other side of Paul's arguments, see Miller, *Corinthian Democracy*.
168. Dinshaw, *Getting Medieval*, 39.

Chapter 3

1. Butler treats this declaration as an exemplary instance of performativity in a few places, including *Bodies That Matter*, 231–32.
2. For one, more informal discussion of the role of religious and even specifically biblical counsel for parents of an intersex child, see Hendricks, "Is It a Boy or a Girl?" The piece is fascinating for a number of reasons, including the way it cycles between doubt and certitude, faith in the medical professionals profiled and faith in God and scriptures. Perhaps these juxtapositions are meant to be primarily associative, as Hendricks appears to miss the dissociation between the prescribed course of action and one parent's theological reaction (that, itself, concludes the piece): "We've come to the conclusion that this is a special child and a member of our family. We trust in God. The world is not perfect" (16). For other ways in which religious arguments or identifications can either support or undermine intersex people, see Diamond and Beh, "The Right to Be Wrong"; and Kerry, "Intersex Individuals' Religiosity."
3. Hillman, *Intersex (For Lack of a Better Word)*.
4. This question is actively considered by the Christians discussed, for instance, in Gross, "Intersexuality and Scripture"; Looy, "Male and Female"; Jung, "Christianity and Human Sexual Polymorphism"; and Cornwall, " 'State of Mind.' "
5. Looy, "Male and Female," 11–12, 16; Jung, "Christianity and Human Sexual Polymorphism," 304; O'Donovan, *Transsexualism*; Colson, "Blurred Biology"; and the reflections in Mollenkott, *Omnigender*, 84–86, 90, 92; and Cornwall, " 'State of Mind.' " For ways that Christians similarly read this narrative into Paul's argumentation in Romans 1 to discuss the "biblical stance on" homosexuality, see Martin, "Heterosexism"; as well as the analysis in chapter 5.
6. "God's Unique Creation" is the tagline on ISGI's main page, and is also prominently featured in the site's Manifesto page, where the contrasting comments reflecting a theology of "The Fall" can also be found. See http://www.xyxo.org/isgi/index.html and http://www.xyxo.org/isgi/Manifesto.html For a narrative that weaves evangelical reflections on scripture with personal experiences of the treatment of intersex people in a "Bible teaching Baptist church," see the Director's Page of ISGI: http://www.xyxo.org/isgi/director.html See also the brief discussions of ISGI in Mollenkott, *Omnigender*, 5; and Preves, *Intersex and Identity*, 93–95.
7. Lebacqz, "Difference or Defect?" 200; Gross, "Intersexuality and Scripture," 74; and Jung, "Christianity and Human Sexual Polymorphism," 299. For a small sample of

some of the treatment of intersex people in church communities, see Looy, "Male and Female," 15. For a substantial approach that is both sympathetic to intersex people and (apologetically) inclined toward conservative evangelical and Roman Catholic audiences (and thus suspicious of the utility of queer approaches), see DeFranza, *Sex Difference*.

8. Gross, "Intersexuality and Scripture," 70.
9. Coan, "Shunned by the Church," http://www.isna.org/pdf/gross2.pdf.
10. Gross, "Intersexuality and Scripture," 70–74. See also the elaborations on Gross in Carden, "Genesis/Bereshit," especially 25–30. One of Looy's friends similarly notes: "this implies that God's fullness includes both male and female aspects. He has wondered, not entirely tongue in cheek, whether this means that intersexes reflect God's image more completely than most, and notes that the Genesis passage states 'male *and* female God created them,' not male *or* female!" (Looy, "Male and Female," 17).
11. Gross, "Intersexuality and Scripture," 74.
12. Mollenkott, *Omnigender*, 90–93; Tanis, *Trans-Gendered*, 61–62.
13. Hendricks, "Is It a Boy," 13.
14. ISGI's Manifesto page http://www.xyxo.org/isgi/Manifesto.html (accessed July 27, 2010). The same quote can be found in Preves, *Intersex and Identity*, 93. (Note that the ISGI website had already moved from isgi.org when I first researched this in 2009 and 2010.) See also at least one of the interviewed intersex Christians in Cornwall, "British Intersex Christians' Accounts," 225. Cornwall's more recent empirical research is compelling for how many affirmative church experiences are communicated by those intersex Christians she interviewed. Here, see also Cornwall, "Asking About What Is Better"; and Cornwall, "Telling Stories." However, the rather small sample size and the requirement that an interview subject continue to self-identify as Christian indicate the potential limitations (or even affirmative tilt) of this (initial) study. On the methodology for this study, see Cornwall, "British Intersex Christians' Accounts," 222.
15. While the Christians in ISGI and in Hendricks's article refer to such passages with confidence and consolation, Gross and the Christians in Looy notably do not.
16. Mollenkott, *Omnigender*, 110–14, 118–22; Tanis, *Trans-Gendered*, 69–79; and Jung, "Christianity and Human Sexual Polymorphism," 305. Mollenkott, for instance, identifies the eunuchs "from birth" with intersex people, those "made eunuchs by others" with postoperative transsexuals, and those "who have made themselves eunuchs for the kingdom of heaven" with pre- and nonoperative transsexuals, transgender, homosexual, and celibate people (*Omnigender*, 120). Reay specifically builds on Mollenkott and Tanis, repeatedly linking intersex to transgender in "Towards a Transgender Theology."
17. Mollenkott, *Omnigender*, vii–ix, 192 (cf. 85, 113–14); cf. Tanis, *Trans-Gendered*, 80–83; and Jung, "Christianity and Human Sexual Polymorphism," 303.
18. I write "as" (earlier) in order to mark this chapter's effort to work in solidarity with wider movements around the visibility and viability of intersex people. In short, whether you, or I, or even they know it, there are intersex people in our lives. After

all, how many of us know, rather than assume or ascribe, the precise chromosomal or hormonal elements of our anatomy? Even our gonadal structures might not be as self-evident as we might think in our routine (and not-so-routine) contact with our bodies. Here, I am also striving not to treat people with intersex conditions as fetish objects, or as an interesting limit case for scholars, theologians, and religious professionals to consider, nor should it be for scholars in women's, gender, and sexuality studies (though I fear that intersex has been and in some cases still is treated this way). In their critical attention to the use of intersex in the women's or gender studies classroom, Koyama and Weasel exhort scholars, teachers, and activists to "use theories to support people, rather than the other way around" ("From Social Construction," 175). As Cornwall narrates ("Introduction"), well-intentioned scholars in religious and theological studies have also used intersex conditions as a test case to "think with," particularly, but not only within ecclesial debates about homosexuality. (Here, Cornwall is referring to Hare, " 'Neither Male Nor Female.' ") I note these instances as a caution against making arguments too abstract or distanced from intersex people, or simply using people to "score points" in other contexts. An engagement with and commitment to addressing the stigmatizing conditions of people with intersex conditions necessitates doing more than just using their bodies as instruments for other purposes.

19. The quote in the heading is from Triea, "Finishing School Dropout," as quoted in Crouch, "Betwixt and Between," 34.
20. Karkazis, *Fixing Sex*, 6–7, 291–92, n. 4.
21. Dreger and Herndon "define a person as intersex if she or he was born with a body that someone decided isn't typical for males or females" ("Progress and Politics," 200). See also the Intersex Society of North America's definition, "What Is Intersex?" (http://www.isna.org/faq/what_is_intersex). For a later definition of intersex, as "disorders of sex development," involving atypical development in chromosomal, gonadal, or anatomical sex, see Lee et al., "Consensus Statement."
22. Reis, for instance, defines intersex conditions as those where there is "discordance between the multiple components of sex anatomy (internal reproductive organs, external genitalia, and sex chromosomes)" ("Divergence or Disorder?," 536). The most common form of intersex is congenital adrenal hyperplasia (CAH), a condition where a person with a 46, XX karyotype and ovaries produces androgens that "virilize" the external genitalia as an infant or at the onset of puberty. The next most common intersex diagnosis is androgen insensitivity syndrome (AIS), a condition where a person with a 46, XY karyotype and testes is partially or completely insensitive to androgens, thus "feminizing" the external genitalia. In another form of androgen insensitivity, 5-alpha-reductase deficiency (5-AR), the body does not "read" testosterone until puberty because of a missing enzyme. The external genitalia appear to be feminine until the "masculinizing" puberty occurs. For brief definitions, descriptions, and statistical frequencies of the various intersex diagnoses, see Kessler, *Lessons*, 165–68; Dreger, *Hermaphrodites*, 37–43; Wilson and Reiner, "Management of Intersex," especially 122–23; Fausto-Sterling, *Sexing the Body*, 50–54; and Karkazis, *Fixing Sex*, 22–26. Roughly 60 percent of diagnoses of atypical or ambiguous genitalia are attributed to CAH (Karkazis, *Fixing Sex*, 19–20;

and Grumbach and Conte, "Disorders of Sex Differentiation," 1360). For an even higher percentage estimate, see Fausto-Sterling, *Sexing the Body*, 53; and Blackless, Charuvastra, Derryck, Fausto-Sterling, Lauzanne, and Lee, "How Sexually Dimorphic Are We?"

23. For exemplary summaries of the now traditional medicalized protocol, see Kessler, *Lessons*, 12–32; Dreger, *Hermaphrodites*, 180–88; Wilson and Reiner, "Management of Intersex," 122–25; Fausto-Sterling, *Sexing the Body*, 30–77; and perhaps most comprehensively, Karkazis, *Fixing Sex*, 47–62.

24. Most of the founding assumptions of this protocol can be traced to the influence of John Money and his colleagues. For example, by Money, Hampson, and Hampson: "Hermaphroditism"; "An Examination"; and "Imprinting and the Establishment of Gender Role." By Money alone, see: "Hermaphroditism" (1952); "Hermaphroditism" (1956); and "Psychologic Consideration of Sex Assignment." Money's work would reach a much wider professional and popular audience through: Money and Ehrhardt, *Man and Woman*.

25. Kessler, *Lessons*, 19, 25; Dreger, "A History of Intersex," 11; and Karkazis, *Fixing Sex*, 159 (cf. 142–55).

26. Note all of the sources quoted in Crouch, "Betwixt and Between," 30, 44; as well as Kessler, *Lessons*, 34, 141; Fausto-Sterling, *Sexing the Body*, 45, 275–76; Karkazis, *Fixing Sex*, 182–85; and Feder, *Family Bonds*, 66.

27. Kessler, *Lessons*, 15. For more on the role of belief in scientific and medical views of intersex, see Fausto-Sterling, *Sexing the Body*.

28. That the rationale for the treatment protocol (the need for male-like genitalia—a longer phallic structure—early in life to ensure stable male gender identity) is inconsistent is made clear by the recommendation against surgery for 5-AR assigned males (Kessler, *Lessons*, 41).

29. For various illustrations of this size standard for infant genitalia, typically depicted in ruler form, see Kessler, *Lessons*, 43, 101; Fausto-Sterling, *Sexing the Body*, 59; as well as a version of the "Phall-O-Meter" used by intersex activists (and created by Triea), "The Phall-O-Meter," http://alicedreger.com/phallometer.html.

30. While there are some signs that surgeons are becoming more reluctant to perform "feminizing" surgeries on those karyotype 46, XY males with micropenises, early genital surgery is still recommended in most intersex cases, especially when the infant is receiving a female gender assignment (Karkazis, *Fixing Sex*, 135–37). In cases where the combination of factors (including gonadal, genital, genetic, chromosomal, and hormonal components) is more mixed or ambiguous than these general descriptions (earlier), the default assignment and treatment is also for a female gender assignment.

31. For succinct summing statements to this effect, see Preves, *Intersex and Identity*, 11, 145, 152. Shame, in particular, runs throughout the key studies as well as the first-person interviews and narratives in: most of the entries in Dreger, ed., *Intersex in the Age of Ethics*; Preves, *Intersex and Identity*; Hester, "Intersex and the Rhetorics of Healing"; and Karkazis, *Fixing Sex*, 216–35, 236–90. Preves's entire monograph is structured around how intersex people deal with shame and social stigmatization, following stresses among activists like Chase: "Surgery inflicts emotional harm

by legitimating the idea that the child is not lovable unless 'fixed' with medically unnecessary plastic surgery carrying significant risks" ("Surgical Progress," 155; cf. 147).

32. Dreger, "A History of Intersex," 19.

33. Preves, *Intersex and Identity*, 72.

34. For examples of firsthand responses to such lies and deception, see Groveman, "The Hanukkah Bush," 26–27; Coventry, "Finding the Words," 72; Preves, *Intersex and Identity*, 68, 73–75; Hester, "Intersex and the Rhetorics of Healing," 53–54, 58; and Karkazis, *Fixing Sex*, 221.

35. Intersex Society of North America, *Hermaphrodites with Attitude* 1:1 (Winter 1994); as quoted in Kessler, *Lessons*, 79–80.

36. Chase, "What Is the Agenda," 240. Karkazis similarly explains that the goals for many intersex people and intersex activists are "to change treatment practices and improve the well-being of others with these conditions. While this goal necessarily involves a broadened understanding of what it means to be male and female, the cornerstone of this argument does not center on gender: intersexuality, these activists argue, is primarily a problem of stigma and trauma, not of gender" (*Fixing Sex*, 247).

37. Some "improvements" in treatment practices still perpetuate such effects through terminological shifts, like the move to label intersex "disorders of sexual development" (DSD) in Consortium on the Management of Disorders of Sex Development, *Clinical Guidelines*. Though such a term is ostensibly meant to eliminate the gendered and sexualized connotations of intersex (apparently to address stigma), it simply shifts to a different and perhaps more stigmatizing term like disorder (as exposed in Reis, "Divergence or Disorder?")!

38. As Chase highlights, it was precisely this that surgical experts claimed for decades: "As recently as 1993, no one publicly disputed surgeon Milton Edgerton when he wrote that in forty years of clitoral surgery on intersexuals, 'not one has complained of loss of sensation, *even when the entire clitoris was removed*'" ("Hermaphrodites with Attitude," 192; quoting Edgerton, "Discussion").

39. Kessler, *Lessons*, 56–57; Wilson and Reiner, "Management of Intersex," 125; Chase, "Surgical Progress," 152; Fausto-Sterling, *Sexing the Body*, 85–87; and Preves, *Intersex and Identity*, 79–80.

40. Preves, *Intersex and Identity*, 74, 79–80, 83–85; and Karkazis, *Fixing Sex*, 216–17, 229–31.

41. As one respondent describes their experience: "I was forced to be surgically mutilated and medically raped at the age of fourteen. And that's exactly what I consider it" (Preves, *Intersex and Identity*, 73). See also Chase, "Hermaphrodites with Attitude," 195; Kessler, *Lessons*, 39–40, 78–79; Crouch, "Betwixt and Between," 34–35; Preves, *Intersex and Identity*, 65; and Karkazis, *Fixing Sex*, 1–3, 133, 199, 210–11, 255. For Chase ("'Cultural Practice'"), the connection to what has been called female genital mutilation (in Africa, for example) is intentional.

42. Kipnis and Diamond comment on the focus of the creator of this protocol: "echoing Freud, Money surmised that the presence or absence of the penis was the critical anatomical factor" ("Pediatric Ethics," 176). Though the protocol proceeds from the

assumption of a clear idea of a "normal" sized clitoris (not penis-sized), female genital size and appearance have rarely been defined outside of vague descriptions. On the long periods of inattention or underrepresentation of the clitoris in medical literature, see Fausto-Sterling, *Sexing the Body*, 85. The first table for neonate clitoral size was not published until twenty-five years after the OGR treatment paradigm had been introduced and practiced—on the claim that doctors were acting on the basis of clitoral size (Karkazis, *Fixing Sex*, 150–51)!

43. Greenburg, "International Legal Developments," 93. Wilson and Reiner concur: "Sexual function for genetic males and fertility for genetic females are the major considerations" ("Management," 123). For similar observations, see Hegarty and Chase, "Intersex Activism," 124; and Roen, "Queer Kids," 263.

44. Holmes, "Queer Cut Bodies," 100.

45. On the lack of concern with female satisfaction with forms of sexual contact, see Greenburg, "International Legal Developments," 97; Holmes, "Rethinking the Meaning," 172. Preves (*Intersex*, 56–57) discusses cases where surgical treatments are withheld until the intersex woman was married or in a monogamous heterosexual relationship.

46. For a first-person account that stresses how surgery is as much for the (future) husband, see Walcutt, "Time," 198 and 199.

47. Hendricks, "Is It a Boy," 15. Though the quote in its original context is unattributed, it was later identified, with regret, as the words of Johns Hopkins surgeon John P. Gearhart (Holmes, "Rethinking the Meaning," 169). Though Gearhart regrets it, those engaged in ethical reflection on these practices should be grateful that he let such a way of thinking slip and, thus, communicate explicitly some of the implicitly misogynist notions in these medical practices.

48. Dreger and Herndon, "Progress," 202.

49. Triea, "Power, 143.

50. Chase, "Hermaphrodites," 207. Karkazis describes the specifically andro- and phallocentric basis for these surgical priorities accordingly: "The assumption is that it would be better to be a woman without a vagina and no reproductive capacity than a man with a small penis" (*Fixing Sex*, 116).

51. As Chase explains it on another occasion: "What you produce is somebody who has a body that is vaguely female, is infertile, doesn't menstruate, probably doesn't have any sexual function, might have genital pain, and has been lied to and shamed. That is supposed to be less painful than having a small dick? I think it is taken to be less painful because female pain is discounted. Once it has been transformed into female pain it doesn't bother us so much" (Hegarty and Chase, "Intersex Activism," 124; cf. Roen, "Queer Kids," 264).

52. Crouch, "Betwixt and Between," 31; and Hester, "Intersex(es) and Informed Consent," 33. Yet, this determination about patient well-being and medical action seems misplaced when it is based on infant genital length, particularly since studies have indicated that there is no direct correspondence between infant and adult genital size (Preves, *Intersex and Identity*, 57; and Karkazis, *Fixing Sex*, 102). Furthermore, it is strange that medical practitioners focus on delivering such specific and more post-pubescent outcomes (penis length or vaginal depth) in early

surgery. As Holmes notes: "An infant has no requirement for a vagina" ("Rethinking the Meaning," 170).

53. Sytsma, "The Ethics of Using Dexamethasone."

54. Preves, *Intersex and Identity*, 49; Reis, "Divergence or Disorder?" 540; and Dreger, Feder, and Tamar-Mattis, "Preventing Homosexuality (and Uppity Women)."

55. For some commonalities between the treatment of childhood gender identity disorder (CGID) and intersex, also as ways of defending masculinity, see Roen, "Queer Kids," 269.

56. Dreger, *Hermaphrodites*; and Feder, "Imperatives," 227, 242.

57. Fausto-Sterling, *Sexing the Body*, 72.

58. Dreger and Herndon, "Progress," 207; cf. Holmes, "Queer Cut Bodies," 84.

59. This is a common, even aphoristic phrase in Pauline interpretation, since "freedom" is commonly seen as a major conceptual theme for the letter to the Galatians, particularly since Luther first focused so much of his own interpretive attention on this letter. Betz sees freedom as the central theological concept: "It is the basic concept underlying Paul's argument throughout the letter" (*Galatians*), 255.

60. Kahl notes, for instance that: "Nobody would question that circumcision is the most burning problem of Galatians" ("No Longer Male," 40). Dunn similarly opens an article (*The New Perspective*, 313) with the declaration: "The central issue in these passages is obviously circumcision." For further arguments about the central role of circumcision in ancient Judaisms and in Paul's letters (like Galatians), see Dunn, *The New Perspective*, 153–71. Martyn's reconstruction of the reason for Paul writing the letter (in *Galatians*, 13–19), for example, revolves around the desire of the audience to be circumcised, in accordance with what "the Teachers" brought to the community (120–26, 303–5, 560–62).

61. See also the same verbal root for "force" or "compel" (*anagkazein*) in Paul's description of the nonnecessity for Titus to be circumcised (2:3) and Cephas's actions toward the Gentiles/nations (2:14).

62. Indeed, the tenor and trajectory of this letter (and scholarly tendencies to identify with Paul's perspective) have led to a whole host of constructions of "opponents," often cast as aggressively invasive and disruptive.

63. For further reflections on a more descriptive (perhaps closer) translation of this verse and especially the term for "uncircumcision," see the discussion later (as well as Lopez, *Apostle to the Conquered*, 146–47).

64. For some of the contours of feminist arguments about circumcision and the status and role of women in early Judaisms and Christianities, see Lieu, "Circumcision."

65. Kahl, "Gender Trouble," 72; cf. Kahl, "No Longer Male," 48–49.

66. Mollenkott draws on feminist theological responses and then follows up on Kahl's set of questions to ask and add her own "omnigendered" vision: "'Maybe a "third sex" in between?' Maybe as irregular as intersexuals? Transsexuals? Transgenderists? In Christ, no male and female: It is time for Christianity to regain Paul's vision" (*Omnigender*, 113–14; cf. Tanis, *Trans-Gendered*, 81–83).

67. Briggs, "Galatians," 218. Stendahl's work on 3:28 (*The Bible and the Role of Women*) has been pivotal in developing the biblical arguments for women's equality.

68. Schüssler Fiorenza, *Rhetoric and Ethic*, 149; cf. Polaski, *A Feminist Introduction*, 64; Gaventa, *Our Mother Saint Paul*, 63. Martin highlights how "the verse had become the *locus classicus* of the debate about gender equality" (*Sex and the Single Savior*, 78).

69. Kahl, "Gender Trouble," 58–59. Cf. Kahl, "Der Brief an die Gemeinden in Galatien"; and Kahl, "No Longer Male." Kahl's view is in contradistinction to Lieu, "Circumcision," 369; Briggs, "Galatians," 220; and Schüssler Fiorenza, *Rhetoric and Ethic*, 157, 166, 169–70; among others.

70. Schüssler Fiorenza, *In Memory of Her*, 210. For discussion of this kind of argument regarding baptism's relation to circumcision, see also Lieu, "Circumcision," 368–70; and Schüssler Fiorenza's own qualifications in Schüssler Fiorenza, *Rhetoric and Ethic*, 156–57. There, Schüssler Fiorenza explains that "I would no longer follow the lead of Paul and connect this assertion [women's full membership] with his debate on circumcision" (157). For further reflections on the compatibilities of such interpretations with anti-Jewish and supersessionist readings, see what follows.

71. Gundry-Volf, "Christ and Gender," 453–55. Gundry-Volf opens and then structures this article in opposition to the conclusions about gender in Boyarin, *A Radical Jew*, and Wire, *The Corinthian Women Prophets*.

72. Malestream interpreters of the letter also recognize the echo of the creation account(s) in this baptismal formula (Meeks, "Image of the Androgyne"; Betz, *Galatians*, 195–200; and Martyn, *Galatians*, 376–81, 403–6).

73. Kahl, "Gender Trouble," 59; and Kahl, "No Longer Male," 38.

74. Schüssler Fiorenza, *Rhetoric and Ethic*, 156. The close of the first creation account (Gen 1:27–28) is often connected to claims about procreative activity and "marriage." Schüssler Fiorenza argues that the formula signifies "the social oneness of the messianic community in which social, cultural, religious, national, and biological gender divisions and status differences are no longer valid" (*Rhetoric and Ethic*, 155; cf. Schüssler Fiorenza, *In Memory of Her*, 205–18, 235–36).

75. Kahl, "No Longer Male," 38–39.

76. For the different ways in which scars (and the identification of them in speech) can be interpreted in the ancient context, see Glancy, "Boasting of Beatings."

77. Lopez, *Apostle to the Conquered*, 135, 137–39, 152–53. Here, Lopez recognizes yet qualifies the reading of Paul's woundedness in Martyn, *Galatians*, 568 (cf. Kahl, *Galatians Re-Imagined*, 21–22, 205).

78. Gaventa, *Our Mother Saint Paul*, 29–39. For further reflections, see also Martyn, *Galatians*, 418–31; Polaski, *A Feminist Introduction*, 24–25; Eastman, *Recovering Paul's Mother Tongue*; and the discussion later.

79. Lopez, *Apostle to the Conquered*, 31–55, 143–46; Kahl, *Galatians Re-Imagined*, 283.

80. Kahl, "Gender Trouble," 60–61, 72; Kahl, "No Longer Male," 42–43; Lopez, *Apostle to the Conquered*, 137, 142–46, 156; and Kahl, *Galatians Re-Imagined*, 261, 274, 283–84.

81. For the citational relevance of Galatians 3:28 in relation to Genesis 1:27 (and 2:23) in contemporary Christian deliberations about intersex, see Jung, "Christianity and Human Sexual Polymorphism," 299, 301, 303, 307.

82. Mollenkott, *Omnigender*, 192.

83. Tanis, *Trans-Gendered*, 3.

84. Martyn, *Galatians*, 478.
85. Betz, *Galatians*, 270.
86. Betz, *Galatians*, 270; Martyn, *Galatians*, 478; as well as Dunn, *A Commentary*, 283; and Elliott, *Cutting Too Close*, 235, 321, 340.
87. For the eunuch as a point of identification among some LGBT interpreters, see especially Wilson, *Our Tribe*, 128–29, 281–85.
88. On the (other) two New Testament appearances of eunuch figures, see Hester, "Eunuchs and the Postgender Jesus"; and Burke, *Queering the Ethiopian Eunuch*.
89. Two examples of broader studies of the eunuch and/or castration over the centuries include Taylor, *Castration*; and Scholz, *Eunuchs and Castrati*. Both works have their idiosyncrasies, though. Taylor is a bit more incisive around modern associations for castration and sterility, but is often more glib than circumspect, particularly when asserting not-entirely-justified generalizations. Scholz has greater strengths with ancient materials, but his focus is shaped by his studies of ancient Egypt. As with Brisson's study of androgyny and hermaphroditism (see the discussion in chapter 2), some of Scholz's insights might be lost in the translation, given especially the potentially confused use of terminologies for and the overlaps (but also differences) between eunuchs, hermaphrodites, sexuality, and androgyny.
90. On these terms, see Guyot, *Eunuchen als Sklaven*, 23; Scholz, *Eunuchs and Castrati*, 112; Stevenson, "The Rise of Eunuchs," 497; Hester, "Eunuchs and the Postgender Jesus," 211; and Burke, *Queering the Ethiopian Eunuch*, 97.
91. In one instance, for example, Pliny attempts to differentiate eunuchs (*spadones*) as results of a surgical practice, from hermaphrodites (*hermaphroditi*), and especially *semiviri*, the latter being those whose testicles were destroyed by causes or injuries not related to surgeries (*Natural History* 11.263). However, as Williams highlights, surgically created eunuchs were described as *semiviri* with some regularity in the Roman context (*Roman Homosexuality*, 329, n. 29).
92. Stevenson suggests this understanding in this case particularly, because the context of this categorization is centered around paternity and inheritance ("The Rise of Eunuchs," 497–98).
93. Philostratus, *Vitae sophistarum* 8.489; discussed in Stevenson, "The Rise of Eunuchs," 503–4.
94. Kuefler, *The Manly Eunuch*, 258.
95. Stevenson, "The Rise of Eunuchs," 495, n. 1. This topic of "biologically produced eunuchs" is one area of confusion and even contradiction within Taylor's discussion (*Castration*, 174, 178).
96. Hester's otherwise excellent discussion is symptomatic in this regard. In one moment, he notes: "The ancient world recognized at least two broad categories of eunuchs: those born so, and those made so" ("Eunuch and the Postgender Jesus," 21). Yet, in what follows he almost exclusively discusses the latter. Work by scholars like Strassfeld ("Classically Queer"; and "Translating the Human") cautions scholars against ignoring the first kind of eunuch.
97. Taylor's discussion is driven by this argument, given the way he defines a eunuch (including himself) as a "sterile human being with a penis" (*Castration*, 3). On the

distance from agrarian settings and the modern unfamiliarity with nonhuman animal gelding, see Taylor, *Castration*, 54–56. Burke seems mostly to follow Taylor's argument: "As Taylor argues, if the goal of castration is to control reproduction, it is only necessary to remove the testicles, not the penis; in fact, amputation of the penis increases the risk of mortality. Greco-Roman texts reflect the assumption that castration usually involves the removal of the testicles, not the penis" (*Queering the Ethiopian Eunuch*, 97). On the latter proposition, however, Burke only refers to one text: Sophocles, *Troilus* frg. 620.

98. Stevenson, "The Rise of Eunuchs," 497.

99. Scholz, *Eunuchs and Castrati*, 31–40. In contrast to Taylor (published around the same time), Scholz proceeds with the assumption that castration requires the removal of the penis. Thus, his study contrasts surgical interventions on different parts of the genitalia: "intentional removal of the testicles, creating 'semi-castrati' or impotent persons, called *spadones* in antiquity. In contrast to the *spadones* were the 'full castrati' who had undergone surgical removal of the penis as well" (*Eunuchs and Castrati*, 16). This likely accounts for the high mortality rate (only one in four surviving castration), according to Scholz, *Eunuchs and Castrati*, 16.

100. Scholz, *Eunuchs and Castrati*, 41–50.

101. For initial reflections on Martial's depictions of *galli*, see Taylor, "Two Pathic Subcultures."

102. This obscene slang for penis can be found forty-eight times in Martial. On *mentula* and its synonyms, see Adams, *The Latin Sexual Vocabulary*, 9–12. Another of Martial's epigrams needles a *gallus* for being impotent before losing his *mentula*: "That dick that wouldn't stand tall for you has been cut off, Glyptus. Fool, what need for the knife? You were a Gallus before" (2.45). In Martial and other texts, *galli* are persistently associated not only with gender difference (as impacted by bodily modification) but also with sexual impropriety. For instance, the first epigram quoted earlier attributes a debased interest in performing oral sex (on men, for *galli* in general, and then, worse in his book, on women, for Baeticus; 3.81.1–2).

103. Taylor, "Two Pathic Subcultures," 331.

104. Freud, *The Standard Edition*, 15.208.

105. Taylor, *Castration*, 52, 67.

106. For instance, Martial 8.39; 9:16; 9:36; and Statius, *Silvae* 3.4.

107. For brief discussions of Sporus, see Scholz, *Eunuchs and Castrati*, 116–18; and Williams, *Roman Homosexuality*, 251–52. Not only were eunuchs used as pawns in attempts at imperial succession but also the laws about eunuchs were deployed in imperial rivalries, as when Domitian (despite enjoying his own eunuch) banned castration (Suetonius *Domitianus* 7.1; Martial 6.2) to differentiate himself from his brother and imperial predecessor, Titus, who also enjoyed them (Dio 67.2.3).

108. For eunuchs as *semiviri*, see Seneca *Epistulae morales* 108.7; Valerius Flacco 6.695; Martial 3.91.2; Silius Italicus 17.20; and Juvenal 6.513.

109. For one reflection of the ancient awareness of this difference in timing, see Galen, *De usu partium* 4.190.16.

110. For instance, Cassius Dio 76.14.14–5.

111. Other satirical depictions of the elite Roman imperial wife's sexual use of such eunuchs can be found in Juvenal, 6.366–67; as well as Martial 10.91.
112. For a discussion emphasizing the castration of slaves, see Glancy, *Slavery in Early Christianity*, 23–29; for an emphasis on eunuchs as slaves, see Burke, *Queering the Ethiopian Eunuch*, 98–99.
113. Patterson, *Slavery and Social Death*.
114. Again, Scholz departs from a great deal of scholarship on eunuchs in arguing that their identification with slavery is mistaken (*Eunuchs and Castrati*, 90). Yet, on the very same page, Scholz also acknowledges that there are two kinds of eunuchs, emasculated priests and castrated slaves, the latter's utility tied to their inability to interfere with one's progeny.
115. Scholz (*Eunuchs and Castrati*, 113–14) especially emphasizes the luxury items aspect of the trade in enslaved eunuchs.
116. Stevenson, "The Rise of Eunuchs," 497–98.
117. Justinian, *Digest* 28.2.6 musters figures holding opposing opinions regarding the possibility of a eunuch's paternity.
118. For a couple of epigrams that reflect this concern about the young male's vulnerability to castration, see Martial 9.6; 9.8.
119. Taylor, *Castration*, 123.
120. Scholz, *Eunuchs and Castrati*, 116–17.
121. For Domitian's decree against castrating young enslaved males, see Suetonius *Domitianus* 7.1, Martial 6.2. Following Dio's account (in 67.2.3), Williams repeats the suggestion that Domitian makes this decree because of "an ongoing rivalry with his brother and predecessor Titus, who had also been fond of eunuchs!" Williams continues: "As the same historian later notes [68.2.4], Domitian's successor Nerva again forbade castration within the Roman Empire; it would seem that Domitian's original degree had not been especially effective" (*Roman Homosexuality*, 276, n. 121). For the later codification of these prohibitions, see Justinian, *Digest* 4.42.2.
122. Taylor, *Castration*, 141; and Burke, *Queering the Ethiopian Eunuch*, 102. While Taylor, Burke, and others remain more circumspect about the historical, even material effect of such laws, Scholz accepts the depiction of the empire made in these legal prescriptions: "Thus it is probable that castration was performed mainly on foreigners and slaves" (*Eunuchs and Castrati*, 112).
123. Scholz, *Eunuchs and Castrati*, 93–110.
124. On the scope of ancient circumcision practices, see Sasson, "Circumcision in the Ancient Near East."
125. Elliott, *Cutting Too Close*, 234–36; and Abusch, "Circumcision and Castration," 82–83.
126. Abusch, "Circumcision and Castration," 79–82. For additional reflections on the variety of meanings ascribed to circumcision by Jews in the first century, and then, in the rabbinic period(s) forward, see Elliott, *Cutting Too Close*, 236–44; and Cohen, *Why Aren't Jewish Women*, 21–54.
127. Linder, *The Jews in Roman Imperial Legislation*, 100–101.
128. Taylor, *Castration*, 163–66.

129. Scholz, *Eunuchs and Castrati*, 79–81.

130. On this rise in representation as a problem of attestation, see Lightfoot, "Sacred Eunuchism."

131. For an extensive overview of the *galli*, see Elliott, *Cutting Too Close*, 159–229. For a sample of stories about Attis and Cybele/Agdistis, see Ovid, *Fasti* 4.215–46; Catullus, 63; and Diodorus Siculus, 3.58–59.

132. On the ways the Romans negotiated visually depicting Attis as the paradigm of self-castration, see Hales, "Looking for Eunuchs."

133. Scholz, *Eunuchs and Castrati*, 96–104; and Elliott, *Cutting Too Close*, 154.

134. Lucian depicts one such scene in Syria in his *De Syria Dea*, 50–51.

135. Scholz, *Eunuchs and Castrati*, 60–61; and Elliott, *Cutting Too Close*, 89, 165–66, 189–95, 202–5. For one depiction of such a scene, see Apuleius, *Metamorphoses* 8.24–49.

136. See the more detailed description in Elliott, *Cutting Too Close*, 163–66.

137. On the cluster of factors that stuck to the figure of the *cinaedus*, see Williams, *Roman Homosexuality*, 172–93.

138. Williams, *Roman Homosexuality*, 128. In elucidating this continuum Williams surveys a number of the same texts as I have thus far, specifically alluding to Suetonius *Divus Augustus* 68; Juvenal 2.115–6; and Apuleius, *Metamorphoses* 8.24–30. Later, Williams elaborates: "the *cinaedus* and above all the *gallus* were ideological scare-figures for Roman men: a man who flaunted the breaking of the rules of masculinity could be said to have taken the first step on the dangerous road toward becoming a castrated priest of the Mother Goddess" (*Roman Homosexuality*, 177, but see also 176). For a different, if problematic proposal for combining urban *cinaedi* and the *galli* (as a "religious subculture") into one kind of sexual identity, see Taylor, "Two Pathic Subcultures."

139. Williams, *Roman Homosexuality*, 128. Williams repeats this characterization in the pages to follow: "Castration is an extreme instance of a conceptual all-or-nothing tendency that pervades Roman texts: softening a male constitutes a direct infringement upon his masculine identity" (*Roman Homosexuality*, 129).

140. Hester, "Eunuchs and the Postgender Jesus," 20.

141. Roller, "Attis on Greek Votive Monuments," especially 253–59.

142. Elliott, *Cutting Too Close*, 133–34.

143. Hales, "Looking for Eunuchs," Beard, "The Roman and the Foreign," and Scholz, *Eunuchs and Castrati*, 96–99.

144. Elliott, *Cutting Too Close*, 189–93.

145. See, for instance, the consideration of this potential double vision in Anatolia in Elliott, *Cutting Too Close*, 173. One particular strength of Elliott's study is her effort to bring the focus back to the localized Anatolian contexts.

146. On *galli* as slaves of Cybele, see Scholz, *Eunuchs and Castrati*, 107; and Elliott, *Cutting Too Close*, 211–20.

147. Admittedly, the later empire (particularly after the first circulation of Paul's letters) negotiated eunuch figures in increasingly complicated ways. On these later developments, including in relation to growing numbers of early Christians, see Gleason, *Making Men*; and Kuefler, *The Manly Eunuch*.

148. Hales, "Looking for Eunuchs," 89.

149. Betz, *Galatians*, 270.

150. Betz, *Galatians*, 253, 270 (following the NEB rendering).

151. Martyn, *Galatians*, 478.

152. On the familiarity with religious practices of self-castration, see Kuefler, *The Manly Eunuch*, 259–60; and Elliott, *Cutting Too Close*, 233.

153. Kuefler, *The Manly Eunuch*, 257. Kuefler, however, almost certainly overstates his case when he argues: "Paul linked castration to circumcision—another genital mutilation he rejected—in various passages" (257). While the link seems to be activated in the case of Paul's efforts to keep Gentiles from getting circumcised in Gal 5:12, Paul does not reject circumcision whole-cloth, particularly among Jewish males. Kuefler also attempts to relate such a dual "rejection" to Philippians 3, by following a long-standing scholarly tendency to project a (misnamed) "Judaizing" opposition as the "mutilation" (3:2). This, of course, ignores that in the following verses Paul claims the term "circumcision" for his constructed "we" and lists his own circumcision as indicating his current (not past) Jewish identity (3:3–6). On the latter passage, see Nanos, "Paul's Reversal."

154. For instance, the opening explication of Elliott's basic contention in *Cutting Too Close*, 14.

155. Elliott, *Cutting Too Close*, 231.

156. Elliott, *Cutting Too Close*, 235. The only other occasion in which Paul's wish for castration is discussed in the body of this study is a brief reference within Elliott's discussion of another passage: Paul's characterization of the "foolish" Galatians as beginning in the spirit, yet acting on the flesh (in 3:3), like the *galli* (*Cutting Too Close*, 340). All other references to this verse are relegated either to footnotes (3, 163, 290) or to figures charting the letter as a whole (306, 321).

157. Kahl, "Gender Trouble" 57; cf. "No Longer Male," 40–41; and *Galatians Re-Imagined*, 79. Here, Kahl notes that this letter (only six chapters long) contains close to 20 percent of New Testament occurrences of these terms ("foreskin," "circumcision," "sperm," "castration").

158. Gaventa, *Our Mother Saint Paul*, 63–64.

159. Kahl, "Gender Trouble," 57; "No Longer Male," 40; and *Galatians Re-Imagined*, 79; Johnson Hodge, *If Sons*, 60–64.

160. Johnson Hodge, *If Sons*, 62; Schmidt, "*akrobustia*"; and Marcus, "The Circumcision."

161. Johnson Hodge, *If Sons*, 62–63.

162. Kahl, "Gender Trouble," 57; "No Longer Male," 40; and *Galatians Re-Imagined*, 79; Johnson Hodge, *If Sons*, 62; cf. Marcus, "The Circumcision," 76.

163. Johnson Hodge, *If Sons*, 6; cf. Meyer, "*peritomē*"; and Marcus, "The Circumcision," 76. On circumcision's relation to male fertility, see Eilberg-Schwartz, *The Savage in Judaism*, 143–47; and Stowers, *A Rereading*, 244.

164. Johnson Hodge, *If Sons*, 43, 47–49, 138.

165. Dunn (*The New Perspective*, 315–20), for example, downplays the distinctiveness of Paul's rhetorical focus and treats as common (or commonsensical) Paul's reduction of groups into "the circumcision" and "the foreskin."

166. Polaski, *A Feminist Introduction*, 13, 15, 25; Jervis, *Galatians*, 107.

167. Johnson Hodge, *If Sons*, 62. Here, Johnson Hodge reflects on key passages from Josephus, like *Jewish Antiquities* 20.41. In the era shortly after Paul's, the rabbis reflected on a changing range of concepts and practices surrounding circumcision, including the possibility of Jewish males with foreskins. See Cohen, *Why Aren't Jewish Women*, 21–28. From an analysis of T. Shabbat 15(16).9 70–72 (and numerous parallels), Cohen shows that, "in rabbinic law, circumcision is not always essential to Jewishness" (*Why Aren't Jewish Women*, 23 (cf. 95–101)).

168. Dunn, *The New Perspective*, 155, 161–63, 167–69, 313–21, 331–33.

169. On the fluid and fixed mixture of birth and behavior in Pauline identity rhetorics, see Johnson Hodge, *If Sons*, 57–58; and Buell and Johnson Hodge, "The Politics of Interpretation." For the most part, rabbinic materials in both ancient and contemporary settings stress that one is Jewish by birth. Again, Cohen argues: "Male and female offspring of a Jewish mother are Jewish by birth under Jewish law; the male offspring are Jewish by birth *even if they are left uncircumcised*" (*Why Aren't Jewish Women*, 22, emphasis added). This viewpoint is in contrast to later Christian ideas and in possible continuity with Roman imperial principles (*Why Aren't Jewish Women*, 103, 141–42).

170. For the ambiguities around the term "Judaizing" (*ioudazein*, Gal 2:14), a term frequently used by scholars to describe various parties different from Paul (the "Judaizers"), see Johnson Hodge, *If Sons*, 56–57; and Nanos, *The Irony of Galatians*, 115–19.

171. Dunn, *The New Perspective*, 318–19.

172. It was only later, in some medieval Jewish mystical texts like the Zohar, that circumcision was viewed as functioning in a manner analogous to Christian baptism (Cohen, *Why Aren't Jewish Women*, 42–45, 54). For further reflections on specifically Jewish histories of circumcision, including its gendered dynamics and its persistence even as it has been increasingly questioned in the modern period, see Hoffman, *Covenant of Blood*.

173. Augustine, for example, emphasized the similarity between circumcision and baptism, particularly in circumcision's anticipation of baptism's saving (and superseding) capacities (in *City of God*, 16.27). Augustine's interiorized reflection on salvation and sin would, in turn, shape Martin Luther, one of the most influential readers of Paul and his letter to the Galatians (Stendahl, "The Apostle Paul").

174. Luther, *A Commentary*, 473. While the commentary on Galatians does not reach the anti-Jewish extremes of works like his *On the Jews and Their Lies*, it is still a rather troubling work given Luther's focus, the presence of core anti-Jewish ingredients and adaptively antagonistic dichotomies, and its continuing influence on Pauline interpretation. For the influence, or use, of Luther in Nazi forms of Christianity, see Steigmann-Gall, *The Holy Reich*; and Heschel, *The Aryan Jesus*.

175. Kahl, *Galatians Re-Imagined*, 35.

176. Elliott, *Cutting Too Close*, 333.

177. Elliott (*Cutting Too Close*, 333) makes this point about even those interpretations that see circumcision and flesh as connected, like Jewett, *Paul's Anthropological Terms*, 96–97.

178. Indeed, the insistence that it is not I (the interpreter) that focuses on penises, but someone else (now or then), exemplified the homosexual "panic" component of many modern arguments at (and after) the rise of heterosexuality and medicalized insistence on dimorphically sexed bodies. For more on the role of such panics, see Boyarin, *Unheroic Conduct*.

179. Kahl, *Galatians Re-Imagined*, 35.

180. Castelli, "Allegories of Hagar."

181. Briggs, "Galatians," 224. For more on the ancient place and use of females, slaves, and enslaved females, see Joshel and Murnaghan, *Women and Slaves*.

182. Kahl, "No Longer Male," 46, 49; Lopez, *Apostle to the Conquered*, 140–41; and Kahl, *Galatians Re-Imagined*, 268, 299.

183. Modern surgeons were not the only ones who thought it was easy to make a female ("a hole"); ancient thinkers of the body were particularly concerned about the many ways in which "male" bodies could and would lose their masculinity through too much feminine behavior. It was too easy to become porously female ("hole-y"), while maintaining one's status as a "man" was a *vir*-tuous trial (much harder to keep the position of "a pole," if you will).

184. Briggs, "Galatians," 224–25.

185. Kahl, *Galatians Re-Imagined*, 247; cf. 15.

186. Scholars like Kahl, Lopez, and Gaventa draw on the immense body of Galatians' interpretation by Martyn, who displays (by Kahl's own account), an "exuberant rhetoric of war" (*Galatians Re-Imagined*, 310, n. 48), particularly when speaking of divine invasion: Martyn, *Galatians*, 97–105, 524–36; and Martyn, *Theological Issues*, 111–23, 251–66.

187. Elliott (*Cutting Too Close*, 313–17) suggests that the vice list in 5:19–21 echoes a range of qualities attributed to the *galli* and/or the cult of the Mother of the Gods.

188. Note here the importance of pleasure and pain in intersex critiques, and the general lack of focus of doctors on their patients' outcomes in terms of pain and pleasure. (Doctors at least claim to minimize the former and preserve the latter; and, yet, like Paul their attention and actions seem directed elsewhere.)

189. In this heading, the admonition, again coined by Triea (as quoted in Holmes, "Queer Cut Bodies," 105), warns people to stop looking for other ancient or mythical bodies to play an imagined equivalent role for intersex people.

190. Holmes, "Queer Cut Bodies," 84.

191. Morland, "Is Intersexuality Real?" 528.

192. Holmes, "Queer Cut Bodies," 104. Emphasis original.

193. Holmes, "Rethinking the Meaning," 174; cf. Roen, "Queer Kids," 275; and Morland, "What Can Queer Theory," 301.

194. On such practices of modifying enslaved bodies, see Glancy, *Slavery in Early Christianity*, 24–29, 87–89.

195. Morland, "What Can Queer Theory," 301.

196. Roen, "Queer Kids," 270.

197. Holmes, "Queer Cut Bodies," 104.

198. Feder, "Imperatives," 240–41; Holmes, "Queer Cut Bodies," 98, 106; and Chase, "Hermaphrodites," 199.

199. For two provocative readings of 1 Corinthians in light of such racial/ethnic differences (for the first and twenty-first centuries), see Liew, *What Is Asian American Hermeneutics?*, 75–114. On the dynamics of racialized emasculation, particularly in perceptions of Asian American males, see Eng, *Racial Castration*.

200. Indeed, these "others" (to the ancient Jews/Judeans/*Ioudaioi*) behave in the exact opposite fashion to how "the nations" are characterized in Israelite and Jewish literature. Contrast, for example, their actions with the account of the city of Sodom: not only are they hospitable, but they do not prey on (by attempting to penetrate) the weak and vulnerable (therefore feminine) visitor.

201. This "autobiographical" narration (which was of course rhetorically shaped for the occasion of his argument) constitutes a strikingly large portion of the letter (1:11–2:14), perhaps reflecting Paul's estimation of the power of his self-presentation. Temporally, this is especially the case, given the power of his past's relation to his depiction of the present, where once he was pursuing, now he was preaching (1:23). Paul also builds this self-portrait by contrasting his relative constancy to Peter's different behavior in the past and present (2:12–14).

202. In a parallel fashion, one could reread the so-called "Jerusalem council" in light of some of the first modern efforts to discern the meaning of hermaphroditic bodies, where doctors gathered to diagnose, but often came to conflicting visions of the body's meaning (Dreger, *Hermaphrodites*).

203. Consider also a related critique of the letter's argumentation about stigma focused on the devaluation of black and brown bodies in Parker, "One Womanist's View."

204. For one, potentially problematic reading of Paul's "silence" regarding women in this letter (and the construction of an exclusivist [kind of] Jewish opposition to Paul), see Wiley, *Paul and the Gentile Women*.

Chapter 4

1. Williams, "'No Longer as a Slave.'"

2. Byron, *Recent Research on Paul and Slavery*.

3. The most persistent and consistent presentation of the sexual use of enslaved people and its impact for understanding biblical materials can be found in Glancy, *Slavery in Early Christianity*. See also Briggs, "Paul on Bondage"; Briggs, "Slavery and Gender"; Harrill, *Slaves in the New Testament*; and Horsley, "Slave Systems." The sexual vulnerability of enslaved people is acknowledged throughout the important *Onesimus Our Brother* collection, but particularly foregrounded in Noel, "Nat Is Back"; Johnson, "Onesimus Speaks"; and Perkinson, "Enslaved by the Text."

4. Unless otherwise noted, all classical references follow the available LCL translations. This translation can be found in Finley, *Ancient Slavery*, 96.

5. The translation of Horace is taken from Williams, *Roman Homosexuality*, 32.

6. This translation can also be found in Finley, *Ancient Slavery*, 96. Several biblical scholars (like Horsley, "Slave Systems," 44–45) highlight a similar set of texts in discussing the ancient conditions of slavery.

7. Williams notes: "Horace recommends to his readers that if they want to play it safe, they will vent their sexual energies on their own slaves; he speaks of male and female slaves indifferently" (*Roman Homosexuality*, 32).

8. The texts more consistently assert the nonproblematic use of enslaved people by male owners, even as they often reflect on the female owner's uses. For further reflections on the complicated presentation and positionality of females as owners and enslaved (and a potential "double standard"), see Joshel and Murnaghan, eds., *Women and Slaves*.

9. Osiek, *Philippians, Philemon*, 137.

10. The adjective *achrēston* also, then, can be translated in several ways to reflect a similar range of descriptions in terms of (a lack of) use, serviceability, and profitability. These comfortably overlap with each other and connect to an owner's view of the enslaved body as a tool for use.

11. Glancy's treatment of this letter is brief and sporadic (as in *Slavery in Early Christianity*, 91–92). In an article considering *porneia* and (mostly) female slaves, Osiek views the case of Onesimus as irrelevant to the topic of obedience and sexuality ("Female Slaves," 270). Horsley devotes a section to the sexual exploitation in an introduction to ancient slave systems ("Slave Systems," 44–46), but then mostly avoids the subject in his treatment of Paul's letters, an avoidance that is complete in the case of his examination of this letter (Horsley, "Paul and Slavery," 178–82).

12. Foucault, *The Use of Pleasure*.

13. Foucault, *The Use of Pleasure*, 215.

14. Richlin, *The Garden of Priapus*, 57–64.

15. Williams, *Roman Homosexuality*, 18.

16. Williams, *Roman Homosexuality*, 18–19; and more broadly, Hallett and Skinner, eds., *Roman Sexualities*.

17. The irony of this passage, like others in the ancient sources, is that it is voiced by an enslaved character (even as, granted, it is written by and for an elite audience). This likely reflects how much owners hoped for and at times worked toward gaining acquiescence and acceptance of the social order.

18. Williams, *Roman Homosexuality*, 30–31.

19. The positionings indicated by the elite free (often imperial) male perspective that predominates on this topic, alongside the range of acceptable receptacles for sexual use, reflect the interwoven dynamics of gender and sexuality within slavery, ethnicity, race, status, and empire. In other words, it exemplifies one element of a kyriarchal order (described in the Prelude).

20. Williams, *Roman Homosexuality*, 31.

21. Finley, *Ancient Slavery*, 95. For references to the sexual use of enslaved people in Homer's *Iliad* (2.1.366; 2.9.128–34; 2.22.164; and 2.23.257–61), see Stumpp, *Prostitution in der römischen Antike*, 26; and Klees, *Sklavenleben im klassischen Griechenland*, 155–75.

22. Finley, *Ancient Slavery*, 95; and McGinn, *Prostitution, Sexuality*, 196.

23. Bradley, *Slavery and Society*, 28.

24. For some discussion of this passage in the context of Herodas's works and slavery, in general, see DuBois, *Slaves and Other Objects*, 99–109.

25. I owe the connection between *Mimes* 5 and 6 to DuBois's study, where she makes the original and provocative link between the use of slaves and dildos (while the repetition in terminology, particularly of *chraomai*, is not particularly stressed in DuBois). Mimes often have connections in terms of subject matter and characters, as reflected by the recurrence not only of the terminology of sexual use (*chraomai*) in *Mimes* 5 and 6, but also of characters like Metro and Kerdon (in *Mimes* 6 and 7) and of the complaints about and physical threats against enslaved people that open all three of these mimes.

26. To be clear, the slaveowning women's actions are depicted as comedic indecency in keeping with Greek mime traditions, which are not generally affirmative of what twenty-first-century audiences might like to see as women's sexual self-determination. Nevertheless, the sexual focus of many of the minimal plot points in these mimes only reinforces the sexual resonance of the "use" of Gastron in 5.6. See, for example, the description of Kerdon (the cobbler/dildo-maker) as one with whom "the late Kylaethis was intimate" (*echrēto*, 6.55) and Koritto's attempts to physically persuade Kerdon to make another dildo by doing many things, including "almost giving him my body to use" (*to sōma mounon ouchi dousa chrēsasthai*, 6.78).

27. DuBois, *Slaves*, 102, 104 respectively.

28. The description of the object of their use as *pais* is potentially ambiguous, since the term can be used to describe a young male. However, in most of the following instances, it is more likely that *puer* and *pais* refer to an enslaved male. This ambiguity, but also discontinuity (between "our" concepts of boy "now" and "then"), will be indicated in the following by placing "boy" in quotes. See, for example, Golden, "*Pais*"; and Garnsey, "Sons, Slaves." It seems likely that an enslaved male is meant in this passage: the absence of courtship rituals for lover-beloved dynamics and the joke at Sophocles's expense (that he lost his cape) indicates a context of expecting to get it "for free," rather than through suasion and gift-offering. Earlier in the same section, for example, when Sophocles is described as "fond of young lads" (603E), he is attracted to a wine-pouring slave described as a handsome boy (*pais*, 603F).

29. Brooten, *Love Between Women*, 245. Here, Brooten also cites the standard dictionary entries for *chrēsis* and *chraomai* in LSJ and BAGD.

30. Brooten, *Love Between Women*, 245, n. 87.

31. For further discussion of this passage, see also Halperin, *How To Do the History*, 89–103. Here, Halperin also reminds that Foucault considered this text in *The Care of the Self*, 190–92, 211–27. Indeed, it is here that Foucault also differentiates the Roman era: "love for boys was practiced for the most part with young slaves, about whose status there was no reason to worry. 'In Rome the freeborn ephebe was replaced by the slave,' says Paul Veyne" (*The Care of the Self*, 190; citing Paul Veyne, "L'Homosexualité à Rome," *L'Histoire* [January 1981]: 77).

32. For example, the dictionary entries on *koinoō* in LSJ and BAGD, and Swancutt, "Sexing the Pauline Body."

33. Brooten's landmark study of female homoeroticism discusses how the sexual use of enslaved people would have fit with common perceptions of "natural" use, acknowledging their role as appropriate receivers as well as formulaic figures for describing

those who are possessed by love (*Love Between Women*, 87–106, 250–51). Brooten founded and continues to direct the Feminist Sexual Ethics Project at Brandeis University, where the relationship between slavery, sexuality, and religion is a major research priority. For some preliminary indications of the scope and analytic of this project, see Brooten with Hazelton, ed., *Beyond Slavery*.

34. Indeed, the youthful and beardless appearance of enslaved males such as these often indicate the likelihood of their castration, reminding one that ancient eunuchs were typically enslaved in this context (see chapter 3).

35. Ironically, Halperin's observations about these slave populations (in *How To Do the History*, 96) called my attention to this passage, even as Halperin failed to more fully consider the significance of enslaved people as included in his consideration of ancient inclinations and more modern orientations.

36. The translation can be found in Williams, *Roman Homosexuality*, 32. (Compare, for example, the more sanitizing translations in the LCL edition of Horace.)

37. Upon translating this passage, Williams elaborates: "The chatty style and appeals to the three basic appetites of food, drink, and sex give a common-sense feeling to his argument. The language itself, with its insistent repetitions of the interrogative particle *num* in tricolon crescendo, seems designed to make an urgent appeal to his readership, to convince them of something that should in any case be obvious to them, that men's slaves are meant to be used and can be used without fear of repercussions" (*Roman Homosexuality*, 32).

38. Achilles Tatius, *Leucippe and Clitophon*, 5.17; Chariton, *Chareas and Callirhoe*, 2.6; Longus, *Daphnis and Chloe*, 4.11–19; and Xenophon, *Ephesian Tale*, 1.16; 2.9; 5.7. For a general introduction to the conventions and repetitive *topoi*, plots, and broader narrative arcs of these novels, see Reardon, ed., *Collected Ancient Greek Novels*, especially 1–16, and the individual introductions to each novel. In ways similar to the advice dispensed in Horace earlier, one finds a distinctly out-of-control version of the food-drink-sex association in Longus, *Daphnis and Chloe*, 4.11. The companion of the master's son, Gnathon, desires Daphnis, as he was "a fellow who knew only eating, drinking until he was drunk, and fornicating after he was drunk, and who was no more than a mouth, a belly, and the parts below the belly" (*Daphnis and Chloe*, 4.11.2).

39. Bradley, *Slavery and Society*, 49. Bradley makes this point in connecting the legal property rights of owners and the events depicted in Chariton's novel, cited in this chapter's introduction and discussed further in what follows.

40. For example, Epictetus prefaces his advice on *chrēsis* by instructing: "In things that pertain to the body take only as much as your bare need requires, I mean such things as food, drink, clothing, shelter, and household slaves; but cut down everything which is for outward show or luxury" (*Encheiridion*, 33.7). See also Epictetus, *Encheiridion*, 41, where he worries over excessive time spent on bodily matters like exercise, eating, drinking, defecating, and sex.

41. Frederickson, "Natural and Unnatural Use," 200–201.

42. Horsley, "The Slave Systems," 44; and Glancy, *Slavery in Early Christianity*, 21.

43. The latter clause translates *all' ēdeōs hekaterō chrētai*. Frederickson cites this passage ("Natural and Unnatural Use," 200) as a demonstration of the "pervasive

interpretation of sexual activity as use." This terminology of use is not applied exclusively to sexual contact with unweddable receptacles, though, as is made clear by
Plutarch's advice to a bride and groom: "Therefore man and wife ought especially to
indulge [*chrēsthai*] in this with circumspection" (*Moralia*, 144B). Thus, control is
not simply a matter of directing *chrēsis* toward appropriate parties, but *chrēsis* itself
is a form of the control of self and others and is a compatible expression of elite male
slaveowning comportment.

44. Suetonius, *Virgil*, 9–11; and the discussion of this passage in Williams, *Roman
Homosexuality*, 33.

45. For a fuller grasp of the often ugly, if colorful, sexual humor of the Romans, see
Richlin, *The Garden of Priapus*. Veyne similarly notes: "A much repeated way of
teasing a slave is to remind him of what his master expects of him, i.e., to get down on
all fours" (Veyne, "Homosexuality in Ancient Rome," 29).

46. On this epigram, see also Bradley, *Slavery and Society*, 49.

47. Finley's work (*Ancient Slavery*) aims to counteract such claims for an exceptional,
compassionate, and/or altruistic form of slavery in antiquity. In Pauline studies, see
Briggs, "Paul on Bondage," especially 111–14, 120, 121. For an argument on the difference between manumission and emancipation, see Callahan, "Paul, *Ekklēsia*."

48. For this strategy of recapitalizing on the original, not declining value of an enslaved
body by requiring the manumitted to earn the cost of a younger, healthier (and far
more valuable) enslaved person, see Hopkins, *Conquerors and Slaves*, 118, 128.

49. Hopkins, *Conquerors and Slaves*, 133–71.

50. Hopkins, *Conquerors and Slaves*, 141–44, 158, 163, 166.

51. On service owed until the death of the owner(s), see Hopkins, *Conquerors and Slaves*,
150, 163. For the ambiguous state of children born to freed people, see also Hopkins,
Conquerors and Slaves, 155–57. Owners tended not to manumit enslaved females
who were still "productive" in terms of birthing new enslaved people.

52. Glancy, *Slavery in Early Christianity*, 10–38. Indeed, the inscriptions at Delphi
(Hopkins, *Conquerors and Slaves*, 142–44) show how slaves are still described mainly
as things, as bodies, even as they are being manumitted.

53. Tacitus, *Annals*, 14.42.3; discussed in Bradley, *Slavery and Society*, 108. The passage
itself is frustratingly ambiguous, even obscure, about the motivations of the enslaved
person and the owner, likely because this incident is only compelling to the Romans
for the debate it provoked as to whether to execute all of the enslaved members of the
household (*Annals*, 14.42–45).

54. This event is also considered in my examination of eunuch figures in the Roman imperial era (see chapter 3), indicating again the significant overlap between enslaved
and castrated figures.

55. The Greek of the second clause is: *hōste kai hekousa kai akousa poēsei to soi dokoun.*
See the previous discussion of the adverbial willingly (*hekousa*) and unwillingly
(*akousa*).

56. As Glancy so succinctly puts it: "Slaves did not have the legal right nor cultural power
to say 'no' to their owners' sexual demands" (*Slavery in Early Christianity*, 52).

57. Patterson, *Slavery and Social Death*; as well as Finley, *Ancient Slavery*, 75.

58. On slavery within conceptions of "family," see Rawson, ed. *The Family in Ancient Rome*; Osiek and Balch, *Families in the New Testament World*; and Balch and Osiek, *Early Christian Families*.

59. The relation of this common triad of "women, children, and slaves" to the elite free male head of household is, of course, reflected in the *Haustafeln* passages of other Second Testament epistles (Col. 3:18–4:1; Eph. 5:21–6:9; and 1 Ptr. 2:18–3:7; cf. 1 Tim. 2:8–15; 5:1–2; 6:1–2; Tit. 2:1–10; 3:1).

60. Saller, "Slavery and the Roman Family," 82.

61. As a result, an insistence on examining the images, conditions, or terminologies of slavery for understanding Philemon (or other letters) is neither contradictory to nor incompatible with the consideration of family images, conditions, or terminologies (as found, for example, in Frilingos, " 'For My Child' ").

62. On status and the sexual use of slaves and prostitutes, see Finley, *Ancient Slavery*, 96; and Stumpp, *Prostitution*, 26. For further context about the Roman legal and economic conditions for prostitution, see McGinn, *Prostitution, Sexuality*; and McGinn, *The Economy of Prostitution*.

63. Williams highlights (*Roman Homosexuality*, 275, nn. 106 and 110) Porphyrio's claim that this warning of Horace (*Epistles* 1.18.75) to Lollius is referring to Virgil's acceptance of the beautiful *puer* Alexander from Pollio (described in Suetonius, *Virgil*, 9, cited earlier). The passage in Suetonius once more displays how the term "boy" (*puer, pais*) is used for enslaved males, as one cannot give just any "boy," but enslaved "boys" can be given.

64. It is unlikely that Paul's Jewishness would have altered his (or other ancient Jews') approaches to slavery, since practices among Jews followed the predominant practices of the Greco-Roman period, including around the presumed sexual vulnerability of enslaved people. See Hezser, *Jewish Slavery*; Martin, "Slavery and the Ancient Jewish Family"; and Satlow, *Jewish Marriage*, 195.

65. Note, though, the hesitation of Glancy around the association of *euchrēston* and *achrēston* with specifically sexual uses of enslaved people, even as she discusses one potential such instance for *achrēston* (Longus, *Daphnis and Chloe*, 4.29.4), in Glancy, "The Utility of an Apostle," especially 78–79.

66. I would actually make the opposite translational recommendation for these two uses of *chrēsis* terms: emphasize the asymmetrical sexual protocol behind Paul's condemnation in Romans 1 by translating those instances with terms of "use," and then more carefully consider in the context of Phlm what makes a person, enslaved, manumitted, or free, "useful" or "good-for-use" to others in the Roman imperial context. On *chrēsis* in Romans 1, see Frederickson, "Natural and Unnatural Use."

67. Since I find no particular set of arguments about the proper "addressee" of this letter (or about the likely owner of Onesimus) completely convincing, I preserve the ambiguity of the letter and Philemon scholarship throughout the following treatment of the letter. The most frequently cited "dissenters" to the traditional position (Philemon as the addressee) are Knox, *Philemon Among the Letters*; and Winter, "Paul's Letter."

68. For example, Bradley, *Slaves and Masters*, 13–14, 113.

69. Hopkins, *Conquerors and Slaves*, 154.

70. See also the role of *splanchna* in its relation to erotic contact and the "heart," "lips," and "mouth" in Achilles Tatius, 2.37.10.

71. Glancy, for instance, considers how Paul would have accepted hospitality from a slaveholder (*Slavery in Early Christianity*, 45).

72. The use of enslaved people for exploitative purposes including sexual satisfaction (for the user) among family members certainly also puts the repetitive use of kinship terms in Paul's letters in another light, worthy of expanded consideration.

73. The reasons for the exchange, selling, or even giving of enslaved people of course include aesthetic and erotic motivations of the recipient-user (as in the gift of the beautiful Alexander from Pollio to Virgil, in Suetonius, *Virgil*, 9).

74. The Greek *koinōnia* terms stress holding something in common and, in this vein, are also used as terms for sexual contact elsewhere (for example, Lucian, *Erōtes*, 27).

75. Xenophon, *Ephesian Tale*, 1.16.3–5. Kittredge (*Community and Authority*, 13–51) has convincingly demonstrated the subordinating force of this term for obedience (*hypakouein*), over and against previous scholarship that would prefer to view Paul as seeking some kind of "free obedience."

76. On the mostly nonaffectionate and hierarchical view of parent–child relations in the ancient world, see Wire, *The Corinthian Women Prophets*, 45–47; and Castelli, *Imitating Paul*, 99–102. Frilingos ("'For My Child.'") emphasizes the interconnection of kinship with power dynamics in Philemon by stressing how the reference to Onesimus as Paul's *technon* (v. 10) acts within Paul's technology (*techno[n]*-ology) of power.

77. Smith, "Utility, Fraternity."

78. Indeed, the Latin term *familia* was used both of the wider household/family and of the household slave (as a result, a *familia* can be within the *familia*).

79. This argument is *contra* the key thesis of Lewis ("An African American Appraisal"), which reads Philemon in light of (at least part of) Galatians and, thus, sees familial language as a mitigation of slavery.

80. It is not uncommon for Paul to argue to establish chains of hierarchical arrangements among the "kin" of the assemblies; being a "brother" does not preclude Paul having a more prominent or authoritative position. For more on Paul's hierarchical argumentation, see Marchal, *Hierarchy, Unity, and Imitation*.

81. For the argument that Paul is here seeking the manumission of Onesimus, see, for example, Schenk, "Der Brief des Paulus"; Knox, *Philemon*, 24–27, 36–37; Bruce, *The Epistles to the Colossians, to Philemon*, 216–21; Winter, "Paul's Letter," 1, 4, 11–12; and Martin, "The Rhetorical Function." For the creative (if rarely affirmed) argument that Onesimus is the actual brother of the addressee, see Callahan, "Paul's Epistle"; and Callahan, *Embassy of Onesimus*.

82. Though it does not seem likely, given some of the details of this letter (and Galatians), it is also not impossible that this difference in Onesimus can be traced to his potential castration! If Onesimus is (newly?) castrated, he is even more alienated from any form of (past or future) kinship, and thus pliable for even greater integration into the addressee's household. Enslaved eunuchs are also prized aesthetically and, thus, erotically by their owner-users (which could account for how Onesimus

is now especially "good-for-use" or "easy-to-use"). For more of the contours around ancient eunuchs, see the discussion in chapter 3. For the concerns about excess, given ancient standards of moderation, see Martin, "Heterosexism."

83. Martin ("Slave Families," 207, 222–30) stresses that slaves can play a variety of "family" roles, roles that simultaneously blur and yet maintain structures of authority.

84. For a variety of reflections about kinship terms in the ancient assembly communities, see Osiek and Balch, eds., *Families in the New Testament World*; Balch and Osiek, ed., *Early Christian Families*; and Moxnes, ed., *Constructing Early Christian Families*.

85. Paul's letters also reflect sexual contact with those who are or are not one's "brother/sister" in the community (1 Cor 7:12–16, 39; and possibly 1 Thess. 4:4). Of course, if there is one idea that seems to have both varied and yet carried over the centuries, it is that males have permissible sexual access to those people that are made their "kin" in particular ways (like the "wife"). Despite common contemporary jokes and discomforts about "imagining one's parents," kinship and sexual use are firmly woven together, if not always and only in a closed and exclusive relation (despite some protestations otherwise).

86. If Paul seems (if inconsistently) to argue against joining community members to those "outside," this raises further questions about what uses of enslaved people are imagined (or "permitted"). If, in fact, it is better to join oneself to an enslaved person within the community (so long as she or he is not a prostitute, 1 Cor 6:15–17), does this explain the especial usefulness of Onesimus now? One should be cautious in reading one of Paul's letters in light of another too much (if at all), though.

87. Bartchy, "Slavery, Greco-Roman," 69; Briggs, "Paul on Bondage," 114–15, 117; Glancy, *Slavery in Early Christianity*, 49, 58, 70; Osiek, "Female Slaves," 269–70, 274.

88. Callahan, *Embassy of Onesimus*, 50.

89. This departs with other instances in Paul's letters where "flesh" (*sarx*) *is* used in a contrastive or adversative fashion. In fact, in one of these instances, *sarx* is associated with both slavery and generation (Gal 4:23). Even as *sarx* plays a different role in the arguments of Galatians 4:21–5:1 and Philemon 14–16, both reflect a similarly casual acceptance of the mechanics of ancient slavery (and Gal comes closest to explicitly reflecting on the sexual use of an enslaved body, see chapter 3). These similarities and differences underscore how important it is to read Paul's arguments in the context of the ancient world but also of each particular letter, not trying to read one letter in light of one or more of the others. (His arguments often run and, thus, function differently.)

90. For one consideration of the phrase "in the flesh" as involving sexual use, see Perkinson, "Enslaved by the Text," 126–29.

91. Much as the interpretive community should need to grapple with the compatibility of such uses of enslaved people with Pauline argumentation, so also should the selection of the term *kyrios* as a key term in the early (and future) communities requires further critical reflection. One could protest that Paul "does not mean" *that* sense of "lord" (the kyriarchal), yet this is precisely the reason why it requires further critical

reflection. It is not unlikely that the power of this term was at least a contributing factor for its use and acceptance. Regardless, its resonance in an imperially gendered slave system cannot be easily extracted or refracted to serve other purposes. This means that one cannot do without at least being vigilant about kyriarchal impulses continuing (consciously or otherwise). Thus, this raises the (perhaps) unhappy idea that the continuing resonance of such a term is not dissonant with or contrary to the ancient *ethos* described here.

92. Further, if Paul were in fact attempting to counter such a presumed affiliation between the embodied use of enslaved people for those in the roles of (those close to) "lords," his argument would have likely required much greater strength and agility than the presumed "subtlety" attributed to him here by scholars who typically read the letter as the height of diplomacy. In short, in order to effectively counter such a predominant protocol, the argument would need to undermine this protocol much more cohesively (or, perhaps, explicitly). As Glancy maintains, if Paul is against such accepted forms of use, it is odd that he leaves no explicit trace of this disapproval (Glancy, *Slavery in Early Christianity*, 70).

93. Williams, " 'No Longer as a Slave,' " 44–45. Martin ("Slave Families," 226, n. 43) also discusses a number of inscriptions (including CIL 6.21787, 6.36351, 6.2233, and 6.11511) that combine *dominus* with familial terms like father, mother, brother, and son. (So, from the perspective of the "other" side as well, one can be a master/lord/owner *and* a "brother.")

94. The same Greek verb (*gennaō*) is used for the production of an enslaved "child" in Philemon 10 as in Galatians 4:23. These expressions are more (rather than less) compatible with the attitude displayed by the "joke" of this passage: "Quirinalis doesn't think he should have a wife, though he wants to have sons, and has found a way to achieve this: he fucks his slave girls and fills town house and country estate with home-born knights. Quirinalis is a true paterfamilias" (Martial, *Epigrams*, 1.84). Such compatibilities might qualify more positive evaluations of Philemon's familial language (and "kinship" with Gal), such as Lewis, "An African American Appraisal."

95. Indeed, the *chrēsis* language that immediately follows this image of "begetting" could be more fully contextualized in light of this particular aim or outcome of the sexual use of enslaved people. One potential implication is that Paul's argumentation could be establishing a competing claim on Onesimus, over against an(other) owner-user, on the basis of being another or better "begetter" of Onesimus.

96. For a reminder of how manumission does not represent a significant change in the dynamics between owner and slave, see DeVos, "Once a Slave." For a different view of manumission as an emancipatory (but not liberatory) strategy, using the space left in the exploitative imperial system, see Callahan, "Paul, *Ekklēsia*"; and Wire, "Response."

97. On this ongoing vulnerability, see Horsley, "Slave Systems," 48–53; Briggs, "Paul on Bondage," 111–13; and Glancy, *Slavery in Early Christianity*, 14.

98. Osiek, *Philippians, Philemon*, 142. Osiek elaborates: "in verse 21 we see the real relationship. As in most Pauline communities, Paul sees himself as the authority who can command" (*Philippians, Philemon*, 141). Even as Callahan differs as to the

relationship between Onesimus and the addressee, he also notes the force of Paul's rhetoric here, stressing that the following verse (prepare hospitality for Paul, v. 22) is a "tacit threat . . . just tentative enough to be imminent without being falsifiable" (*Embassy of Onesimus*, 64).

99. On patronage and friendship in Paul's letters and the Roman imperial context, see Fitzgerald, "Paul and Friendship"; and Marchal, "'With Friends Like These . . . :'"

100. For similar arguments regarding the strategic use of family rhetorics, competing claims on Onesimus, and the stress on Paul's status in this letter, see also Frilingos, "'For My Child,'" 101–4.

101. In what follows I will tend to use the term BDSM for these practices and participants, except where I am discussing specific examples in the literature. In those instances I will be following the often subtly shifting acronyms or descriptions given by whatever participant, theorist, writer, and/or scholar referenced at that point.

102. "Safe, Sane, and Consensual" was first coined by david stein in 1983, for the Gay Male S/M Activists (GMSMA). One version of the originating essay by stein can be found in "Safe, Sane, Consensual." "Risk Aware Consensual Kink" was coined by Gary Switch for The Eulenspiegel Society (TES), sometime in the later 1990s, and was posted to their e-mail list in an essay titled "Origin of RACK; RACK vs. SSC." For further context on both acronyms, see Weiss, *Techniques of Pleasure*, 80–84.

103. SAMOIS, ed., *Coming to Power*. Among some practitioners the clinical and potentially pathologizing resonance of sadomasochism (and its predecessors, sadism and masochism) led to the relabeling of SM as "sensuality and mutuality," while some of the more spiritually inclined participants redubbed it "sex magic" (Thompson, "Introduction," xix–xx).

104. In many ways BDSM has been with queer studies from its start, and possibly even before it, since these practices play a key role in Rubin's ground-breaking proposal for a radical theory and politics of sexuality in "Thinking Sex."

105. Califia, *Public Sex*, 158.

106. Foucault, "Sex, Power," 387–88.

107. Califia, *Public Sex*, 169.

108. McClintock, "Maid to Order."

109. For instance, the range of contributions in Thompson, ed., *Leatherfolk*. More theoretically inclined materials make similar utopic claims about BDSM, as Halperin argues: "Fist-fucking and sadomasochism appear in this light as utopian political practices, insofar as they disrupt normative sexual identities and thereby generate . . . means of resistance to the discipline of sexuality, a form of counterdiscipline" (*Saint Foucault*, 97).

110. MacKendrick, *Counterpleasures*, 110, italics original.

111. MacKendrick, *Counterpleasures*, 113. This sort of antieconomic understanding of BDSM recurs in Carrette, "Intense Exchange."

112. The preference for bottoming resounds throughout the literature on, from, or about BDSM participants. Califia, for instance, highlights: "It's a truism in the S/M community that bottoms outnumber tops about ten to one . . . .This would certainly seem to imply that one role is potentially more rewarding than the other" ("The Limits of the S/M Relationship," 222).

113. Truscott, "S/M: Some Questions," 19; cf. 26, 29.

114. This approach is inspired by, even as it departs from the approaches that work from or toward the perspective of Onesimus, including most of the contributions in Johnson, Noel, and Williams, eds., *Onesimus Our Brother*.

115. These instabilities are particularly pronounced for the Romans, given the elite males' insecurities about the potential to become debased and effeminized in a range of ways, including becoming enslaved. That there were not (enough) obvious differences between enslaved, manumitted, and free people made the cultural and political work of marking these differences so important in this context. In some similar ways, Paul's arguments were also inherently unstable, requiring as they did the audience's acceptance. Paul's efforts to persuade reflect (but have also historically obscured) his uncertainty, vulnerability, and instability in claims to power and authority.

116. On the various forms of slave resistance, see Callahan and Horsley, "Slave Resistance."

117. Indeed, it is this tension, between the widespread sexual use of enslaved people and Paul's (other) arguments about erotic conduct, that puzzles and drives some of the more sensitive and careful analyses (Glancy, *Slavery in Early Christianity*, 57–70; Osiek, "Female Slaves," 268–74).

118. There is considerable ambiguity as to whether visiting a brothel (with a *pornē*) would be viewed as *porneia* in the Roman imperial context. This ambiguity around *porneia* is not exactly resolved in the case of 1 Corinthians (or 1 Thessalonians), since Paul never clearly delineates what *porneia* is, only that it is problematic. See Briggs, "Paul on Bondage," 116–17; Glancy, *Slavery in Early Christianity*, 49–50, 58–66; and Osiek, "Female Slaves," 268–70.

119. For example, Briggs, "Paul on Bondage," 114–15, 117; Glancy, *Slavery in Early Christianity*, 35, 49, 59, 68, 70; Osiek, "Female Slaves," 269–70, 274.

120. On the "dim, ad hoc flashes of the lives of slaves," and the ambiguity of this letter, see Martin, "The Eyes Have It," 224, 230.

121. Sharpe, *Monstrous Intimacies*, 26. Sharpe provides a further contextualization of the everyday intimacies disavowed yet embodied at the heart of slavery and its haunting aftermaths, "the sadomasochism of everyday black life" (in 1–23).

122. Williams, " 'No Longer as a Slave,' " 37; cf. Callahan, *Embassy of Onesimus*, 2–4.

123. Williams, " 'No Longer as a Slave,' " 35–45. For more on the relationship between African Americans and the bible and the development of African American biblical hermeneutics, see Wimbush, ed., *African Americans and the Bible*; and Brown, *Blackening the Bible*.

124. Noel notes, for instance: "Within this cultural framework of US history, the Philemon text cannot but be both racialized and gendered" ("Nat Is Back," 76). On the racialized discipline of biblical studies, see Kelley, *Racializing Jesus*.

125. Hartman, *Scenes of Subjection*, 79–90.

126. For the relationship of these enslaved and segregated figures to present-day practices and, then, contemporary sexualized images for females and males, see Collins, *Black Sexual Politics*, 53–85, 119–80. On "controlling images" and black women's responses to them, see Collins, *Black Feminist Thought*, 69–96, 123–48.

127. Douglas, *Sexuality and the Black Church*, 31–61.

128. On the terrible silences buried in enslaving texts and traditions, see Johnson, "Onesimus Speaks," especially 95.

129. Cohen's "Punks, Bulldaggers, and Welfare Queens." As scholars engaged in queer of color critique (like Ferguson, *Aberrations in Black*) increasingly highlight, one of the longest critical engagements of the operations of sexuality as it intersects with a wide range of social dynamics can be found in the work of "women of color feminists" like Lorde, Smith, and Anzaldúa.

130. This is so commonplace in many contemporary BDSM contexts, that one of the more recent long-range and monograph-length ethnographic studies of BDSM quite noticeably marginalizes any consideration of race (Newmahr, *Playing on the Edge*). Newmahr notes the whiteness of the community considered, and mentions "race play" once in passing, but the subversion or reinforcement of racialized categories or practices are treated no further. This absence is all the more striking considering Newmahr's persistent concern with experiences of violence and evaluating to what degree sadomasochistic practices are subversive of another structuring social category: gender. By way of a brief contrast, the insistence on the separation or even absence of racist or problematic slave dynamics is foregrounded and critically assessed throughout Weiss, *Techniques of Pleasure*, but especially in the fifth chapter: "Sex Play and Social Power," 187–231.

131. Hopkins, "Rethinking Sadomasochism," 123.

132. Hopkins, "Rethinking Sadomasochism," 123.

133. Hopkins, "Rethinking Sadomasochism," 124.

134. It is ironic that this stress on the "newness" in imagining BDSM's utopic possibilities can be found in Foucault and a major interpreter of his legacy (Halperin), considering Foucault's own theorization of the disciplinary force within ideas of freedom. There is something about BDSM that makes it an exception or special case but, I argue, we should consider it further in the light of a Foucauldian apparatus (contra Foucault's own reflections on such practices).

135. This, of course, is likely a function of the pitched "battles" between different feminist views of the meaning and political significance of the forms of sexual and bodily contact in BDSM (as well as sex work and pornography). Theoretical or practical cautions about the resistant or disruptive effects of BDSM practices are clearly not limited to feminists. Bersani, for instance, maintained: "S/M profoundly—and in spite of itself—argues for the continuity between political structures of oppression and the body's erotic economy" ("Foucault, Freud," 18–19).

136. For example, Califia, *Public Sex*, 169.

137. Rubin, "The Leather Menace," 224.

138. Spillers, "Mama's Baby." For some reflections on the importance of this particular work as an overlooked, yet defining text, see Spillers, "'Whatcha Gonna Do?'"; Scott, *Extravagant Abjection*, especially 16, 155–65; Holland, *The Erotic Life of Racism*, especially 13, 45–59, 87–93; and Nash, *The Black Body in Ecstasy*, 39–43. For one work that traces how slavery and the production of racialized gender provide an alternative trajectory for the understanding of gender as mutable or transitive, see Snorton, *Black on Both Sides*.

139. Spillers, "Mama's Baby," 73.

140. Spillers, "Mama's Baby," 74–75. Again, Spillers charts and reflects on these dynamics years before more prominent thinkers (classed as queer, like Butler, *Antigone's Claim*) reconsidered the relation of kinship to cultural change.

141. For Spillers ("Mama's Baby," 75–76) the experiences of both Frederick Douglass and Malcolm X are examples of such "disremembering." (On the "ruins of a dismembered past," see also Hartman, *Scenes of Subjection*, 11.)

142. For the relations of Hartman's work to Spillers, see "'Whatcha Gonna Do?,'" 300, 303–5; Scott, *Extravagant Abjection*, 156–65; Holland, *The Erotic Life of Racism*, 45–46; and Hartman, *Scenes of Subjection*, 82–86.

143. Hartman, *Scenes of Subjection*, 4.

144. Hartman, *Scenes of Subjection*, 5.

145. For other complexities and complications around consent, especially for our understanding of biblical texts, see Graybill, "Fuzzy, Messy, Icky."

146. Hartman, *Scenes of Subjection*, 80.

147. Hartman, *Scenes of Subjection*, 79–94

148. Hartman, *Scenes of Subjection*, 102–12.

149. Jacobs, *Incidents in the Life of a Slave Girl*, 55; discussed in Hartman, *Scenes of Subjection*, 104–5 (as well as Sharpe, *Monstrous Intimacies*, 9–13; and Scott, *Extravagant Abjection*, 155–57).

150. Hartman, *Scenes of Subjection*, 103–9.

151. Hartman, *Scenes of Subjection*, 111.

152. Butler, *Undoing Gender*, 1, 15; and the discussion in chapter 1.

153. Hartman, *Scenes of Subjection*, 5.

154. Jacobs, *Incidents in the Life of a Slave Girl*, 55.

155. For instance, the reflections of Portillo, a self-described "S/M dyke of color" in "I Get Real"; and of Williams, in Weiss, *Techniques of Pleasure*, 210–13. (Both of these are women of color who reflect on their preferred submissive or bottoming activities in their BDSM communities.) Since Weiss interviewed Williams for her project (in 2002), Williams has become an increasingly public and expert educator in BDSM communities (Harrington and Williams, *Playing Well with Others*). For further reflections on BDSM for work specifically on Black female sexuality, see Cruz, *The Color of Kink*.

156. Portillo, "I Get Real," 50. Note, however, that later Portillo distances her preferred roles and practices from these historical resonances: "Now that I get to do real S/M, I no longer use historical fantasies—although they *were* a handy tool to get me off when I was still trying to 'convert' my vanilla lovers" ("I Get Real," 51). (Indeed, it might be worth considering the initiating role that historically based scenarios play in getting people involved in a scene that somehow "clicks" or works for them.)

157. For further consideration of these kinds of scenes, especially within a community imagined to be "postracial" or otherwise not racially marked, see Weiss, *Techniques of Pleasure*, 190–219.

158. Delores Williams's trailblazing theological work reflected on the sexual exploitation and coerced surrogacy of Hagar as a prototype and a parallel to the situation of more recently enslaved women and their African American descendants (*Sisters*

in the Wilderness). Traci West traces the historical legacy of slavery as a continuing trauma of intimate violence against Black women (*Wounds of the Spirit*). See also the work of Renita Weems, Emilie M. Townes, Cheryl Townsend Gilkes, Katie Geneva Cannon, and Monica A. Coleman.

159. "Sadomasochism" and "masochism," for example, are decried in Cannon, "Sexing Black Women," especially 20; Copeland, "Body, Representation," especially 109; and Copeland, "'Wading Through Many Sorrows," especially 151; cf. See also Johnson, "Onesimus Speaks," 96, 98.

160. The earlier definitions of "womanist" by Alice Walker, for example, stress these qualities: "'You acting womanish', i.e., like a woman. Usually referring to outrageous, audacious, courageous or willful behavior. Wanting to know more and in greater depth than is considered 'good' for one" (*In Search*, xi). Of course, other aspects of these early definitions also stress the potential for same-sex eroticism between (Black) women. On womanist approaches to biblical materials, see Smith, ed., *I Found God*; and Byron and Lovelace, eds., *Womanist Interpretations*.

161. For a few intriguing reconsiderations of deviance and respectability, see Clay, "Confessions of a Ex-Theological Bitch"; Miller, "'I Am a Nappy-Headed Ho;'" Davis, "The Invisible Women"; and Lovelace, "'We Don't Give Birth." For one reflection that specifically (if momentarily) reconsiders BDSM in Black religious studies, see Pinn, "Embracing Nimrod's Legacy."

162. Douglas (*Sexuality and the Black Church*), for instance, insists that Black religious thinking on sexuality uses a wider set of sources, including broader literary, cultural, and artistic materials. For queer of color critique, see works like Muñoz, *Disidentifications*; Ferguson, *Aberrations in Black*; and especially for African American or Black queer perspectives, Johnson and Henderson, eds., *Black Queer Studies*.

163. See, not only the studies quoted earlier, but especially Weiss, *Techniques of Pleasure*. Weiss's productive concern with historical structures of exploitation (and her accompanying characterization of BDSM communities) would be further complicated by considering the cultural work alluded to and discussed in what follows.

164. This project will consider the example of filmmaker Isaac Julien further, but other readers might be more interested in how these racialized aspects of BDSM have been (re)considered in the works of Toni Morrison, Gayl Jones, Gary Fisher, Rotimi Fani-Kayode, and Robert Reid-Pharr, among others. Some of the most useful work on these figures can be found in Reid-Pharr, *Black Gay Man*; Stockton, *Beautiful Bottom*; Freeman, "Turn the Beat Around"; Sharpe, *Monstrous Intimacies*; and Basu, *The Commerce of Peoples*. Slightly earlier, but still compelling to consider are Mercer, "Skin Head Sex Thing"; and Sedgwick, "Afterword."

165. Sharpe, *Monstrous Intimacies*.

166. On whiteness as a racialized position that denies its racialization and claims a kind of transparency, while also being intimately intertwined to and within constructions of racial minoritizations (African, Latino, and Asian, for instance), see Reid-Pharr, *Black Gay Man*, 88–89. On the "historical baggage" of the whip, particularly as it arrives in Julien's short film *The Attendant* in a piece of leather baggage, see Freeman, "Turn the Beat Around," 56–58.

167. Still, the significance of racial and/or ethnic categories for ancient contexts like the biblical (ones) is not as straightforwardly distant as scholarship has historically been inclined to proclaim. See Byron, *Symbolic Blackness*; and Buell, *Why This New Race*.

168. Sharpe provides a careful, threefold caution about common ways to misread, object to, or otherwise misuse Julien's film (*Monstrous Intimacies*, 122–23).

169. Sharpe's project, for instance, focuses on subjectivities that are said "to be surviving the pasts of slavery, that is not yet past" (*Monstrous Intimacies*, 26).

170. Cruz, Deitcher, and Frankel, eds., *The Film Art of Isaac Julien*.

171. Julien's films have been the focus of several projects in race-critical and queer studies, but here I tend to be more convinced by and thus especially draw on the readings of Sharpe (*Monstrous Intimacies*, 111–52), Freeman ("Turn the Beat Around"), and secondarily Stockton (*Beautiful Bottom*, 117–23). For some of Julien's own reflections on *The Attendant* specifically, see "Confessions of a Snow Queen."

172. Thus, these black leather implements highlight that it is not this, my specific project that "brings race into" a discussion of BDSM, since race is already "here" and "there" in various complicated ways. In the leather community's simulation of black skin (and in Robert Mapplethorpe's photographic depiction of both Black men and leather men), for instance, one sees the eroticization of certain kinds of racialized difference (and the traffic between them). See especially Mercer, "Skin Head Sex Thing," 174–75; and Freeman, "Turn the Beat Around," 59–60.

173. Julien, for instance, discusses how contemporary BDSM practices transform elements of slavery, demonstrating how meanings are not simply fixed in time: "Although the current images of 'whips' and 'chains' in the representational practices of s/ m have been borrowed from this colonial iconography, the refashioning of these accoutrements (i.e., rubberisation, polished surfaces, latex, polished metal) has transformed them into sexualised, stylised fetish clothing for the queer body. The imperialist slave iconography is appropriated and repositioned" ("Confessions of a Snow Queen," 80–81).

174. Again, Julien notes: "The legacy of slave imperialism persists, and the world is haunted by its traumatic and ineradicable memory" ("Confessions of a Snow Queen," 80).

175. Julien, "Confessions of a Snow Queen," 81.

176. Julien, "Confessions of a Snow Queen," 81.

177. Sharpe, *Monstrous Intimacies*, 119–20.

178. As the work of Buell persistently makes clear ("God's Own People"; "Cyborg Memories"; and "Hauntology Meets Posthumanism"), the disciplines of New Testament and early Christian studies are haunted by legacies of racialization, particularly in their pursuit for pure origins.

179. Freeman, "Turn the Beat Around," 43. For similar reflections, particularly explicit considerations of fraught desires, including, though not exclusively focused on interracial BDSM, see Reid-Pharr, *Black Gay Man*, 1–18, 85–98, 135–49.

180. Freeman, "Turn the Beat Around," 53.

181. See the similar connections made by Basu: "Our historical endeavor, then, is to retrieve the past and not be trapped by it, but instead to use it to build a future. The

historical process, then, is remarkably similar to sadomasochistic performance" (*The Commerce of Peoples*, 138).

182. For another careful negotiation of the traumatic, even hysterical elements of an inquiry into the perspective of Onesimus, see Johnson, "Onesimus Speaks." On the traumatic impacts of and within "early Christian" literature, see Kotrosits, *Rethinking Early Christian Identity*.

183. Freeman, "Turn the Beat Around," 34–35. For reflections on how BDSM practices can respond to, reorganize, and recast other kinds of trauma, even toward healing ends, see Hart, *Between the Body and the Flesh*; and Cvetkovich, *An Archive of Feelings*.

184. This is just one way of restating and restaging the false alternatives of dealing with potentially damaging biblical interpretation, named by Stone (*Practicing Safer Texts*, 8–13), as inspired by his reading of Schüssler Fiorenza (*Rhetoric and Ethic*, 17–30). For my own considerations of these two interventions, see Marchal, "Responsibilities to the Publics."

185. Much of my reflections on this opera, and the aria within it, rely on the illuminating information and analysis found in Freeman, "Turn the Beat Around," 52–54.

186. Both Freeman ("Turn the Beat Around," 63) and Sharpe (*Monstrous Intimacies*, 120–23) are interested in the ways *The Attendant* offer different ways of viewing or alternative uses of official histories.

187. Shaner's analysis of this passage (*Enslaved Leadership*, 42–62) particularly emphasizes the importance of this verb for revealing the ambiguities of Onesimus functioning as an "enslaved leader" within the assembly community.

188. It is important to grapple with white sexual paranoia and fantasies around Black bodies (see Noel, "Nat Is Back," 76–77). Outside of religious studies, several works (like Scott, *Extravagant Abjection*, Nash, *The Black Body in Ecstasy*, and Musser, *Sensational Flesh*) imagine other uses for the horrors and abjections, the potentials and impossibilities of remembrance of slavery. There is, of course, much more to do with(in) biblical interpretation, perhaps especially because we may still have only prologues to queer of color critiques and uses of biblical texts and traditions (as in Thomas, "The Futures Outside"). A recent issue of *Black Theology* signals some womanist routes for rethinking the politics of pleasure for Black women and/in the Black church (and opens with explicit reflections on Nash, *The Black Body in Ecstasy*): Lomax, "Black Bodies in Ecstasy"; Cooper, "How Sarah Got Her Groove Back"; Day, " 'I Am Dark and Lovely' "; Jones, "The Will to Adorn"; Moultrie, "Putting a Ring on It"; Russaw, "Veils and Lap Cloths"; and Lomax, "Theorizing the Distance."

Chapter 5

1. Exemplary are Brooten, *Love Between Women*; and, then, Martin, "Heterosexism"; and Martin, "*Arsenokoitēs* and *Malakos*." The focus on these texts and the belief that they are especially "about homosexuality" are both products of a particular historical moment, shaped as much by "liberals" as "conservatives" (see White, *Reforming Sodom*).

2. Longenecker, *Apostle of Liberty*; Buckmaster, *Paul: A Man Who Changed the World*; Bruce, *Paul: Apostle of the Heart Set Free*.

3. Wright, *Pauline Perspectives*; and Dunn, *The New Perspective*.

4. Bassler, *Navigating Paul*; and Roetzel, *The Letters of Paul*.

5. Badiou, *Saint Paul*; Žižek, *The Puppet and the Dwarf*; and Agamben, *The Time That Remains*. For helpful engagements, see Blanton, *A Materialism for the Masses*; Dunning, *Christ Without Adam*; and Welborn, *Paul's Summons*.

6. Sanders, *Paul, the Law*, 123–36; and Räisanen, *Paul and the Law*, 97–109.

7. Puar and Rai, "Monster, Terrorist, Fag"; Puar, "Queer Times"; and Puar, *Terrorist Assemblages*.

8. Puar explains: "Exceptionalism paradoxically signals distinction from (to be unlike, dissimilar) as well as excellence (imminence, superiority), suggesting a departure from yet mastery of linear teleologies of progress" (*Terrorist Assemblages*, 3). In Puar's work, Muslim and Sikh bodies (racially figured as "terrorist") are the Others to the exceptional citizens (both heterosexuals and homosexuals figured as "patriots").

9. For instance, Massad, "Re-Orienting Desire"; Shah, "Between 'Oriental Depravity'"; Shah, *Stranger Intimacy*; and Somerville, "Sexual Aliens."

10. Agamben, *Homo Sacer*; Agamben, *State of Exception*; and Butler, *Precarious Life*.

11. Puar explicitly asserts: "discussions of American exceptionalism rarely take up issues of gender and sexuality" (*Terrorist Assemblages*, 5).

12. Puar, *Terrorist Assemblages*, 4.

13. Puar, *Terrorist Assemblages*, 10.

14. Puar, *Terrorist Assemblages*, 2. On this mode of exceptionalism in the modern US nation-state, see Reddy, *Freedom with Violence*.

15. Puar, *Terrorist Assemblages*, 10; cf. Puar and Rai, "Monster, Terrorist, Fag."

16. Puar, *Terrorist Assemblages*, 27, 35.

17. Puar, *Terrorist Assemblages*, 165 (cf. xii). On the dual moves of quarantining and corrective incorporation, see also Puar and Rai, "Monster, Terrorist, Fag," 121–30.

18. As a result, Puar argues: "Race, ethnicity, nation, gender, class, and sexuality disaggregate gay, homosexual, and queer national subjects who align themselves with U.S. imperial interests from forms of illegitimate queerness that name and ultimately propel populations into extinction" (*Terrorist Assemblages*, xi–xii).

19. Puar, *Terrorist Assemblages*, xxiii–xxiv, 55, 165.

20. Puar, *Terrorist Assemblages*, 132–33.

21. The biopolitical is elaborated in Foucault's first volume of *The History of Sexuality*, 135–59; and Foucault, "*Society Must Be Defended*," 239–64. For the necropolitical, see Mbembe, "Necropolitics." On the "bare life" of these populations, see Agamben, *Homo Sacer*.

22. Alexander, *Pedagogies of Crossing*, 239.

23. Alexander, *Pedagogies of Crossing*, 23–25, 53.

24. Alexander, *Pedagogies of Crossing*, 26–27, 57–64.

25. Alexander, *Pedagogies of Crossing*, 62.

26. Alexander, *Pedagogies of Crossing*, 41.

27. Alexander, *Pedagogies of Crossing*, 51–53.

28. Alexander, *Pedagogies of Crossing*, 58; cf. 66–88. Just in the context of South Africa, Barnard ("The United States in South Africa"; and *Queer Race*) has carefully traced very similar dynamics to the racialized and imperial tropes for gay tourism (cf. Boone, "Vacation Cruises").

29. Alexander, *Pedagogies of Crossing*, 79. This is why Alexander's work has a recurrently dual focus: "against hegemonic discourses produced within metropolitan countries, and even within oppositional lesbian, gay, and bisexual communities that position the so-called Third World as barbaric—in contrast to American civilized democracy" (*Pedagogies of Crossing*, 28).

30. Alexander (*Pedagogies of Crossing*, 181–254) examines the US sexual exceptionalism (also) described by Puar in the twenty-first century, the Spanish colonization of the Americas by Balboa in the sixteenth century, and the criminalization of lesbian and gay sex in the Caribbean during the twentieth century.

31. Alexander, *Pedagogies of Crossing*, 192, cf. 196.

32. Alexander, *Pedagogies of Crossing*, 239.

33. Alexander, *Pedagogies of Crossing*, 195.

34. Puar, *Terrorist Assemblages*, 184–87; as well as Ahmed, "Affective Economies."

35. Alexander, *Pedagogies of Crossing*, 235–36.

36. Thus, in certain ways, this work links back to Rubin's reflections on moral panics and their effects (in "Thinking Sex"). As Alexander argues: "This (white) originary citizen is in sharp contradistinction to the (dark) naturalized citizen, the dark immigrant, or even the dark citizen born of the dark immigrant whose (latent) 'loyalty' is perennially suspect and, therefore, ultimately threatening" (*Pedagogies of Crossing*, 235).

37. Puar, *Terrorist Assemblages*, 5; and Alexander, *Pedagogies of Crossing*, 234.

38. Puar, *Terrorist Assemblages*, 7–9. Here, Puar presents a rather different reflection on singularity and universalism than Badiou (who attempts his reading of Paul on such terms in *Saint Paul*).

39. Two examples from within Hebrew Bible scholarship have considered the relationship between the state of exception and the contemporary resonance of biblical concepts: Sherwood, "The God of Abraham"; and Runions, "Empire's Allure."

40. For a related argument about biblical figures operating toward sexualized discipline and dehumanizing enemies (but focused on Babel/Babylon), see Runions, *The Babylon Complex*, especially 179–212.

41. Indeed, Martin ("Heterosexism," especially 333–39) contends that Paul has in mind a very specific historical narrative here, claiming that all humans had knowledge of one deity in the past, but the more polytheistic people(s) actively turned away from (or defied) this knowledge at one point, thus explaining their decline. On the cognitive language in this passage, see Brooten, *Love Between Women*, 222–28. On these "decline of civilization" narratives, see Stowers, *A Rereading*, 85–100.

42. Martin ("Heterosexism," 336, 341–49) locates the argument within the ancient concern for excess and thus translates this phrase as "*beyond* nature."

43. Countryman, *Dirt, Greed, and Sex*, 110–11.

44. Indeed, there is a strange agency attributed to God, in causing the behavior (the sexual activities, yes, but also a long string of offenses, including murder and all manner of evil) that is being condemned.

45. For two other, instructive readings of this passage in light of intersecting gender, sexual, ethnic, and imperial dynamics, see briefly, Kwok, "A Postcolonial Reading," especially 39–45; and, at greater length in relation to British colonialism, Moore, *God's Beauty Parlor*, 133–72.

46. Stowers, *A Rereading*, 109.

47. This reading of the impact of universalism in Paul's argumentation contrasts significantly with the one found in Lopez's reading of Galatians (*Apostle to the Conquered*).

48. On the biopolitics of biblical figurations, see Runions, *The Babylon Complex*.

49. Sedgwick, *Epistemology of the Closet*.

50. On the relationship between ethnoracial (stereo)typing and claims about sexual transgression (like associating idolatrous "heathen" as sexually aberrant), see Bailey, "They're Nothing but Incestuous Bastards."

51. Indeed, Paul's arguments about "the law" in Romans reflect a similar coexistence of minoritizing and universalizing viewpoints. It is simultaneously something that only a certain people, the *Ioudaioi*, have in relation to the divine (3:1–2, minoritizing), but it is something the other nations can "know" by doing, without having it, as all humans should (2:14–15, universalizing). Furthermore, Paul argues that all are "justified" through a divine action (universalizing), yet the benefits of this action can only be gained by those who negotiate the proper relationship of *pistis* (loyalty, obedience) with the divine (minoritizing, 3:21–26).

52. Countryman (*Dirt, Greed, and Sex*, 116–17) has argued that the judgment of death in 1:32 does not directly follow on 1:26–27, and thus only applies as a punishment for those judged in the third part of the cause-effect cycle and described in the vice list in 1:29–31.

53. The minoritizing and universalizing models about the uses of divine knowledge and the practices of excessive erotics also correspond to particular views of time in "history." The minoritizing views tend to reflect on an already present: only some use divine knowledge properly and only some have been handed over to certain problematic practices. The universalizing views seem to aim toward the not yet, an anticipatory potential future, that could, in fact, turn in either direction: all could gain and thus properly use the divine knowledge or not and become like the various negative types (of Romans 1 and throughout Paul's letters); all could accept their "justification" and display a constrained and moderate comportment or not and descend like the nations into excessive erotic practices (that comport with improper gender crossings). These particular, if broad trends in Paul's argumentation could be the result of a dualistic (and apocalyptically influenced) worldview, still recognizable at various sites of argumentation where "all or nothing" scenarios are invoked. (This likely requires further queer reflection about argumentative strategies, their heritages, and their intended and unintended effects.) On recent developments of the "antisocial thesis," which may provide provocative links to Paul's deployments of apocalyptic and limits on kinship, see Edelman, *No Future*; and Bersani, *Homos*.

54. In what follows, I will increasingly use terms like "ethnoracial," or pair "race" with "ethnicity," following the practice of Buell (*Why This New Race*, especially 5–29), despite the occasional claims that their use would be anachronistic. Consider also Byron, *Symbolic Blackness*.

55. For one, at times problematic, survey of the variety of meanings attributed to these two terms, see Elliott, "No Kingdom." The clearest and most convincing explanation of the known (if objectionable) or unknowable meanings of these two terms remains Martin, "*Arsenokoitēs* and *Malakos*."

56. One of the clearest explications of the rhetorical context for these vice lists, both within the letter and the ancient Greco-Roman world, is Ivarsson, "Vice Lists."

57. The reference to "his father's woman" could indicate that the man has taken a step-mother who was relatively closer to him in age (Wire, *The Corinthian Women Prophets*, 76–78) and/or or his father's enslaved or freed woman (Glancy, *Slavery in Early Christianity*, 63–65).

58. Of course, this also has the potential to indicate that, once driven out, the one-time insiders are now the kind of outsiders to be judged apocalyptically by (this version of) the deity.

59. Zaas, "Catalogues and Context"; and Ivarsson, "Vice Lists."

60. Indeed, Ivarsson ("Vice Lists," 167–68) stresses that such interrelation (or stickiness) is characteristic of vice lists.

61. On the specific significance of *malakoi* as connoting softness and effeminacy (and the genuine difficulty of determining the meaning of *arsenokoitai*), see Martin, "*Arsenokoitēs* and *Malakos*."

62. Ivarsson, "Vice Lists," 176.

63. On the combined or alternating dynamics of fixity and fluidity in these letters, see Buell and Johnson Hodge, "The Politics of Interpretation"; and Johnson Hodge, *If Sons*.

64. Hall, *Inventing the Barbarian*.

65. Hall, *Inventing the Barbarian*, 4–5. Jonathan Hall (*Ethnic Identity*, 44–47) also marks the wars with the Persians as a turning point in Greek constructions of their own ethnicity: where once it was aggregative, now it was oppositional.

66. Hall, *Inventing the Barbarian*, 4–9.

67. Even as Hall argues that language itself can only be an indicium, rather than a criterion for ethnicity, he concedes the original linguistic connotation of the term *barbaros* (*Ethnic Identity*, 45).

68. Hall delineates eight main factors in describing the function of ethnicity (*Ethnic Identity*, 32–33), but particularly stresses subjective and ascriptive claims about territory and descent as more important than language for differentiating ancient ethnicities (*Ethnic Identity*, 24–25).

69. Hall, *Ethnic Identity*, 45.

70. Dauge, *Le Barbare*. See also the massive coverage of Greek and Roman "proto-racist" views of their others in Isaac, *The Invention of Racism*. For another, intentionally anachronistic collection of relevant sources, see Kennedy, Roy, and Goldman, *Race and Ethnicity*.

71. Boatwright, *Peoples*, 8–12; and Ferris, *Enemies of Rome*, 4.

72. Edwards, "Incorporating the Alien."

73. Edwards and Woolf, "Cosmopolis"; and Boatwright, *Peoples*, 47–53.

74. Hall, *Inventing the Barbarian*, 201.

75. Hall, *Inventing the Barbarian*, 2, 209; Ferris, *Enemies of Rome*, 180; Boatwright, *Peoples*, 12; and Mattern, *Rome and the Enemy*, 73–74.

76. Mattern, *Rome and the Enemy*, 71. On Roman ethnography in general, see Lund, *Zum Germanenbild*.

77. Said, *Orientalism*, 29.

78. Hall, *Inventing the Barbarian*, 99.

79. Ferris, *Enemies of Rome*, 180.

80. On Medea as a paradigmatic barbarian and/as transgressive woman, see Hall, *Inventing the Barbarian*, 203; Kennedy, Roy, and Goldman, *Race and Ethnicity*, 322. Euripides stresses that Medea is from a barbarian land (*Medea*, 1331–33); Seneca associates her with other barbaric monsters (*Medea*, 42–54, 116–34); and Ovid stressed that Medea's actions have made her into a barbarian to Jason (*Heroides*, 12.103–6).

81. Hall maintains: "Femaleness, barbarism, luxury, and hubris are thus ineluctably drawn into the same semantic complex, as interconnected aspects of all that Greek manhood should shun" (*Inventing the Barbarian*, 206).

82. Hallett, "Female Homoeroticism"; Swancutt, "*Still* Before Sexuality."

83. The argument throughout Swancutt, "*Still* Before Sexuality," but especially 33.

84. Williams, *Roman Homosexuality*, 135.

85. Ferris, *Enemies of Rome*, 165.

86. Lopez, *Apostle to the Conquered*, 26–55.

87. Lopez, *Apostle to the Conquered*, 103–5.

88. Lopez, *Apostle to the Conquered*, 44–45.

89. Hall, *Inventing the Barbarian*, 209.

90. Stevenson, "The Rise of Eunuchs," 502.

91. Williams, *Roman Homosexuality*, 128.

92. Williams, *Roman Homosexuality*, 177.

93. Williams, *Roman Homosexuality*, 177.

94. Aristotle, *Politics*, 1.1.5; 1.2.18–19; and the discussion in Isaac, *The Invention of Racism*, 177–79; and Kennedy, Roy, and Goldman, *Race and Ethnicity*, 63–64.

95. Hall, *Inventing the Barbarian*, 201.

96. Hall, *Inventing the Barbarian*, 80–84, 125–33.

97. See Trogus (Justin) 41.2.5–6; Plutarch *Crassus* 21.6; and the discussion in Mattern, *Rome and the Enemy*, 70.

98. On the use of Roman imperial marriage laws to establish such standards and activities, see D'Angelo, "Early Christian Sexual Politics."

99. Williams (*Roman Homosexuality*, 18) has described the insertive role as "the prime directive of masculine sexual behavior" for the Romans. See also Richlin, *The Garden of Priapus*, 57–64; as well as the discussion in chapter 4.

100. Walters, "Invading the Roman Body," 41, cf. 36–37.

101. McClintock, *Imperial Leather*.

102. Richlin, "Not Before Homosexuality," 553.

103. The prime directive of penetration reveals itself, then, as about more than just masculinity or sexuality: "A sexual protocol that proclaims itself to be about

gender-appropriate behavior turns out to be part of a wider pattern of social status, where the violability or inviolability of the body is a privileged marker of such status" (Walters, "Invading the Roman Body," 41).

104. Williams, *Roman Homosexuality*, 160–81; and Walters, "Invading the Roman Body," 33.

105. On the relation of unmen or non-men to wo/men in the lower regions of kyriarchal orders (particularly as enslaved or freed), see Marchal, "Slaves as Wo/men and Unmen."

106. Moore, "Que(e)rying Paul," 261.

107. On the attribution of sexual perversity to the outsider and colonized people as an imperial rationale, see Said, *Orientalism*; and Knust, *Abandoned to Lust* (though Knust stresses the persistence of the insider-outsider elements of this dynamic, more than the imperial-colonial aspects).

108. Williams, *Roman Homosexuality*, 135–37.

109. Williams, *Roman Homosexuality*, 179.

110. For various accusations, innuendos, implications, and stagings of elite public figures as sexually improper, see Williams, *Roman Homosexuality*, 163–65, 173–81, 188–209, 276. On the depiction of Roman matrons as *tribades*, and the dual concern with controlling both distant and proximate others, see Swancutt, "*Still* Before Sexuality," 13, 34–37.

111. For two more optimistic readings of Paul's critique (possibly of the emperors), see Jennings, *Outlaw Justice*, 36–40; and Elliott, *The Arrogance of Nations*, 79–82. Paul is not different from the empire by critiquing the emperors, but his rhetorics are steeped in the same thought world. Rhetorically constructing and targeting a figure around improper erotic conduct, like unnatural use (1:26–27), is not a challenge to the imperially gendered system that claims racial/ethnic and religious superiority on the basis of sexual exceptionalism; this can be merely echoing one expression of its inner workings.

112. Ivarsson, "Vice Lists," 176. Ivarsson also suggests that several other passages in Paul's letters stereotype Gentiles, including Romans 1:23–32; 1 Corinthians 5:1; 10:7–10; Galatians 4:8–9; and 1 Thessalonians 4:4–5.

113. Knust, *Abandoned to Lust*, 51–87.

114. Similar concerns might also be at work in Philippians, where Paul deploys antimodels as points of contrast who focus on mutilating the flesh (3:2), glorying in shame, and treating their belly as a god (3:19) destined for destruction (3:19). Indeed, the reference to the surrounding world as a "crooked or perverse generation" (2:15) might reflect similar presumptions at work in 1 Corinthians 5–6 about the relationship between the assembly community and the rest of the world.

115. Indeed, these reflections could further problematize and resituate a number of dualisms fundamental to Pauline argumentation, like flesh/spirit or death/eternal life (or even the past/present, before/after), as intersecting with or otherwise shaped by these sexual, gender, and ethnoracial figurations.

116. Runions, too, attempts to read figures of sublime alterity otherwise, particularly for their potential for disruption (*The Babylon Complex*, 213–16, 231–45).

117. Matthews's treatment of this passage ("A Feminist Analysis"), however, aims to foreground an explicitly intersectional reading in terms of status, race, and ethnicity, alongside and within gender and sexuality. In organizing my current project this way, I am trying to indicate (perhaps too retrospectively) that these arguments about gender-variant females, castrated males, and enslaved people were also already racialized.

118. Their withdrawal from sex (Wire, *Corinthian Women Prophets*; and Marchal, "How Soon") could have been the implicit reason why males who cannot maintain Paul's particular brand of sexual austerity claimed a need for contact with sexually immoral females (or prostitutes). Of course, males with their own available spouses also made frequent use of other sexual receptacles without significant or consistent condemnation in the ancient Roman imperial setting.

119. This order was distinctly gendered (Wire, *The Corinthian Women Prophets*; Økland, *Women in Their Place*; and Miller, *Corinthian Democracy*).

120. On the potentially racialized dynamics to this argument about barbaric tongues, see Tupamahu, "Language Politics."

121. Though notice Paul's willingness to cast audience members as immature and childish figures in their thoughts and speech (14:20, but also in 1 Cor 1–4).

122. Cicero, *De finibus* 2.49; cf. *De divinatione* 1.84.

123. Josephus, *Jewish War* 5.17; *Jewish Antiquities* 4.12; 11.229; 16.177; Philo, *On the Life of Moses* 2.12.19ff.; *On Rewards and Punishments* 165; *On the Special Laws* 2.165ff.

124. Of course, it is even contested whether Romans 1:26 refers to female-female sexual behavior (Swancutt, "*Still* Before Sexuality"). Unlike the narration of the divine punishment of males (who are consumed with passion for each other, committing shameless acts with other males), "their females" are described as a collective, but not described in a strictly parallel fashion akin to males. They are not described as consumed with passion for each other, or as committing shameless acts with other females.

125. Brooten, *Love Between Women*, 238–58.

126. This is certainly the case in later decades and centuries (MacDonald, *Early Christian Women*).

127. For all of its strengths, Knust's examination of the sexualized rhetoric in Paul's letters (*Abandoned to Lust*) remain mostly incurious about the recipients, "opponents," or quite simply the other assembly members.

128. On the possible backgrounds and descriptions of these figures, see Lampe, *From Paul*, especially 164–83; and Hanks, "Romans," 583–84, 604–5.

129. For initial insights on the women named (and unnamed), including Phoebe, Prisca, Mariam, Junia, Tryphaena and Tryphosa, Persis, Julia, the mother of Rufus, the sister of Nereus, and possibly the sisters greeted with the others mentioned in v. 14, see their entries in Meyers, ed. *Women in Scripture*, 106–7, 119–20, 134–37, 165–66, 469–40. Indeed the dictionary is just one indicator of the advances of various feminist approaches to reconstructing historical information about women in and through biblical argumentation, and a potent signal of what queer approaches can learn, share, and adapt from feminist historical methods. See also Brooten,

"Junia...Outstanding"; Schüssler Fiorenza, "Missionaries, Apostles"; and Schüssler Fiorenza, "The 'Quilting' of Women's History."

130. Feminist biblical scholars who have attended to the rhetorical dynamics of these letters (like Wire, *The Corinthian Women Prophets*; Schüssler Fiorenza, *Rhetoric and Ethic*; Kittredge, "Rethinking Authorship"; and Marchal, *The Politics of Heaven*) have stressed that one cannot begin with a position of simple acceptance or acquiescence (either in historical presuppositions about the past community or ethical-political considerations of the present and the future). Paul's authority is (and was) far from final or ultimate, but his arguments reflect that he is one out of many. This might indicate the utility of feminist historical conceptualizations for a range of interrogatory practices, as it pluralizes the visions and authorities of and in structures of the ancient assembly communities.

131. On Phoebe, the titles used, and her status, see Schüssler Fiorenza, "Missionaries, Apostles," 423–27; Schüssler Fiorenza, "The 'Quilting' of Women's History," 44–48; MacDonald, "Reading Real Women," 207–9; and Gaventa, *When in Romans*, 9–14.

132. On the rather problematic way Acts frames Paul in terms of Jewish-Gentile difference, see Matthews, *Perfect Martyr*.

133. Lampe, *From Paul*, 11–14, 75; Oakes, *Reading Romans*, 74.

134. On the different diasporic migrant strategies attributed to Paul, see the discussions in Aymer, "Rootlessness and Community"; and Agosto, "Islands, Borders."

135. Some scholars see Prisca's economic status as relatively high (Meeks, *The First Urban Christians*, 59; MacDonald, "Reading Real Women," 204; Stowers, *A Rereading*, 75–79, Jewett, *Romans*, 64–65), while others situate the couple as relatively low, with perhaps only a moderate surplus in comparison to other craftworking people (Lampe, *From Paul*, 187–95; Friesen, "Poverty," 353). Oakes takes them as a model for what the Roman assembly communities might be like: a Gentile craftworker (tentmaking) house church (*Reading Romans*, 79).

136. On the potential of this "mixed marriage," see Jewett, *Romans*, 956. On Jewish-Gentile intermarriage in the communities addressed by Paul's letters, see also Johnson Hodge, "Married to an Unbeliever." Within his arguments to these assembly communities, Paul uses an aggregative argument around race/ethnicity (not creating a third ethnoracial category, as Sechrest, *A Former Jew*, claims), offering to fold Gentiles into his view of Abrahamic descent (Buell, *Why This New Race*, 75–76, 201; Johnson Hodge, *If Sons*, 67–116).

137. It seems overstated to assume (given references in Rom 16:5 and 1 Cor 16:19) that they own homes in multiple places. The assembly could be meeting in their rented apartment and/or tenement quarters (Lampe, *From Paul*, 187–95; Friesen, "Poverty," 353; Oakes, *Reading Romans*, 89–97).

138. Brooten, "Junia . . . Outstanding," 142. The masculinization of the name simply relied upon circular reasoning: because a woman could not be an apostle, the letter's greeting of a woman called an apostle must be mistaken, thus Junia[s] must not have been a woman. For further treatment, see also Epp, *Junia*.

139. Schüssler Fiorenza, "Missionaries, Apostles," 430; Brooten, "Junia," 107; Lampe, *From Paul*, 176; and Epp, *Junia*, 23.

140. Brooten, "Junia," 107; MacDonald, "Reading Real Women," 209; Lampe, *From Paul*, 75, 168.

141. Wansink, *Chained in Christ*; Standhartinger, "Letter from Prison."

142. MacDonald, "Reading Real Women," 203; Jewett, *Romans*, 957–58; Diogenes Laertius *Lives of Eminent Philosophers* 4.11.

143. It is unlikely that the support provided by Prisca and Aquila was "merely" some sort of economic sponsorship of Paul, then, given the risk of drawing the attention of Roman imperial authorities.

144. On imprisonment and the role of Junia in particular, see Fox, "Decentering Paul."

145. Lampe, *From Paul*, 164–65.

146. Lampe, *From Paul*, 171–83.

147. D'Angelo, "Women Partners."

148. Schüssler Fiorenza, "Missionaries, Apostles," 428; Lampe, *From Paul*, 179–80.

149. D'Angelo, "Women Partners," 75, 83.

150. D'Angelo, "Tryphaena," 165–66. For reflections on biblical texts by and with sex workers, see Ipsen, *Sex Working and the Bible*.

151. D'Angelo, "Women Partners," 83.

152. D'Angelo argues to this effect: "Perhaps the vehemence of Paul's condemnation of female and male homoeroticism in Rom 1:26–27 is in part apologetic, arising from the need to defend the early Christian mission's practice of missionary couples, including both his own practice and the women attested in Rom. 16:12" ("Women Partners," 84).

153. A longer exposition of the people besides Paul cited in the opening and closing of 1 Corinthians would need to reconsider the "people belonging to Chloe" (1:11), Crispus and Gaius (1:14), the household of Stephanas (1:16; 16:15), Stephanas and Fortunatus and Achaicus (16:17), and Aquila and Prisca (16:19), alongside the depiction of Paul in relation to Apollos. See, initially, Concannon, "*When You Were Gentiles*."

154. Again, on alternating claims of fixity and fluidity, see Buell and Johnson Hodge, "The Politics of Interpretation"; and Johnson Hodge, *If Sons*.

155. Cohen, *The Beginnings of Jewishness*; and Eisenbaum, *Paul Was Not a Christian*, 99–115.

156. Cohen, *The Beginnings of Jewishness*, 27–37.

157. Cohen, *The Beginnings of Jewishness*, 39–49; and the fuller discussion in Cohen, *Why Aren't Jewish Women*.

158. Cohen, *The Beginnings of Jewishness*, 53–62, 140–74.

159. Cohen structures his analysis around seven different practices (*The Beginnings of Jewishness*, 140–74), and notes the continuing ambiguities around proselytes (or "converts") (157–62).

160. Eisenbaum, *Paul Was Not a Christian*, 104–105; Cohen, *The Beginnings of Jewishness*, 37–39.

161. Eisenbaum, *Paul Was Not a Christian*, 107–15.

162. Lampe, *From Paul*, 69–70.

163. "Paul's interaction with Gentiles should not be seen as the radical step it is typically perceived to be" (Eisenbaum, *Paul Was Not a Christian*, 115).

164. Liew (*What Is Asian American Biblical Hermeneutics?*, 75–97, 175–88) develops a particularly convincing explanation of Paul's gender, sexual, and racialized arguments in light of a colonized consciousness.

165. Liew thus describes the arguments in 1 Corinthians: "Paul's stigmatization of sexually dissident bodies (whether Jewish or Greco-Roman) in particular and his claim to be 'more Greco-Roman' than others only end up reduplicating and reinforcing colonial ideologies . . . Paul projects his own abjection and stigmatization as being 'feminine' and 'morally corrupt' onto women and other sexual dissidents. By duplicating and displacing colonial abjection onto people who are also in different ways already subjected, Paul greatly compromises his resistance against colonization and racialization. He has, in a sense, himself become those who oppress him or what he hates. He is building community on the backs of those whom 'everyone' can agree to marginalize and stigmatize" (*What Is Asian American Hermeneutics?*, 95).

166. Eisenbaum parenthetically, but frankly notes: "I want to stress that I am in no way endorsing Paul's damning view of Gentiles. It is important to realize that this is just a bias of Paul's" (*Paul Was Not a Christian*, 236).

167. For further possibilities, see Hoke, "Unbinding Imperial Time."

168. Cohen, *The Beginnings of Jewishness*, 346; Eisenbaum, *Paul Was Not a Christian*, 105.

169. Consider, for instance, Lopez, *Apostle to the Conquered*; Marchal, *The Politics of Heaven*; and Liew, *What Is Asian American Hermeneutics?* For (similar) connections between these ancient contexts and exceptionalist politics in the age of US dominance, see Runions, *The Babylon Complex*.

170. Memmi, *The Pillar of Salt*, 165.

171. Slabodsky, *Decolonial Judaism*, 1, 10, 115–43.

172. On Abu Ghraib, sexual degradation, and Babylonian ("Muslim") differentiations, see Runions, *The Babylon Complex*, 208–10.

173. For some initial directions where postcolonial and queer forms of biblical interpretation might intersect or interact, see Punt, "Queer Theory."

174. Dinshaw, *Getting Medieval*, 12. Though Brooten only briefly treats the figures named in Romans 16, before embarking on an extensive and detailed commentary of 1:18–32 (*Love Between Women*, 218–19), her work also seems to be propelled by similar questions about who were the targets and audience(s) of Paul's letter and how we can know them. See also Brooten's imaginative evoking of an ancient context where various parties receive Paul's letter to the Romans differently (*Love Between Women*, 300–302).

175. Warner, *The Trouble with Normal*.

176. Puar, *Terrorist Assemblages*, 22.

177. For one nuanced, queerly biblical reflection on the potential for complicity, see Huber, "Gazing at the Whore."

178. For one, beautiful rumination on this practice, and the persistence of the queerly stigmatized figure, see Brintnall, "Who Weeps."

Epilogue

1. For another, perhaps even more illuminating set of temporal, political, sexualized, racialized, and scripturalized disorientations, see Hidalgo, *Revelation in Aztlán*; and Hidalgo, "'*Our* Book of Revelation . . . .'"
2. Dinshaw, *Getting Medieval*, 167.
3. Dinshaw, *Getting Medieval*, 39.
4. Dinshaw, *Getting Medieval*, 1.
5. Butler, *Gender Trouble*, 136–49.
6. Freeman, "Packing History," 728; cf. Freeman, "Time Binds," 66; Freeman, "Still After"; and Freeman, "Time Binds," 62.
7. Freeman, "Packing History," 729.
8. Freccero, *Queer/Early/Modern*, 69–73.
9. Freeman, "Time Binds," 66.
10. Love, *Feeling Backward*, 43.
11. Freeman, "Packing History," 729.
12. Wire, *The Corinthian Women Prophets*, 119–26.
13. For some discussion of how the prophetic females were defined by a new creation (that has already happened in them), see Wire, *The Corinthian Women Prophets*, 125–26, 128–29, 176, 184–86.
14. Morland, "What Can Queer Theory," 300.
15. Freeman, "Packing History," 729.
16. Hartman, *Scenes of Subjection*.
17. Spillers, "Mama's Baby."
18. Morland, "What Can Queer Theory," 295–98, 304–5.
19. For a helpful discussion of how haunting redirects concerns about anachronism, see Buell, "Hauntology Meets Post-Humanism."
20. Ahmed, *Willful Subjects*.

Bibliography

Abusch, Ra'anan. "Circumcision and Castration under Roman Law in the Early Empire." Pages 75–86 in *The Covenant of Circumcision: New Perspectives on an Ancient Jewish Rite*. Edited by Elizabeth Wyner Mark. Hanover, NH: Brandeis University Press, 2003.

Adams, Edward, and David G. Horrell, eds. *Christianity at Corinth: The Quest for the Pauline Church*. Louisville: Westminster John Knox, 2004.

Adams, J. N. *The Latin Sexual Vocabulary*. Baltimore: Johns Hopkins University Press, 1982.

Agamben, Giorgio. *Homo Sacer: Sovereign Power and Bare Life*. Translated by Daniel Heller-Roazen. Stanford: Stanford University Press, 1988.

Agamben, Giorgio. *State of Exception*. Translated by Kevin Attell. Chicago: University of Chicago Press, 2005.

Agamben, Giorgio. *The Time That Remains: A Commentary on the Letter to the Romans*. Translated by Patricia Dailey. Stanford: Stanford University Press, 2005.

Agosto, Efraín. "Islands, Borders, and Migration: Reading Paul in Light of the Crisis in Puerto Rico." Pages 149–70 in *Latinxs, the Bible and Migration*. Edited by Efraín Agosto and Jacqueline Hidalgo. New York: Palgrave, 2018.

Ahmed, Sara. "Affective Economies." *Social Text* 22:2 (2004): 117–39.

Ahmed, Sara. *Willful Subjects*. Durham: Duke University Press, 2014.

Alexander, M. Jacqui. *Pedagogies of Crossing: Meditations on Feminism, Sexual Politics, Memory, and the Sacred*. Durham: Duke University Press, 2005.

Anzaldúa, Gloria. *Borderlands/La Frontera: The New Mestiza*. San Francisco: Aunt Lute Books, 1987.

Armour, Ellen T., and Susan M. St. Ville, eds. *Bodily Citations: Religion and Judith Butler*. New York: Columbia University Press, 2006.

Aymer, Margaret. "Rootlessness and Community in Contexts of Diaspora." Pages 46–71 in *Fortress Commentary on the Bible: New Testament*. Edited by Margaret Aymer, Cynthia Briggs Kittredge, and David A. Sánchez. Minneapolis: Fortress, 2014.

Badiou, Alain. *Saint Paul: The Foundation of Universalism*. Translated by Ray Brassier. Stanford: Stanford University Press, 2003.

Bailey, Randall C. "They're Nothing but Incestuous Bastards: The Polemical Use of Sex and Sexuality in Hebrew Canon Narratives." Pages 121–38 in *Reading from This Place*, Vol. 1. *Social Location and Biblical Interpretation in the United States*. Edited by Fernando F. Segovia and Mary Ann Tolbert. Minneapolis: Fortress, 1995.

Balch, David L., and Carolyn Osiek, eds. *Early Christian Families in Context: An Interdisciplinary Dialogue*. Grand Rapids, MI: Eerdmans, 2003.

Barnard, Ian. *Queer Race: Cultural Interventions in the Racial Politics of Queer Theory*. New York: Lang, 2004.

Barnard, Ian. "The United States in South Africa: (Post)Colonial Queer Theory?" Pages 129–38 in *Postcolonial and Queer Theories: Intersections and Essays*. Edited by John C. Hawley. Westwood, CT: Greenwood, 2001.

Barrett, C. K. *A Commentary on the First Epistle to the Corinthians.* 2nd ed. BNTC. London: A&C Black, 1971.

Bartchy, S. Scott. "Slavery, Greco-Roman." Pages 65–73 in *Anchor Bible Dictionary*, Vol. 6. Edited by David Noel Freedman. Garden City, NY: Doubleday, 1992.

Bassler, Jouette. *Navigating Paul: An Introduction to Key Theological Concepts.* Louisville: Westminster John Knox, 2007.

Basu, Biman. *The Commerce of Peoples: Sadomasochism and African American Literature.* Lanham, MD: Lexington, 2012.

Beard, Mary. "The Roman and the Foreign: The Cult of the 'Great Mother' in Imperial Rome." Pages 165–90 in *Shamanism, History, and the State.* Edited by Nicholas Thomas and Caroline Humphrey. Ann Arbor: University of Michigan Press, 1994.

Bersani, Leo. "Foucault, Freud, Fantasy, and Power." *GLQ* 2:1–2 (1995): 11–33.

Bersani, Leo. *Homos.* Cambridge, MA: Harvard University Press, 1995.

Bersani, Leo. "Is the Rectum a Grave?" Pages 197–222 in *AIDS: Cultural Analysis/Cultural Activism.* Edited by Douglas Crimp. Cambridge, MA: MIT Press, 1987.

Betz, Hans Dieter. *Galatians: A Commentary on Paul's Letter to the Churches in Galatia.* Hermeneia. Philadelphia: Fortress, 1979.

Blackless, Melanie, Anthony Charuvastra, Amanda Derryck, Anne Fausto-Sterling, Karl Lauzanne, and Ellen Lee. "How Sexually Dimorphic Are We?" *American Journal of Human Biology* 12:2 (2000): 151–66.

Blanton, Ward. *A Materialism for the Masses: Saint Paul and the Philosophy of Undying Life.* New York: Columbia University Press, 2014.

Boatwright, Mary T. *Peoples of the Roman World.* Cambridge: Cambridge University Press, 2012.

Boone, Joseph A. "Vacation Cruises, or, the Homoerotics of Orientalism." *PMLA* 110:1 (1995): 89–107.

Bornstein, Kate. *Gender Outlaw: On Men, Women, and the Rest of Us.* New York: Vintage, 1995.

Boswell, John. *Christianity, Social Tolerance, and Homosexuality: Gay People in Western Europe from the Beginning of the Christian Era to the Fourteenth Century.* Chicago: University of Chicago Press, 1980.

Boyarin, Daniel. *A Radical Jew: Paul and the Politics of Identity.* Berkeley: University of California Press, 1994.

Boyarin, Daniel. *Unheroic Conduct: The Rise of Heterosexuality and the Invention of the Jewish Man.* Berkeley: University of California Press, 1997.

Bradley, Keith. *Slavery and Society at Rome.* Cambridge: Cambridge University Press, 1994.

Bradley, Keith. *Slaves and Masters in the Roman Empire: A Study in Social Control.* New York: Oxford University Press, 1987.

Briggs, Sheila. "Galatians." Pages 218–36 in *Searching the Scriptures: A Feminist Commentary*, Vol. 2. Edited by Elisabeth Schüssler Fiorenza with Ann Brock and Shelly Matthews. New York: Crossroad, 1994.

Briggs, Sheila. "Paul on Bondage and Freedom in Imperial Roman Society." Pages 110–23 in *Paul and Politics: Ekklesia, Israel, Imperium, Interpretation. Essays in Honor of Krister Stendahl.* Edited by Richard A. Horsley. Harrisburg, PA: Trinity, 2000.

Briggs, Sheila. "Slavery and Gender." Pages 171–92 in *On the Cutting Edge: The Study of Women in Biblical Worlds. Essays in Honor of Elisabeth Schüssler Fiorenza.* Edited by Jane Schaberg, Alice Bach, and Esther Fuchs. New York: Continuum, 2003.

Brintnall, Kent L. "Queer Studies in Religion." *Critical Research on Religion* 1:1 (2013): 51–61.

Brintnall, Kent L. "Who Weeps for the Sodomite?" Pages 145–60 in *Sexual Disorientations: Queer Temporalities, Affects, Theologies*. Edited by Kent L. Brintnall, Joseph A. Marchal, and Stephen D. Moore. New York: Fordham University Press, 2018.

Brintnall, Kent L., Joseph A. Marchal, and Stephen D. Moore, eds. *Sexual Disorientations: Queer Temporalities, Affects, Theologies*. New York: Fordham University Press, 2018.

Brisson, Luc. *Sexual Ambivalence: Androgyny and Hermaphroditism in Graeco-Roman Antiquity*. Translated by Janet Lloyd. Berkeley: University of California Press, 2002 [1997].

Brooten, Bernadette J. "Junia." Page 107 in *Women in Scripture: A Dictionary of Named and Unnamed Women in the Hebrew Bible, The Apocryphal/Deuterocanonical Books, and the New Testament*. Edited by Carol Meyers, with Toni Craven and Ross S. Kraemer. Grand Rapids, MI: Eerdmans, 2000.

Brooten, Bernadette J. "Junia . . . Outstanding Among the Apostles (16:7)." Pages 141–44 in *Women Priests: A Catholic Commentary on the Vatican Declaration*. Edited by Leonard Swidler and Arlene Swidler. New York: Paulist Press, 1977.

Brooten, Bernadette J. "Lesbian Historiography Before the Name?" *GLQ* 4:4 (1998): 557–630.

Brooten, Bernadette J. *Love Between Women: Early Christian Responses to Female Homoeroticism*. Chicago: University of Chicago Press, 1996.

Brooten, Bernadette J. "Response to 'Corinthian Veils and Gnostic Androgynes.'" Pages 291–96 in *Images of the Feminine in Gnosticism*. Edited by Karen L. King. Philadelphia: Fortress, 1988.

Brooten, Bernadette J., with Jacqueline L. Hazelton, eds. *Beyond Slavery: Overcoming Its Religious and Sexual Legacies*. New York: Palgrave, 2010.

Brown, Michael Joseph. *Blackening the Bible: The Aims of African American Biblical Scholarship*. Harrisburg, PA: Trinity, 2004.

Brown, Wendy. *Politics Out of History*. Princeton: Princeton University Press, 2001.

Bruce, F. F. *The Epistles to the Colossians, to Philemon, and to the Ephesians*. Grand Rapids, MI: Eerdmans, 1984.

Bruce, F. F. *Paul: Apostle of the Heart Set Free*. Grand Rapids, MI: Eerdmans, 1977.

Buckmaster, Henrietta. *Paul: A Man Who Changed the World*. New York: McGraw-Hill, 1965.

Buell, Denise Kimber. "Cyborg Memories: An Impure History of Jesus." *BibInt* 18:4–5 (2010): 313–41.

Buell, Denise Kimber. "God's Own People: Specters of Race, Ethnicity, and Gender in Early Christian Studies." Pages 159–90 in *Prejudice and Christian Beginnings: Investigating Race, Gender, and Ethnicity in Early Christian Studies*. Edited by Elisabeth Schüssler Fiorenza and Laura Nasrallah. Minneapolis: Fortress, 2009.

Buell, Denise Kimber. "Hauntology Meets Post-Humanism: Some Payoffs for Biblical Studies." Pages 29–56 in *The Bible and Posthumanism*. Edited by Jennifer L. Koosed. Atlanta: SBL, 2014.

Buell, Denise Kimber. *Why This New Race: Ethnic Reasoning in Early Christianity*. New York: Columbia University Press, 2005.

Buell, Denise Kimber, and Caroline Johnson Hodge. "The Politics of Interpretation: The Rhetoric of Race and Ethnicity in Paul." *JBL* 123:2 (2004): 235–51.

Burke, Peter, ed. *New Perspectives on Historical Writing*. 2nd ed. University Park: Pennsylvania State University Press, 2001.

Burke, Sean D. *Queering the Ethiopian Eunuch: Strategies of Ambiguity in Acts*. Minneapolis: Fortress, 2013.

Butler, Judith. "Against Proper Objects." *differences* 6:2–3 (2004): 1–26.

Butler, Judith. *Antigone's Claim: Kinship Between Life and Death*. New York: Columbia University Press, 2000.

Butler, Judith. *Bodies That Matter: On the Discursive Limits of "Sex"*. New York: Routledge, 1993.

Butler, Judith. *Gender Trouble: Feminism and the Subversion of Identity*. New York: Routledge, 1990.

Butler, Judith. "Imitation and Gender Insubordination." Pages 13–31 in *Inside /Out: Lesbian Theories, Gay Theories*. Edited by Diana Fuss. New York: Routledge, 1991.

Butler, Judith. *Precarious Life: The Power of Mourning and Violence*. London: Verso, 2004.

Butler, Judith. *Undoing Gender*. New York: Routledge, 2004.

Byron, John. *Recent Research on Paul and Slavery*. Sheffield: Sheffield Phoenix, 2008.

Byron, Gay L. *Symbolic Blackness and Ethnic Difference in Early Christian Literature*. London: Routledge, 2002.

Byron, Gay L., and Vanessa Lovelace, eds. *Womanist Interpretations of the Bible: Expanding the Discourse*. Atlanta: SBL, 2016.

Califia, Patrick. "The Limits of the S/M Relationship, or Mr. Benson Doesn't Live Here Anymore." Pages 221–32 in *Leatherfolk: Radical Sex, People, Politics, and Practice*, 3rd ed. Edited by Mark Thompson. Los Angeles: Daedalus, 2004 [1991].

Califia, Patrick. *Public Sex: The Culture of Radical Sex*. Pittsburgh: Cleis, 1994.

Callahan, Allen Dwight. *Embassy of Onesimus: The Letter of Paul to Philemon*. Valley Forge, PA: Trinity, 1997.

Callahan, Allen Dwight. "Paul, *Ekklēsia*, and Emancipation in Corinth: A Coda on Liberation Theology." Pages 216–23 in *Paul and Politics: Ekklesia, Israel, Imperium, Interpretation. Essays in Honor of Krister Stendahl*. Edited by Richard A. Horsley. Harrisburg, PA: Trinity, 2000.

Callahan, Allen Dwight. "Paul's Epistle to Philemon: Toward an Alternative Argumentum." *HTR* 86 (1993): 357–76.

Callahan, Allen Dwight, and Richard A. Horsley. "Slave Resistance in Classical Antiquity." *Semeia* 83–84 (1998): 133–51.

Cannon, Katie G. "Sexing Black Women: Liberation from the Prisonhouse of Anatomical Authority." Pages 11–30 in *Loving the Body: Black Religious Studies and the Erotic*. Edited by Anthony B. Pinn and Dwight N. Hopkins. New York: Palgrave, 2004.

Cantarella, Eva. *Bisexuality in the Ancient World*. 2nd ed. Translated by Cormac Ó Cuilleanáin. New Haven: Yale University Press, 2002 [1988].

Carden, Michael. "Genesis/Bereshit." Pages 21–60 in *The Queer Bible Commentary*. Edited by Deryn Guest, Robert E. Goss, Mona West, and Thomas Bohache. London: SCM, 2006.

Carrette, Jeremy R. "Intense Exchange: Sadomasochism, Theology and the Politics of Late Capitalism." *Theology and Sexuality* 11:2 (2005): 11–30.

Castelli, Elizabeth A. "Allegories of Hagar: Reading Galatians 4.21–31 with Postmodern Feminist Eyes." pages 228–50 in *The New Literary Criticism and the New Testament*. Edited by Edgar V. McKnight and Elizabeth Struthers Malbon. Valley Forge, PA: Trinity, 1994.

Castelli, Elizabeth A. *Imitating Paul: A Discourse of Power*. Louisville: Westminster/John Knox, 1991.

Chase, Cheryl. "'Cultural Practice' or 'Reconstructive Surgery'? U.S. Genital Cutting, the Intersex Movement, and Medical Double Standards." Pages 126–51 in *Genital Cutting and Transnational Sisterhood: Disputing U.S. Polemics*. Edited by Stanlie M. James and Claire C. Robertson. Urbana: University of Illinois Press, 2002.

Chase, Cheryl. "Surgical Progress Is Not the Answer to Intersexuality." Pages 147–59 in *Intersex in the Age of Ethics*. Edited by Alice Domurat Dreger. Hagerstown, MD: University Publishing Group, 1999.

Chase, Cheryl. "What Is the Agenda of the Intersex Patient Advocacy Movement?" *Endocrinologist* 13:3 (May/June 2003): 240–42.

Clay, Elonda. "Confessions of a Ex-Theological Bitch: The Thickness of Black Women's Exploitation Between Jacquelyn Grant's 'Backbone' and Michael Eric Dyson's 'Theological Bitch.'" Pages 93–106 in *Ain't I a Womanist, Too? Third-Wave Womanist Religious Thought*. Edited by Monica A. Coleman. Minneapolis: Fortress, 2013.

Coan, Stephen. "Shunned by the Church." *The Natal Witness*. February 25, 2000.

Cohen, Cathy J. "Punks, Bulldaggers, and Welfare Queens: The Radical Potential of Queer Politics." *GLQ* 3:4 (1997): 437–65.

Cohen, Shaye J. D. *The Beginnings of Jewishness: Boundaries, Varieties, Uncertainties*. Berkeley: University of California Press, 1999.

Cohen, Shaye J. D. *Why Aren't Jewish Women Circumcised? Gender and Covenant in Judaism*. Berkeley: University of California Press, 2005.

Collins, Patricia Hill. *Black Feminist Thought: Knowledge, Consciousness, and the Politics of Empowerment*. Revised Tenth Anniversary Edition. New York: Routledge, 2000.

Collins, Patricia Hill. *Black Sexual Politics: African Americans, Gender, and the New Racism*. New York: Routledge, 2005.

Collins, Raymond F. *1 Corinthians*. Sacra Pagina 7. Collegeville, MN: Liturgical Press, 1999.

Colson, Chuck. "Blurred Biology: How Many Sexes Are There?" *Breakpoint*. October 16, 1996.

Concannon, Cavan W. *"When You Were Gentiles": Specters of Ethnicity in Roman Corinth and Paul's Corinthian Correspondence*. New Haven: Yale University Press, 2014.

Consortium on the Management of Disorders of Sex Development. *Clinical Guidelines for the Management of Disorders of Sex Development in Childhood*. Rohnert Park, CA: Intersex Society of North America, 2006.

Conzelmann, Hans. *1 Corinthians: A Commentary on the First Epistle to the Corinthians*. Hermeneia. Translated by James W. Leitch. Philadelphia: Fortress Press, 1975.

Cooper, Brittney. "How Sarah Got Her Groove Back, or Notes Toward a Black Feminist Theology of Pleasure." *Black Theology* 16:3 (2018): 195–206.

Copeland, M. Shawn. "Body, Representation, and Black Religious Discourse." Pages 98–112 in *Womanist Theological Ethics: A Reader*. Edited by Katie Geneva Cannon, Emilie M. Townes, and Angela D. Sims. Louisville: Westminster John Knox, 2011.

Copeland, M. Shawn. "'Wading Through Many Sorrows': Toward a Theology of Suffering in a Womanist Perspective." Pages 135–54 in *Womanist Theological Ethics: A Reader*. Edited by Katie Geneva Cannon, Emilie M. Townes, and Angela D. Sims. Louisville: Westminster John Knox, 2011.

Cornwall, Susannah. "Asking About What Is Better: Intersex, Disability, and Inaugurated Eschatology." *Journal of Religion, Disability, and Health* 17 (2013): 369–92.

Cornwall, Susannah. "British Intersex Christians' Accounts of Intersex Identity, Christian Identity and Church Experience." *Practical Theology* 6:2 (2013): 220–36.

Cornwall, Susannah. *Controversies in Queer Theology*. London: SCM, 2010.

Cornwall, Susannah. "Introduction: Troubling Bodies?" Pages 1–26 in *Intersex, Theology, and the Bible: Troubling Bodies in Church, Text, and Society*. Edited by Susannah Cornwall. New York: Palgrave, 2015.

Cornwall, Susannah. "'State of Mind' Versus 'Concrete Set of Facts': The Contrasting of Transgender and Intersex in Church Documents on Sexuality." *Theology and Sexuality* 15:1 (2009): 7–28.

Cornwall, Susannah. "Telling Stories About Intersex and Christianity: Saying Too Much or Not Saying Enough?" *Theology* 117:1 (2014): 24–33.

Countryman, L. William. *Dirt, Greed, and Sex: Sexual Ethics in the New Testament and Their Implications for Today*. Philadelphia: Fortress, 1990.

Coventry, Martha. "Finding the Words." Pages 71–76 in *Intersex in the Age of Ethics*. Edited by Alice Domurat Dreger. Hagerstown, MD: University Publishing Group, 1999.

Cromwell, Jason. "Queering the Binaries: Transsituated Identities, Bodies, and Sexualities." Pages 509–20 in *The Transgender Studies Reader*. Edited by Susan Stryker and Stephen Whittle. New York: Routledge, 2006.

Crouch, Robert A. "Betwixt and Between: The Past and Future of Intersexuality." Pages 29–49 in *Intersex in the Age of Ethics*. Edited by Alice Domurat Dreger. Hagerstown, MD: University Publishing Group, 1999.

Cruz, Amada, D. Deitcher, and D. Frankel, eds. *The Film Art of Isaac Julien*. Annandale-on-Hudson, NY: Bard College, Center for Curatorial Studies, 2000.

Cruz, Ariane. *The Color of Kink: Black Women, BDSM, and Pornography*. New York: New York University Press, 2016.

Currah, Paisley, and Susan Stryker, eds. *Postposttranssexual: Key Concepts for a Twenty-First-Century Transgender Studies*. TSQ 1:1–2 (2014).

Cvetkovich, Ann. *An Archive of Feelings: Trauma, Sexuality, and Lesbian Public Cultures*. Durham: Duke University Press, 2003.

Daly, Mary. *Gyn/Ecology: The Metaethics of Radical Feminism*. Boston: Beacon, 1978.

D'Angelo, Mary Rose. "Early Christian Sexual Politics and Roman Imperial Family Values: Rereading Christ and Culture." Pages 23–48 in *The Papers of the Henry Luce III Fellows in Theology*. Volume 6. Edited by Christopher I. Wilkins. Pittsburgh: ATS, 2003.

D'Angelo, Mary Rose. "Tryphaena." Pages 165–66 in *Women in Scripture: A Dictionary of Named and Unnamed Women in the Hebrew Bible, The Apocryphal/Deuterocanonical Books, and the New Testament*. Edited by Carol Meyers, with Toni Craven and Ross S. Kraemer. Grand Rapids, MI: Eerdmans, 2000.

D'Angelo, Mary Rose. "Veils, Virgins, and the Tongues of Men and Angels: Women's Heads in Early Christianity." Pages 131–64 in *Off with Her Head! The Denial of Women's Identity in Myth, Religion, and Culture*. Edited by Howard Eilberg-Schwartz and Wendy Doniger. Berkeley: University of California Press, 1995.

D'Angelo, Mary Rose. "Women Partners in the New Testament." *JFSR* 6 (1990): 65–86.

Dauge, Yves Albert. *Le Barbare: Recherches sur la conception romaine de la barbarie et de la civilization*. Brussels: Latomus, 1981.

Davis, Stacy. "The Invisible Women: Numbers 30 and the Politics of Singleness in Africana Communities." Pages 21–47 in *Womanist Interpretations of the Bible: Expanding the Discourse*. Edited by Gay L. Byron and Vanessa Lovelace. Atlanta: SBL, 2016.

Day, Keri. "'I Am Dark and Lovely': Let the Shulammite Woman Speak." *Black Theology* 16:3 (2018): 207–17.

Dean, Tim. *Beyond Sexuality*. Chicago: University of Chicago Press, 2000.

Dean, Tim. *Unlimited Intimacy: Reflections on the Subculture of Barebacking.* Chicago: University of Chicago Press, 2009.

DeFranza, Megan K. *Sex Difference in Christian Theology: Male, Female, and Intersex in the Image of God.* Grand Rapids, MI: Eerdmans, 2015.

Derrida, Jacques. *Specters of Marx: The State of the Debt, the Work of Mourning, and the New International.* Translated by Peggy Kamuf. London: Routledge, 1994.

DeVos, Craig S. "Once a Slave, Always a Slave? Slavery, Manumission and Relational Patterns in Paul's Letter to Philemon." *JSNT* 82 (2001): 89–105.

Diamond, Milton, and Hazel Glenn Beh. "The Right to Be Wrong: Sex and Gender Decisions." Pages 103–13 in *Ethics and Intersex.* Edited by Sharon E. Sytsma. Dordrecht: Springer, 2006.

Dinshaw, Carolyn. *Getting Medieval: Sexualities and Communities, Pre- and Postmodern.* Durham: Duke University Press, 1999.

Dinshaw, Carolyn. "Got Medieval?" *Journal of the History of Sexuality* 10:2 (2001): 202–12.

Douglas, Kelly Brown. *Sexuality and the Black Church: A Womanist Perspective.* Maryknoll, NY: Orbis, 1999.

Dover, K. J. *Greek Homosexuality.* Cambridge, MA: Harvard University Press, 1989.

Dreger, Alice Domurat. *Hermaphrodites and the Medical Invention of Sex.* Cambridge, MA: Harvard University Press, 1998.

Dreger, Alice Domurat. "A History of Intersex: From the Age of Gonads to the Age of Consent." Pages 5–22 in *Intersex in the Age of Ethics.* Edited by Alice Domurat Dreger. Hagerstown, MD: University Publishing Group, 1999.

Dreger, Alice Domurat, ed. *Intersex in the Age of Ethics.* Hagerstown, MD: University Publishing Group, 1999.

Dreger, Alice Domurat, Ellen Feder, and Anne Tamar-Mattis. "Preventing Homosexuality (and Uppity Women) in the Womb?" *Bioethics Forum.* June 29, 2010.

Dreger, Alice Domurat, and April M. Herndon. "Progress and Politics in the Intersex Rights Movement: Feminist Theory in Action." *GLQ* 15:2 (2009): 199–224.

DuBois, Page. *Slaves and Other Objects.* Chicago: University of Chicago Press, 2003.

Duggan, Lisa. "The New Homonormativity: The Sexual Politics of Neoliberalism." Pages 175–94 in *Materializing Democracy: Toward a Revitalized Cultural Politics.* Edited by Russ Castronovo and Dana D. Nelson. Durham: Duke University Press, 2002.

Dunn, James D. G. *A Commentary on the Epistle to the Galatians.* BNTC. London: A & C Black, 1993.

Dunn, James D. G. *The New Perspective on Paul.* Rev. ed. Grand Rapids, MI: Eerdmans, 2008 [2005].

Dunning, Benjamin H. *Christ Without Adam: Subjectivity and Sexual Difference in the Philosophers' Paul.* New York: Columbia University Press, 2014.

Dunning, Benjamin H. *Specters of Paul: Sexual Difference in Early Christian Thought.* Philadelphia: University of Pennsylvania Press, 2011.

Eastman, Susan. *Recovering Paul's Mother Tongue: Language and Theology in Galatians.* Grand Rapids, MI: Eerdmans, 2007.

Edelman, Lee. *No Future: Queer Theory and the Death Drive.* Durham: Duke University Press, 2004.

Edgerton, Milton T. "Discussion: Clitoroplasty for Clitoromegaly due to Adrenogenital Syndrome Without Loss of Sensitivity (by Nobuyuki Sagehashi)." *Plastic and Reconstructive Surgery* 91 (1993): 956.

Edwards, Catherine. "Incorporating the Alien: The Art of Conquest." Pages 44–70 in *Rome the Cosmopolis*. Edited by Catherine Edwards and Greg Woolf. Cambridge: Cambridge University Press, 2003.

Edwards, Catherine. *The Politics of Immorality in Ancient Rome*. Cambridge: Cambridge University Press, 1993.

Edwards, Catherine, and Greg Woolf. "Cosmopolis: Rome as World City." Pages 1–20 in *Rome the Cosmopolis*. Edited by Catherine Edwards and Greg Woolf. Cambridge: Cambridge University Press, 2003.

Eilberg-Schwartz, Howard. *The Savage in Judaism: An Anthropology of Israelite Religion and Ancient Judaism*. Bloomington: Indiana University Press, 1990.

Eisenbaum, Pamela. *Paul Was Not a Christian: The Original Message of a Misunderstood Apostle*. New York: HarperOne, 2009.

Elliott, John H. "No Kingdom of God for Softies? or, What Was Paul Really Saying? 1 Corinthians 6:9–10 in Context." *BTB* 34 (2004): 17–40.

Elliott, Neil. *The Arrogance of Nations: Reading Romans in the Shadow of the Empire*. Minneapolis: Fortress, 2008.

Elliott, Susan. *Cutting Too Close for Comfort: Paul's Letter to the Galatians in Its Anatolian Cultic Context*. London: T&T Clark, 2003.

Eng, David L. *Racial Castration: Managing Masculinity in Asian America*. Durham: Duke University Press, 2001.

Enke, A. Finn, ed. *Transfeminist Perspectives in and Beyond Transgender and Gender Studies*. Philadelphia: Temple University Press, 2012.

Epp, Eldon Jay. *Junia: The First Woman Apostle*. Minneapolis: Fortress, 2005.

Fabian, Johannes. *Time and the Other*. New York: Columbia University Press, 2002.

Fausto-Sterling, Anne. *Sexing the Body: Gender Politics and the Construction of Sexuality*. New York: Basic, 2000.

Feder, Ellen K. *Family Bonds: Genealogies of Race and Gender*. New York: Oxford University Press, 2007.

Feder, Ellen K. "Imperatives of Normality: From 'Intersex' to 'Disorders of Sex Development.'" *GLQ* 15:2 (2009): 225–47.

Feinberg, Leslie. "Transgender Liberation: A Movement Whose Time Has Come." Pages 205–20 in *The Transgender Studies Reader*. Edited by Susan Stryker and Stephen Whittle. New York: Routledge, 2006.

Ferguson, Roderick A. *Aberrations in Black: Toward a Queer of Color Critique*. Minneapolis: University of Minnesota Press, 2003.

Ferris, Iain M. *Enemies of Rome: Barbarians Through Roman Eyes*. Somerset: Sutton, 2000.

Finley, Moses I. *Ancient Slavery and Modern Ideology*. New York: Viking Press, 1980.

Fitzgerald, John T. "Paul and Friendship." Pages 319–43 in *Paul in the Greco-Roman World: A Handbook*. Edited by J. Paul Sampley. Harrisburg, PA: Trinity, 2003.

Fitzmyer, Joseph A. *First Corinthians: A New Translation with Introduction and Commentary*. Anchor Yale Bible. New Haven: Yale University Press, 2008.

Foucault, Michel. *Discipline and Punish: The Birth of the Prison*. Translated by Alan Sheridan. New York: Vintage, 1979.

Foucault, Michel. *The History of Sexuality, Volume 1: An Introduction*. Translated by Robert Hurley. New York: Vintage Books, 1990.

Foucault, Michel. *The History of Sexuality, Volume 2: The Use of Pleasure*. Translated by Robert Hurley. New York: Random House, 1990.

Foucault, Michel. *The History of Sexuality, Volume 3: The Care of the Self*. Translated by Robert Hurley. New York: Random House, 1988.

Foucault, Michel. "Sex, Power, and the Politics of Identity." Pages 382–90 in *Foucault Live: Interviews, 1961–84*. Translated by Lysa Hochroth and John Johnston. Edited by Sylvere Lotringer. New York: Semiotext(e): 1996.

Foucault, Michel. *"Society Must Be Defended": Lectures at the Collège de France, 1975–1976*. Edited by Mauro Bertani and Alessandro Fontana. Translated by David Macey. New York: Picador, 1997.

Fox, Arminta. "Decentering Paul, Contextualizing Crimes: Reading in Light of the Imprisoned." *JFSR* 33:2 (2017): 37–54.

Fradenburg, Louise, and Carla Freccero. "Introduction: Caxton, Foucault, and the Pleasures of History." Pages xiii–xxiv in *Premodern Sexualities*. Edited by Louise Fradenburg and Carla Freccero. New York: Routledge, 1996.

Fradenburg, Louise, and Carla Freccero. "Preface." Pages vii–xii in *Premodern Sexualities*. Edited by Louise Fradenburg and Carla Freccero. New York: Routledge, 1996.

Freccero, Carla. *Queer/Early/Modern*. Durham: Duke University Press, 2006.

Frederickson, David E. "Natural and Unnatural Use in Romans 1:24–27: Paul and the Philosophic Critique of Eros." Pages 197–222 in *Homosexuality, Science, and the "Plain Sense" of Scripture*. Edited by David L. Balch. Grand Rapids, MI: Eerdmans, 2000.

Fredriksen, Paula. "How Later Contexts Affect Pauline Content, or: Retrospect Is the Mother of Anachronism." Pages 17–51 in *Jews and Christians in the First and Second Centuries: How to Write Their History*. Edited by Peter J. Tomson and Joshua Schwartz. Leiden, Brill: 2014.

Fredriksen, Paula. "Mandatory Retirement: Ideas in the Study of Christian Origins Whose Time Has Come to Go." *SR* 35 (2006): 231–46.

Freeman, Elizabeth. "Packing History, Count(er)ing Generations." *New Literary History* 31 (2000): 727–44.

Freeman, Elizabeth. "Still After." *South Atlantic Quarterly* 106:3 (2007): 495–500.

Freeman, Elizabeth. "Time Binds, or, Erotohistoriography." *Social Text* 23:3–4 (2005): 57–68.

Freeman, Elizabeth. *Time Binds: Queer Temporalities, Queer Histories*. Durham: Duke University Press, 2010.

Freeman, Elizabeth. "Turn the Beat Around: Sadomasochism, Temporality, History." *differences* 19:1 (2008): 32–70.

Freud, Sigmund. *The Standard Edition of the Complete Psychological Works of Sigmund Freud*. Translated by James Strachey. London: Hogart, 1953–1974.

Friesen, Steven J. "Poverty in Pauline Studies: Beyond the So-Called New Consensus." *JSNT* 26:3 (2004): 323–61.

Frilingos, Chris. "'For My Child, Onesimus': Paul and Domestic Power in Philemon." *JBL* 119:1 (2000): 91–104.

Gardner, Jane F. *Women in Roman Law and Society*. Bloomington: Indiana University Press, 1986.

Garnsey, Peter. "Sons, Slaves—and Christians." Pages 101–21 in *The Roman Family in Italy: Status, Sentiment, and Space*. Edited by Beryl Rawson and Paul Weaver. Oxford: Clarendon, 1997.

Garnsey, Peter, and Robert Saller. *The Roman Empire: Economy, Society, and Culture*. Berkeley: University of California Press, 1987.

Gaventa, Beverly Roberts. *Our Mother Saint Paul.* Louisville: Westminster John Knox, 2007.

Gaventa, Beverly Roberts. *When in Romans: An Invitation to Linger with the Gospel According to Paul.* Grand Rapids, MI: Baker Academic, 2016.

Glancy, Jennifer A. "Boasting of Beatings (2 Corinthians 11:23–25)." *JBL* 123 (2004): 99–135.

Glancy, Jennifer A. *Slavery in Early Christianity.* Minneapolis: Fortress, 2006.

Glancy, Jennifer A. "The Utility of an Apostle: On Philemon 11." *JECH* 5:1 (2015): 72–86.

Gleason, Maud. *Making Men: Sophists and Self-Presentation in Ancient Rome.* Princeton: Princeton University Press, 1995.

Gleason, Maud W. "The Semiotics of Gender: Physiognomy and Self-Fashioning in the Second Century C.E." Pages 389–415 in *Before Sexuality: The Construction of Erotic Experience in the Ancient Greek World.* Edited by David M. Halperin, John J. Winkler, and Froma I. Zeitlin. Princeton: Princeton University Press, 1990.

Goldberg, Jonathan. "After Thoughts." *South Atlantic Quarterly* 106:3 (2007): 501–10.

Goldberg, Jonathan, and Madhavi Menon. "Queering History." *PMLA* 120.5 (2005): 1608–17.

Golden, Mark. "*Pais,* 'Child' and 'Slave.'" *L'Antiquite Classique* 54 (1985): 91–104.

Gordon, Avery F. *Ghostly Matters: Haunting and the Sociological Imagination.* Minneapolis: University of Minnesota Press, 2008.

Gordon, Pamela. "The Lover's Voice in *Heroides* 15: Or, Why Is Sappho a Man?" Pages 274–91 in *Roman Sexualities.* Edited by Judith P. Hallett and Marilyn B. Skinner. Princeton, Princeton University Press, 1998.

Graybill, Rhiannon. "Fuzzy, Messy, Icky: The Edges of Consent in Hebrew Bible Rape Narratives and Rape Culture." *Bible and Critical Theory* 15:2 (2019): 1–27.

Green, Jamison. "Look! No, Don't!: The Visibility Dilemma for Transsexual Men." Pages 499–508 in *The Transgender Studies Reader.* Edited by Susan Stryker and Stephen Whittle. New York: Routledge, 2006.

Greenburg, Julie A. "International Legal Developments Protecting the Autonomy Rights of Sexual Minorities: Who Should Determine the Appropriate Treatment for an Intersex Infant?" Pages 87–101 in *Ethics and Intersex.* Edited by Sharon E. Sytsma. Dordrecht: Springer, 2006.

Gross, Sally. "Intersexuality and Scripture." *Theology and Sexuality* 11 (1999): 65–74.

Groveman, Sherri A. "The Hanukkah Bush: Ethical Implications in the Clinical Management of Intersex." Pages 23–28 in *Intersex in the Age of Ethics.* Edited by Alice Domurat Dreger. Hagerstown, MD: University Publishing Group, 1999.

Grumbach, M. M., and F. A. Conte. "Disorders of Sex Differentiation." Pages 1303–1435 in *Williams Textbook of Endocrinology.* 9th ed. Edited by J. D. Wilson et al. Philadelphia: Saunders, 1998.

Guest, Deryn. 2016. "Modeling the Transgender Gaze: Performances of Masculinities in 2 Kings 9–10." Pages 45–80 in *Transgender, Intersex, and Biblical Interpretation.* Teresa J. Hornsby and Deryn Guest. Atlanta: SBL, 2016.

Gundry-Volf, Judith M. "Christ and Gender: A Study of Difference and Equality in Gal 3, 28." Pages 439–77 in *Jesus Christus als die Mitte der Schrift: Studien zur Hermeneutik des Evangeliums.* Edited by Christof Landmesser, Hans-Joachim Eckstein, and Hermann Licthenberger. Berlin: Walter de Gruyter, 1997.

Guyot, Peter. *Eunuchen als Sklaven und Freigelassene in der griechisch-römischen Antike.* Stuttgart Klett-Cotta, 1980.

Halberstam, J. Jack. *Gaga Feminism: Sex, Gender, and the End of Normal.* Boston: Beacon, 2012.

Halberstam, Judith. "F2M: The Making of Female Masculinity." Pages 210–28 in *The Lesbian Postmodern.* Edited by Laura Doan. New York: Columbia University Press, 1994.

Halberstam, Judith. *Female Masculinity.* Durham: Duke University Press, 1998.

Halberstam, Judith. "The Good, the Bad, and the Ugly: Men, Women, and Masculinity." Pages 343–67 in *Masculinity Studies and Feminist Theory: New Directions.* Edited by Judith Kegan Gardiner. New York: Columbia, 2002.

Halberstam, Judith. *In a Queer Time and Place: Transgender Bodies, Subcultural Lives.* New York: New York University Press, 2005.

Halberstam, Judith. *Queer Art of Failure.* Durham: Duke University Press, 2011.

Halberstam, Judith. "Transgender Butch: Butch/FTM Border Wars and the Masculine Continuum." *GLQ* 4:2 (1998): 287–310.

Hales, Shelley. "Looking for Eunuchs: The *Galli* and Attis in Roman Art." Pages 87–103 in *Eunuchs in Antiquity and Beyond.* Edited by Shaun Tougher. London: Duckworth, 2002.

Haley, Shelly P. "Lucian's 'Leaena and Clonarium': Voyeurism or a Challenge to Assumptions." Pages 286–303 in *Among Women: From the Homosocial to the Homoerotic in the Ancient World.* Edited by Nancy Sorkin Rabinowitz and Lisa Auanger. Austin: University of Texas Press, 2002.

Hall, Edith. *Inventing the Barbarian: Greek Self-Definition Through Tragedy.* Oxford: Clarendon, 1989.

Hall, Jonathan M. *Ethnic Identity in Greek Antiquity.* Cambridge: Cambridge University Press, 1997.

Hallett, Judith P. "Female Homoeroticism and the Denial of Roman Reality in Latin Literature." *Yale Journal of Criticism* 3 (1989): 209–27.

Hallett, Judith P. "Women as *Same* and *Other* in Classical Roman Elite." *Helios* 16:1 (1989): 59–78.

Hallett, Judith P., and Marilyn B. Skinner, eds. *Roman Sexualities.* Princeton: Princeton University Press, 1997.

Halperin, David M. *How to Do the History of Homosexuality.* Chicago: University of Chicago Press, 2002.

Halperin, David M. *One Hundred Years of Homosexuality: And Other Essays on Greek Love.* New York: Routledge, 1990.

Halperin, David M. *Saint Foucault: Towards a Gay Hagiography.* New York: Oxford University Press, 1995.

Hanks, Thomas. "Romans." Pages 582–605 in *The Queer Bible Commentary.* Edited by Deryn Guest, Robert E. Goss, Mona West, and Thomas Bohache. London: SCM, 2006.

Haraway, Donna J. "The Promises of Monsters: A Regenerative Politics for Inappropriate/d Others." Pages 295–337 in *Cultural Studies.* Edited by Lawrence Grossberg, Cary Nelson, and Paula A. Treichler. New York: Routledge, 1992.

Hare, John. "'Neither Male Nor Female': The Case of Intersexuality." Pages 98–111 in *An Acceptable Sacrifice? Homosexuality and the Church.* Edited by Duncan Dormor and Jeremy Morris. London: SPCK, 2007.

Harrill, J. Albert. *Slaves in the New Testament: Literary, Social, and Moral Dimensions.* Minneapolis: Fortress, 2006.

Harrington, Lee, and Mollena Williams. *Playing Well with Others: Your Field Guide to Discovering, Exploring and Navigating the Kink, Leather and BDSM Communities.* Gardena, CA: Greenery, 2012.

Hart, Lynda. *Between the Body and the Flesh: Performing Sadomasochism*. New York: Columbia University Press, 1998.

Hartman, Saidiya V. *Scenes of Subjection: Terror, Slavery, and Self-Making in Nineteenth-Century America*. New York: Oxford University Press, 1997.

Hegarty, Peter, and Cheryl Chase. "Intersex Activism, Feminism and Psychology: Opening a Dialogue on Theory, Research and Clinical Practice." *Feminism and Psychology* 10:1 (2000): 117–32.

Hendricks, Melissa. "Is It a Boy or a Girl?" *Johns Hopkins Magazine* (November 1993): 10–16.

Heschel, Susannah. *The Aryan Jesus: Christian Theologians and the Bible in Nazi Germany*. Princeton: Princeton University Press, 2008.

Hester, J. David. "Eunuchs and the Postgender Jesus: Matthew 19.12 and Transgressive Sexualities." *JSNT* 28:1 (2005): 13–40.

Hester, J. David. "Intersex and the Rhetorics of Healing." Pages 47–71 in *Ethics and Intersex*. Edited by Sharon E. Sytsma. Dordrecht: Springer, 2006.

Hester, J. David. "Intersex(es) and Informed Consent: How Physicians' Rhetoric Constrains Choice." *Theoretical Medicine and Bioethics* 25:1 (2004): 21–49.

Hezser, Catherine. *Jewish Slavery in Antiquity*. Oxford: Oxford University Press, 2005.

Hidalgo, Jacqueline M. "'Our Book of Revelation . . . Prescribes our Fate and Releases Us from It': Scriptural Disorientations in Cherríe Moraga's *The Last Generation*." Pages 113–32 in *Sexual Disorientations: Queer Temporalities, Affects, Theologies*. Edited by Kent L. Brintnall, Joseph A. Marchal, and Stephen D. Moore. New York: Fordham University Press, 2018.

Hidalgo, Jacqueline M. *Revelation in Aztlán: Scriptures, Utopias, and the Chicano Movement*. New York: Palgrave, 2016.

Hillman, Thea. *Intersex (For Lack of a Better Word)*. San Francisco: Manic D, 2008.

Hines, Sally. "Feminism." *TSQ* 1:1–2 (2014): 84–86.

Hoffman, Lawrence A. *Covenant of Blood: Circumcision and Gender in Rabbinic Judaism*. Chicago: University of Chicago Press, 1996.

Hoke, James N. "Unbinding Imperial Time: Chrononormativity and Paul's Letter to the Romans." Pages 68–89 in *Sexual Disorientations: Queer Temporalities, Affects, Theologies*. Edited by Kent L. Brintnall, Joseph A. Marchal, and Stephen D. Moore. New York: Fordham University Press, 2018.

Holland, Sharon Patricia. *The Erotic Life of Racism*. Durham: Duke University Press, 2012.

Holmes, Morgan. "Queer Cut Bodies." Pages 84–100 in *Queer Frontiers: Millennial Geographies, Genders, and Generations*. Edited by Joseph A. Boone et al. Madison: University of Wisconsin Press, 2000.

Holmes, Morgan. "Rethinking the Meaning and Management of Intersexuality." *Sexualities* 5:2 (2002): 159–80.

Hopkins, Keith. *Conquerors and Slaves*. Cambridge: Cambridge University Press, 1978.

Hopkins, Patrick D. "Rethinking Sadomasochism: Feminism, Interpretation, and Simulation." *Hypatia* 9:1 (1994): 116–41.

Hornsby, Teresa J. "The Annoying Woman: Biblical Scholarship After Judith Butler." Pages 71–92 in *Bodily Citations: Religion and Judith Butler*. Edited by Ellen T. Armour and Susan M. St. Ville. New York: Columbia University Press, 2006.

Horrell, David G., and Edward Adams. "Introduction: The Scholarly Quest for Paul's Church at Corinth: A Critical Survey." Pages 1–43 in *Christianity at Corinth: The Quest for the Pauline Church.* Edited by Edward Adams and David G. Horrell. Louisville: Westminster John Knox, 2004.

Horsley, Richard A. *1 Corinthians.* ANTC. Nashville: Abingdon, 1998.

Horsley, Richard A. "Paul and Slavery: A Critical Alternative to Recent Readings." *Semeia* 83/84 (1998): 153–200.

Horsley, Richard A. "The Slave Systems of Classical Antiquity and Their Reluctant Recognition by Modern Scholars." *Semeia* 83/84 (1998): 19–66.

Huber, Lynn R. "Gazing at the Whore: Reading Revelation Queerly." Pages 301–20 in *Bible Trouble: Queer Reading at the Boundaries of Biblical Scholarship.* Edited by Teresa J. Hornsby and Ken Stone. Atlanta: SBL, 2011.

Hull, Gloria T., Patricia Bell Scott, and Barbara Smith, eds. *All the Women Are White, All the Blacks Are Men, But Some of Us Are Brave: Black Women's Studies.* Old Westbury, NY: Feminist Press, 1982.

Ingleheart, Jennifer. "Introduction: Romosexuality: Rome, Homosexuality, and Reception." Pages 1–35 in *Ancient Rome and the Construction of Modern Homosexual Identities.* Edited by Jennifer Ingleheart. Oxford: Oxford University Press, 2015.

Intersex Society of North America. *Hermaphrodites with Attitude* 1:1 (1994).

Ipsen, Avaren. *Sex Working and the Bible.* London: Equinox, 2008.

Isaac, Benjamin. *The Invention of Racism in Classical Antiquity.* Princeton: Princeton University Press, 2004.

Ivarsson Fredrik. "Vice Lists and Deviant Masculinity: The Rhetorical Function of 1 Corinthians 5:10–11 and 6:9–10." Pages 163–84 in *Mapping Gender in Ancient Religious Discourses.* Edited by Todd Penner and Caroline Vander Stichele. Leiden: Brill, 2007.

Jacobs, Harriet A. *Incidents in the Life of a Slave Girl, Written by Herself.* Edited by Jean Fagan Yellin. Cambridge: Harvard University Press, 1987 [1861].

Jakobsen, Janet R., and Ann Pellegrini. *Love the Sin: Sexual Regulation and the Limits of Religious Tolerance.* New York: New York University Press, 2003.

Jennings, Theodore W., Jr. *Outlaw Justice: The Messianic Politics of Paul.* Stanford: Stanford University Press, 2013.

Jervell, Jacob. *Imago Dei: Gen 1, 26f im Spätjudentum, in der Gnosis und in den paulinischen Briefen.* Göttingen: Vandenhoeck & Ruprecht, 1960.

Jervis, L. Ann. *Galatians.* NIBCNT. Peabody, MA: Hendrickson, 1999.

Jewett, Robert. *Paul's Anthropological Terms: A Study of Their Use in Conflict Settings.* Leiden: Brill, 1971.

Jewett, Robert. *Romans: A Commentary.* Hermeneia. Minneapolis: Fortress, 2007.

Johnson, E. Patrick, and Mae G. Henderson, eds. *Black Queer Studies: A Critical Anthology.* Durham: Duke University Press, 2005.

Johnson, Matthew V. "Onesimus Speaks: Diagnosing the Hys/Terror of the Text." Pages 91–100 in *Onesimus Our Brother: Reading Religion, Race, and Culture in Philemon.* Edited by Matthew V. Johnson, James A. Noel, and Demetrius K. Williams. Minneapolis: Fortress, 2012.

Johnson, Matthew V., James A. Noel, and Demetrius K. Williams, eds. *Onesimus Our Brother: Reading Religion, Race, and Culture in Philemon.* Minneapolis: Fortress, 2012.

Johnson Hodge, Caroline. *If Sons, Then Heirs: A Study of Kinship and Ethnicity in the Letters of Paul.* New York: Oxford University Press, 2007.

Johnson Hodge, Caroline. "Married to an Unbeliever: Households, Hierarchies, and Holiness in 1 Corinthians 7:12–16." *HTR* 103:1 (2010): 1–25.

Johnson-DeBaufre, Melanie, and Laura S. Nasrallah. "Beyond the Heroic Paul: Toward a Feminist and Decolonizing Approach to the Letters of Paul." Pages 161–74 in *The Colonized Apostle: Paul Through Postcolonial Eyes*. Edited by Christopher D. Stanley. Minneapolis: Fortress, 2011.

Jones, Melanie C. "The Will to Adorn: Beyond Self-Surveillance, Toward a Womanist Ethic of Redemptive Self-Love." *Black Theology* 16:3 (2018): 218–30.

Joshel, Sandra R., and Sheila Murnaghan, eds. *Women and Slaves in Greco-Roman Culture: Differential Equations*. London: Routledge, 1998.

Julien, Isaac. "Confessions of a Snow Queen: Notes on the Making of *The Attendant*." Pages 79–83 in *The Film Art of Isaac Julien*. Edited by Amada Cruz, D. Deitcher, and D. Frankel. Annandale-on-Hudson, NY: Bard College, Center for Curatorial Studies, 2000.

Jung, Patricia B. "Christianity and Human Sexual Polymorphism: Are They Incompatible?" Pages 293–309 in *Ethics and Intersex*. Edited by Sharon E. Sytsma. Dordrecht: Springer, 2006.

Kahl, Brigitte. "Der Brief an die Gemeinden in Galatien: Vom Unbehagen der Geschlechter und anderen Problemen des Andersseins." Pages 603–11 in *Kompendium feministischer Bibelauslegung*. Edited by Luise Schottroff and Marie-Theres Wacker. Gütersloh: Chr. Kaiser Gütersloher Verlagshaus, 1998.

Kahl, Brigitte. *Galatians Re-Imagined: Reading with the Eyes of the Vanquished*. Minneapolis: Fortress, 2010.

Kahl, Brigitte. "Gender Trouble in Galatia? Paul and the Rethinking of Difference." Pages 57–73 in *Is There A Future for Feminist Theology?* Edited by Deborah F. Sawyer and Diane M. Collier. Sheffield: Sheffield Academic, 1999.

Kahl, Brigitte. "No Longer Male: Masculinity Struggles Behind Galatians 3:28?" *JSNT* 79 (2000): 37–49.

Karkazis, Katrina. *Fixing Sex: Intersex, Medical Authority, and Lived Experience*. Durham: Duke University Press, 2008.

Kelley, Shawn. *Racializing Jesus: Race, Ideology, and the Formation of Modern Biblical Scholarship*. London: Routledge, 2002.

Kennedy. Rebecca F., C. Sydnor Roy, and Max L. Goldman, eds. *Race and Ethnicity in the Classical World: An Anthology of Primary Sources in Translation*. Indianapolis: Hackett, 2013.

Kerry, Stephen. "Intersex Individuals' Religiosity and Their Journey to Wellbeing." *Journal of Gender Studies* 18:3 (2009): 277–85.

Kessler, Suzanne J. *Lessons from the Intersexed*. New Brunswick, NJ: Rutgers University Press, 1998.

King, Helen. *The One-Sex Body on Trial: The Classical and Early Modern Evidence*. Burlington, VT: Ashgate, 2013.

King, Karen L. *What Is Gnosticism?* Cambridge, MA: Harvard University Press, 2003.

Kipnis, Kenneth, and Milton Diamond. "Pediatric Ethics and the Surgical Assignment of Sex." Pages 173–93 in *Intersex in the Age of Ethics*. Edited by Alice Domurat Dreger. Hagerstown, MD: University Publishing Group, 1999.

Kittredge, Cynthia Briggs. *Community and Authority: The Rhetoric of Obedience in the Pauline Tradition*. Harrisburg, PA: Trinity, 1998.

Kittredge, Cynthia Briggs. "Feminist Approaches: Rethinking History and Resisting Ideologies." Pages 117–33 in *Studying Paul's Letters: Contemporary Perspectives and Methods*. Edited by Joseph A. Marchal. Minneapolis: Fortress, 2012.

Kittredge, Cynthia Briggs. "Rethinking Authorship in the Letters of Paul." Pages 318–33 in *Walk in the Ways of Wisdom: Essay in Honor of Elisabeth Schüssler Fiorenza*. Edited by Shelly Matthews, Cynthia Briggs Kittredge, and Melanie Johnson-DeBaufre. New York: Continuum, 2003.

Klees, Hans. *Sklavenleben im klassischen Griechenland*. Stuttgart: Franz Steiner, 1998.

Knox, John. *Philemon Among the Letters of Paul: A New View of Its Place and Importance*. Rev. ed. New York: Abingdon, 1959 [1935].

Knust, Jennifer Wright. *Abandoned to Lust: Sexual Slander and Ancient Christianity*. New York: Columbia University Press, 2005.

Kotrosits, Maia. *Rethinking Early Christian Identity: Affect, Violence, and Belonging*. Minneapolis: Fortress, 2015.

Koyama, Emi, and Lisa Weasel. "From Social Construction to Social Justice: Transforming How We Teach About Intersexuality." *Women's Studies Quarterly* 30:3–4 (2002): 169–78.

Kraemer, Ross Shepard, and Mary Rose D'Angelo, eds. *Women and Christian Origins*. Oxford: Oxford University Press, 1999.

Kuefler, Mathew. *The Manly Eunuch: Masculinity, Gender Ambiguity, and Christian Ideology in Late Antiquity*. Chicago: University of Chicago Press, 2001.

Kwok Pui-lan. "A Postcolonial Reading: Sexual Morality and National Politics: Reading Biblical 'Loose Women.'" Pages 21–46 in *Engaging the Bible: Critical Readings from Contemporary Women*. Edited by Choi Hee An and Katheryn Pfisterer Darr. Minneapolis: Fortress, 2006.

Lampe, Peter. *From Paul to Valentinus: Christians at Rome in the First Two Centuries*. Translated by Michael Steinhauser. Edited by Marshall D. Johnson. Minneapolis: Fortress, 2003.

Laqueur, Thomas. *Making Sex: Body and Gender from the Greeks to Freud*. Cambridge, MA: Harvard University Press, 1990.

Latour, Bruno. *We Have Never Been Modern*. Translated by Catherine Porter. Cambridge, MA: Harvard University Press, 1993.

Lebacqz, Karen. "Difference or Defect? Intersexuality and the Politics of Difference." *Annual of the Society of Christian Ethics* 17 (1997): 213–29.

Lee, Peter A., et al. "Consensus Statement on Management of Intersex Disorders." *Pediatrics* 118 (2006): 814–15.

Lewis, Lloyd A. "An African American Appraisal of the Philemon-Paul-Onesimus Triangle." Pages 232–46 in *Stony the Road We Trod: African American Biblical Interpretation*. Edited by Cain Hope Felder. Minneapolis: Fortress, 1991.

Lieu, Judith M. "Circumcision, Women, and Salvation." *NTS* 40 (1994): 358–70.

Liew, Tat-Siong Benny. *What Is Asian American Biblical Hermeneutics? Reading the New Testament*. Honolulu: University of Hawai'i Press, 2008.

Lightfoot, J. L. "Sacred Eunuchism in the Cult of the Syrian Goddess." Pages 71–86 in *Eunuchs in Antiquity and Beyond*. Edited by Shaun Tougher. London: Duckworth and The Classical Press of Wales, 2002.

Linder, Amnon. *The Jews in Roman Imperial Legislation*. Detroit: Wayne State University Press, 1987.

Lochrie, Karma. *Heterosyncrasies: Female Sexuality When Normal Wasn't*. Minneapolis: University of Minnesota Press, 2005.

Lomax, Tamura. "Black Bodies in Ecstasy: Black Women, the Black Church, and the Politics of Pleasure: An Introduction." *Black Theology* 16:3 (2018): 189–94.

Lomax, Tamura. "Theorizing the Distance Between Erotophobia, Hyper-moralism, and Eroticism: Toward a Black Feminist Theology of Pleasure." *Black Theology* 16:3 (2018): 263–79.

Longenecker, Richard N. *Apostle of Liberty*. New York: Harper & Row, 1964.

Looy, Heather. "Male and Female God Created Them: The Challenge of Intersexuality." *Journal of Psychology and Christianity* 21:1 (2002): 10–20.

Lopez, Davina C. *Apostle to the Conquered: Reimagining Paul's Mission*. Minneapolis: Fortress, 2008.

Lorde, Audre. *Sister Outsider: Essays and Speeches*. Berkeley, CA: Crossing Press, 1984.

Love, Heather. *Feeling Backward: Loss and the Politics of Queer History*. Cambridge, MA: Harvard University Press, 2007.

Love, Heather. "Queer." *TSQ* 1:1–2 (2014): 172–76.

Love, Heather. "'Spoiled Identity': Stephen Gordon's Loneliness and the Difficulties of Queer History." *GLQ* 7:4 (2001): 487–519.

Lovelace, Vanessa. "'We Don't Give Birth to Thugs': Family Values, Respectability Politics, and Jephthah's Mother." Pages 239–61 in *Womanist Interpretations of the Bible: Expanding the Discourse*. Edited by Gay L. Byron and Vanessa Lovelace. Atlanta: SBL, 2016.

Lund, Allan A. *Zum Germanenbild der Römer: Eine Einführung in die antike Ethnographie*. Heidelberg: C. Winter, 1990.

Luther, Martin. *A Commentary on Saint's Paul's Epistle to the Galatians*. Grand Rapids, MI: Baker Book House, 1979.

MacBain, Bruce.*Prodigy and Expiation: A Study in Religion and Politics in Republican Rome*. Brussels: Latomus, 1982.

MacDonald, Dennis Ronald. "Corinthian Veils and Gnostic Androgynes." Pages 276–92 in *Images of the Feminine in Gnosticism*. Edited by Karen L. King. Philadelphia: Fortress, 1988.

MacDonald, Dennis Ronald. *There Is No Male and Female: The Fate of a Dominical Saying in Paul and Gnosticism*. Philadelphia: Fortress, 1981.

MacDonald, Margaret Y. *Early Christian Women and Pagan Opinion: The Power of the Hysterical Woman*. Cambridge: Cambridge University Press, 1996.

MacDonald, Margaret Y. "Reading Real Women Through the Undisputed Letters of Paul." Pages 199–220 in *Women and Christian Origins*. Edited by Ross Shepard Kraemer and Mary Rose D'Angelo. New York: Oxford University, 1999.

MacGregor, Kirk R. "Is 1 Corinthians 11:2–16 A Prohibition of Homosexuality?" *Bibliotheca Sacra* 166/662 (2009): 201–16.

MacKendrick, Karmen. *Counterpleasures*. Albany: State University of New York Press, 1989.

Marchal, Joseph A. "The Corinthian Women Prophets and Trans Activism: Rethinking Canonical Gender Claims." Pages 223–46 in *Bible Trouble: Queer Reading at the Boundaries of Biblical Scholarship*. Edited by Teresa J. Hornsby and Ken Stone. Atlanta: SBL, 2011.

Marchal, Joseph A. *Hierarchy, Unity, and Imitation: A Feminist Rhetorical Analysis of Power Dynamics in Paul's Letter to the Philippians*. Atlanta: SBL, 2006.

Marchal, Joseph A. "Homosexual/Queer." Pages 336–44 in *The Oxford Encyclopedia of the Bible and Gender Studies*. Edited by Julia M. O'Brien. Oxford: Oxford University Press, 2014.

Marchal, Joseph A. "How Soon Is (This Apocalypse) Now? Queer Velocities After a Corinthian Already and a Pauline Not Yet." Pages 45–67 in *Sexual Disorientations: Queer Temporalities, Affects, Theologies*. Edited by Kent L. Brintnall, Joseph A. Marchal, and Stephen D. Moore. New York: Fordham University Press, 2018.

Marchal, Joseph A. *The Politics of Heaven: Women, Gender, and Empire in the Study of Paul*. Minneapolis: Fortress, 2008.

Marchal, Joseph A. "Queer Approaches: Improper Relations with Pauline Letters." Pages 209–27 in *Studying Paul's Letters: Contemporary Perspectives and Methods*. Edited by Joseph A. Marchal. Minneapolis, Fortress, 2012.

Marchal, Joseph A. "Queer Studies and Critical Masculinity Studies in Feminist Biblical Studies." Pages 304–27 in *Feminist Biblical Studies in the Twentieth Century: Scholarship and Movement*. Edited by Elisabeth Schüssler Fiorenza. Atlanta: SBL, 2014.

Marchal, Joseph A. "Responsibilities to the Publics of Biblical Studies and Critical Rhetorical Engagements for a Safer World." Pages 101–15 in *Secularism and Biblical Studies*. Edited by Roland Boer. London: Equinox, 2010.

Marchal, Joseph A. "Slaves as Wo/men and Unmen: Reflecting upon Euodia, Syntyche, and Epaphroditus in Philippi." Pages 141–76 in *The People Beside Paul: The Philippian Assembly and History from Below*. Edited by Joseph A. Marchal. Atlanta: SBL, 2015.

Marchal, Joseph A. "'With Friends Like These . . .': A Feminist Rhetorical Reconsideration of Scholarship and the Letter to the Philippians." *JSNT* 29:1 (September 2006): 77–106.

Marcus, Joel. "The Circumcision and Uncircumcision in Rome." *NTS* 35 (1989): 67–81.

Martin, Clarice J. "The Eyes Have It: Slaves in the Communities of Christ-Believers." Pages 221–39 in *Christian Origins: Volume 1 of A People's History of Christianity*. Edited by Richard A. Horsley. Minneapolis: Fortress, 2005.

Martin, Clarice J. "The Rhetorical Function of Commercial Language in Paul's Letter to Philemon (Verse 18)." Pages 321–37 in *Persuasive Artistry: Studies in New Testament Rhetoric in Honor of George A. Kennedy*. Edited by Duane F. Watson. Sheffield: Sheffield Academic, 1991.

Martin, Dale B. "*Arsenokoitēs* and *Malakos*: Meanings and Consequences." Pages 117–36 in *Biblical Ethics and Homosexuality: Listening to Scriptures*. Edited by Robert L. Brawley. Louisville: Westminster John Knox, 1996.

Martin, Dale B. *The Corinthian Body*. New Haven: Yale University Press, 1995.

Martin, Dale B. "Heterosexism and the Interpretation of Romans 1:18–32." *BibInt* 3 (1995): 332–55.

Martin, Dale B. "Paul Without Passion: On Paul's Rejection of Desire in Sex and Marriage." Pages 201–15 in *Constructing Early Christian Families: Family as Social Reality and Metaphor*. Edited by Halvor Moxnes. London: Routledge, 1997.

Martin, Dale B. *Sex and the Single Savior: Gender and Sexuality in Biblical Interpretation*. Louisville: Westminster John Knox, 2006.

Martin, Dale B. "Slave Families and Slaves in Families." Pages 207–30 in *Early Christian Families in Context: An Interdisciplinary Dialogue*. Edited by David L. Balch and Carolyn Osiek. Grand Rapids, MI: Eerdmans, 2003.

Martin, Dale B. "Slavery and the Ancient Jewish Family." Pages 113–29 in *The Jewish Family in Antiquity*. Edited by Shaye J. D. Cohen. Atlanta: Scholars, 1993.

Martyn, J. Louis. *Galatians: A New Translation with Introduction and Commentary*. AB 33A. New York: Doubleday, 1998.

Martyn, J. Louis. *Theological Issues in the Letters of Paul*. London: T&T Clark, 1997.

Massad, Joseph. "Re-Orienting Desire: The Gay International and the Arab World." *Public Culture* 14:2 (2002): 361–85.

Mattern, Susan P. *Rome and the Enemy: Imperial Strategy in the Principate*. Berkeley: University of California Press, 1999.

Matthews, Shelly. "A Feminist Analysis of the Veiling Passage (1 Corinthians 11:2–16): Who Really Cares That Paul Was Not a Gender Egalitarian After all?" *Lectio Difficilior* 2 (2015).

Matthews, Shelly. *Perfect Martyr: The Stoning of Stephen and the Construction of Christian Identity*. New York: Oxford University Press, 2010.

Matthews, Shelly. "'To be one and the same with the woman whose head is shaven' (1 Cor 11:5b): Resisting the Violence of 1 Corinthians 11:2–16 from the Bottom of the Kyriarchal Pyramid." Pages 31–51 in *Sexual Violence and Sacred Texts*. Edited by Amy Kalmanofsky. Cambridge: Feminist Studies in Religion Books, 2017.

Mbembe, Achille. "Necropolitics." *Public Culture* 15:1 (2003): 11–40.

McCabe, Susan. "To Be and to Have: The Rise of Queer Historicism." *GLQ* 11:1 (2005): 119–34.

McClintock, Anne. *Imperial Leather: Race, Gender and Sexuality in the Colonial Conquest*. New York: Routledge, 1995.

McClintock, Anne. "Maid to Order: Commercial Fetishism and Gender Power." *Social Text* 37 (1993): 81–116.

McGinn, Thomas A. J. *The Economy of Prostitution in the Roman World: A Study of Social History and the Brothel*. Ann Arbor: University of Michigan Press, 2004.

McGinn, Thomas A. J. *Prostitution, Sexuality, and the Law in Ancient Rome*. New York: Oxford University Press, 1988.

McIntosh, Mary. "The Homosexual Role." *Social Problems* 16:2 (1968): 182–92.

Meeks, Wayne A. *The First Urban Christians: The Social World of the Apostle Paul*. New Haven: Yale University Press, 1983.

Meeks, Wayne A. "Image of the Androgyne: Some Uses of a Symbol in Earliest Christianity." *History of Religions* 13 (1974): 165–208.

Meier, John P. "On the Veiling of Hermeneutics (1 Cor 11:2–16)." *CBQ* 40:2 (1978): 212–26.

Memmi, Albert. *The Pillar of Salt*. Translated by Edouard Roditti. New York: Beacon, 1992 [1966].

Menéndez-Antuña, Luis. "Is There a Room for Queer Desires in the House of Biblical Scholarship? A Methodological Reflection on Queer Desires in the Context of Contemporary New Testament Studies." *BibInt* 23 (2015): 399–427.

Mercer, Kobena. "Skin Head Sex Thing: Racial Difference and the Homoerotic Imaginary." Pages 169–210 in *How Do I Look? Queer Film and Video*. Edited by Bad Object-Choices. Seattle: Bay Press, 1991.

Meyer, Rudolf. "*peritomē*." Pages 73–74 in *Theological Dictionary of the New Testament*, Vol. 6. Translated by G. W. Bromiley. Edited by G. Kittel and G. Friedrich. Grand Rapids, MI: Eerdmans, 1964–76.

Meyers, Carol, with Toni Craven, and Ross S. Kraemer, eds. *Women in Scripture: A Dictionary of Named and Unnamed Women in the Hebrew Bible, the Apocrypha/Deuterocanonical Books, and the New Testament*. Grand Rapids, MI: Eerdmans, 2000.

Miller, Anna C. *Corinthian Democracy: Democratic Discourse in 1 Corinthians*. Eugene, OR: Pickwick, 2015.

Miller, Monica R. "'I Am a Nappy-Headed Ho': (Re)Signifying 'Deviance' in the Haraam of Religious Respectability." Pages 123–37 in *Ain't I a Womanist, Too? Third-Wave Womanist Religious Thought*. Edited by Monica A. Coleman. Minneapolis: Fortress, 2013.

Mitchell, Margaret M. *Paul and the Rhetoric of Reconciliation: An Exegetical Investigation of the Language and Composition of 1 Corinthians*. Louisville: Westminster John Knox, 1991.

Mollenkott, Virginia Ramey. *Omnigender: A Trans-Religious Approach*. Cleveland: Pilgrim, 2001.

Money, John. "Hermaphroditism: An Inquiry into the Nature of a Human Paradox." PhD dissertation, Harvard University, 1952.

Money, John. "Hermaphroditism: Recommendations Concerning Case Management." *Journal of Clinical Endocrinology and Metabolism* 16:4 (1956): 547–56.

Money, John. "Psychologic Consideration of Sex Assignment in Intersexuality." *Clinics in Plastic Surgery* 1:2 (1974): 215–22.

Money, John, and Anke A. Ehrhardt. *Man and Woman, Boy and Girl: The Differentiation and Dimorphism of Gender Identity from Conception to Maturity*. Baltimore: Johns Hopkins University Press, 1972.

Money, John, Joan G. Hampson, and John L. Hampson. "An Examination of Some Basic Sexual Concepts: The Evidence of Human Hermaphroditism." *Bulletin of the Johns Hopkins Hospital* 97:4 (1955): 301–19.

Money, John, Joan G. Hampson, and John L. Hampson. "Hermaphroditism: Recommendations Concerning Assignment of Sex, Change of Sex, and Psychologic Management." *Bulletin of the Johns Hopkins Hospital* 97:4 (1955): 284–300.

Money, John, Joan G. Hampson, and John L. Hampson. "Imprinting and the Establishment of Gender Role." *Archives of Neurology and Psychiatry* 77:3 (1957): 333–36.

Moore, Stephen D. *God's Beauty Parlor: And Other Queer Spaces in and Around the Bible*. Stanford: Stanford University Press, 2001.

Moore, Stephen D. "Que(e)rying Paul: Preliminary Questions." Pages 249–74 in *Auguries: The Jubilee Volume of the Sheffield Department of Biblical Studies*. Edited by David J. A. Clines and Stephen D. Moore. Sheffield: Sheffield Academic, 1998.

Moore, Stephen D., Kent L. Brintnall, and Joseph A. Marchal. "Queer Disorientations: Four Turns and a Twist." Pages 1–44 in *Sexual Disorientations: Queer Temporalities, Affects, Theologies*. Edited by Kent L. Brintnall, Joseph A. Marchal, and Stephen D. Moore. New York: Fordham University Press, 2017.

Moraga, Cherríe, and Gloria Anzaldúa, eds. *This Bridge Called My Back: Writings by Radical Women of Color*. Watertown, MA: Persephone, 1981.

Morland, Iain. "Is Intersexuality Real?" *Textual Practice* 15:3 (2001): 527–47.

Morland, Iain. "What Can Queer Theory Do for Intersex?" *GLQ* 15:2 (2009): 285–312.

Moultrie, Monique. "Putting a Ring on It: Black Women, Black Churches, and Coerced Monogamy." *Black Theology* 16:3 (2018): 231–47.

Moxnes, Halvor, ed. *Constructing Early Christian Families: Family as Social Reality and Metaphor*. London: Routledge, 1997.

Muñoz, José Esteban. *Disidentifications: Queers of Color and the Performance of Politics*. Minneapolis: University of Minnesota Press, 1999.

Murib, Zein. "LGBT." *TSQ* 1:1–2 (2014): 118–20.

Murphy-O'Connor, Jerome. "Sex and Logic in 1 Corinthians 11:2–16." *CBQ* 42:4 (1980): 482–500.

Musser, Amber Jamilla. *Sensational Flesh: Race, Power, and Masochism*. New York: New York University Press, 2014.

Namaste, Vivian K. "Genderbashing. Sexuality, Gender, and the Regulation of Public Space." *Society and Space* 14:2 (1996): 221–40.

Namaste, Vivian K. *Invisible Lives: The Erasure of Transsexual and Transgendered People*. Chicago: University of Chicago Press, 2000.

Nanos, Mark D. *The Irony of Galatians: Paul's Letter in First-Century Context*. Minneapolis: Fortress, 2002.

Nanos, Mark D. "Paul's Reversal of Jews Calling Gentiles 'Dog' (Philippians 3:2): 1600 Years of an Ideological Tale Wagging an Exegetical Dog?" *BibInt* 17 (2009): 448–82.

Nash, Jennifer C. *The Black Body in Ecstasy: Reading Race, Reading Pornography*. Durham: Duke University Press, 2014.

Newmahr, Staci. *Playing on the Edge: Sadomasochism, Risk, and Intimacy*. Bloomington: Indiana University Press, 2011.

Noel, James A. "Nat Is Back: The Return of the Re/Oppressed in Philemon." Pages 59–90 in *Onesimus Our Brother: Reading Religion, Race, and Culture in Philemon*. Edited by Matthew V. Johnson, James A. Noel, and Demetrius K. Williams. Minneapolis: Fortress, 2012.

Oakes, Peter. *Reading Romans in Pompeii: Paul's Letter at Ground Level*. Minneapolis: Fortress, 2009.

O'Donovan, Oliver. *Transsexualism and Christian Marriage*. Nottingham: Grove, 1982.

Økland, Jorunn. *Women in Their Place: Paul and the Corinthian Discourse of Gender and Sanctuary Space*. London: T&T Clark, 2004.

Osiek, Carolyn. "Female Slaves, *Porneia*, and the Limits of Obedience." Pages 255–74 in *Early Christian Families in Context: An Interdisciplinary Dialogue*. Edited by David L. Balch and Carolyn Osiek. Grand Rapids, MI: Eerdmans, 2003.

Osiek, Carolyn. *Philippians, Philemon*. ANTC. Nashville: Abingdon, 2000.

Osiek, Carolyn, and David L. Balch. *Families in the New Testament World: Households and House Churches*. Louisville: Westminster John Knox, 1997.

Parker, Angela N. "One Womanist's View of Racial Reconciliation in Galatians." *JFSR* 34:2 (2018): 23–40.

Patterson, Orlando. *Slavery and Social Death: A Comparative Study*. Cambridge, MA: Harvard University Press, 1982.

Pellegrini, Ann. "Touching the Past. or, Hanging Chad." *Journal of the History of Sexuality* 10:2 (2001): 185–94.

Perkinson, James W. "Enslaved by the Text: The Uses of Philemon." Pages 121–41 in *Onesimus Our Brother: Reading Religion, Race, and Culture in Philemon*. Edited by Matthew V. Johnson, James A. Noel, and Demetrius K. Williams. Minneapolis: Fortress, 2012.

Pinn, Anthony B. "Embracing Nimrod's Legacy: The Erotic, the Irreverence of Fantasy, and the Redemption of Black Theology." Pages 157–77 in *Loving the Body: Black Religious Studies and the Erotic*. Edited by Anthony B. Pinn and Dwight N. Hopkins. Basingstoke: Palgrave, 2004.

Pintabone, Diane T. "Ovid's Iphis and Ianthe: When Girls Won't Be Girls." Pages 256–85 in *Among Women: From the Homosocial to the Homoerotic in the Ancient World*. Edited by Nancy Sorkin Rabinowitz and Lisa Auanger. Austin: University of Texas Press, 2002.

Polaski, Sandra Hack. *A Feminist Introduction to Paul*. St. Louis: Chalice, 2005.

Pomeroy, Sarah B. *Goddesses, Whores, Wives, and Slaves: Women in Classical Antiquity*. New York: Schocken, 1975.

Portillo, Tina. "I Get Real: Celebrating My Sadomasochistic Soul." Pages 49–55 in *Leatherfolk: Radical Sex, People, Politics, and Practice*, 3rd ed. Edited by Mark Thompson. Los Angeles: Daedalus, 2004 [1991].

Preves, Sharon E. *Intersex and Identity: The Contested Self*. New Brunswick, NJ: Rutgers University Press, 2003.

Prosser, Jay. "Judith Butler: Queer Feminism, Transgender, and the Transsubstantiation of Sex." Pages 21–60 in *Second Skins: The Body Narratives of Transsexuality*. New York: Columbia University Press, 1998.

Puar, Jasbir K. "Queer Times, Queer Assemblages." *Social Text* 23:3–4 (2005): 121–39.

Puar, Jasbir K. *Terrorist Assemblages: Homonationalism in Queer Times*. Durham: Duke University Press, 2007.

Puar, Jasbir K., and Amit S. Rai. "Monster, Terrorist, Fag: The War on Terrorism and the Production of Docile Patriots." *Social Text* 20:3 (2002): 117–48.

Punt, Jeremy. "Queer Theory, Postcolonial Theory, and Biblical Interpretation: A Preliminary Exploration of Some Intersections." Pages 321–41 in *Bible Trouble: Queer Reading at the Boundaries of Biblical Scholarship*. Edited by Teresa J. Hornsby and Ken Stone. Atlanta: SBL, 2011.

Räisanen, Heiki. *Paul and the Law*. Philadelphia: Fortress, 1983.

Rawson, Beryl, ed. *The Family in Ancient Rome: New Perspectives*. Ithaca: Cornell University Press, 1986.

Raymond, Janice. *The Transsexual Empire: The Making of the She-Male*. Boston: Beacon, 1979.

Reardon, B. P., ed. *Collected Ancient Greek Novels*. Berkeley: University of California Press, 1989.

Reay, Lewis. "Towards a Transgender Theology: Que(e)rying the Eunuchs." Pages 148–67 in *Trans/formations*. Edited by Marcella Althaus-Reid and Lisa Isherwood. London: SCM, 2009.

Reddy, Chandan. *Freedom with Violence: Race, Sexuality, and the US State*. Durham: Duke University Press, 2011.

Reid-Pharr, Robert F. *Black Gay Man: Essays*. New York: New York University Press, 2001.

Reis, Elizabeth. "Divergence or Disorder? The Politics of Naming Intersex." *Perspectives in Biology and Medicine* 50:4 (2007): 535–43.

Richlin, Amy. *The Garden of Priapus: Sexuality and Aggression in Roman Humor*. New Haven: Yale University Press, 1992 [1983].

Richlin, Amy. "Not Before Homosexuality: The Materiality of the *Cinaedus* and the Roman Law Against Love Between Men." *Journal of the History of Sexuality* 3:4 (1993): 523–73.

Roen, Katrina. "Queer Kids: Toward Ethical Clinical Interactions with Intersex People." Pages 259–77 in *Ethics of the Body: Postconventional Challenges*. Edited by Margrit Shildrick and Roxanne Mykitiuk. Cambridge: MIT, 2005.

Roetzel, Calvin. *The Letters of Paul: Conversations in Context*. 6th ed. Louisville: Westminster John Knox, 2015.

Roller, Lynn E. "Attis on Greek Votive Monuments: Greek God or Phrygian?" *Hesperia* 63 (1994): 245–62.

Rubin, Gayle. "Of Catamites and Kings: Reflections on Butch, Gender, and Boundaries." Pages 466–82 in *The Persistent Desire: A Femme-Butch Reader*. Edited by Joan Nestle. Boston: Alyson, 1992.

Rubin, Gayle. "The Leather Menace: Comments on Politics and S/M." Pages 194–229 in *Coming to Power: Writings and Graphics on Lesbian S/M*. Edited by SAMOIS. Boston: Alyson, 1987 [1981].

Rubin, Gayle. "Thinking Sex: Notes for a Radical Theory of the Politics of Sexuality." Pages 267–319 in *Pleasure and Danger: Exploring Female Sexuality*. Edited by Carole S. Vance. London: Pandora, 1989.

Runions, Erin. *The Babylon Complex: Theopolitical Fantasies of War, Sex, and Sovereignty*. New York: Fordham University Press, 2014.

Runions, Erin. "Empire's Allure: Babylon and the Exception to Law in Two Conservative Discourses." *JAAR* 77:3 (2009): 680–711.

Russaw, Kimberly D. "Veils and Lap Cloths: The Great Cover Up of Bynum and the Bible in Black Churches." *Black Theology* 16:3 (2018): 248–62.

Said, Edward W. *Orientalism*. Rev. ed. New York: Vintage, 1994 [1978].

Saller, Richard. "Slavery and the Roman Family." *Slavery and Abolition* 8 (1987): 65–87.

SAMOIS, ed. *Coming to Power: Writings and Graphics on Lesbian S/M*. Boston: Alyson, 1987 [1981].

Sanders, E. P. *Paul, the Law and the Jewish People*. Philadelphia: Fortress, 1977.

Sasson, Jacob M. "Circumcision in the Ancient Near East." *JBL* 85 (1966): 473–76.

Satlow, Michael L. *Jewish Marriage in Antiquity*. Princeton: Princeton University Press, 2001.

Schenk, Wolfgang. "Der Brief des Paulus und Philemon in der neueren Forschung (1945–1987)." *ANRW* 2.25.4 (1987): 3439–95.

Schippert, Claudia. "Implications of Queer Theory for the Study of Religion and Gender: Entering the Third Decade." *Religion and Gender* 1:1 (2011): 66–84.

Schmidt, K. L. "*akrobustia*." Pages 225–26 in *Theological Dictionary of the New Testament*, Vol. 1. Translated by G. W. Bromiley. Edited by G. Kittel and G. Friedrich. Grand Rapids, MI: Eerdmans, 1964–76.

Scholz, Piotr O. *Eunuchs and Castrati: A Cultural History*. Translated by John A. Broadwin and Shelley L. Frisch. Princeton: Markus Weiner, 2001 [1999].

Schüssler Fiorenza, Elisabeth. *In Memory of Her: A Feminist Theological Reconstruction of Christian Origins*. Tenth Anniversary Edition. New York: Crossroad, 1994 [1983].

Schüssler Fiorenza, Elisabeth. "Missionaries, Apostles, Coworkers: Romans 16 and the Reconstruction of Women's Early Christian History." *Word and World* 6 (1986): 420–33.

Schüssler Fiorenza, Elisabeth. "Paul and the Politics of Interpretation." Pages 40–57 in *Paul and Politics: Ekklesia, Israel, Imperium, Interpretation. Essays in Honor of Krister Stendahl*. Edited by Richard A. Horsley. Harrisburg, PA: Trinity, 2000.

Schüssler Fiorenza, Elisabeth. *The Power of the Word: Scripture and the Rhetoric of Empire*. Minneapolis: Fortress, 2007.

Schüssler Fiorenza, Elisabeth. "The 'Quilting' of Women's History: Phoebe of Cenchrae." Pages 35–49 in *Embodied Love: Sensuality and Relationship as Feminist Values*. Edited by Paula M. Cooey, Sharon A. Farmer, and Mary Ellen Ross. San Francisco: Harper, 1987.

Schüssler Fiorenza, Elisabeth. *Rhetoric and Ethic: The Politics of Biblical Studies*. Minneapolis: Fortress, 1999.

Schüssler Fiorenza, Elisabeth. *Wisdom Ways: Introducing Feminist Biblical Interpretation*. Maryknoll, NY: Orbis, 2001.

Scott, Darieck. *Extravagant Abjection: Blackness, Power, and Sexuality in the African American Literary Imagination*. New York: New York University Press, 2010.

Scott-Dixon, Krista, ed. *Trans/forming Feminisms: Trans/feminist Voices Speak Out*. Toronto: Sumach: 2006.

Scroggs, Robin. "Paul and the Eschatological Woman." *JAAR* 40:3 (1972): 283–303.

Sechrest, Love. *A Former Jew: Paul and the Dialectics of Race.* London: T&T Clark, 2009.

Sedgwick, Eve Kosofsky. "Afterword." Pages 273–91 in *Gary in Your Pocket: Stories and Notebooks of Gary Fisher.* Edited by Eve Kosofsky Sedgwick. Durham: Duke University Press, 1996.

Sedgwick, Eve Kosofsky. *Between Men: English Literature and Male Homosocial Desire.* New York: Columbia University Press, 1985.

Sedgwick, Eve Kosofsky. *Epistemology of the Closet.* Berkeley: University of California Press, 1990.

Sedgwick, Eve Kosofsky. *Tendencies.* Durham: Duke University Press, 1993.

Seesengood, Robert Paul. *Paul: A Brief History.* Malden, MA: Wiley, 2010.

Serano, Julia. *Whipping Girl: A Transsexual Woman on Sexism and the Scapegoating of Femininity.* Berkeley: Seal, 2007.

Shah, Nayan. "Between 'Oriental Depravity' and 'Natural Degenerates': Spatial Borderlands and the Making of Ordinary Americans." *American Quarterly* 57:3 (2005): 703–25.

Shah, Nayan. *Stranger Intimacy: Contesting Race, Sexuality, and the Law in the North American West.* Berkeley: University of California Press, 2011.

Shaner, Katherine A. *Enslaved Leadership in Early Christianity.* New York: Oxford University Press, 2018.

Sharpe, Christina. *Monstrous Intimacies: Making Post-Slavery Subjects.* Durham: Duke University Press, 2010.

Sherwood, Yvonne. "The God of Abraham and Exceptional States, or The Early Modern Rise of the Whig/Liberal Bible." *JAAR* 76:2 (2008): 312–43.

Singer, T. Benjamin. "From the Medical Gaze to *Sublime Mutations*: The Ethics of (Re) Viewing Non-normative Body Images." Pages 601–20 in *The Transgender Studies Reader.* Edited by Susan Stryker and Stephen Whittle. New York: Routledge, 2006.

Skinner, Marilyn B. "Introduction: *Quod multo fit aliter in Graecia* . . . ." Pages 3–25 in *Roman Sexualities.* Edited by Judith P. Hallett and Marilyn B. Skinner. Princeton: Princeton University Press, 1997.

Skinner, Marilyn B. *Sexuality in Greek and Roman Culture.* Malden, MA: Blackwell, 2005.

Slabodsky, Santiago. *Decolonial Judaism: Triumphal Failures of Barbaric Thinking.* New York: Palgrave, 2014.

Smith, Barbara. *Toward a Black Feminism Criticism.* New York: Out & Out Books, 1977.

Smith, Barbara, ed. *Home Girls: A Black Feminist Anthology.* New York: Kitchen Table/ Women of Color Press, 1983.

Smith, Mitzi J. "Utility, Fraternity, and Reconciliation: Ancient Slavery as a Context for the Return of Onesimus." Pages 47–58 in *Onesimus Our Brother: Reading Religion, Race, and Culture in Philemon.* Edited by Matthew V. Johnson, James A. Noel, and Demetrius K. Williams. Minneapolis: Fortress, 2012.

Smith, Mitzi J., ed. *I Found God in Me: A Womanist Biblical Hermeneutics Reader.* Eugene, OR: Cascade, 2015.

Snorton, C. Riley. *Black on Both Sides: A Racial History of Trans Identity.* Minneapolis: University of Minnesota Press, 2017.

Somerville, Siobhan B. "Sexual Aliens and the Racialized State: A Queer Reading of the 1952 U.S. Immigration and Nationality Act." Pages 75–91 in *Queer Migrations: Sexuality, U.S. Citizenship, and Border Crossings.* Edited by Eithne Luibhéid and Lionel Cant Jr. Minneapolis: University of Minnesota Press, 2005.

Spade, Dean. "Mutilating Gender." Pages 315–32 in *The Transgender Studies Reader*. Edited by Susan Stryker and Stephen Whittle. New York: Routledge, 2006.

Spillers, Hortense. "Mama's Baby, Papa's Maybe: An American Grammar Book." *Diacritics* 17:2 (1987): 65–81.

Spillers, Hortense. "'Whatcha Gonna Do?'—Revisiting 'Mama's Baby, Papa's Maybe: An American Grammar Book'" A Conversation with Hortense Spillers, Saidiya Hartman, Farah Jasmine Griffin, Shelly Eversley, and Jennifer L. Morgan, *Women's Studies Quarterly* 35:1–2 (2007): 299–309.

Standhartinger, Angela. "Letter from Prison as Hidden Transcript: What It Tells Us About the People at Philippi." Pages 107–140 in *The People Beside Paul: The Philippian Assembly and History from Below*. Edited by Joseph A. Marchal. Atlanta: SBL, 2015.

Steigmann-Gall, Richard. *The Holy Reich: Nazi Conceptions of Christianity, 1919–1945*. Cambridge: Cambridge University Press, 2004.

Stendahl, Krister. "The Apostle Paul and the Introspective Conscience of the West." Pages 78–96 in *Paul Among Jews and Gentiles, and Other Essays*. Minneapolis: Fortress, 1976.

Stendahl, Krister. *The Bible and the Role of Women: A Case Study in Hermeneutics*. Philadelphia: Fortress, 1966.

Stevenson, Walter. "The Rise of Eunuchs in Greco-Roman Antiquity." *Journal of the History of Sexuality* 5 (1995): 495–511.

Stockton, Kathryn Bond. *Beautiful Bottom, Beautiful Shame: Where "Black" Meets "Queer"*. Durham: Duke University Press, 2006.

Stone, Ken. "The Garden of Eden and the Heterosexual Contract." Pages 48–70 in *Bodily Citations: Religion and Judith Butler*. Edited by Ellen T. Armour and Susan M. St. Ville. New York: Columbia University Press, 2006.

Stone, Ken. *Practicing Safer Texts: Food, Sex and Bible in Queer Perspective*. London: T&T Clark, 2005.

Stone, Ken. "Queer Theory and Biblical Interpretation: An Introduction." Pages 11–34 in *Queer Commentary and the Hebrew Bible*. Edited by Ken Stone. Cleveland: Pilgrim, 2001.

Stowers, Stanley K. *A Rereading of Romans: Justice, Jews and Gentiles*. New Haven: Yale University Press, 1994.

Strassfeld, Max. "Classically Queer: Eunuchs and Androgynes in Rabbinic Literature." PhD dissertation: Stanford University, 2013.

Strassfeld, Max. "Translating the Human: The *Androginos* in Tosefta Bikurim." *TSQ* 3:3–4 (2016): 587–604.

Stryker, Susan. "(De)Subjugated Knowledges: An Introduction to Transgender Studies." Pages 1–17 in *The Transgender Studies Reader*. Edited by Susan Stryker and Stephen Whittle. New York: Routledge, 2006.

Stryker, Susan. "My Words to Victor Frankenstein Above the Village of Chamounix: Transgender Rage." *GLQ* 1:3 (1994): 237–54.

Stryker, Susan. *Transgender History*. Berkeley: Seal, 2008.

Stryker, Susan, and Stephen Whittle, eds. *The Transgender Studies Reader*. New York: Routledge, 2006.

Stumpp, Bettina Eva. *Prostitution in der römischen Antike*. Berlin: Akademie, 1998.

Suleri, Sara. *The Rhetoric of English India*. Chicago: University of Chicago Press, 1992.

Sullivan, Nikki. "Transmogrification: (Un)Becoming Other(s)." Pages 552–64 in *The Transgender Studies Reader*. Edited by Susan Stryker and Stephen Whittle. New York: Routledge, 2006.

Swancutt, Diana M. "Sexing the Pauline Body of Christ: Scriptural Sex in the Context of the American Christian Culture War." Pages 65–98 in *Toward a Theology of Eros: Transfiguring Passion at the Limits of Discipline*. Edited by Virginia Burrus and Catherine Keller. New York: Fordham University Press, 2006.

Swancutt, Diana M. "*Still* Before Sexuality: 'Greek' Androgyny, the Roman Imperial Politics of Masculinity and the Roman Imperial Invention of the *Tribas*." Pages 11–61 in *Mapping Gender in Ancient Religious Discourses*. Edited by Todd Penner and Caroline Vander Stichele. Leiden: Brill, 2007.

Sytsma, Sharon E. "The Ethics of Using Dexamethasone to Prevent Virilization of Female Fetuses." Pages 241–58 in *Ethics and Intersex*. Edited by Sharon E. Sytsma. Dordrecht: Springer, 2006.

Tanis, Justin. *Trans-Gendered: Theology, Ministry, and Communities of Faith*. Cleveland: Pilgrim, 2003.

Taylor, Gary. *Castration: An Abbreviated History of Western Manhood*. New York: Routledge, 2000.

Taylor, Rabun. "Two Pathic Subcultures in Ancient Rome." *Journal of the History of Sexuality* 7 (1997): 319–71.

Thistelton, Anthony C. *The First Epistle to the Corinthians: A Commentary on the Greek Text*. NIGTC. Grand Rapids, MI: Eerdmans, 2000.

Thomas, Eric A. "The Futures Outside: Apocalyptic Epilogue Unveiled as Queer Africana Prologue." Page 90–112 in *Sexual Disorientations: Queer Temporalities, Affects, Theologies*. Edited by Kent L. Brintnall, Joseph A. Marchal, and Stephen D. Moore. New York: Fordham University Press, 2018.

Thompson, Mark. "Introduction." Pages xv–xxiv in *Leatherfolk: Radical Sex, People, Politics, and Practice*. 3rd ed. Edited by Mark Thompson. Los Angeles: Daedalus, 2004 [1991].

Townsley. Gillian. "*Gender Trouble* in Corinth: Que(e)rying Constructs of Gender in 1 Corinthians 11.2–16." *Bible and Critical Theory* 2:2 (2006): 17.1–17.14.

Townsley, Gillian. "*The Straight Mind* in Corinth: Problematizing Categories and Ideologies of Gender in 1 Corinthians 11:2–16." Pages 247–81 in *Bible Trouble: Queer Reading at the Boundaries of Biblical Scholarship*. Edited by Teresa J. Hornsby and Ken Stone. Atlanta: SBL, 2011.

Townsley, Gillian. The Straight Mind *in Corinth: Queer Readings across 1 Corinthians 11:2–16*. Atlanta, SBL, 2017.

Treggiari, Susan. *Roman Marriage: "Iusti Coniuges" from the Time of Cicero to the Time of Ulpian* (Oxford: Clarendon Press, 1991).

Triea, Kiira. "Power, Orgasm, and the Psychohormonal Research Unit." Pages 141–44 in *Intersex in the Age of Ethics*. Edited by Alice Domurat Dreger. Hagerstown, MD: University Publishing Group, 1999.

Truscott, Carol. "S/M: Some Questions and a Few Answers." Pages 15–36 in *Leatherfolk: Radical Sex, People, Politics, and Practice*. 3rd edition. Edited by Mark Thompson. Los Angeles: Daedalus, 2004 [1991].

Tupamahu, Ekaputra. "Language Politics and the Constitution of Racialized Subjects in the Corinthian Church." *JSNT* 41:2 (2018): 223–45.

Twomey, Jay. "The Pastor and His Fops: Gender Indeterminacy in the Pastor and His Readers." Pages 283–300 in *Bible Trouble: Queer Reading at the Boundaries of Biblical Scholarship*. Edited by Teresa J. Hornsby and Ken Stone. Atlanta: SBL, 2011.

Vander Stichele, Caroline, and Todd Penner. "Paul and the Rhetoric of Gender." Pages 287–310 in *Her Master's Tools? Feminist and Postcolonial Engagements of Historical-Critical Discourse*. Edited by Caroline Vander Stichele and Todd Penner. Atlanta: SBL, 2005.

Veyne, Paul. "Homosexuality in Ancient Rome." Pages 26–35 in *Western Sexuality: Practice and Precept in Past and Present Times*. Edited by Philippe Ariès and Andre Béjin. Oxford: Oxford University Press, 1985.

Volcano, Del LaGrace. *Sublime Mutations*. Tübingen: Konkursbuch Verlag, 2000.

Volcano, Del LaGrace, and Judith "Jack" Halberstam. *The Drag King Book*. London: Serpent's Tail, 1999.

Walcutt, Heidi. "Time for a Change." Pages 197–200 in *Intersex in the Age of Ethics*. Edited by Alice Domurat Dreger. Hagerstown, MD: University Publishing Group, 1999.

Walker, Alice. *In Search of Our Mothers' Gardens*. San Diego: Harcourt Brace Jovanovich, 1983.

Walters, Jonathan. "Invading the Roman Body: Manliness and Impenetrability in Roman Thought." Pages 29–46 in *Roman Sexualities*. Edited by Judith P. Hallett and Marilyn B. Skinner. Princeton: Princeton University Press, 1997.

Walters, Jonathan. "'No More Than a Boy': The Shifting Construction of Masculinity from Ancient Greece to the Middle Ages." *Gender and History* 5 (1991): 20–33.

Wansink, Craig S. *Chained in Christ: The Experience and Rhetoric of Paul's Imprisonments*. Sheffield: Sheffield Academic, 1996.

Warner, Michael. *The Trouble with Normal: Sex, Politics, and the Ethics of Queer Life*. Cambridge: Harvard University Press, 1999.

Weeks, Jeffrey. *Making Sexual History*. Cambridge: Polity, 2000.

Weeks, Jeffrey. *Sex, Politics, and Society: The Regulation of Sexuality Since 1800*. London: Longman, 1981.

Weheliye, Alexander G. *Habeas Viscus: Racializing Assemblages, Biopolitics, and Black Feminist Trajectories of the Human*. Durham: Duke University Press, 2014.

Weismantel, Mary. "Toward a Transgender Archaeology: A Queer Rampage Through Prehistory." Pages 319–34 in *The Transgender Studies Reader 2*. Edited by Susan Stryker and Aren Z. Aizura. New York: Routledge, 2013.

Weiss, Margot. *Techniques of Pleasure: BDSM and the Circuits of Pleasure*. Durham: Duke University Press, 2011.

Welborn, L. L. *Paul's Summons to Messianic Life: Political Theology and the Coming Awakening*. New York: Columbia University Press, 2015.

West, Traci. *Wounds of the Spirit: Black Women, Violence, and Resistance Ethics*. New York: New York University Press, 1999.

White, Heather R. *Reforming Sodom: Protestants and the Rise of Gay Rights*. Chapel Hill: University of North Carolina Press, 2015.

Wilchins, Riki Ann. *Read My Lips: Sexual Subversion and the End of Gender*. Milford, CT: Firebrand, 1997.

Wiley, Tatha. *Paul and the Gentile Women: Reframing Galatians*. New York: Continuum, 2005.

Williams, Craig A. *Roman Homosexuality: Ideologies of Masculinity in Classical Antiquity*. New York: Oxford University Press, 1999.

Williams, Delores S. *Sisters in the Wilderness. The Challenge of Womanist God-Talk*. Maryknoll, NY: Orbis, 1993.

Williams, Demetrius K. "'No Longer as a Slave': Reading the Interpretation History of Paul's Epistle to Philemon." Pages 11–46 in *Onesimus Our Brother: Reading Religion, Race, and Culture in Philemon*. Edited by Matthew V. Johnson, James A. Noel, and Demetrius K. Williams. Minneapolis: Fortress, 2012.

Williams, Michael Allen. *Rethinking "Gnosticism": An Argument for Dismantling a Dubious Category*. Princeton: Princeton University Press, 1999.

Wilson, Bruce E., and William G. Reiner. "Management of Intersex: A Shifting Paradigm." Pages 119–35 in *Intersex in the Age of Ethics*. Edited by Alice Domurat Dreger. Hagerstown, MD: University Publishing Group, 1999.

Wilson, Nancy. *Our Tribe: Queer Folks, God, Jesus, and the Bible*. San Francisco: HarperSanFrancisco, 1995.

Wimbush, Vincent L., ed. *African Americans and the Bible: Sacred Texts and Social Textures*. New York: Continuum, 2000.

Winter, Sara B. C. "Paul's Letter to Philemon." *NTS* 33 (1987): 1–15.

Wire, Antoinette Clark. *The Corinthian Women Prophets: A Reconstruction Through Paul's Rhetoric*. Minneapolis: Fortress, 1990.

Wire, Antoinette Clark. "Response: Paul and Those Outside Power." Pages 224–26 in *Paul and Politics: Ekklesia, Israel, Imperium, Interpretation. Essays in Honor of Krister Stendahl*. Edited by Richard A. Horsley. Harrisburg, PA: Trinity, 2000.

Wright, N. T. *Pauline Perspectives: Essays on Paul, 1978–2013*. Minneapolis: Fortress, 2013.

Zaas, Peter S. "Catalogues and Context: 1 Corinthians 5 and 6." *NTS* 34 (1988): 622–29.

Žižek, Slavoj. *The Puppet and the Dwarf: The Perverse Core of Christianity*. Cambridge, MA: MIT Press, 2003.

Index